The Professional's Book of
ROTTWEILERS

TS-147

Title page: **Tasha of Lakeview owned by Tanya Jones Oldham.**

Distributed in the UNITED STATES by T.F.H. Publications, Inc., One T.F.H. Plaza, Neptune City, NJ 07753; in CANADA to the Pet Trade by H & L Pet Supplies Inc., 27 Kingston Crescent, Kitchener, Ontario N2B 2T6; Rolf C. Hagen Ltd., 3225 Sartelon Street, Montreal 382 Quebec; in CANADA to the Book Trade by Macmillan of Canada (A Division of Canada Publishing Corporation), 164 Commander Boulevard, Agincourt, Ontario M1S 3C7; in ENGLAND by T.F.H. Publications, The Spinney, Parklands, Portsmouth PO7 6AR; in AUSTRALIA AND THE SOUTH PACIFIC by T.F.H. (Australia) Pty. Ltd., Box 149, Brookvale 2100 N.S.W., Australia; in NEW ZEALAND by Ross Haines & Son, Ltd., 82 D Elizabeth Knox Place, Panmure, Auckland, New Zealand; in the PHILIPPINES by Bio-Research, 5 Lippay Street, San Lorenzo Village, Makati, Rizal; in SOUTH AFRICA by Multipet Pty. Ltd., P.O. Box 35347, Northway, 4065, South Africa. Published by T.F.H. Publications, Inc. Manufactured in the United States of America by T.F.H. Publications, Inc.

The Professional's Book of
ROTTWEILERS

ANNA KATHERINE NICHOLAS

Ch. Doroh's Headline, C.D., owned by Mary Ellen Moehler.

Acknowledgments

The author takes this opportunity to thank all owners and contributors to this book who so graciously provided photographs and invaluable information. To these Rottweiler troopers this volume is dedicated.

We are especially proud of our guest chapters and the selfless contribution of the following individuals: Dr. Evelyn M. Ellman, Mr. and Mrs. Frank Fiorella, Dorothea Gruenerwald, Eve and Manson Johnson, Patricia J. Hall, Keith and Jo Peckham, Catherine M. Thompson and Arthur Twiss. Without these special folk, this book could not have been possible.

Anna

Contents

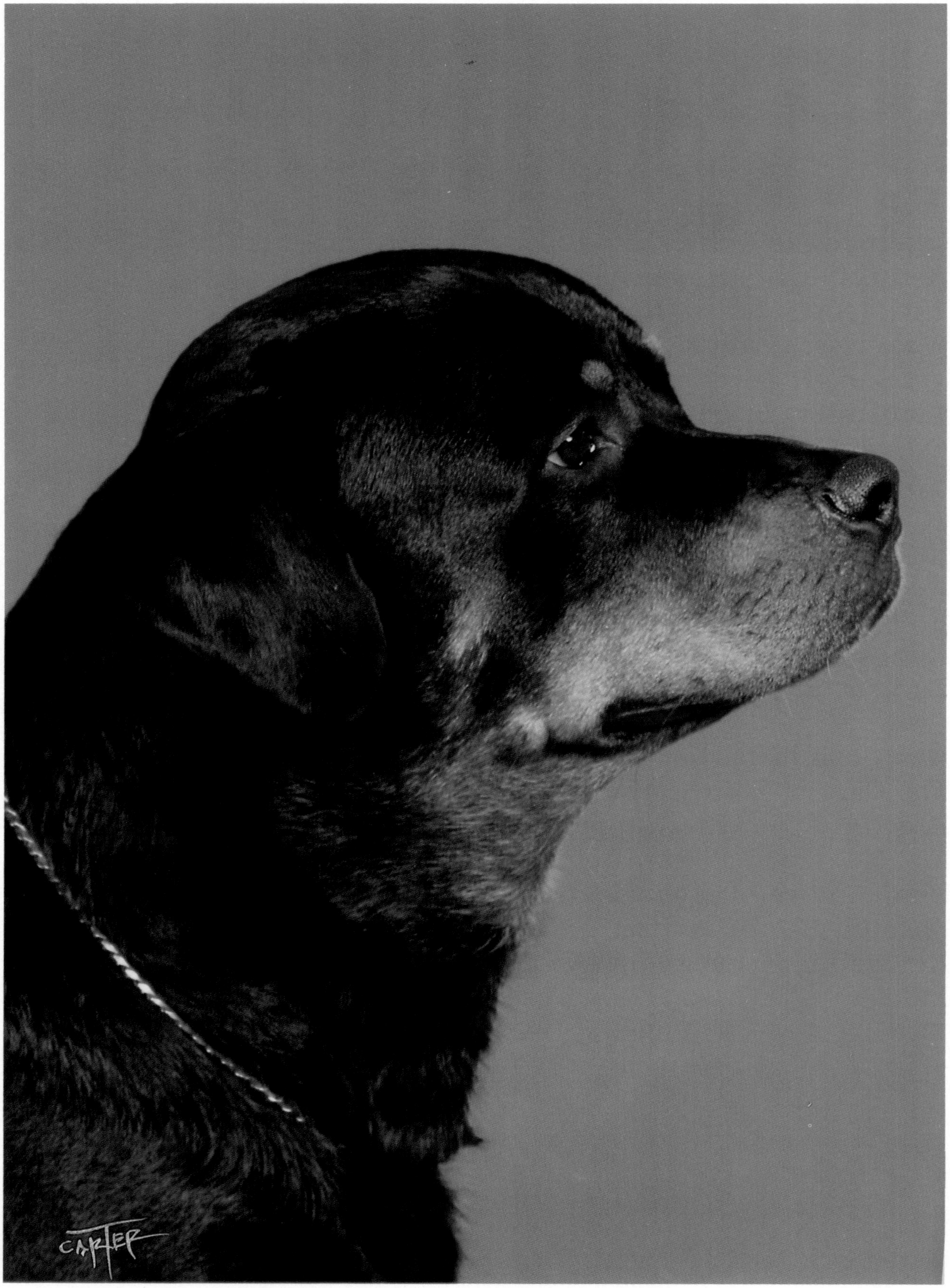
CARTER

Origin of the Rottweiler

Although the belief is widespread that Germany is the native country of the Rottweiler, this is not the entire truth. While the breed was developed in Germany, the Rottweiler's ancestors originated in Roman territory where several different mastiff-type strains of canine have existed for many hundreds of years.

These original canines include a big, black, harsh-coated dog of large size and tremendous power, one so respected in the Roman Empire that the Emperor Nero is said to always have kept several around his palace for guard dog purposes.

When the Roman troops made their raids on Europe, many of these mastiff types accompanied them for the dual purpose of herding the cattle used to feed the army and protecting the camp from marauders while the troops slept.

The route taken by the Romans toward southern Germany was through the Alps. There is little doubt to the infusion of Greater Swiss Mountain Dog mixing with the original Roman dogs during that period. Then, upon travel and settlement in Germany, what seems likely was still another cross, this time with German Pinschers (*pinscher* is the German word for terrier).

All this has led historians away from the original theory and to the point of view that almost without question the early Rottweilers were actually a combination of the Mastiff forebearers, the Greater Swiss Mountain Dog, and the German Pinscher.

The area of Rottweil, where the dogs mostly settled, was lush farming country. The Romans built a villa there of red tile. The city of Rottweil itself was built over ground which, when excavated, was discovered to contain red tile from the ancient Roman baths—"*das Rote Wil.*" A Christian church was erected on the site of the Roman baths, and the town was named Rottweil due to the red tiles which had preceded it on that land.

As things finally settled back again into a normal German country area, the farmers became better acquainted with a number of dogs left behind by the troops. These dogs were found to be superior in their abilities for the work which the farmers needed— the herding of cattle, the pulling of milk carts, and the protection of home and family. Of course, they were encouraged to stay.

As the busy community grew into an important trading area, the dogs became continuously more useful. Among their special and most

Opposite: Head study of Ch. Bourbon's Anvil von Mirko, C.D. Anvil, following in the pawprints of his famous sire, Int., Am. Ch. Mirko von Steinkopf, C.D.X., SchH. III, I.P.O. III, F.H., Registered Therapy Dog, is also a Registered Therapy Dog. Owners, Donna and Karl Rice, Hallsville, TX.

needed duties was the accompaniment of their masters to town to sell the cattle and produce. What a comfort it must have been to be accompanied by these herding dogs who were hardy enough for the trip across the country into town, and to have their protection for the trip home with their earnings. Needless to say, robberies were frequent during the lonely trips, but those who cleverly attached their money bags firmly to the collars of their Rottweiler dogs had few if any problems while en route. It would take considerable temerity for even the boldest thief to lay hands on a money bag dangling so near the mouth of one of these fearless dogs. That fact made life, we are sure, far simpler for the farmers and less worrisome for the wives and children at home.

Life proceeded peacefully for awhile in the area of Rottweil. Progress was taking over the city fast, creating a big and important cultural and trading center, and the population kept increasing. Soon the Old German Empire city of Rottweil took on quite a different atmosphere as new inventions and discoveries changed the way of life for many.

One of these changes might well have wiped out our Rottweiler. This was the innovation of the railroad—and the use of it (government owned and by orders of same) for transportation of the cattle. The result was that no more dogs herded cattle across the countryside! As if that were not enough, a better way was found for handling the products which had been Rottweiler-drawn by cart. Numbers of the breed diminished

The ancestors back in Rottweil would be proud of Ch. Roja's A Gumbo File, U.D., T.T., H.I.C., and the technique with which this herding job is being done at Country Storer Ranch, of which Liebenswert Kennels is a division at Alleyton, TX.

Aust. Ch. Stromhall Lord Lutz, bred, owned and handled by Pat Hall, was Best Exhibit at the R.C. of N.S.W. Championship Show in 1989.

rapidly. Fortunately, however, there were some Rottweiler owners who loved their dogs and kept a few for that reason, although the keeping of dogs as pets unless they had other uses was not popular at that time.

Among those whose association with Rottweilers continued, there grew up a fiercely competitive "my dog's better than your dog" spirit. This grew among them as a few litters were born, and an effort was made to impress with the merits of each puppy.

Despite the fact that a few were still being cared for, the truth of the matter was that Rottweilers were then unemployed, and that something had to come along to

replace their former occupation or the breed would sink into complete extinction.

If it had not been thought of earlier (one would almost think that impossible considering the obvious suitability of Rottweiler dogs for this type of work), the usefulness of Rotties for police work was brought home to the people of Hamburg one evening at the beginning of the 20th century. An off-duty policeman was walking his dog past a waterfront bar when he and the dog became aware of a loud and fairly violent brawl taking place inside. He and the people involved in the brawl discovered each other at about the same moment, and the fight, which had

Top:
Am., Can. Ch. Birch Hill's Nanna v. Brader pulls the cart in the tradition of her breed at the Brookfield, Illinois, Zoo's "Animals on Parade" in 1984. Her owner, Frank Braden, looks on.
Bottom:
A hind view of the Rott Trot 1988, at the start of the race. This event is becoming increasingly popular in the Rottweiler fancy.

been concerned until then with a most attractive young lady, moved its focal point from them to the man with the dog.

True to his Rottweiler instinct, the dog immediately evaluated the situation and took action when the mob of brawling sailors started toward his master. Quicker than a wink, several of the sailors were flat on the ground, having been knocked down by the Rottie—the others scrambled to leave the area before it became their turn. The massive substance, aura of power, and confident self-assurance were far too obvious for any argument, and the men who had been brawling so lustily disappeared into the shadows, probably hoping never again to encounter a Rottweiler.

Yden's Dutch von Adler Rock, 18-month-old son of Ch. Gentle Thor of Kinderfox ex Am., Can. Ch. Von Brula v. Yden, Am., Can. C.D., T.T., is owned by Sandra Al Moses, Adler Rock Rottweilers.

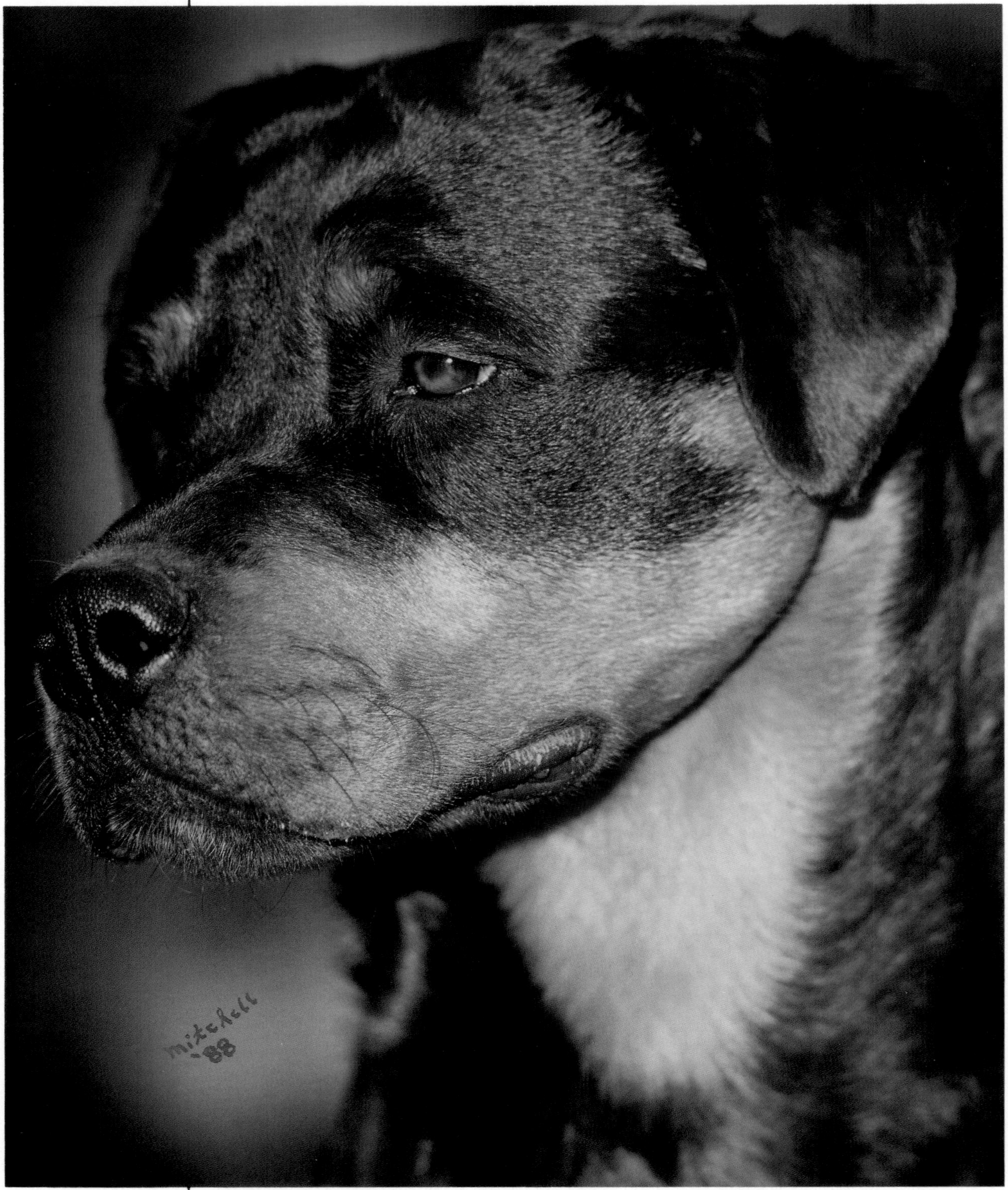
mitchell
'88

Rottweiler Development in Germany

It has been almost 90 years now since that historic occasion on which the Heidelberg Dog Show took place, where the president of the sponsoring organization gave the two co-chairmen, Albert Graf and Karl Knauf, an assignment to fulfill for him: to find him a dog "of unusual breeding and admirable character" which he would enjoy owning.

Feeling flattered at the president's confidence in them and anxious to do a good job, Herr Graf and Herr Knauf determined that they must discover not just a satisfactory dog but an extraordinary one. Early discussion on the subject brought them to the assets of the Rottweiler and the determination to set about a complete study of these dogs in order to qualify themselves to choose the very best.

Being aware that there were some good general books on dogs available, they felt it would be quite simple to read up on the breed. That thought soon passed into oblivion, however, as it was quickly found that not one word on Rottweilers was included in any of these works.

In the course of events, it was determined that since so little was generally available to help the dog-loving public learn about Rottweilers, a club should be formed on the breed's behalf. This would bring together a group of Rottweiler owners who could pool their knowledge and share it with others, at the same time protecting and promoting the best interests of the future of the breed.

So it was that on January 13, 1907, a group of fanciers assembled to discuss the situation and plans for forming the original German Rottweiler Club (the D.R.K.). This took place in Heidelberg, the city that soon became known as the "true birthplace of the breed." Perhaps the 13th was not the best date to have chosen, as very quickly problems in the membership arose involving the expulsion of a member for what was considered to be an infringement on the basic principles of good sportsmanship. The offended member, with his friends, lost no time in resigning and starting a second club in protest and for the express intention of wiping out the original.

The second club also had its headquarters in Heidelberg. For its name, it chose the South German Rottweiler Club, and began operation April 26, 1907, only three months after the D.R.K. A stormy course followed, with

Opposite: Head study of Summerfield's Special Moment, owned by Paula A. Cingota of Summerfield Rottweilers, Jamul, CA. Photo courtesy of Mike Mitchell.

This is the crest of the German town of Rottweil. Photo courtesy of Eve and Manson Johnson.

differences of opinion so strong and so widely separated that any unification of the two groups was obviously impossible.

The next step was the appearance of still a third Rottweiler Specialty Club, the International Rottweiler Club (I.R.K.). Those people associated with the South German Club were gradually absorbed into this one, putting an end to that group and leaving only the D.R.K. and I.R.K. in operation.

At the time of the foundation of the original German Rottweiler Club, a most positive step had been taken on behalf of the breed: that of seeking the interest and support of the police department for Rottweilers, and bringing to their attention the numerous assets this breed offers for work with the police. Having lost their occupation as cattle dogs and then as cart dogs, Rottweilers were in

need of a formal working career, and considering their splendid ability and inborn tendencies for guard work, why shouldn't this be developed as a possibility for making them police assistants?

The police in Hamburg thought that such a plan might be both successful and beneficial; several dogs were immediately recruited for the experiment. Max von der Stahlenberg (breed book 48) and Flock von Hamburg led the way so capably and so successfully that in 1910, the breed became the fourth one recognized for this work by the German Police Association. The German Rottweiler Club (D.R.K.), of course, lost no time in becoming affiliated with the Police Association as Rottweilers began actively working in this capacity.

Efforts were re-introduced during 1913, although unsuccessfully, towards the unification of the D.R.K. and the

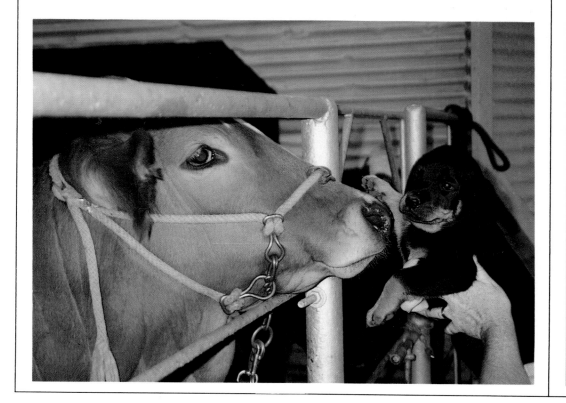

Top:
Two outstanding Rottweilers owned by Windcastle Rottweilers, Carolyn and Bert Kaufmann, Arroyo Grande, CA. They are Ch. Windcastle's California Kid and Am., Can. Ch. Windcastle's X-tra Special, T.T.
Bottom:
Nine-week-old puppy, Wiseguy von Wilken, being introduced to Elmer, 9-month-old steer. Owners, Hellmann Kennels, Robstown, TX.

I.R.K. Seven years then passed until it was again brought up in 1920, by which time there was evidence of a softening trend between the two factions. There is considerable truth to the "United We Stand" school of thought and that working as one organization could produce more positive results.

Ratification was finally achieved at a meeting in Gassel on July 4,

(2,340 listings) filling two volumes, the second of which, however, having included 770 entries from the wavering D.R.K.

It is especially interesting to note the differences in the stud book listings of the two early groups. The D.R.K. was dominated by Sieger Ralf vom Necker and Rottweilers of the Strahlenburg line; thus, in this group, working tendencies took precedence over

At home in the Netherlands, the internationally titled Ch. Barto sits thoughtfully by the door at V.T. Straotje Kennels, his birthplace. Barto's breeders and the owners of this kennel, Ton and Wil Emmers, are now enjoying success with Barto's progeny, including a youngster who has won Best in Show over a German Klubsieger. This photo courtesy of Barto's American owner, Frank J. Fiorella.

1921, and the following month a general meeting was held for the establishment of the General German Rottweiler Club (A.D.R.K.), under whose leadership the breed continues to flourish right up to the present time.

Stud books, of course, had been kept by the D.R.K. and I.R.K., and they had to be consolidated as a foundation for the new A.D.R.K. D.R.K. had but one volume which included listings on 286 dogs and 214 bitches. I.R.K. had been the more popular, with registrations

show quality. The I.R.K. listings were dominated by the Teck lines. We understand that this is the group which placed emphasis on correct type and conformation in the breed.

There was surely much to be accomplished in various breeding programs once the A.D.R.K. had taken the situation in hand, with emphasis placed on a combination of excellent working ability and beauty of type. Heads were particularly in need of improvement at that period, as

True Lee Heika of Khetaqua, bred by Lee McKenney, is by Ch. Altar's Gunner of Woodland ex Ashby v. Foxcroft, C.D. Priscilla Drake Qua, owner, Center Ossipee, NH.

Black Velvet von Dorow at age 3 years. Breeder-owner, Nancy C. Estes, Von Dorow Rottweilers, Midland, TX.

well as incorrect bites and steep hindquarters, which were very much in evidence. The breed has assuredly prospered under the astute leadership of the A.D.R.K., a fact which can be well appreciated as one surveys the magnificent Rottweilers of modern times!

The correct full title for the A.D.R.K. is the Allgemeiner Deutscher Rottweiler Club. It is a member of the Verband für das Deutsche Hundewesen (V.D.H.) and of the Fédération Cynologique Internationale (F.C.I.), being governed by their rules. As is the case in all countries where the popularity of a breed prospers, there are now numerous local and regional clubs also working diligently for their breed.

Stuttgart, Germany, is now the home of A.D.R.K., and now as in the beginning there is truly an involved group of people working diligently for whatever it believes to be best for breed. Their activities are world famous and highly esteemed; their help, wherever it is needed, is always available.

In 1942, the *Körung* (selection for breed suitability) went into effect. Since that time in Germany, only dogs with *Körung* or *Zuchttauglichkeitsprüfung* can be registered. Approval for *Körung* is gained by taking the dog or bitch to an approved judge who examines the dog for appearance, health, bearing, expression, and conformation. The manner in which the dog moves (gait) is evaluated, as is temperament, and also a study of the pedigree is taken into due consideration. A dog who has been *Körung*-approved for breeding then has his statistics published in the stud book, creating a permanent record.

Such a record is, of course, tremendously valuable to breeders who wish to review the background of the dog or dogs they are considering purchasing, especially since the listings frequently include notations and recommendations regarding what type bitch might be most suitable for breeding with a particular dog.

A training degree which has been earned in advance is also required for a *Körung*, as well as obvious good health and an absence of hereditary faults. The dog must excel in working tendencies and ability.

The *Zuchttauglichkeitsprüfung* is also an A.D.R.K. breeding requirement—a stern test of character intended to eliminate from breeding dogs who are shy, nervous, or lacking in fighting instinct. For qualification, it is required that the dog be sharp and possess obvious fighting instincts. Mere protectiveness is insufficient; iron nerves and fighting spirit are requisites. Reapproval for the degree must be applied for at three-year intervals.

Rottweilers applying for the *Körung* test must be accompanied by an *Ahnentafel* certificate issued by the A.D.R.K. This certificate brings with it the pedigree and vital statistics of the dog. Two classes of *Körung* are obtainable: No. 1, which is reissued periodically; or No. 2, which is permanent, remaining throughout the lifetime of the dog.

Top: Edgar Kaltenbach, a very prominent and successful Schutzhund and police dog trainer in Germany, working on "bite" practice with Amboss vom Konigssiek, SchH. III, F.H., I.P.O. III, Gekort. Photo courtesy of Eve and Manson Johnson. *Middle:* Sunning themselves, Am., Can. Ch. The Chena Wilderness, age 6 years, with her son, Am., Can. Ch. Wilderness Kobuk v. Forstwald, age 3½ years. Owner-bred by JoAnn Harnish. *Bottom:* Timberline's Keystone Kop, by Hasso v. Hennekamp ex Merrymoore's Pride and Joy. This dog is a working partner with Sheridan County, WY, County Deputy Kelly Hamilton.

Ch. Lindenwood's Anaconda, C.D., T.T., bred by Linda and Bill Michels, Whitmore Lake, MI.

The Modern Rottweiler in Germany

The following remarks, thoughts, and opinions regarding the Rottweilers of present-day Germany have been sent to us through the courtesy of Manson and Eve Johnson, dedicated breeders from Land O' Lakes, Florida. Their Evman Kennels are based on and conducted along the German methods of breeding and raising these wonderful dogs.

Eve and Manson have had the rare distinction of watching their dogs make prestigious wins in the keenest of German competition. They are frequent visitors to these events, thus their fingers are constantly on the pulse of developments in the homeland of the Rottie.

On September 3 and 4, 1988, an event of special significance took place in the town of Rottweil on the southernmost border of West Germany. It was the 18th Annual A.D.R.K. Klubsieger Show, appropriately taking place where Rottweiler dogs were developed as a breed. It was also the occasion on which Eve and Manson Johnson placed in competition the American-German United Friendship Trophy, designed and presented by them as a rotating trophy to be presented annually to the Top Stud Dog of the Year in Germany. It is a token of the desire to salute America's and Germany's mutual admiration for the Rottweiler.

In addition to the donation of the trophy, there was another exciting reason for the Johnsons' presence there—the fact that they owned three of the Rottweilers entered into competition at this fabulous occasion.

Excitement was high-pitched as the evening prior to the big day arrived. It seemed as though the entire population of this small town on the southernmost border of West Germany had turned out, plus hordes of enthusiasts not only from Germany and the U.S. but from England, Scotland, Spain, Portugal, France, Italy, Denmark, Finland, Australia, South Africa, Canada, Mexico, and Brazil. The head of the East German Rottweiler Klub was the guest of the A.D.R.K..

Saturday morning, opening day, found the 18th Anniversary Klubsieger Show getting underway. It took more than eight straight hours of judging for the evaluation of more than 134 dogs in competition. Each dog is critically evaluated as to conformation and movement, the latter calling for *many* laps around the ring, as opposed to the few times which are accepted in the United States. Dog

"Excitement was high-pitched as the evening prior to the big day arrived. It seemed as though the entire population of this small town on the southernmost border of West Germany had turned out . . ."

and handler continue until the dog's condition, stamina, strength, lasting power, and topline have been thoroughly evaluated.

In Germany, the dogs are presented naturally, with no attempts made to alter appearance—not even the clipping of whiskers or removal of front dewclaws. Nor is there evidence of excessive grooming. Over-handling is not permitted. The judge does not use his hands on the mouth. The handler presents the dog's teeth and mouth.

Sunday was the show's finale—especially exciting for the Johnsons, as it was then that their own winning dogs appeared in the ring. When the smoke of battle had cleared at the end of a strenuous day, Gary vom Grutenblick had been named *Klubsieger* and Cita von der Nonnenhohle the *Klubsiegerin.* Tasco vom Zimmerplatz was *Klubjugendsieger* and Jenny von der Silberdistel (owned by the Johnsons) the *Klubjugendsiegerin.* The Top Stud Dog of the Year and winner of the American-German United Friendship Trophy was Iwan vom Fusse der Eifel, owned by Heinz Esser.

In 1989, Manson Johnson visited the Bundessieger Zuchtschau, held by the German V.D.H. on May 6 and 7, in 1989, at Dortmond, West Germany. Here the winners of the show are awarded the *Bundessieger* for Best Adult Male and the *Bundessiegerin* for Best Adult Female. A total of 86 Rottweilers were entered, of which 12 were

Top: **At Storer Ranch, carting is not only for horses. Ch. Liebenswert Designer Genes, T.T., HIC, starting off to do the rounds. Pat Storer, owner, Alleyton, TX.** *Middle:* **Am., Can. Ch. Ebonstern Lorelei v.d. Liebe, Can. C.D., pictured at 14 months. By Am., Can Ch. Ebonstern Black Bart ex Ebonstern Bryt Promise. Cheryl Wagner, Mount Vernon, WA, owner.** *Bottom:* **Six Alouette Rottweilers at "Rottie Walk" in May, 1987, Maple Ridge, B.C., Canada.**

Top: Ch. Nelson v.d. Brabantpark, Dutch import, 1988 Top Ten Rottweiler, Best in Show, multi-Group winner, American R.C. Specialty winner. Owned by Powderhorn/Wencrest Rottweilers, Inc., Hollywood, CA.

Bottom: Best of Breed and Winners Bitch was a family affair at Evelyn Kenny Kennel and Obedience Club in August, 1988. Best of Breed was awarded Can. Ch. Hildegruen's Dauntless Frisco, C.D.; Winners Bitch, completing her championship, Can. Ch. Mink Hollow's Briana, C.D.

"Of this event, Manson Johnson says that it was certainly prestigious, and this in his opinion the Klubsieger is, of course, the most so..."

absent, leaving a total of 74 actually present divided among seven classes.

Of this event, Manson Johnson says that it was certainly prestigious, and this in his opinion the Klubsieger is, of course, the most so, the Bundessieger second, and the Europasieger Show third among the A.D.R.K. conformation events.

Unfortunately, we understand that the show was held in tight quarters in two inadequately sized small rings in a huge, smoke-filled and overcrowded building with a floor far too slippery to make a fair evaluation of the dog's gait or movement possible. This seems such a shame.

The 1989 *Bundessjugendsieger* (Best Puppy Dog) was Heit von Hennekamp, born February 27, 1988, sired by Iwan vom Fusse der Eifel ex Sheila vom Hause Lohnert.

The *Bundessjugendsiegerin* (Best Puppy Bitch) was won by Vroni vom Hennekamp, a littermate to the Puppy Dog. This seems to support all the opinions I have heard expressed regarding the superiority of their sire, Iwan vom Fusse der Eifel, as a stud dog of superiority and importance.

The 1989 *Bundessieger* (Best Rottweiler Male) was Chris vom Obergrombacher Schloss, SchH. III, born July, 1985, by Hassan Konigsgarten ex Berta von KleinVach. The 1989 *Bundessiegerin* (Best Rottweiler Female) was Ina von Silberdistel, born May, 1986, by Lord vom Schilfeck ex Niky vom Steinkopf.

The award for the Most Beautiful Dog in Show was gained by Rambo vom Hennekamp, born December, 1987, also by Iwan vom Fusse der Eifel, his dam Ines vom Hennekamp.

Manson Johnson has written us provocatively about German Rottweilers in general and particularly the manner in which they are bred. He has answered several questions which are surely pertinent, a discussion of which we believe belongs in this coverage of the breed.

The questions regard the reasons Americans, even after all these years, return in hopes of buying Rottweilers in Germany, especially West Germany, which seems to be the source of some of the best even nowadays. How does it happen that only comparatively few American-bred Rotties seem able to gain the Schutzhund III degree, while this is quite often taken for granted in Germany?

Manson's answer is both simple and complex. In simplistic terms, he feels that all of these questions can be answered by the statement that Germans must adhere to the quite strict breeding regulations of the Allgemeiner Deutscher Klub, and in order to fully understand this statement, more must be known about the purposes of the A.D.R.K. Put quite simply, the A.D.R.K. is the only breed group responsible for definition, promotion, and enforcement of the German Rottweiler standard and the issuance of *Ahnentafels* (pedigrees).

Goals of the A.D.R.K. are as follows:

1) The preservation, consolidation, and strengthening of the peculiar characteristics of the Rottweiler breed, and the enhancement of its physical attributes and character.
2) The supervision of the breeding and training of Rottweilers, with special emphasis on the Rottweiler as a suitable dog for use in the public sector; as a guide dog for the blind; as a guard dog to protect life and property; and as a first aid dog in times of emergency or disaster. In taking precedence as it does, A.D.R.K. is a steadying influence on breed quality and character.
3) Defining the German standard for the Rottweiler, making assistance and advice available to all members in the matters of breeding, rearing and care of Rottweilers. Also included in this is the acquistion and disposal of Rottweilers.

Portrait in yarn by Chris Brown of Am., Can. Ch. Von Gailingen's Dassie Did It, U.D.T., Can. C.D., and Am., Bda. Ch. Von Gailingen's Dark Delight, U.D.T., Bda. C.D.X., Can. C.D. Both bred, owned, and handled to their splendid records by Mrs. Catherine M. Thompson, Von Gailingen Rottweilers, Freehold, NJ.

4) Bringing the Rottweiler to people's attention, especially in the case of the younger generation, and for promoting interest in breeding, general usefulness and versatility.

5) The establishment of rules for breeding and judging Rottweilers. The conducting of tests for breeding suitability, performance and conformation shows and the publication of such awards are all under A.D.R.K. jurisdiction, as is the promotion of the participation of man and his dog in controlled and systematic training programs for the Rottweiler.

6) The promotion of scientific research in the canine field in general.

7) Last but far from least is the cooperation with Rottweiler lovers from all parts of the world.

Manson Johnson makes special note that all aspects of the rules and regulations of A.D.R.K. place emphasis on its original slogan, "Rottweiler breeding is and remains the breeding of *Working Dogs.*"

The minimum age for breeding Rottweilers under A.D.R.K. suitability requirements is 20 months for females and 24 months for males. The maximum age for breeding is eight years for females and nine years for males. Although Americans are not under A.D.R.K. regulations, there is wisdom and experience in these requirements

Apache Hill's Gusher, by Ch. Cannon River Gusher ex Ch. Excalibur's B. Apache War Song, C.D. Gusher is now a police dog with the San Diego Police Department. Photo courtesy of Irene Castillo, Abilene, TX.

and these limitations should be followed in your own breeding of Rottweilers wherever you may live, as they are for the purpose of assuring strong, healthy young stock. It is the actual mating date which is used in determining whether the dog is too young or too old to be bred.

Under A.D.R.K. requirements, a male Rottweiler may not service more than two females within one week, nor more than 40 females during one year. All breedings, including those with females from foreign countries, must be reported to the A.D.R.K. stud book office. In complying with the breeding regulations of the V.D.H., the A.D.R.K. female Rottweilers are allowed to bear only one litter per calendar year. The breeder is allowed to freely choose the breeding partners within the regulations of the A.D.R.K., but it is recommended for his own good that he seek the advice of the local breed warden, who then should recommend at least two eligible select males from which the breeder can choose for the breeding of the female. It is the responsibility of the owners of the male and of the female to make certain, before mating, that both partners possess A.D.R.K. pedigrees and that they have passed a breed suitability test.

Members of the A.D.R.K. are only allowed to breed registered Rottweilers that have passed a *Zuchttauglichkeitsprüfungen* or Breed Suitability Test. At the time of mating, one of the partners must have at least a Schutzhund I degree and one must have *Körung* or select hip joints meaning HD− or HD+/−. The minimum age requirement at the time of mating is 24 months.

The *Zuchttauglichkeitsprüfung*, or Breed Suitability Test, consists of conformation examination and temperament evaluation. The purpose of the BST is to select Rottweilers which are suitable for breeding and to exclude those who are unsuitable. The minimum age for taking the Breed Suitability Test is 18 months for both males and females. The judge evaluates the males first and then the females. Each dog is measured thoroughly from head to toe in various positions and then weighed. His overall conformation is recorded, with special attention given to eye color, bite, number of teeth, topline, rear angulation, coat, etc. Structure as related to movement is very important in the evaluation.

The dog's temperament is then tested. Two gunshots are fired approximately 20 feet from the dog as he is walked off lead. The dog must not react shyly or aggressively to the gunshot. The dog is walked into a group of people and is told to sit. The dog should be indifferent to the group. Once again, shyness and aggressiveness are grounds for failure. An attack on the handler occurs, whereby the dog must react by attacking an agitator who is wearing a protective suit. The dog bites the sleeve while being driven gestures with the stick and sleeve. The dog takes two pronounced stick hits while being driven by the agitator. A Rottweiler that fails the Breed Suitability Test may enter again as often as the owner desires.

Members of the A.D.R.K. wishing

Ch. Alfa vom Whithaus at age 16 months. This daughter of Int. Ch. Mirko vom Steinkopf, SchH. III, ex Ch. Hanni vom Bakkes, SchH. I, V-2. A champion at only 17 months, she displays significant maturity and character that are typical of the intelligent expression of the Rottweiler. Alfa is from the "A" litter of Mirko and Hanni and is owned by Dr. and Mrs. Jack Whitman, Whithaus Rottweilers, Ponte Vedra Beach, FL.

off by the agitator, and takes two controlled stick hits. The final part of the Temperament Test is called the Courage Test, whereby the dog must go after an agitator who is running straight away from the dog. As the dog comes within 50 feet of the agitator, the latter turns and faces the dog, making threatening to breed dogs are encouraged to choose only the best possible dogs for the purpose. It is important that Germany's standard for the Rottweiler be upheld with its emphasis on unambiguous sexual characteristics, health and vitality, perseverance, good strong body and bone structure, scissors bite and correct dentition, steady nerves, self-confidence, courage, and steadfast character. Hip dysplasia is a degenerative trait with a strong hereditary link which can sadly decrease the animal's working ability. Therefore, each and every reputable breeder must only breed dogs with select hip joints. Matings producing litters with hereditary faults must not be repeated. The head breed warden is obligated to ban such matings and, should this action not be heeded, to see to it that registration of the litter does not take place.

Ch. Lindenwood's Anaconda, C.D., T.T., bred by Linda and Bill Michels, Whitmore Lake, MI.

The *Körung*, or Breeding Qualification Tests, are the most selective breeding tests for Rottweilers. According to A.D.R.K., the purpose of the *Körung* is "to select the best from among the dogs suitable for breeding, thus enabling these dogs to be utilized most intensely in the breeding programs." The minimum age requirements for *Körung* are 30 months for females and 36 months for males. Only the best-of-the-best among Rottweilers are permitted to try for the *Körung*. The dogs chosen must excel in conformation competition by being rated at least Very Good (*Sehr Gut*/SG) at three conformation shows under at least two different judges. The dogs must have achieved working titles, either Schutzhund or I.P.O. Males must have a Schutzhund III and females must have at least a Schutzhund I. The dogs must have succeeded in their Breed Suitability Test with hip ratings in the highest categories. The dogs also must have passed a 12-mile endurance test called AD (*Ausdaurprufung*). Another important requirement is that dogs used for breeding must possess very dark mouth pigmentation and eye color.

It is in the spring and fall each year that the *Körung* is offered, the actual test being similar to that for Breed Suitability, although more intensified. It is not unusual for less than half of those trying to pass the test to meet with success. Those who do pass the *Körung* are awarded the designation for a period of two years (the *Angekort*). During this same two-year period, offspring of such a dog are examined, and if the offspring are high quality, then the parent becomes eligible to try for the highest breeding rating, that of "Breeding Qualified until end of the breeding utilization age," abbreviation for which is *Gekort bis EzA*. A minimum of three good-quality litters is the basis on which this distinction is attained by a stud dog. For a brood bitch, one good litter suffices.

Gretel von der Silberdistel SchH. III, I.P.O. III, AD, Gekort, placing V-1 at the Klubsieger Show with breeder Franz Olbricht. Owners, Eve and Manson Johnson.

TERMS SEEN IN ROTTWEILER PEDIGREES

As you study the pedigrees of Rottweilers, read about them, or discuss the breed with others who are also interested in it, there are certain terms encountered with such frequency that we feel an explanation of some of them here may prove useful.

The following list of terms which you will see frequently in the pedigrees of Rottweilers is used here with the permission of *Rottweil Xpress*, the magazine for which it was prepared. Our thanks to Joe McGinnis and Duane Doll for sharing it with us.

AD: Has passed the Endurance Test.

A.D.R.K.: Allgemeiner Deutscher Rottweiler Klub, the parent club for the breed in Germany.

BISA: Was awarded Best in Show at an AKC-licensed all-breed conformation show.

BISS: Was awarded Best Rottweiler at a licensed Specialty Show.

Ch.: Has completed the requirements to be entitled an American Kennel Club Champion of Record. When championship title was earned in a foreign country, Ch. must be preceded with country of origin of award, i.e., Mex. Ch., Bda. Ch., etc.

C.D.: Has completed the requirements for the Companion

Glacier Valley Ruffian, by Am., Can. Ch. Bryloukis Great Expectations, C.D., ex Panamint Polar Delight. Breeder-owner, P. Adriane Schaefer, Alaska.

Dog obedience degree by receiving a qualifying score three separate times in the Novice Obedience Class.

C.D.X.: Has completed the requirements for the Companion Dog Excellent obedience degree by receiving qualifying scores in the Open Obedience Class.

FH: *Fahrtenhund*; advanced Tracking degree.

***Gekort*:** Suitable for breeding for a period of two years; subject to reevaluation. Obtained at three years of age.

***Gekort bis EzA*:** Is rated suitable for breeding for the duration of Breeding Utilization Age: nine years in males, eight years in females. Obtained at five years of age.

H.D. –: (H.D. free) No indication of hip dysplasia.

H.D. ±: (H.D. good) Transition stage.

H.D. +: (H.D. fair) Mild indication of hip dysplasia.

H.D. + +: X-rays show positive hip dysplasia. Breeding is prohibited.

H.D. + + +: Severely dysplastic. Breeding is prohibited.

I.P.O.: *Internationale Prufungsordnung*. International Working Order. International Trials incorporating tracking, obedience and protection. Similar to Schutzhund with slight variations. Three levels: I.P.O. I (minimum age 14 months); I.P.O. II (16 months); I.P.O. III (20 months).

***Korüng*:** Has met strict requirements in all areas; breed suitability, conformation, working, protection, is free from hip dysplasia. Dog or bitch is suitable for breeding (*gekort*) for a period of two years; after that time dog and progeny are reevaluated.

LS: *Leistungszucht*. Parents and grandparents have SchH. degrees and *Korüng*.

Pink Papers: Uninterrupted Schutzhund lineage.

SchH.: Schutzhund, the working degree requiring extensive abilities in the areas of tracking, obedience, and protection. There are three levels of Schutzhund—SchH. I: Beginning Schutzhund (minimum age 14 months); SchH. II: Intermediate Schutzhund (16 months); and SchH. III: Advanced Schutzhund (18 months). After attaining the degree at any level, the dog must wait six months before being eligible for competition at the next higher level. Upon reaching SchH. III, dog is eligible for competition at any time.

***Sieger*:** Male champion at a particular show (i.e., *1989 Klubsieger*, winner of the 1989 A.D.R.K. Specialty Show).

***Siegerin*:** Female champion at a particular show.

T.D.: Has passed an A.K.C.-

licensed Tracking test. May be combined with Utility Degree: U.D.T.

T.D.X.: Has passed an A.K.C.-licensed Tracking Dog Excellent test. May be combined with Utility Degree: U.D.T.X.

U.D.: Has attained the Utility Dog degree by receiving three qualifying scores in Utility Class. May be combined with Tracking Degree: U.D.T.

WH: *Wachhund* (Guard dog). Obedience/Guard test. No bite work is involved in this training.

Z.T.P.R.: Has passed the Breed Suitability Test in Germany.

GERMAN STANDARD FOR THE ROTTWEILER

The following standard for the breed was prepared by the A.D.R.K. and is the German standard for the Rottweiler. It was first adopted in Germany during the early 1900s, where the general type has remained practically unchanged over the years, as has breed character.

General Appearance and Character—The Rottweiler is a robust dog rather above the medium size, neither plump nor light, neither spindle-shanked nor like a Greyhound. His figure, which is short, compact, and strong in proportion, gives every indication not only of high intelligence but also of wonderful devotion,

Top: **Ch. Gemstone's Blitz Meister, T.T., by Ch. Rodsden's Berte v. Zederwald, C.D.X., ex Evo Regnant of Gemstones, C.D., belongs to Karen and Harold Riddle, Jr., Fall Branch, TN.**
Middle: **Aust. Ch. Stromhall Picka Pack, owned by Pat Hall. Photo courtesy of Powderhorn/Wencrest.** *Bottom:* **Glen vom Markgraflerland, SchH. III, having his measurements taken at the 1988 Korung in Germany. Photo courtesy of Eve and Manson Johnson.**

Top: Ch. Pioneer das Bedazzled at age 16 months. Winners Bitch at the 1985 A.R.C. National Specialty from Bred-by-Exhibitor Class. Finished in 11 shows. A Best of Breed winner; a Group placer; and dam of both conformation and obedience title holders. Bred and owned by Virginia Aceti and Sheryl Hedrick. *Bottom:* Southwind Dempsey of True Lee, son of Ch. Altar's Gunner of Woodland ex Ashby v. Foxcroft, C.D. Bred by Lee McKenney, this Rottie is owned by Priscilla Drake Qua, Kehtaqua Kennels.

eagerness, and joy in work. A tractable dog with considerable power and stubborn endurance. His general appearance immediately proclaims him to be of determination and courage; his calm glance indicates his good humor and his unswerving fidelity. His nature exhibits no traces of disquietude, hastiness, or indecision. Treachery, maliciousness and falseness are entirely foreign to his nature.

Head—Of medium length; the skull broad between the ears and moderately arched in the line of forehead when viewed from the side. The frontal depression is well emphasized. The occipital point is well developed, although it does not in any way protrude. The cheeks are well covered with muscle without being excessively so. The zygomatic arch is well pronounced.

The straight bridge of the nose is not very long. The length from the root to the tip is not longer than the upper part of the head (epicranium) from the occipital bone to the frontal depression.

The tip of the nose is well formed, rather broad than round, with comparatively large nostrils, and always black in color.

The flews are also black and firm; they fall gradually away towards the corners of the mouth which do not protrude excessively.

The teeth are strong, engaging one over the other like a scissors. The incisors grip in front of the lower jaw.

The medium-sized eyes are of a

Ch. HawkHaven's Abbon Danza, by Rodsden's Strawland Tyr ex HawkHaven's Thea. Owned by Barbara Kellett, Crystal Lake, IL.

perceptible dewlap or superfluous skin.

Forequarters—Show long, well-set shoulders. The upper arm is well set, but not too close to the body. The lower arm is well developed, powerful and muscular. The fetlocks, which are slightly "springy," are powerful and not too steeply set. The paws are round, very compact, and arched. The soles are very hard, the dark nails short and strong. The forelegs when viewed from all sides are straight and are not set too narrow.

Trunk—Breast is roomy, broad and deep; rather round than oval. The back is straight and firm, rather short than long. The part in the region of the kidneys is short, powerful and deep; the flanks are very slightly drawn up. The buttocks are short and broad and do not fall away.

Hindquarters—The upper parts of the thigh are short, broad, and well covered with muscle. The shanks are very long and very muscular above; they are sinewy below and powerful. The hocks have a good angle but not exaggerated, and still less steep. The paws are somewhat longer than those of the forelegs, but are very compact with strong toes and without dewclaws.

Tail—(stumpy tail) is carried perpendicular as much as possible. It is short, set high, and prolongs the line of back in a perpendicular direction. The dog is often born with this stumpy tail, called "bobtail." It is, however, to be subsequently docked if it is too long.

Hair—The so-called bristly hair, is short, rough and strong. The underdown, which must be found on the neck and thighs, must on no account protrude from the outer hair. The hair is somewhat long on the fore and hind as well as on the tail. Otherwise it is rather short than long, sitting close and firm.

Color—Black with very distinct and dark markings on the cheeks, the muzzle, the breast, and the legs as well as over each eye; these markings are from mahogany

dark brown color and expressive of good humor and self-confidence. The eyelids close down well.

The ears are small and triangular and stand away from each other as much as possible; they are set high and appear to give breadth to the upper part of the head; they are carried well forward and afford a good covering for the ear hole.

The scalp is tightdrawn and sits well everywhere; at most, it only forms folds when the dog is on the alert.

The neck is powerful, round and broad, with plenty of muscle and slightly arched line rising from the shoulders, fairly spare without any

brown to yellow in color. Small white markings on the chest and belly are not exactly faults but neither are they desirable.

Size—In the case of dogs, height at shoulder is 24–27½ inches. In bitches from 22–26, always in good proportion.

Numerous faults are listed by the A.D.R.K., ranging from dogs who are ineligible to compete at all, which includes those being monorchids or cryptorchids; having bad mouths; strongly marked reversal of sexual characteristics (doggy bitches and bitchy dogs); nervousness, cowardice or stupidity; long and curly coats or too smooth a coat with undercoat lacking.

Slightly less serious than the above faults are those which are considered to be "working faults" in that they affect the dog's usefulness and ability to work as well as appearance; and a number of what might be called "minor" faults.

Ch. Merrymoore's Imp von Dorow, T.T. American R.C. Top Ten Bitch, 1985, a Group winner; 16 times Best of Breed, 38 times Best of Opposite Sex. By Merrymoore's V.I.P. ex Tasha von Huntshof.

Certified Pedigree

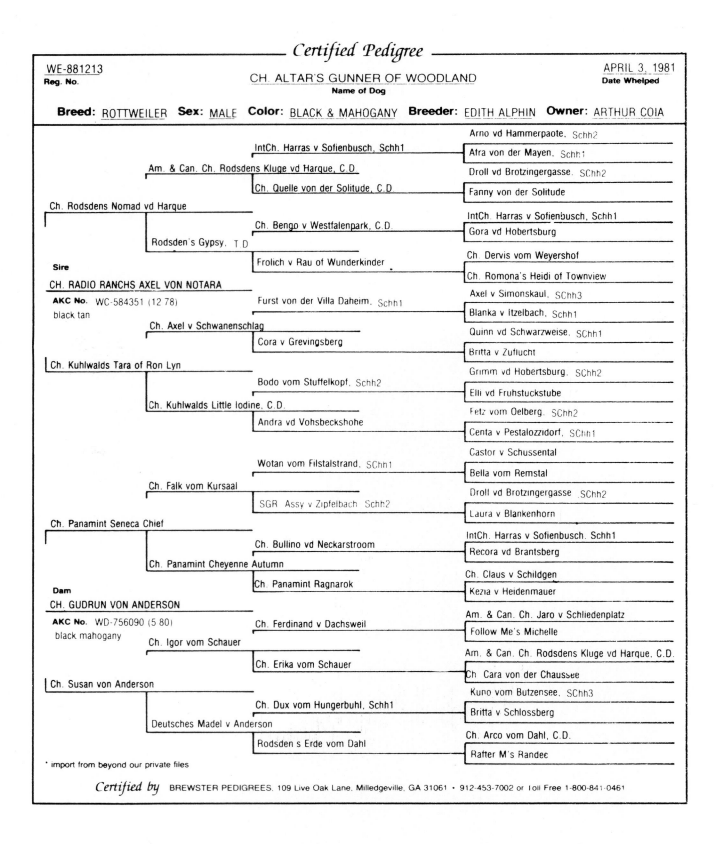

WE-881213
Reg. No.

CH. ALTAR'S GUNNER OF WOODLAND
Name of Dog

APRIL 3, 1981
Date Whelped

Breed: ROTTWEILER **Sex:** MALE **Color:** BLACK & MAHOGANY **Breeder:** EDITH ALPHIN **Owner:** ARTHUR COIA

Sire

CH. RADIO RANCHS AXEL VON NOTARA

AKC No. WC-584351 (12 78)
black tan

Ch. Rodsdens Nomad vd Harque

- Am. & Can. Ch. Rodsdens Kluge vd Harque, C.D.
  - IntCh. Harras v Sofienbusch, Schh1
    - Arno vd Hammerpaote, Schh2
    - Afra von der Mayen, Schh1
  - Ch. Quelle von der Solitude, C.D.
    - Droll vd Brotzingergasse, SChh2
    - Fanny von der Solitude
- Rodsden's Gypsy, T.D.
  - Ch. Bengo v Westfalenpark, C.D.
    - IntCh. Harras v Sofienbusch, Schh1
    - Gora vd Hobertsburg
  - Frolich v Rau of Wunderkinder
    - Ch. Dervis vom Weyershof
    - Ch. Romona's Heidi of Townview

Ch. Kuhlwalds Tara of Ron Lyn

- Ch. Axel v Schwanenschlag
  - Furst von der Villa Daheim, Schh1
    - Axel v Simonskaul, SChh3
    - Blanka v Itzelbach, Schh1
  - Cora v Grevingsberg
    - Quinn vd Schwarzweise, SChh1
    - Britta v Zuflucht
- Ch. Kuhlwalds Little Iodine, C.D.
  - Bodo vom Stuffelkopf, Schh2
    - Grimm vd Hobertsburg, SChh2
    - Elli vd Fruhstuckstube
  - Andra vd Vohsbeckshohe
    - Fetz vom Oelberg, SChh2
    - Centa v Pestalozzidorf, SChh1

Dam

CH. GUDRUN VON ANDERSON

AKC No. WD-756090 (5 80)
black mahogany

Ch. Panamint Seneca Chief

- Ch. Falk vom Kursaal
  - Wotan vom Filstalstrand, SChh1
    - Castor v Schussental
    - Bella vom Remstal
  - SGR Assy v Zipfelbach Schh2
    - Droll vd Brotzingergasse, SChh2
    - Laura v Blankenhorn
- Ch. Panamint Cheyenne Autumn
  - Ch. Bullino vd Neckarstroom
    - IntCh. Harras v Sofienbusch, Schh1
    - Recora vd Brantsberg
  - Ch. Panamint Ragnarok
    - Ch. Claus v Schildgen
    - Kezia v Heidenmauer

Ch. Susan von Anderson

- Ch. Igor vom Schauer
  - Ch. Ferdinand v Dachsweil
    - Am. & Can. Ch. Jaro v Schliedenplatz
    - Follow Me's Michelle
  - Ch. Erika vom Schauer
    - Am. & Can. Ch. Rodsdens Kluge vd Harque, C.D.
    - Ch. Cara von der Chaussee
- Deutsches Madel v Anderson
  - Ch. Dux vom Hungerbuhl, Schh1
    - Kuno vom Butzensee, SChh3
    - Britta v Schlossberg
  - Rodsden s Erde vom Dahl
    - Ch. Arco vom Dahl, C.D.
    - Rafter M's Randee

* import from beyond our private files

Certified by BREWSTER PEDIGREES, 109 Live Oak Lane, Milledgeville, GA 31061 • 912-453-7002 or Toll Free 1-800-841-0461

36

AKC WD402051
INDIVIDUAL REG. NO.

LITTER REG. NO.

Certified Pedigree

Darra
CALL NAME

AKC
REGISTERED WITH

CH. DARRA MICHAELA VON STOLZENFELS, CD
REGISTERED NAME OF DOG

ARC Bronze Pro- duction Award Winner

BREED Rottweiler   **DATE WHELPED** April 20, 1976   **SEX** Bitch

BREEDER Jack P. & Dr. Evelyn M. Ellman **ADDRESS** 16757 E. Ft. Custer Dr., Augusta, Mi. 49012

OWNER Jack P. & Dr. Evelyn M. Ellman **ADDRESS** 16757 E. Ft. Custer Dr., Augusta, Mi. 49012

GENERAL DESCRIPTION black with mahagony markings

SIRE

Igor vom Kursaal

- BS Blitz v. Schloss Westerwinkel SchH 3
  - Axel v.d. Kappenbergerheide, SchH 2
    - BS Igor v. Kohlwald, SchH 1
    - Dolli von der Immenruh
  - Asta vom Afirahaus
    - Rex v. Kohlwald, SchH 3
    - Birke von Eggau, SchH 3
- Herta vom Kursaal, SchH 2
  - Arko vom Martinsberg, SchH1
    - Arno v. Schafenberg, SchH 1
    - BS Vroni v. Gaisburg, SchH 3
  - Jutta vom Burgtobel
    - Arras v.d. Schweizergrenze
    - Elli v. Burgtobel

Ch. Kavon Mr. Murphy A/C CD
Dog World Award Winner, Obedience
REG. NO. WB906860

Kavon Lony

- Kavon Kano
  - Igor v. Kursaal
    - BS Blitz v. Schloss Westerwinkel SchH 3
    - Herta v. Kursaal, SchH 2
  - Follow Me's Doreen
    - Ch. Follow Me's Xerxes
    - Rita
- Kuhlwald Ida
  - Bodo vom Stüffelkopf
    - Grimm v.d. Hobertsburg, SchH 1
    - Elli v.d. Frühstücksstube
  - Andra v.d. Vohsbeckshöhe
    - Fetz vom Oelberg, SchH 2
    - Centa v. Pestalozzidorf SchH 1

DAM

BS Ferro v.d. Löwenau SchH 2

- Arno v. Stüffelkopf, SchH 2
  - Pio v.d. Solitude, SchH 2
    - Droll v.d. Brötzingergasse SchH 2
    - Fanny v.d. Solitude
  - Elli v.d. Frühstücksstube
    - Amor v. Sonnenhof, SchH 1
    - Kari Eulenspiegel
- Dunja v.d. Löwenau, SchH 1
  - Bär v. Schloss Westerwinkel
    - Axel v.d. Kappenbergerheide SchH 2
    - Asta vom Afirahaus
  - Pedra von Hohenreissach
    - Lando v. Jakobsbrunnen, SchH 3
    - Diana v. Remstal, SchH 1

Gunda von Ingenhof, AD
ARC Bronze Production Award Winner
REG. NO. WD 107350

Käthe vom Kursaal, SchH 2

- BS Blitz v. Schloss Westerwinkel, SchH 3
  - Axel v.d. Kappenbergerheide, SchH 2
    - BS Igor v. Kohlwald, SchH 1
    - Dolli von der Immenruh
  - Asta vom Afirahaus
    - Rex vom Kohlwald, SchH 3
    - Birke v. Eggau, SchH 3
- BS/Swiss Sg. Assy v. Zipfelbach, SchH I
  - Droll v.d. Brötzingergasse SchH 2
    - Alex vom Glastal, SchH 1
    - Asta v.d. Brötzingergasse, SchH 1
  - Laura vom Blankenhorn
    - Arno v.d. Wanne, SchH 2
    - Bertel v. Nuifra, SchH 1

I HEREBY CERTIFY THAT THIS PEDIGREE IS TRUE AND CORRECT
TO THE BEST OF MY KNOWLEDGE AND BELIEF

SIGNED *Dr. Evelyn M. Ellman*

DATE January 25 19 89

THE KENNEL CLUB

CERTIFIED PEDIGREE
EXTRACTED FROM
KENNEL CLUB RECORDS

1 CLARGES STREET, LONDON, W1Y 8AB

Pedigree for **POTTERSPRIDE PURE N'FREE**	Registration No **0157BX**
Breed **ROTTWEILER**	Breeder **MRS V E SLADE**
Colour **BLACK & GOLD**	Sex **DOG** Born **1/05/86**

SIRE 1: CAPRIDO MINSTREL OF POTTERSPRIDE CH
4991BR

3 CHESARA DARK CHARLES CH
0712BQ

7 CHESARA DARK HEROD
B2214401B10

CHESARA DARK JULIETTE OF VONMARK
8 C2275705C10

4 LYRIC FROM CAPRIDO
2232BN

9 CHESARA DARK JORIS
2169BK

TRENCHARD BIANCA
10 B0099782B12

DAM 2: POTTERSPRIDE SUPER EBONY
H0942404H06

5 GAMEGARDS EVER READY
3537BQ

11 GAMEGARDS FIRE'N RAIN
3259BG

SCHUTZ OF GAMEGARDS CH
12 3452BI

6 CASSES LASS OF POTTERSPRIDE CH
1950BK

13 PRINCE GELERT OF BHALUK CH
3236BI

AARON'S FUGUE
14 063190/71

MRS V E SLADE
POTTERSPRIDE MEADOW LODGE
WIMBISH LOWER GREEN
SAFFRON WALDEN ESSEX CB10 2XH

Registered Owner

The Seal of The Kennel Club embossed hereon certifies that
this pedigree has been compiled from official records.
This is not an export document.

Date Issued: **20/10/88**

Certificate of Pedigree

Registered Name	JOUKONHEIMO SULLA
Kennel Name	Sulla
Sex	Male
Breed	Rottweiler
C.K.C. Individual Registration No.	
Fin: SF22060/88	
C.K.C. Litter No.	
Date of Birth	July 25, 1988
Birthplace	Finland
Breeder	J.A.U. Yrjola
Address	Pajamaentie 7 C 33
City	00360 Helsinki 36
Province	Finland
Postal Code	

GENERAL DESCRIPTION

Color and Markings Black/Tan

Weight
Height at Shoulder
Temperament
House-broken?
Field-broken?
Head
Muzzle
Eyes
Ears
Body
Forelegs
Hindlegs
Coat
Tail
Feather
Peculiarities

Sire: (1) Rocky
C.K.C. No. SF13506/86 *

Dam: (2) Joukonheimo Ofelia
C.K.C. No. SF12703G

OWNER
FINNROTTI KENNEL
Markus Maenpaa
Box 353
Nipigon, Ont., Can.
P0T-2J0
(807)886-2409

Grand Parents

V-83
Haukkukallion Tarro
C.K.C. No. SF13503F/78

Onnimannin Blackberry
C.K.C. No. SF08623F/82 *

Fin.+Swed. Ch.
Von Urbano Leopold
C.K.C. No. SF08433V/78 *

Joukonheimo Gloria
C.K.C. No. SF10315E/79

Great Grand Parents

Matador
C.K.C. No. SF012544/74 *

Haukkukallion Susanna
C.K.C. No. SF07519S/74

Fandangos Dan
C.K.C. No. SF16300N/78 *

Onnimannin Strawberry
C.K.C. No. SF044187/79 *

Adlers Puck
C.K.C. No. SF12073P/76 *

Vom Heidenmoor Perle
C.K.C. No. SF18404H/73

Joukonheimo Domitianus
C.K.C. No. SF21577A/76 *

Joukonheimo Cleopatra
C.K.C. No. SF10853J/75 *

Great Great Grand Parents

Ger. IMP.
Gerry Eulenspiegel
Nisitan Mangamilla
Suolan Jumbo
C.K.C. No. SF70973/73
Merilain
(Swed.) Fandangos Tico
(Swed.) Fandangos Beda
Int.,Fin., Swed.Ch.
Mustan Murinan Junior
C.K.C. No. SF17626M/77
Tahvan Tassun Biamadonna
C.K.C. No. SF3816C/76*
(Ger.)
Droll V. St.Andreasberg
C.K.C. No. SF3915/74 *
Int. Ch.
Sabine V. Heidenmoor
Oidipus
Gitta V. Heidenmoor
(Swed.) Faunus Demon
C.K.C. No. SF41823/73
Lorelei V. Heidenmoor
C.K.C. No. SF6087D/72
Meko
Lorelei V. Heidenmoor
C.K.C. No. SF 6087D/72

Great Great Great Grand Parents

Alex V. Kloster Disibodenberg
Barbel V. Grevinsberg
Dieter V. Heidenmoor
Nisitan Harriman
Attalos Janne
Nurkkanienen Ella
Bingo
Paivin Susanna
Alfan Batman
Fandangos Skimmer
Fandangos Gyller
Hassleholms Beda
Nor.V.Ch.Black Hurricane
Mustan Murinan Astanda
Fin.Ch. Attalos Adolf
Tahvan Tassun Adessa
Falko V. Grunsfeld
Anne V. Bauergraben
Artemis *
Krambambuli V.Heidenmoor
Tito V. Jollasheim
Lotte de Lortto
Dieter V.Heidenmoor
Xantippa V.Heidenmoor
Swed.Ch Saltsjoborgs Ben Hogan
Faunus Arana
Antoni SF339/65T
Fin.Ch Cora V.Heidenmoor
Hallanvaara Carax Max
Dear Favorite Dora
Antoni SF339/65T
Fin.Ch Cora V.Heidenmoor

38

CH. PRINCE GELERT OF BHALUK
Date of Birth 23 AUGUST 1972

Breeder: Mrs. Reeve   Top Dog 1975   Owner Violet Slade
12CCs 3 Res. CCs

Ch. Gamegards Bulli v.d. Waldachquelle BVA/KC HD Cert.	Bullu v. Hungerbuhl Sch.H3	Kuno v. Butzensee Sch.H3
		Britta v. Schlossberg
	Anka v. Reichenbachle	BS '63 Blitz v. Schloss Westerwinkel Sch.H3
		Antje v. Wegscheide
Bhaluk Princess Delilah	Gamegards Lars v.d. Hobertsberg	Caro v. Kupferdach Sch.H3
		Adda v. Dahl Sch.H3
	Elsa from Blackforest	Rintelna The Bombardier CDX, UDX
		Anouk from Blackforest

CH. RICH BITCH OF POTTERSPRIDE
Date of Birth 8 March 1983

Breeder: Mrs. L. Shaw
Junior Warrant   Top Champion Bitch 1985   Owner: Violet Slade
5 CCs, Res CCs

Ch. Caprido Minstrel of Potterspride	Ch. Chesara Dark Charles	Chesara Dark Herod
		Chesara Dark Juliet Vonmark
	Lyric from Caprido	Chesara Dark Joris
		Trenchard Bianca
Potterspride Bronze Angel	Ch. Linguards Jupiter	Poirot Brigadier
		Bassenthwait Carol
	Ch. Cass'es Lass of Potterspride	Ch. Prince Gelert of Bahluk
		Aarons Fugue

To be suitable as a stud or dam, a Rottweiler must possess the physical characteristics as well as the pedigree, which make him/her both phenologically and geneologically suitable for breeding purposes.

Pedigree

Little Flower Kennels

Frank & Val Fiorella
76 Woodcrest Road
Boxford, Mass. 01921

Tel. (617) 887-8887

INT. CH. *BARTO V 'T STRAOTJE, IPO III, RO-16980T
Registered Name of Dog

Date Whelped __July 16, 1983__   Sex __Male__

Breeder __A. L. Emmers__   Address __The Netherlands__

Owner __Frank & Val Fiorella__   Address __Boxford, Massachusetts__

PARENTS	GRANDPARENTS	GREAT-GRANDPARENTS	GREAT-GREAT-GRANDPARENTS
SIRE: Dingo v d Marorie SchH 1 HD Tc Utrecht	Klubsg., World Sg., Bundessieger Dingo v Schwaiger Wappen, SchH III HD Free Utrecht	1977 Europa Sieger Int. Ch. Ives Eulenspiegel SchH 3 HD Free, ADRK	Astor Vom Landgraben
			Dina Vom Kaiserberg
		Anja vom Schwaiger Wappen SchH 1	Attila V.D.VierbenDonaub
			Anka Vom Lohauserholz
	Bonny v Beckum, IPO III HD Tc Utrecht	Axel v d Nedermolen SchH 2 HD Tc Utrecht	Elko V Kastanienbaum
			Anca (NHSB SBGOID)
		Dushka v d Kaempe HD Free Utrecht	Gerlach VH Brabantpark
			Anda V D Kaempe
DAM: International Ch. Belgian Ch. Quinty v 't Straotje IPO I HD Tc Utrecht	Young Klubsg. 1974 Astor v Fusse der Eifel, SchH 3 HD Free Utrecht	Int. Ch., KS Bulli v Hungerbuhl SchH 2	Kuno V Butzensee
			Britta V Schlossberg
		Cora v d Simonskaul HD Free ADRK	Donar V Mackgraflerland
			Anuschka V Marienberg
	Floortje Winner '81, Club Show Winner '80 HD Tc Utrecht	Dutch Ch. Floris HD Free Utrecht	Nino VD Brantsberg
			Tarzan
		Bonny v d Hoge Zijde HD Tc Utrecht	Kasper VD Keizerlanden
			Carla VD Leenheer

40

PEDIGREE OF STROMHALL NAYAH

Whelped: November 20, 1984   AKC# WF 690855   O.F.A.   #RO-12064

Critique from Medallion Rottweiler Club Specialty - June 12 & 13, 1987 - j. Dieter Hoffmann of Germany:

Medium to large sized, harmonious bitch. Calm, attentive. Powerful head. Medium sized ears, well carried. Round, medium brown eyes. Scissors bite. P-1 upper left doubled. Gumline dark rose. Muscular, firm neck. Well pronounced chest with forechest. Well placed shoulders. Well positioned front, feet well knuckled. Firm back. Well positioned, muscular rear. Trotter. Good coat. Slightly rusty markings. Winners Bitch.

PARENTS	GRANDPARENTS	GREAT-GRANDPARENTS	GREAT-GREAT-GRANDPARENTS
Ch. Stromhall Torrey, UDTD HD Normal	Chesara Dark Nobleman	Chesara Akilles	Ch. Fandangos Fair Boy
			Dackes Ina
		Chesara Dark Memory	Ch. Chesara Luther
			Chesara Dark Desire
	Ch. Anverdon's Olympia, CD HD Normal	Ch. Heatherglen Franz, CDX	Heatherglen Rudi
			Chesara Dark Wishful
		Ch. Grunwalds Dark Mumtaz, CD HD Normal	Montoya Tacitus
			Brentano Heidi
Stromhall Pushy Peta HD Normal	Powderhorn's Fetz of Wencrest HD Normal	A/D/B Ch. Oscar vh Brabantpark OFA #RO-1428	Gerlach vh Brabantpark HD Free
			Ch. Onsbessy vd Brantsberg HD Free
		Ilona v Haus Schottroy OFA #RO-1650	Chris v Wildberger Schloss/II HD-
			Afra v Haus Schottroy/I HD+/-
	Ch. Stromhall Skana, CDX HD Normal	Ch. Stromhall Torrey, UDTD HD Normal	Chesara Dark Nobleman
			Ch. Anverdon's Olympia, CD HD Normal
		Kerusgal Black Quest	Leoleon Pinto, CDX TD
			Ch. Kerusgal Black Belle

MRS. CLARA HURLEY
3320 Wonderview Plaza
Hollywood, CA 90068
(213) 851-3174

Inquiries to Owners
POWDERHORN/WENCREST ROTTWEILERS, INC.

MICHAEL S. GROSSMAN
6594 E. Pinion Street
Agoura, CA 91301
(818) 889-9514

Von Brader Rottweilers

PEDIGREE

WM998341
Litter Reg. No.

WF587970
Individual Reg. No.

Multi BiS
BiSS (CRC 1988) CH VON BRADERS EIGER- RO-11086

Award of Merit-1988 **Registered Name of Dog**   MRC Hall of Fame

Date Whelped __July 26, 1984__   Sex __Male__

Breeder/   Frank and Mary Brader   (312) 964-7688
Owner   406 67th Court
             Downers Grove, IL 60516

PARENTS	GRANDPARENTS	GREAT-GRANDPARENTS	GREAT-GREAT-GRANDPARENTS
SIRE:			
CH Eiko vom Schwaiger Wappen (Import) SchH3 CDX RO-3068 1986 Top Producer	Igor vom Kastanienbaum SchH 3, FH, ADRK HD-Free Gekort ADRK #47 541	Int CH Bulli v Hunger-buhl,SchH 1 Gekort BIS Eza ADRK#42 465 Schw Sg 71 & 72, Klubsg 71 & Weltsg 73	Kuno v Butzensee, SchH 3 ADRK #40 415
			Britta v Schlossberg ADRK #39 075
		Gitta vom Bucheneck SchH 1, ADRK HD-Free ADRK #44 776	Furst v d Villa Daheim SchH 1 ADRK #42 204
			Indra v Schloss Wester-Winkel SchH 1 ADRK #40 758
	Int. CH Anka vom Lohauserholz, SchH3, FH Gekort BIS Eza ADRK# 46 801 Klubsg. 74 Europasg. 74, Bundessg. 75, VDH-Siegerin	Dack von der Meierei SchH3, ADRK #44 531 Gekort HD-Free	Alex v Kloster Disibodenberg SchH 2, ADRK #40 961
			Bardel v Grevingsberg, SchH 1 ADRK HD-Free ADRK #42 342
		Tilla vom Kursaal SchH 2, ADRK #44 811	Ero v Haus Westphal, SchH 3 ADRK HD-Free Gekort BIS Eza ADRK #43 172
			Wilma v Kursaal ADRK #39 011
DAM:			
A/C CH Birch Hill's Nanna v Brader TD Ro-4362-T BOS 1983 MRC Specialty MRC Honor Roll MRC Hall of Fame Multiple Group Placements 1986 Top Producer	A/C CH Rodsden's Elko Kastanienbaum A/C CD, Amer. CDX TD WD 694350 RO-1448	Int. CH Elko vom Kastanienbaum, SchH 1 46 34 C HD-Free, Utrecht	Elko vom Kaiserberg 44 352 SchH 1
			Gitta vom Bucheneck 44 776 SchH 1 HD-Free
		CH Gundi vom Reichenbachle 48 086 RO-846 HD-Free, Utrecht	Berno vom Albtal 42 673 SchH 3 FH
			Antje von der Wegscheide 41 225
	CH Rodsden's Birch Hill Bess CD TD WD 363207 RO-1174	CH Dux vom Hungerbuhl SchH 1 RO-234 WC 018804	Kuno vom Butzensee SchH 3 40 415
			Britta vom Schlossberg 39 075
		CH Rodsden's Frolich Burga, CD TD RO-649 WC 589812	CH Max von der Hobertsburg WC 308208 RO-320
			CH Rodsden Willa vd Harque UDT WB 854722 RO-321

PIONEER

WM 547782
_____
Litter Reg. No.

Bitch
_____
Sex

PEDIGREE

WE 188771
_____
Individual Reg. No.

CH. ROBIL MARTA VON DONNAJ   RO-2513-GOOD
_____
Registered Name of Dog

Breeder ___ Janet Putnam, Pepperell, Mass.

Owner ___ Virginia Aceti and Sheryl Hedrick, Pioneer Rottweilers, Hollis, NH

PARENTS	GRANDPARENTS	GREAT-GRANDPARENTS	GREAT-GREAT-GRANDPARENTS
sire: AMER/CAN CH. DONNAJ VT YANKEE OF PAULUS CDX TT WD 139569 OFA RO-964-T All-Breed BIS BISS ARC National Spec. 1981 BOB CRC Spec. 1977,79,80 ARC Gold Sire	CH. AXEL VOM SCHWANENSCHLAG RO-166 ARC Silver Sire	FURST VON DER VILLA DAHEIM SchH I	AXEL VOM SIMONSKAUL SchH III
			BLANKA VOM ITZELBACH SchH I
		CORA VOM GREVINGSBERG	QUINN VON DER SCHWARZWEISE SchH I
			BRITTA VON DER ZUFLUCHT
	CH. AMSEL VON ANDAN CD RO-300 MRC Hall of Fame ARC Silver Dam	A/C CH. RODSDEN'S KATO VON DONNAJ CDX TD BIS All-Breed RO-37 MRC Hall of Fame	CH. RODSDEN'S KLUGE VON DER HARQUE CD RO-50
			CH. FRANZI VOM KURSAAL MRC Honor Roll
		EHRENWACHES ANDERNACHE MRC Honor Roll RO-111	FETZ VOM OELBERG SchH II HD – RO-25
			RODSDEN'S UBERMUTIG KARLA CD
dam: DONNAJ TOUCH OF CLASS OFA RO-1320 WD 464995	CH. RODSDEN'S IKON VON DER HARQUE CD RO-355 WD,BW, 1973 MRC Specialty	CH. RODSDEN'S KLUGE VON DER HARQUE CD MRC Hall of Fame RO-50 ARC Gold Sire	Int.Ch.-Schon. HARRAS VOM SOFIENBUSCH SchH I BS.1960-61-62 MRC Hall of Fame
			CH. QUELLE VON DER SOLITUDE CD MRC Hall of Fame BOS CRC Spec. 1963
		CH. RODSDEN'S ERICKA DEIRDRE DAHL RO-157	CH. ARCO VOM DAHL CDX SchH III WD,BW MRC Spec.1969 RO-73
			RAFTER M'S RANDEE RO-109
	AMER/CAN CH. NORTHWIND'S HELGA RO-802	A/C CH. RODSDEN'S KATO VON DONNAJ CDX TD BIS All-Breed RO-37 MRC Hall of Fame	CH. RODSDEN'S KLUGE VON DER HARQUE CD MRC Hall of Fame RO-50
			CH. FRANZI VOM KURSAAL MRC Honor Roll
		A/C CH. NORTHWIND'S DANKA A/C CD MRC Honor Roll RO-208 ARC Silver Dam	CH. RODSDEN'S KLUGE VON DER HARQUE CD MRC Hall of Fame RO-50
			CAN CH. NORTHWIND'S TINA

PIONEER ROTTWEILERS
P.O. BOX 805
HOLLIS, NH 03049

VIRGINIA ACETI
SHERYL HEDRICK
603-465-2028

43

AHNENTAFEL FÜR DEN ROTTWEILER

aus ~~Körzucht~~ Leistungszucht

Name des Hundes: **P e t z   v o m   H e g e s t r a u c h**

Farbe:	schwarz/braun	Wurftag: 15. Mai 1982	Geschlecht: R ü d e
Züchter des Hundes:	Günter Weber, Gladenbacher Str. 9, 6301 Biebertal 4	Wurfjahr in Buchstaben: Neunzehnhundertzweiundachtzig

Erläuterungen über den Wurf
zu dem dieser Hund gehört

	Rüden	Hündinnen
Wurfstärke bei der Geburt	4	3
Totgeboren	0	1
verendet bis zur Eintragung		
Zum Zuchtbuch gemeldet	4	2

Eingetragen
in das Zuchtbuch des **A D R K**

Band: L   XVI   Nummer: 59 955

Tätowier-Nr.: 59 955

Eintragungs- und Prüfungsbestätigung

Der hier beschriebene Rottweiler ist
am 15. November 1982 in das Zuchtbuch
des Allgemeinen Deutschen Rottweiler-Klub
unter der Nr. 59 955 eingetragen worden.

Die Abstammungsangaben sind nachgeprüft und
ihre Richtigkeit wird hiermit bestätigt.

Die Zuchtbuchstelle des ADRK

Züchter-Bestätigung

Für die Richtigkeit der Angaben an die Zuchtbuchstelle zur
Ausfertigung dieser Urkunde bürgt als Züchter durch Unterschrift:

Datum: 19. November 1982

Unterschrift des Züchters:
(Ohne Unterschrift des Züchters nicht gültig)

Name: Günter Weber

Wohnort: 6301 Biebertal 4
Gladenbacher Str. 9

Eigentumswechsel

1) am _____ 19__ an _____
in _____
(Unterschrift des Verkäufers)

2) am _____ 19__ an _____
in _____
(Unterschrift des Verkäufers)

3) am _____ 19__ an _____
in _____

Untersuchung auf HD

Datum: 1.6.83   Tätowier-Nr.: i

Unterschrift der Röntgenstelle: _____

Ergebnis der Röntgenauswertung:
Zucht- und körfähig _____
Zur Zucht geeignet _____

Porta Westfalica 4, den _____

Ergebnis der Zuchttauglichkeitsprüfung
in Neuwied 1   am 27.11.1983

Zuchttauglich _____   6404
Körmeister oder Richter: _____
Bestätigung der Zuchtbuchstelle des ADRK: Willi Hedtke

Porta Westfalica 4, den 12. Dezember 1983

1. Körung in _____   am _____

Für die Dauer von zwei Jahren angekört
(bis einschließlich _____)

Körmeister: _____
Bestätigung der Zuchtbuchstelle des ADRK: _____

Porta Westfalica 4, den _____

2. Körung in _____   am _____

Auf Lebenszeit angekört

Körmeister: _____
Bestätigung der Zuchtbuchstelle des ADRK: _____

Porta Westfalica 4, den _____

Vater

Bär vom Hegestrauch, 55 801

ZtPr.-Bericht: Groß, kräftig,knochen-
stark, guter Rüdenkopf, kleines hoch-
angesetztes Ohr, gut getrag., dklbr.
Auge, leicht rosa Zahnleiste, genüg.
Vorbrust, gute Brusttiefe,gute Schul-
terlage, Pfoten geschloss.erwünscht,
kräft.Hals, Rücken nicht ganz fest,
kurze Kruppe, Hinterhand genüg.kräf-
tig, Winkelung gut,grobes Stockhaar,
rostbraune satte Abzeich.,gut.Traber
Scherengebiß; Selbstsicherh.und Auf-
merksamk.hoch, Mut, Kampf- u.Schutz-
trieb sehr hoch, Härte hoch, schuß-
gleichgültig.

SchH I

Kein Hinweis für HD - körfähig.

Mutter

Gabi vom Forstwald, 51 034

ZtPr.-Bericht: Gebiß einwandfr.,klein
in gut.Substanz u.Knochenstärke, etw.
knapper Stirnabsatz, Augen dunkel-b.
mittelbraun, Ohren seitl.tief anges.,
etw.groß, gut getragen, Brand gut in
der Farbe, Mittelhandknoch.sollte etw.
straffer sein, Pfoten gut geknöchelt,
gute Rückenlinie, breite Keulen, Hinterhand gut gewinkelt, frei u.flüssig
i.d.Bewegung; Selbstsicherheit u.Auf-
merksamkeit hoch,Mut,Kampf- u.Schutz-
trieb sehr hoch, Härte hoch, schuß-
gleichgültig.

SchH I

HD Übergangsform - körfähig.

3

Cito vom Schwaiger Wappen, 50 884
ZtPr.-Ber.:Sehr schön,lebh.,knochen-
st.Rüde i.sehr gut.Verfass.,s.schön.,
etw.gedrung.Kopf m.kleinem,gut getr.
Ohr,d.Auge dkl,kräft.Nack.,Brust und
Schult.i.Ordn.,s.g.Rückenlin.,s.gute
Winkel.,Pfot.gut geschloss.,freies,aus-
greif.Gangw.,s.schöner,satter Brand;
Selbstsicherh.,Aufmerks.u.Härte hoch,
Mut,Kampf- u.Schutztr.sehr hoch,schuß-
glchglt. SchH II,kein Hinw.f.HD-körf.

4

Venus vom Rodenstein, 50 783
ZtPr.-Ber.:Mittelgr.,s.harmon.,natürl.
Aufbau,mittl.Wink.,typ.Kopfform,gutes
Geschlechtsgepr.,voll.Fang,sattbr.Auge,
gut getr.Ohr,etw.helle Innenlefz.,gut
verteil.,a.Brust u.Läuf.etw.helle Abz.
etw.leicht auswärtsgest.Vorderläufe,
etw.flache Vorderpfot.,übr.Pigm.i.Ord-
nung,s.geräum.u.behend.Gangw.;Selbst-
sicherh.,Aufmerks.,Mut u.Härte hoch,
tr.mittel,schußglchglt. SchH I, kein

5

Cuno vom Georgshof, 43 936
Körper:Kräft.,rob.,muskul.,s.g.Ge-
samterschein.,g.Knoch.,s.g.Typ,g.Rü-
denkopf,Auge dkl.,Ohr gut getr.,Schul-
tergut.könn.fest.sein,hint.Winkel.gut,
Haar u.Abz.gut,Rück.fest.erwün.,Ge-
samtanlagen gut;lebh.,aufmerks.,furcht-
los,nervenf.,rottweilermäßig,Schärfe
gut.
SchH III, HD leicht positiv - körfähig.

6

Afra vom Forstwald, 46 20?
ZtPr.-Bericht:Kräft.,knochenst.Hündin,
i.richt.Größe,korrek.aufgeb.,liegt gut
i.Typ,trock.,etw.leicht.Kopf m.dklbr.
Auge u.kl.gut getr.Ohr,der Fang müßte
voll.s.,Brust,Schulter i.Ordn.,s.g.Rü-
kenlin.,Winkel.richt.,i.d.Beweg.fr.,geht
hint.etw.hackeneng,Haar u.Farbe etw.
matt,steht i.Haarwech.,Scherengeb.;gut
art.,aufmerks.,furchtl,Schutz-u.Kampf-
tr.reichl.vorh.,Draufg.,schußglchglt.

7

Cuno v.Georgshof,
43 936, SchH III,
HD leicht pos.-körf.

8

Anka v.Lohauserholz,
46 801, SchH III, FH,
KS 74,ES 74,BS 75,VDH-
Sieg.,Int.Champ.-Schön.
HD 1.pos.-gek.b.EzA.

9

Dux v.Kastanienbaum,
46 293, SchH III,
HD frei - körfähig.

10

Mona v.Rodenstein,
45 295,
kein Hinw.f.HD - körf.

11

Quick v.d.Solitude,
38 608,SchH III,FH,
HD frei-körfähig.LS.66,
gekört bis EzA.

12

Cora v.Welherbrünnele,
40 282, SchH I

13

Berno v.Albtal,42 673
SchH III, FH,
HD 1.pos.- körfähig.
Gekört bis EzA.

14

Cora v.Schwanenhurst,
42 498,SchH I,
HD leicht pos.-körf.
SchH III,HD fr.-körf.

15

Quick v.d.Solitude,LS,
38 608, SchH III, FH

16

Cora v.Welherbrünnele
40 282, SchH I

17

Dack v.d.Meierei,44 5?
SchH III

18

Tilla v.Kursaal, 44 81
SchH II

19

Arko v.Georgshof,42 36
SchH III,FH, gek.b.EzA

20

Iris v.Markgräflerland
44 397

21

Dolf v.Welherbrünnele,
40 631,SchH III,FH,gek.

22 EzA
Burga v.d.Bergkirche,
42 878

23 EzA
Droll v.d.Brötzingergas
se,36 212, SchH II

24

Manny v.d.Solitude,
35 565

25

Basso v.Schifferstadt,
37 586, SchH I

26

Freya v.d.Hardt, 36 941

27

Wasso v.Oelberg,39 223,
SchH III,gek.b.EzA.

28

Heidi v.Dürrbach,?9 916

29

Cito v.Schloßberg,
39 888

30

Ange v.Oelberg, 39 538

45

What is Schutzhund?

Although not recognized or approved by the American Kennel Club, Schutzhund Trials and the training of Rottweilers and of other large German breeds have been met steadily with increasing popularity. In the United States, a great many fanciers are following the European custom of training their dogs for Schutzhund work; there are now a number of trials for this type work being conducted. The American Rottweiler Club holds a Schutzhund Class in conjunction with the National Specialties. The Medallion Rottweiler Club also presents this feature at their Specialties, and the United States Rottweiler Club sponsors *Seiger*-type Specialty events at which Schutzhund Classes are, in the German tradition, included. The U.S.R.C. is also known as the Rottweiler Performance Club, and holds its shows under A.D.R.K. rules, officiated over by judges from the A.D.R.K. who come to America specifically for this purpose.

Schutzhund training is actually an advanced form of obedience training, going further in its range as it includes attack (or protection) training in addition to the basic obedience and tracking necessary for obedience degrees under A.K.C. rules. The basis of Schutzhund work is obedience, however, as every step of the way depends on the dog's willingness and ability to follow an assortment of commands.

In Germany, Schutzhund training is almost a way of life for the Rottweiler, and one who does not have a degree, or degrees, earned in this manner is looked upon with little respect (as you will realize upon further pursuit of the subject, for example, by reading the breeding requirements for A.D.R.K.-registered Rottweilers in Europe). With such extreme emphasis placed upon the subject, Germany naturally has scores of well-qualified Schutzhund trainers, a condition not existent in the United States. Enthusiasm is riding right along, however (although there are indeed some very strong holdouts against this type of training for the dogs), and with new training schools and new capable trainers gaining in numbers, there is little doubt that more and more Schutzhund-trained Rotties will be appearing on the scene.

It must be remembered that a *capable* trainer, who really knows the subject well, is a *must* if the dog is to be successfully trained. A partially trained Schutzhund Dog can be a problem, as can one that

Opposite: Best in Show and multi-Best in Specialty winner, Am., Can. Ch. Mad River's Magnum von Worley, Top Ten in U.S. 1986 (A.R.C.) and 1987 (Group system). This handsome dog is owned and treasured by Dawn and Jim Worley, Newark, OH.

has been mistreated in the process and that has not learned what is expected. So before engaging the services of anyone for this purpose, check the person out by contacting others whose dogs the person has trained to learn of their satisfaction or lack thereof. There is no shortage of reliable, capable handlers, so do not hesitate to make a change if it seems necessary.

I am sure that you who are reading this book are acquainted by now with the fact that there are three levels of training in the earning of the Schutzhund degrees:

Schutzhund I (SchH. I), Schutzhund II (SchH. II), and Schutzhund III (SchH. III). The exercises involved under obedience include: heeling on leash; heeling off leash; sitting from motion; down in motion from recall; retrieving on flat ground; retrieving over a jump; proceeding ahead of the handler, during which the dog drops down upon command; long down under distraction; and protection in the form of holding an agitator at bay by barking without biting; and a courage test, where the dog is sent after a running agitator who turns to attack the dog, at which time the

Apache Hill's Oil Gusher, by Ch. Cannon River Oil Tanker, C.D., ex Ch. Excalibur's B. Apache War Song, C.D., with his "boss," friend, trainer, and owner-handler Ron Smithson. Ron and Gusher are both esteemed and valued members of the San Diego police force. Photo courtesy of Irene Castillo.

"Bear" and his partner Roger Jernigan. Einsamstadt Rottweilers in Westfield, MA, are very proud of the three Working K-9s from one of their litters of which Bear is a member. Bear "is the talk of the department both because of his size (126 pounds) and because of his discipline," says Roger, who is Deputy Sheriff in Sarasota County, FL.

dog must get a firm grip on the agitator's arm without actually biting. Should the agitator move to attack the handler, the dog is then required to bite and hold on through two hits from a switch. When the agitator freezes, the dog then releases his grip on the arm. As a courage test, the dog must chase the running agitator, bite hard when this person turns to attack the dog, and hold on until the agitator ceases to fight. The dog is then awarded points of credit and praised for overall courage and hardness in protection. These are the requirements with which a SchH. I degree is attained.

In the next steps, Schutzhund II and Schutzhund III go on from there through more difficult versions of the above, and with stronger emphasis on protection, including locating and barking at the agitator in hiding until commanded to heel, at which time the handler searches out the agitator under the dog's watchful eye. The agitator attempts to escape, upon which the dog bites hard to prevent this from happening. The dog releases only when the agitator freezes, but again bites hard when the agitator again threatens the dog with the switch. The handler then searches for the agitator under the dog's watchful eye, and orders the dog to heel and signals the agitator to walk on ahead. During this transfer, the agitator attacks the handler; this attack ceases after the first bite, when the handler calls off the dog. The agitator walks away about 50 paces, then, turning, makes threatening gestures towards the dog, who immediately retaliates by biting hard. The agitator is then transported back to the judge. Full points in this category can only be allotted to dogs demonstrating exceptional hardness and courage. At this point in his training, if his efforts have earned sufficient points, the dog will be awarded the Schutzhund II degree.

For the ultimate—Schutzhund III (SchH. III)—a more complicated tracking session must be successfully completed and further advancement in the protection segment made evident. More

control and accuracy in Schutzhund III exercises are required than in SchH. I and SchH. II.

In order to qualify for any of the Schutzhund degrees, all dogs entered must pass a temperament test. Dogs failing to do so will be disqualified from the trial.

Our friends Eve and Manson Johnson, who live at Land O' Lakes, Florida, are closely in touch with and devoted advocates of the German Schutzhund training system. Their knowledge on the subject is particularly reliable since they are involved with it first-hand, having several dogs of their own trained and winning in German trials as well as in those held in their area in the United States.

The Johnsons frequently visit the leading German Rottweiler events, where they often have dogs of their own in competition—and among the winners. So deeply

Langhoffen's Eike executing the "bark and hold" command, with helper Willie Pope. Coco Steinford, breeder, owner and trainer.

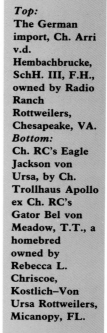

Top:
The German import, Ch. Arri v.d. Hembachbrucke, SchH. III, F.H., owned by Radio Ranch Rottweilers, Chesapeake, VA.
Bottom:
Ch. RC's Eagle Jackson von Ursa, by Ch. Trollhaus Apollo ex Ch. RC's Gator Bel von Meadow, T.T., a homebred owned by Rebecca L. Chriscoe, Kostlich–Von Ursa Rottweilers, Micanopy, FL.

WHAT IS SCHUTZHUND?

Am., Can., Mex. Ch. Quick von Siegerhaus, C.D., Z.T.P.R., working on Schutzhund bite. Owned by Thomas and Carol Woodward of Corning, CA. Photo by Mitchell.

impressed are they with the program that they want   to support it with something more tangible than just their presence and the entries of their dogs. As a gesture of admiration, friendship, and good faith, they now contribute annual friendship trophies, which they travel over to present personally to the Deutsch Meistershaft.

In describing the Deutsch Meistershaft, which is held annually in October and has continued over a span of close to 40 years, the Johnsons comment as follows: "Picture a Schutzhund Trial with 40 excellent working Rottweilers tracking, performing almost perfectly in obedience, and doing the protection routine part of Schutzhund as though it comes naturally (which of course it does through all the generations behind them), and you are envisioning the

Deutsch Meistershaft. In order to participate in this event, each Rottweiler must excel in its own region and attend a trial participating in Schutzhund III, during which each must qualify by earning the highest scores, which score must be high enough to qualify—85 in obedience, 85 in tracking, and 85 in protection, which in the latter case must also include an A. The minimum score is 279.

"From the 15 Landesgruppes, only 12 had scores high enough to qualify. The other 28 competing entries, which made the total of 40 accepted for competition, were selected. The winner of last year's trial is also allowed to return. This year the Besirksgruppe-Burlo Club volunteered to put on the Meistershaft for the A.D.R.K., located just before the border of Holland." Mrs. Johnson continues, "I was very amazed to see some top contenders in conformation also participating and scoring well in this trial. Morris vom Rauchfang, having won the 1985 Bundessieger, competed and placed seventh at this trial. Ambassador vom Frienfels, a beautiful top-producing male, placed eighth. Twenty dogs participated the first day, the majority scoring very high, which made it tough for the second day's contenders."

The above gives you an exciting picture of a leading Schutzhund event in Germany. Faint question or doubt exists regarding the advisability of having one's Rottie trained for attack in Schutzhund. In the U.S., however, I have heard some reservation expressed. Although it is claimed that the attack training makes for a steadier, more reliable dog, there are still questions in the American mind about whether or not it actually works out that way. We have had incidents of conformation judges being growled at or actually bitten and even attacked in the ring; we are getting some mighty frightening publicity involving incidents where family pet Rottweilers have been deemed dangerous to the public, particularly children (who normally they dearly love). We have heard ominous grumblings comparing their intentions to those of which pit bulls are accused.

It is hard to decide what the answer should be. Does not the Rottie, left to follow his natural instincts, possess, by breeding, the instinct to protect, making this part of training superfluous? Or is that really, as many protest, actually *not* the case, these people assuring everyone that the situation is quite the opposite—that temperament benefits by familiarity with all the phases of Schutzhund, including attack training and protection.

Quite frankly I do not know the answer. It is up to the breeders and owners of Rotties to do a bit of soul searching to decide. The fad of owning "macho dogs," so prevalent a few years back, has become considerably subdued of late, owing, I am sure, to all the adverse publicity showered upon anything even faintly resembling a "bull and terrier" breed.

Now let it *not* switch from there to our wonderful Rottweilers, nor widen its horizons to include them.

My own observation from conversation with my fellow judges, some of whom officiate for Rotties in the conformation ring, is that it is more likely that a problem

At the Klubsieger show in Germany, 1988, Gretel von der Silberdistel and trainer Edgar Kaltenbach, after placing V-1 for owners, Eve and Manson Johnson.

Janny von der Gruberheide, SchH. III, F.H., T.T., B.H., A.D., Z.T.P.R., "V" rated, is by one of the most titled of all German Rottweilers, Int. Ch. Nero vom Schloss Reithem SchH. III, from Int. Ch. Hexe von der Gruberheide, SchH. I. Photo courtesy of Eve and Manson Johnson.

can be raised by a foreign-bred dog than by one of American stock with a few generations in between. Just a coincidence probably, but it makes you wonder, do you *really* want to risk a latent desire to attack, or even just *bite* people, in light of the witch hunts against various canines which are now taking place? A hand raised to award a ribbon can be misunderstood and lead a keenly trained dog to attack a judge or anyone else making such a gesture toward the dog's handler.

It is assured that *any* breed of dog is happier and better for *obedience* training, which makes it a more responsible citizen; but for a dog intended as a family dog and companion to children, I wonder if it is wise to go further? All Rottweiler owners must think seriously about this before it becomes too late. We never want to see the noble, loving, beautiful Rottweiler relegated to a position of being barred from certain cities, towns, and states, which we now know can happen. Why let your breed become an addition to the list of vicious breeds—especially as they do not deserve any such loss of esteem.

Tracking Rottweilers

Increasingly we have noted indications that the Rottweiler has written quite a success story in the United States as a Tracking Dog, with steadily increasing numbers of them proudly wearing the letters "T.D." or "T.D.X." following their names.

In view of this rising interest, we have asked an outstanding authority on the subject, Arthur Twiss, from Reading, Massachusetts, to discuss the subject, later in the chapter, for you, tell you what has taken place over the years, and give you some ideas on how to go about enjoying tracking with your own Rottweiler. Mr. Twiss is a breed pioneer on this subject, well experienced and well qualified by first-hand experience.

To appreciate the Rottweiler's participation in today's American Kennel Club-approved Tracking Dog and Tracking Dog Excellent (T.D. and T.D.X.) events, one needs a brief lesson in history.

Tracking as a competitive sport had its origin in Germany. Its introduction to the United States came about through the efforts of two Poodle fanciers, Ms. Blanche Saunders and Mrs. Whitehouse Walker, who are generally credited with having originally convinced the A.K.C. in 1936 to offer tracking as a new competitive event in conjunction with the obedience work in which these two ladies were so deeply involved.

Tracking initially was one of the requirements for earning the Utility Dog degree (U.D.). This requirement was later revised to a Tracking title becoming necessary for dogs aiming to compete in Utility Classes. In 1947, the American Kennel Club took a further step by separating tracking from any of the other obedience events. Nevertheless, today tracking still remains governed by the Obedience Regulations of the A.K.C.

Between 1936 and 1943 the person laying the track was permitted to back-track when so doing. Since 1942, however, the person laying the track to be used by the dogs must single track.

A bitch named Sting vom Felsebmeer whelped a litter in January, 1931, which was to become the first A.K.C.-registered litter of Rottweilers. This was at about the same time that tracking was being introduced to the dog fancy in America. It seemed destined that in only a matter of time the two would get together and a handler with a Rottweiler would accept the challenge of trying to attain a Tracking Dog degree.

1936—1980

The first Rottweiler to achieve the distinction of a Tracking Dog degree was Gero v. Rabenhurst, who successfully completed his tracking tests in August, 1941. Then for a

> "Tracking as a competitive sport had its origin in Germany. Its introduction to the United States came about through the efforts of two Poodle fanciers..."

Lymington Rottweilers on their farm in Brazil. Half-bred Rottweiler is in the lead. She has a great herding instinct and helps take the sheep to the various pastures.

period of 28 years no other Rottweiler earned a similar degree until October, 1969, when a Rottie bitch (the first of her sex) did so. She was Russell's Herzchen.

The following year, in September, 1970, Ch. Axel v.d. Taverne, U.D.T., became the first champion-U.D.T.-titled Rottweiler of record.

INVOLVEMENT BY CLUBS

The American Rottweiler Club sponsored its first tracking test in June, 1982, as part of the events on the program of their second National Specialty Show which was held in San Francisco, California.

Top honors for a Rottweiler Club which has done much to promote tracking during the 1980s must, Mr. Twiss points out, be awarded to the Medallion Rottweiler Club of Wheaton, Illinois. This group of fanciers sponsored its 12th T.D.–T.D.X. Trial in June, 1989—certainly an admirable record. This is

especially so considering that it can be difficult for a club to find the interest and workers to arrange and put on a tracking test. Yet, these dedicated people have presented a combined T.D.–T.D.X. Trial since June, 1984, on the same day at which five Rotties passed the T.D. and two of three competing passed the T.D.X.

Those who watched the tracking event in May, 1987, held in conjunction with the the American Rottweiler Club's National Specialty, had the opportunity to see the organization's first combined T.D.–T.D.X. Trial at which three out of three passed T.D., but unfortunately the only two in T.D.X. did not make it.

In May, 1989 the Colonial Rottweiler Club sponsored its first T.D. test, this at the Mapleton Campus of the Deverex Foundation in Malvern, Pennsylvania. Three out of four passed that day.

Recall for a moment that the title of Tracking Dog Excellent (T.D.X.)

became effective on March 1, 1980. Did the first T.D.X. title in this country go to a Rottweiler? No, it did not. It went to a Dachshund bitch, Gretel von Ruppmur, U.D.T., on March 15, 1980, at a trial held in Florida. But the second T.D.X. was awarded to a Rottweiler dog, Barsoms de Jak Thoris, C.D.T., on March 30, 1980, at Winston-Salem Dog Club Trial.

There have been some other very distinguished tracking accomplishments which we are also happy to record. Margaret Teague deserves special kudos for having trained and handled 11 dogs to the T.D. Of that number, ten passed on the first try with the other one doing so on the second.

Jane F. Weidel, Stockton, Illinois, had the first champion U.D.T. bitch in Ch. Rodsden Willa v.d. Harque, U.D.T., whose litter brother, Rodsden's Wotan v.d. Harque, C.D.X, T.D., also trained by Mrs. Weidel, became the first Rottweiler in the United States to be used for search and rescue work. Mrs. Weidel plays an important role in the Medallion Rottweiler Club's tracking program and is also a highly respected judge of T.D.–T.D.X. events.

Laura Young, Springfield, Missouri, is well known for her work with her male Rottie, Hi Vue Deacon of Quallenhaus, who, at the time of accomplishment, was the youngest male to obtain his T.D., just three days past six months. Also, at age one year to the day, he was the youngest to earn T.D.X.

Top: Yden's Ama Morgan in the protective stage of Schutzhund training. Yvette M. Forest, owner, New Ipswich, NH.
Middle: Being given some pointers on tracking by the "old master" himself, a willing pupil with Trollengen's Berg. Owner, trainer, and handler, D.R. Carlson, Langley, B.C., Canada.
Bottom: On the right is Amboss vom Konigssiek, SchH. III, F.H., I.P.O., Gekort, winning the Werital Sieger in Germany. On the left is Int. Ch. Iwan von Fusse der Eifel, SchH. III, F.H., I.P.O. III, Gekort. Owners, Eve and Manson Johnson.

The very famous Grunberg's Brummel v.d. Adle, Am., Can. T.D., who holds the record for 13-times winner in 13 consecutive trials—the most consecutive wins of any Tracking Dog in the breed. Photo was taken in 1967 at age 10 months. Brummel was owned by Mr. and Mrs. Arthur Twiss and was a true trailblazer for what a Rottie can accomplish in tracking.

Cindy Neale, Ozark, Missouri, is another success story, having successfully handled two T.D. title holders and a T.D.X. dog at Medallion's first combined T.D.–T.D.X. in June, 1984.

Louise Carlson owner-trained her Sophie's Magnolia May On Lake, T.D., who was the youngest bitch at the time to gain a T.D., 17 days past six months of age. This bitch, "Maggie," is Utah's youngest tracking-titled dog, and the first Rottweiler in Utah to earn this degree, which she did in April, 1989.

Grunberg v.d. Adel, Am., Can. T.D., entered and passed his first Tracking Test at the Concord, Massachusetts, Dog Training Club's tracking test in October, 1970. During that period, when tracking was just getting started on the East Coast, it was possible for dogs to gain entry into tests after having earned their titles. Therefore, Brummel was eligible to gain, as he did, the honor of passing more of these tracking tests than any other dog of any other breed. During the same period he earned his

Canadian T.D. and started training for his Canadian T.D.X. Brummel's career coincided with the growing demand of tracking devotees to get a T.D.X. test accepted and approved by the A.K.C. Every method heard of and discussed at this stage was tried out on Brummel, who cooperated fully. It is unfortunate that this great dog died one week prior to competing for the Mountain City Obedience Club T.D.X. test in Montreal, Canada, which probably would have given him still another honor.

Brummel's record of 13 A.K.C. tracking tests entered and 13 passed, with never so much as a single failure, stands today as unbroken and unapproached by other Rottweilers.

Throughout the United States were quickly added a variety of "firsts" to the early history of Rottweiler tracking. Among them Mr. James. H. Fowler of West Chicago, Illinois, as owner-trainer-handler of Gero v. Sofienbusch, took his dog through an impressive career of title earning which included Int., Am., Can. and Mex. Ch.; Am., Can. and Mex. U.D.T.; Can. U.D.T.X.; and a Schutzhund I degree with a "V" rating. Jim Fowler is still active with the Medallion Rottweiler Club today.

On June 24, 1978, an historic milestone was recorded at the Emerald Dog Obedience Club in Eugene, Oregon, when five Rottweilers were entered for tracking and all five of them passed,

1980 TO THE PRESENT

Today's heightened interest in tracking can be credited to the blending of three major factors. First, credit must go to all the hard work done by the early tracking teams who proved that the Rottweiler is indeed a very capable tracking dog; this at the same time as promoting the sport within the Rottweiler fancy.

Second, the efforts of the breeders

Ch. Sophe's Magnolia May On Lake, T.D., in her time the youngest bitch to attain the T.D. degree, which she did at 6½ months of age. "Maggie" is a daughter of the great Best in Show Ch. Nelson v.h. Brabantpark ex Select Ch. Sophe v. Bergenhof, C.D. Bred by Joan Harrison, owned by Lou Carlson and Stan Funicelli. She was the first Rottweiler in Utah to gain the Tracking degree.

which was particularly notable as this was the first test competed in by each of these Rotties. The distinguished five were: Panamint Sultan v. Rheintal, C.D.X., handler Margaret Teague; Ch. Panamint Anytime Anywhere, C.D., handler Dennis Teague; De Reimer's Mariken, handler Rocky Rothrock; and Panamint Saphir v. Rheintal, handler Lucy Ang.

Barbara Hoard Dillon's Panamint Ideal Impression gained her Tracking Dog degree at age seven months at the Orange Empire Dog tracking test in January, 1979.

must be credited. Since the Rottweiler is a working dog, our best breeders strive to produce not only conformation champions but dogs who are capable of earning titles and degrees at *both* ends of their names. These breeders are also encouraging their puppy purchasers to try for a variety of honors which enhance the pleasures of Rottweiler ownership.

Finally, the A.K.C. Board of Directors must be acknowledged for having approved the title of Tracking Dog Excellent (T.D.X.) which became effective on March 1, 1980.

Linda Schuman, with Frolic 'n

Imported as a puppy, Ch. Basko vom Aschafftal, C.D.X., T.D.X., SchH. II, F.H., A.D., here is winning Best of Breed from the classes in an entry of 98 dogs. Trained and handled by M. Teague to all working titles.

Sundance Kid, T.D., lives in Redmond, Washington. "The Kid" was the first dog on the track at the American Rottweiler Club's first Tracking Test (June, 1982), and he passed getting his T.D. at the young age of nine months.

Doroh's Grenda von Arba, Am., Can. T.D., and Doroh's Regina, both owner-handled by Art Twiss of Reading, Massachusetts, obtained their respective T.D.X. and T.D. titles on their first attempt at the Medallion Rottweiler Club's combined T.D.–T.D.X. Trial in June, 1989, in Naperville, Illinois. This was a first for the breed and for an individual owner, since both dogs are the result of Dorothy Wade's breeding program (Doroh, Reg.). Orenda also became the first T.D.X. bitch in New England as a result of her win.

GETTING YOURSELF STARTED IN TRACKING
by Arthur Twiss

You will soon discover that training a Rottweiler to track is a very individualized and subjective undertaking. What motivates your dog may not apply to my dog. A hilly hayfield in New England is in sharp contrast to the desert lands of Arizona. Weather conditions fluctuate to extremes all over the country.

Try to find someone who has trained a dog to the T.D. level and work with that individual. Local obedience and/or breed clubs are a good source for names. Check the latest A.K.C. Judges' Directory. Maybe a judge lives within driving distance of your home. Get books at your library or go to a book store, dog show or pet store. Obtain and study

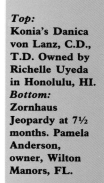

Top:
**Konia's Danica
von Lanz, C.D.,
T.D. Owned by
Richelle Uyeda
in Honolulu, HI.**
Bottom:
**Zornhaus
Jeopardy at 7½
months. Pamela
Anderson,
owner, Wilton
Manors, FL.**

Can. Ch. Wyndhurst's Jessie and Can. Ch. Wyndhurst's von Kaira are examples of what Wyndhurst Rottweilers of Alta., Canada, strive to produce.

the latest A.K.C. Obedience Regulations and Guidelines for Obedience Judges.

It is outside the scope of this book to offer minute details on how to start tracking. Ask 100 people how to train for tracking and you'll probably get 100 varied answers on a specific topic. Tips on how I would start a dog are offered for your consideration.

Let's pretend for the moment that you have a new 8–10–12–week-old puppy and that it has been with you for at least a week. Your starting needs are simple—a non-restrictive puppy harness, a training lead, and an understanding friend.

Go to a local field and let your friend hold the leashed puppy and let him watch you leave as you call his name to get his attention. Disappear behind a predetermined object—a large rock, a maple tree, a dry creek bed. Let the dog immediately find you. Reward the puppy with lavish praise and food treats. Let the puppy rest for 10–15 minutes, then move to another spot

in the field and repeat the exercise. *Rest the puppy.*

For the final exercise that day, change your technique. Leave your dog but have him facing in the opposite direction and *do not* call out his name. When everything is ready, have your friend turn the puppy around, tell him to "find," and start walking slowly toward your location with the dog on a short leash. Keep the dog moving but at the same time gauge the walking so you have the handler moving only when the dog's head is down and he is tracking you. When found, more praise and more food goodies are given for a job well done. Don't overdo it. Always go home on a positive note and resume the lesson the next weekend. I seldom train more than once a week.

I find the following supplies to be adequate for T.D. training. The assumption has been made that your dog is now more mature, i.e., out of the 2–6 month category.

a) An adjustable, non-restrictive harness. You can generally buy

Ch. Little Bit of Cash taking Best of Winners en route to the title. Owned by Billy Arrington.

Here are three Rotties at the Helvoorts' having fun romping with Pat Scott.

Ch. Bulli's Molly von Stolzenfels, handled by owner, Erika Beqaj, taking BOS at Westbury K.A.

Fun in the water for these two splendid young Rotties owned by the Van Helvoorts.

Ch. Hanni vom Bakkes, foundation bitch at Whithaus Rottweilers.

Here at Lakeview Rottweilers, Dawson Springs, KY. Rotties enjoy water sports.

Apache Hill's Merry Deja Vu; Peyote Odyssey, C.D., T.T.; and Flash Back 'N' Time, C.D.

These litter sisters, Abba vom Gampp and Anna von Gampp are owned by Paula Gampp.

Wilderness Epic of Rodan at age 15 months. Bred by JoAnne Harnish. Owned by Rick and Dawn Naylor.

Am., Hol., and Lux. Ch. Quanto v.h. Brabantpark, a Dutch import, pictured winning the 1980 Golden State R.C. Specialty. Quanto is by Gerlach v.h. Brabantpark ex Ch. Onsbessy v.d. Branstberg. Owned by Powderhorn/Wencrest Rottweilers, Inc.

them at pet shops, dog show concessions, or mail order houses. A properly fitted harness will last a lifetime.

b) Lead. I prefer to use a 30-foot × ⅝-inch wide cotton web lead and knot it at the 25-foot point. A lead wider than this tends to be too heavy and awkward to handle. Tracking a Rottweiler with a narrow nylon braided cord will tend to cut your hands.

c) Flags. Make up about ten. Wooden dowels ⅜ inch × 3 or 4 feet are available at your local lumber yard. Point one end with a hatchet, but for a uniform tip do it with a manual pencil sharpener. Don't laugh! The Tracking Club of Massachusetts has over 150 flags which were tipped that way. Buy enough cloth material so that you can use a 10–12-inch square piece per dowel. A solid, contrasting color to your local vegetation works the best.

d) Articles. Use a glove or wallet,

dark in color (color is optional in training) because they are the "approved" items the A.K.C. Obedience Regulations amended to June 1, 1987.

I prefer to start beginner dogs on calm days when the air is still cool, since Rottweilers tend to track better in cool weather. A light rain is acceptable. I lay starting legs crosswind. Why? If you lay the leg into the wind, the dog smells the food treat/article and will have a tendency to track with his head up. A wind from behind you will "contaminate" the track and could confuse the dog.

For now, double lay your own track and leave your article at the end with a piece of food under it. In tracking, the article on the field *must* belong to the tracklayer.

The dog's short lead will be in my left hand and I'll direct the dog's movements with my right hand, held close to the ground. A.K.C. tracking does not require that the dog work exactly on top of the track, but I want to train the dog to be as close as possible.

Aging the track: what constitutes proper aging is a highly subjective topic. I will double track between the flags and age it two to five minutes. The second time I'll age it five to eight minutes. Rottweilers are quick learners, so I will continue to double track but extend the track beyond the second flag for about 15–25 yards. I will then start the dog after a five-minute delay. Most likely your dog will dash to the second flag, search for the article, and when it is not found will lower his head and follow the track to the article. After you have done this for a few times, do the same exercise again but single track. Always reward the dog for a well-done job.

Vary the age of the track as you vary the length of the track. Try for four or five consistent performances up to 15–20 minutes old and up to 100 yards in total leg length before you do a corner. Lay some yourself and have a "stranger" (a non-owner) lay a few tracks.

Your first corner:

1. Make the corner 90° and be aware of the wind direction.
2. Make each leg at least 50 yards.
3. Mark your corner with a flag, if necessary, a colored tape or cloth or an obvious ground marker.
4. Double lay the track at the beginning of this training phase and drop your time back to about five to ten minutes until the dog learns the lesson. Single track when appropriate.

Ch. Doroh's New Wave, C.D., with owner-handler Veronica Wade.

Morris vom Rauchfang, SchH. III, A.D., Gekort, 1985 Bundessieger, demonstrating excellent temperament with this little girl. Photo courtesy of Eve and Manson Johnson.

Opposite: Head study of Dente Ilse von Smiladon. Owned by Dr. Francis Cutwright of Carlsbad, CA. Photo by Mitchell.

5. Draw yourself a map to reinforce what you are doing and where you are going.

Learn the ground spot. Vary the distance and time. Your goal: consistently correct performances up to 15–25 minutes. Now try a second corner to the opposite of your first corner.

The A.K.C. is fully committed to the sport of tracking. They put on tracking seminars around the country, and I strongly urge you to attend should one be given in your area. Mr. John Bernard was the first of the three current Field Representatives for tracking events. Major revisions of tracking regulations have been made by the A.K.C. and that information was published in the *A.K.C. Gazette*. All accepted changes became effective on January 1, 1990. It is now easier to get test dates and locations approved by the A.K.C.

Tracking by its very nature will never appeal to all the tens of thousands of dog owners, but it does offer dog owners the opportunity to test one aspect of their dog's working ability. That fact is becoming well known throughout the dog fancy and the sport of tracking will most definitely grow in stature in the coming years.

The Rottweiler has proven to be an above-average tracking dog in a relatively short period of time, and I strongly believe that we must perpetuate that ability. Train your dog and participate in what will become the most dynamic tracking period in history.

Mitchell
'88

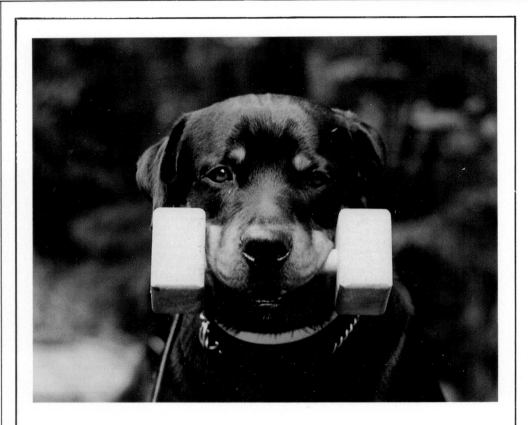

Top:
Yden's Ama Morgan, C.D., owned by Yvette M. Forest, New Ipswich, NH.
Bottom:
Obedience exercise during the Rottie Walk in 1987 in Maple Ridge, B.C., Canada. Photo courtesy of Alouette Kennels.

Rottweilers in Obedience

Everyone at all familiar with my opinions pertaining to responsibility of dog owners must by now be well aware of my stand that all dogs *must* be taught at least simple obedience, for the dog's own safety and for your control of the dog. This is especially important in a breed of the size and substance of a Rottweiler, who should never be entirely out of control when within the range of his owner's voice.

Many owners, as they take their Rotties through this basic training during puppyhood, develop intense admiration for the intelligence and response with which the dog reacts to these early lessons, and thus are encouraged to embark on a training program with the purpose in mind of entering Obedience Trial competition with the dog. The obedience folks derive tremendous enjoyment from this work with their dogs, as, apparently (a conclusion reached after watching some of them at work) do the dogs.

A patient, even-tempered person who enjoys working with his/her own dog can derive satisfaction from the rapport between owner and dog as they learn to work together. If you lack confidence or do not wish to take the time, you can, of course, hire a trainer or enroll the dog to work with one; but I hope you will at least try

doing it yourself first, since much of the satisfaction and the close bond developed between you and your dog results from you yourself working with him.

A patient person who loves being with his dog can, with study and a

Camas Valley Anna vom Ali takes the jump with ease. She is in the Medallion R.C. Hall of Fame. Bred by D. and D. Kutz, owned by Jim and Rachel Murray.

Top:
Am., Can. Ch. Von Bruka Indra v. Yden, Am., Can. C.D., T.T., winning First Place in Novice A at the 1988 Colonial R.C. Specialty Show to complete her C.D. Yvette M. Forest, owner.
Bottom:
Ch. Srigo's I Am Invincible, T.D., Best in Sweepstakes at the Colonial R.C. Specialty. Brother to Srigo's Imitation of Life, Best in Match at the A.R.C. Specialty Match. Owner, Ms. Felicia E.H. Luburich, East Brunswick, NJ.

Ch. RC's Magnum Force von Ursa. Bred, owned and handled by Rebecca L. Chriscoe.

Ch. Doroh's Just Grand, T.D. First bitch to win BIS at A.R.C. National Specialty. Handled by Veronica Wade.

Am., Can. Ch. Ebonstern Gunslinger v. Abra, co-owned by Cheryl Wheeler and Lynn Labore.

Ch. Doroh's Janus Erdelied, C.D. Owner-handled by C.L. "Surely" Rawlings.

Am., Can. Ch. Ebonstern Itzabear v.d. Leibe. Owner, Cheryl Wheeler, Mount Vernon, WA.

Bluefox Abelmann von Siegen and Bluefox Aaronhoff von Siegen. Susan Sheilds, handler. Cheryl Kienast, owner.

Ch. Von Hawthorne's Murray-M, under judge Mrs. Jane Forsyth. Bred by A.J. Hahn; owned by K. and P. Murray.

Ch. Doroh's Hess v. Hopp finished championship owner-handled by S. and N. Miller. Handled here by Dorothy A. Wade.

Ch. Von Riddle's Gabriele v. Eisen, C.D., T.T. Owned by W. and M. Williams and K. Riddle.

bit of reading (there are many splendid books about obedience available), quite easily become a real expert on the subject and a proficient, successful trainer-handler. Some basic rules for success are that you remain confidently calm during the procedure and that you never frighten your dog, turning him against the whole procedure by losing your temper and punishing him too harshly or unjustly. Never, never resort to cruelty. A cowed-down, miserably unhappy dog is hardly a credit to you.

Be immediate and extravagantly lavish with your praise when your instructions are correctly followed. Make the whole thing a fun experience for your dog and, who knows, you may wind up with a famous and admired "star."

As you and the dog become more proficient, it is almost certain that you will wish to try your hand in the Obedience Class at an A.K.C. dog show. If you are working with a class, the information of "where and how" will be available to you. If you are working on your own, it may be necessary for you to contact the A.K.C. (51 Madison Ave., New York, N.Y. 10010) for a list of obedience trials scheduled for your area. If the breeder of your dog is from your area, he may be a source of the information; or perhaps your veterinarian would know.

Throughout the kennel stories appearing in this book, those from the different countries represented, you will read of a long series of beautiful, intelligent, distinguished Rottweilers from around the world who have gained triumphant success as obedience dogs. It is, and I am sure you will agree, thrilling to see and admire their photographs and read of their triumphs. The fact that the Rottweiler is a *working* dog is very obvious as one notes their attainments, true to the tradition of their forebears.

Epic's Burning Desire, C.D.X., was bred by Robert Hogan and Jan Marshall and is owned by Pam Anderson and Mary Fielding. Showing off the excellent form which helped to earn the obedience degrees.

Top: Am., Can. Ch. Way-Mar's Brooks Dawg von Jos, C.D.; Ch. Srigo's Rainbow Wilderness; Am., Can. Ch. The Chena Wilderness; and Am., Can. Ch. Wilderness Kobuk v. Forstwald. All are members of the family at Wilderness Rottweilers, JoAnn Harnish, owner.
Bottom: Weikerhaus Early Edition, U.D., 1985 No. 1 A.R.C. Open Division; No. 2 Schuman; No. 5 Delany System. 1986 A.R.C. Top Ten Open Dog; and No. 4 Schuman. Bred by Rita Welker. Owned and trained by Pepperhaus Rottweilers, Sandy Peppers-Phillips, Fallon, NV.

Top:
Inca von Konigsberg at age 7 represents the Kahlerbald lines; owned by Konigsberg Rottweilers®, Peter and Tammy Mehnert, Lindsay, Ont., Canada.
Bottom:
Am., Can. Ch. Dina von der Brunnleithe, a German import owned by Douglas K. Loving of Kelton, PA. Dina is a daughter of Citto v.d. Pinter, SchH. III, from Anka vom Naabtalblick SchH. I. Dina was bred to Am., Int. Ch. Santo vom Schwaiger Wappen to produce Ero vom Konigsadler, owned by J. Patrick Green.

Establishment of the Rottweiler in the United States

Ch. Einmin Immortelle v. Rottdan, the foundation bitch at Rita McMahon's Freyan Rottweilers, Lakeport, CA.

Many famous people and many magnificent dogs have played important roles in the development of the Rottweiler in the United States. The breed is not one of the longest established here by any means. It wasn't until the mid-1920s that the first mention of it appeared in an American dog publication and the 1930s before any dog show activity was recorded. This makes the extent of the popularity and admiration these dogs have attained all the more remarkable. Stina v. Felsonmeer was the first member of the Rottweiler breed to have been registered with the American Kennel Club, and in 1931 she was the first to whelp an A.K.C.-registered litter. Irma v. Steinbach, an American-bred bitch owned by Robert Sieber of Forest Hills, New York, was born in 1929, thus it would be assumed that she was from one of the earliest litters whelped in this country. Irma was shown at Westminster on one or more occasions during the 1930s. Her breeder was J. Kocker, and she was a daughter of Franzl v.d. Kinzeg ex Zilly v.d. Steinbach. Another Rottie, this one a dog, Prince by name, was home-bred

Ch. Von Hawthorne's Murray is 5 times a Winner of First in the Working Group with numerous additional Group placements to his credit. Owned by Kenneth T. Murray, Murfreesboro, TN.

Opposite: Shikari von Dular at age 3 years. By Ch. RC's Eagle Jackson von Ursa ex Tanja vom Marchenwald (German import). A granddaughter of RC's Gator Bel von Meadow, a No. 1 Producing Rottweiler in the nation we are told, with 18 champions to her credit. Shikari belongs to Tonya Jones Oldham, Lakeview Rottweilers.

and owned by Mr. Sieber and was a son of Jank v. Steinbach ex Nora v.d. Landeck. These first notes of Rotties in the States all take us to the New York area; they are not very informative beyond making us aware that some activity was stirring in the breed then.

Around the beginning of the 1940s, the breed started to stir in California. It was here that the first Rottweiler Club of America took shape and the first American Rottie champions gained titles.

A noted professional handler, Noel Jones, was associated with all these developments. It was Mr. Jones, in conjunction with Barbara Hoard Dillon, a devoted fancier of the breed, who organized and hosted successful Match Shows and

started the original Rottweiler Club of America on its way.

Mr. Jones finished the first two recorded A.K.C.-listed Rottweiler champions of record. He had preceded those two with a stunning dog who swept through to his 15 required points in no time. He never received acknowledgment of a title, however, as his papers from Germany had not cleared when he did so, nor had special permission been requested to show this dog despite that fact; consequently, the wins were cancelled. The dogs that were actually the second and third to finish have gone down in history as the first and second due to this unhappy event. Confusing, but understandable. So far as A.K.C. records are concerned, a dog

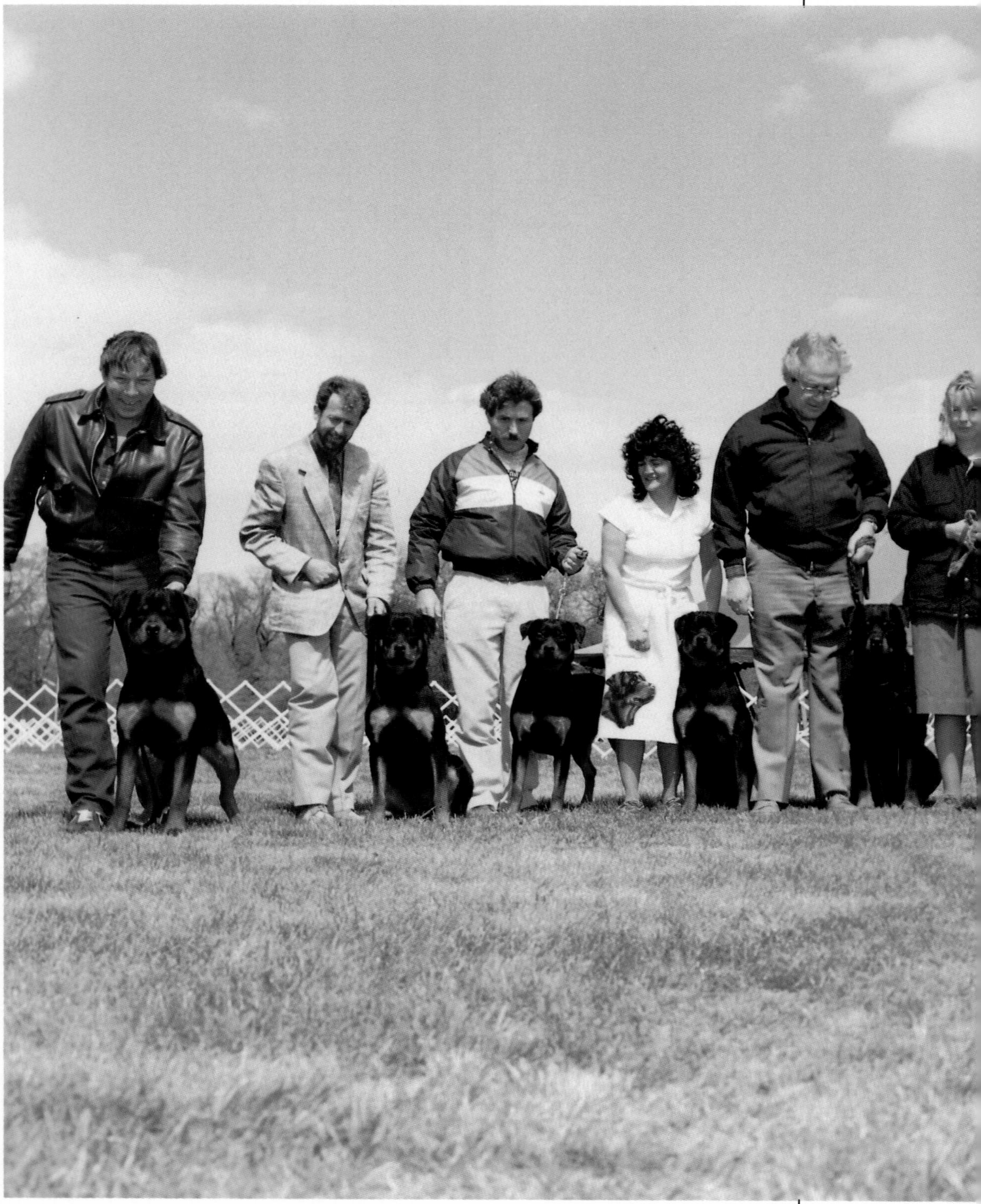

named Ch. Zero became America's first Rottweiler to hold the title, and Champion Cita v.d. Hohenzollern the second, despite the fact that Astra von Weinsberger-Tal actually preceded them by fulfilling the requirements first.

Mr. Jones's own first Rottweiler was Cuna v.d. Schwartzen Eiche, who was sired by Herlinde v.d. Schwartzen Eiche, this dog having gone forth to earn Obedience, Utility and Tracking Dog degrees here. Mr. Eichler, who owned Herlinde and bred Cuna, was a breeder from Wisconsin who did well with some truly quality dogs.

As the 1940s progressed, so did the interest in and popularity of Rottweilers. Among those sharing in these early successes were Barbara Hoard Dillon, owner of Panamint Kennels, and Mrs. Margaretta McIntyre, whose family in Sweden had owned Rottweilers, and who acquired her very own first Rottie when she came to America in 1950, although she had shared those of her family since 1935. Mrs. McIntyre returned to her native Sweden, leaving many friends who miss her deeply in addition to some notable accomplishments in the Rottweiler world.

Rodsden Kennels became active in the Rottweiler world in 1945, owned at that time by D.R. Rademacher and R.F. Klem. In 1978, following Richard Klem's death, ownership was transferred to P.G. Rademacher and Joan R. (Rademacher) Klem. Rodsden has imported, bred, and owned an impressive array of superlative dogs. Their contribution to this breed has been tremendous and thoroughly beneficial all the way. It would be impossible to overstate all that this kennel has accomplished for the good of the breed.

William Stahl, from New Jersey, was a loyal and tenacious early breeder, providing background for at least several others who founded their bloodlines on dogs purchased from Mr. Stahl.

This is the Windwalker "A" litter: *Left to right:* Can. Ch. Windwalker's Austin v. Mirko, C.D., B.H., SchH. I; Windwalker Willsden's Ande, C.D.; Can. Ch. Windwalker's Anje v. Mirko, T.T.; Am., Can. Ch. Windwalker's Ada v. Mirko, T.T.; Am., Int. Ch. Mirko vom Steinkopf, C.D.X, SchH. III, I.P.O. III, F.H.; Windwalker's Alex The Great, C.D., T.T.; Windwalker's Adonis v.d. Mirko; Can. Ch. Windwalker's Asa v. Mirko, Can. C.D., B.H., T.D.; and Windwalker's Adam v. Mirko, C.D., T.T.

One of the most respected ladies in the American fancy, Mrs. Bernard Freeman, Muriel to her hosts of friends, became a pioneer Rottweiler breeder widely noted for greatness in her Rottweilers. She is keenly interested in the breed and is one of the most sought-after judges in America.

Full particulars on the early dogs can be found in the books written for TFH Publications, *The Book of the Rottweiler* and *The World of Rottweilers*, where these and other older successful kennels are covered in depth. Following the American breed standard we bring you updates on kennels appearing in our pages for the first time—from all parts of the world.

We are pleased and proud that our breed publication enjoys the distinction of being the first to present the 1990 Rottweiler Standard of the American Kennel Club.

OFFICIAL AKC STANDARD FOR THE ROTTWEILER

General Appearance
The ideal Rottweiler is a medium large, robust and powerful dog, black with clearly defined rust markings. His compact and substantial build denotes great strength, agility and endurance. Dogs are characteristically more massive throughout with larger frame and heavier bone than bitches. Bitches are distinctly

Top: Ch. Falko v. Waldblick, SchH. I, German import, took the Breed from the Classes, Beverly Hills K.C. Owned by Powderhorn/Wencrest Rottweilers, Inc. *Middle:* Ch. Einmin Immortelle v. Rottdan with a friend at the beach. "Mishka" is one of the Rotties belonging to Rita McMahan, Freyan Rottweilers, Lakeport, CA. *Bottom:* Brother and sister, Ch. Misty Lakes Awol Kid and Ch. Misty Lakes Afternoon D'Light, owned by Dr. Eric and Amelia M. Jimeniz, Bridgewater, CT.

Opposite: Glacier Valley Man 'O War, by Am., Can. Ch. Bryloukis Great Expectations, C.D., ex Panamint Polar Delight, C.D. Owner, P. Adriane Schaefer.

feminine, but without weakness of substance or structure.

Size, Proportion, Substance
Dogs—24 inches to 27 inches. Bitches— 22 inches to 25 inches, with preferred size being mid-range of each sex. Correct proportion is of primary importance, as long as size is within the standard's range. The length of the body, from prosternum to the rearmost projection of the rump, is slightly longer than the height of the dog at the withers, the most desirable proportion of the height to length being 9 to 10. The Rottweiler is neither coarse nor shelly. Depth of chest is approximately fifty percent (50%) of the height of the dog. His bone and muscle mass must be sufficient to balance his frame, giving a compact and very powerful appearance. **Serious Faults**—Lack of proportion, undersized, oversized, reversal of sex characteristics (bitchy dogs, doggy bitches).

Head
Of medium length, broad between the ears; forehead line seen in profile is moderately arched; zygomatic arch and stop well developed with strong broad upper and lower jaws. The desired ratio of backskull to muzzle is 3 to 2. Forehead is preferred dry, however some wrinkling may occur when dog is alert. *Expression* is noble, alert, and self-assured. *Eyes* of medium size, almond shaped with well fitting lids, moderately deep-set, neither protruding nor receding. The desired color is a uniform dark brown. **Serious Faults**—Yellow (bird of prey) eyes, eyes of different color or size, hairless eye rim. *Disqualification*—Entropion. Ectropion. *Ears* of medium size, pendant, triangular in shape; when carried alertly the ears are level with the top of the skull and appear to broaden it. Ears are to be set well apart, hanging forward with the inner edge lying tightly against the head and terminating

Am., Can. Ch. Von Bruka Indra v. Yden, Am., Can. C.D., T.T., and her daughter, Ch. Yden's Blythe Spirit, owned by Yvette M. Forest.

Top:
Ch. Brash Bear von Pioneer, C.D., co-owned by Kandy Galotti and Sheryl Hedrick, North Andover, MA. Baer is a multiple Best of Breed winner and Group placer. He is also the sire of many champions and C.D.X. winners. By Ch. Graudstark's Luger, C.D., ex Ch. Robil Marta von Donnaj.
Bottom:
True Lee Chelsea v. Gunner, Am., Can. C.D., pictured at age 11 months. By Ch. Altar's Gunner of Woodland ex Ashby v. Foxcroft, C.D. True Lee Rottweilers, Lee McKenney, Revere, MA.

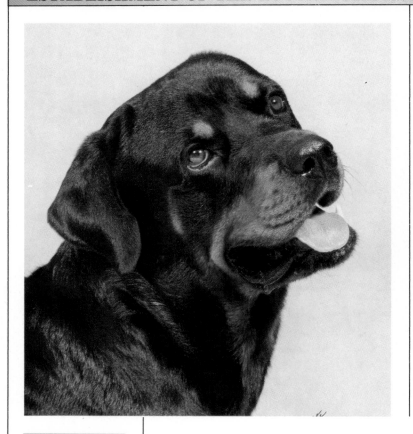

at approximately mid-cheek. **Serious Faults**—Improper carriage (creased, folded or held away from cheek/head). *Muzzle*—Bridge is straight, broad at base with slight tapering towards tip. The end of the muzzle is broad with well developed chin. Nose is broad rather than round and always black. Lips—Always black; corners closed; inner mouth pigment is preferred dark. **Serious Faults**—Total lack of mouth pigment (pink mouth). *Bite and Dentition*—Teeth 42 in number (20 upper, 22 lower) strong, correctly placed, meeting in a scissors bite—lower incisors touching inside of upper incisors. **Serious Faults**—Level bite; any missing tooth. *Disqualifications*—Overshot, undershot (when incisors do not touch or mesh); wry mouth; two or more missing teeth.

Neck, Topline, Body
Neck—Powerful, well muscled, moderately long, slightly arched

Above: Zornhaus Exzacht, C.D., age 2 years. Owned by Pamela Anderson, Wilton Manors, FL. *Right:* Ch. Cannon River's Oil Tanker, C.D., is the winner of an unprecedented 21 all-breed Best in Shows and 2 Specialty Bests. He is owned by George and Elfi Rice, Faribault, MN. Tanker combines the most outstanding of Rottie greats in his pedigree, and is himself siring puppies of exceptional merit.

and without loose skin. *Topline*—The back is firm and level, extending in a straight line from behind the withers to the croup. The back remains horizontal to the ground while the dog is moving or standing. *Body*—The chest is roomy, broad and deep, reaching to elbow, with well pronounced forechest and well sprung, oval ribs. Back is straight and strong. Loin is short, deep and well muscled. Croup is broad, of medium length and only slightly sloping. Underline of a mature Rottweiler has a slight tuck-up. Males must have two normal testicles properly descended into the scrotum. *Disqualification*—Unilateral cryptorchid or cryptorchid males. *Tail*—Tail docked short, close to body, leaving one or two tail vertebrae. The set of the tail is more important than length. Properly set, it gives an impression of elongation of topline; carried slightly above horizontal when the dog is excited or moving.

Forequarters
Shoulder blade is long and well laid back. Upper arm equal in length to shoulder blade, set so elbows are well under body. Distance from withers to elbow and elbow to ground is equal. Legs are strongly developed with straight, heavy bone, not set close together. Pasterns are strong,

Top: **Ch. Srigo's Billet Doux, by Ch. Srigo's Opportunity And How ex Ch. Srigo's Xclusive v. Kurtz. Top Producing Dam in the entire Working Group, 1979. Owned by Ms. Felicia E.H. Luburich.**
Middle: **This handsome young dog, "Justice," is a younger brother to Ch. Powsell's Rambo De Jaco, and one who shows great promise. Owned by Deborah Moneque, Lake Worth, FL.**
Bottom: **Einsamstadt Brie, C.D., T.T., Registered Therapy Dog, owned by Catherine Goldman, Dorchester, MA. Brie here is taking the Triple Bar Spread obstacle from an Agility Demonstration at the Bay Colony Cluster, Boston, 1988, sponsored by the New England Agility Team. Photo coutesy of Judith M. Sherman.**

Ch. Rodsden's Cossack von Brader, C.D., is owned by Goldeiche Rottweilers, Ted W. Grisell, Cicero, IN.

springy and almost perpendicular to the ground. Feet are round, compact with well arched toes, turning neither in nor out. Pads are thick and hard. Nails short, strong and black. Dewclaws may be removed.

Hindquarters
Angulation of hindquarters balances that of forequarters. Upper thigh is fairly long, very broad and well muscled. Stifle joint is well turned. Lower thigh is long, broad and powerful, with extensive muscling leading into a strong hock joint. Rear pasterns are nearly perpendicular to the ground. Viewed from the rear hind legs are straight, strong and wide enough apart to fit with a properly built body. Feet are somewhat longer than the front feet, turning neither in nor out, equally compact with well arched toes. Pads are thick and hard. Nails short, strong, and black. Dewclaws must be removed.

Coat
Outer coat is straight, coarse, dense, of medium length and lying flat. Undercoat should be present on neck and thighs, but the amount is influenced by climatic conditions. Undercoat should not show through outer coat. The coat

is shortest on head, ears and legs, longest on breeching. The Rottweiler is to be exhibited in the natural condition with no trimming. **Fault**—Wavy coat. **Serious Faults**—Open, excessively short, or curly coat; total lack of undercoat; any trimming that alters the length of the natural coat. ***Disqualification***—Long coat.

Color
Always black with rust to mahogany markings. The demarcation between black and rust is to be clearly defined. The markings should be located as follows: a spot over each eye; on cheeks; as a strip around each side of muzzle, but not on the bridge of the nose; on throat; triangular mark on both sides of prosternum; on forelegs from carpus downward to the toes; on inside of rear legs showing down the front of the stifle and broadening out to front of rear legs from hock to toes, but not completely eliminating black from rear of pasterns; under tail; black penciling on toes. The undercoat is gray, tan, or black. Quantity and location of rust markings is important and should not exceed ten percent of body color. **Serious Faults**—Straw-colored, excessive, insufficient or sooty markings; rust marking other than described

above; white marking any place on a dog (a few rust or white hairs do not constitute a marking).

Disqualifications—Any base color other than black; absence of all markings.

Gait

The Rottweiler is a trotter. His movement should be balanced, harmonious, sure, powerful and unhindered, with strong forereach and a powerful rear drive. The motion is effortless, efficient, and ground-covering. Front and rear legs are thrown neither in nor out, as the imprint of hind feet should touch that of forefeet. In a trot the forequarters and hindquarters are mutually coordinated while the back remains level, firm and relatively motionless. As speed increases the legs will converge under body towards a center line.

Temperament

The Rottweiler is basically a calm, confident and courageous dog with a self-assured aloofness that does not lend itself to immediate and indiscriminate friendships. A Rottweiler is self-confident and responds quietly and with a wait-and-see attitude to influences in his environment. He has an inherent desire to protect home and family, and is an intelligent dog of extreme hardness and adaptability with a strong willingness to work, making him especially suited as a companion, guardian and general all-purpose dog.

The behavior of the Rottweiler in the show ring should be controlled, willing and adaptable, trained to submit to examination of mouth, testicles, etc. An aloof or reserved dog should not be penalized, as this reflects the accepted character of the breed. An aggressive or belligerent attitude towards other dogs should not be faulted.

A judge shall excuse from the ring any shy Rottweiler. A dog shall be judged fundamentally shy if, refusing to stand for examination, it shrinks away from the judge. A dog that in the opinion of the judge menaces or threatens him/her, or exhibits any sign that it may not be safely approached or examined by the judge in the normal manner, shall be excused from the ring. A dog that in the opinion of the judge attacks any person in the ring shall be disqualified.

Summary

Faults

The foregoing is a description of the ideal Rottweiler. Any structural fault that detracts from the above described working dog must be penalized to the extent of the deviation.

Disqualifications

Entropion, ectropion. Overshot, undershot (when incisors do not touch or mesh); wry mouth; two or more missing teeth. Unilateral cryptorchid or cryptorchid males. Long coat. Any base color other than black; absence of all markings. A dog that in the opinion of the judge attacks any person in the ring.

Approved May 8, 1990

Roma's Ultra von Siegerhaus, age 10½ months. Sired by Am., Can., Mex. Ch. Quick von Siegerhaus, Z.T.P.R., Am., Can. C.D., T.T., ex Nacht Music von Siegerhaus, Am., Can. C.D. Ultra matured to complete her championship at 26 months of age. Owned by Gary and Roberta Martin, Roma Rottweilers, Chico, CA.

Chinguacousy Dog Fanciers' Association

Top: Ch. Ingrid von Krauss was the first champion Rottweiler owned by Brenda and John Jayne, Dayton, OH. *Middle:* Eichehaus Baronin von Darak at just over 7 months of age, taking Best of Winners at Chinguacousy Dog Fanciers' Association, Toronto, Ontario, March, 1989. Owned by Dr. P.K. and Shelley St. John, Roborott Kennels, Welland, Ont., Canada. *Bottom:* Ch. Rassentreu Krazy Kate v. Jaro is owned by Bill and Lilly Lavender, Boulder House, Pioneertown, CA.

ALPEN HAUS

Alpen Haus Rottweilers in Round Top, New York, are owned by Laura Krutsch, whose interest in and admiration for the breed dates back to the early 1950s, when she was living in Austria. However, it was not until 25 years later that she obtained her first Rottie bitch. Her name was Lyndhausen's Belle, C.D.; she became Laura's best friend and companion for nearly 13 years, and was the foundation for Alpen Haus Rottweilers.

Belle was bred to American and Canadian Ch. Donnaj Vermont Yankee of Paulus. This produced Laura's first champion, Adelheid vom Alpen Haus, who became a Top Producer and was bred to Ch. Luger, leading three champions in the first litter.

The principal bloodlines at Alpen Haus are Graudstark, Northwind, Rodsden, and of course, the old German imports.

Laura Krutsch is a member of the A.D.R.K. in Germany as well as the American Rottweiler Club. She enjoys working and training as well as handling her own dogs, and takes pride in the champions and working-degree holders her kennel has produced.

ANTREN ROTTWEILERS

Antren Rottweilers in Lynbrook, New York, are owned and loved by Karen and Anthony DiCicco and have been a successful venture right from the very beginning.

Foundation bitch here, Ch. Doroh's Jaegerin v. Noblehaus, C.D., T.T., was bred to Ch. Noblehaus Beretta, T.T., thus producing Ch. Antren's Anything Goes, T.T. "Zado," co-owned with Chet and Teri Radd, finished with three majors and became a multiple Best of Breed over specials winner and a high Group placer from the classes—always breeder/owner-handled, which makes this success all the more enjoyable.

This "A" litter also included the major-pointed (with a Best of Opposite Sex over specials) Antren's All That Jazz, C.D., T.T., and Antren After The Storm, T.T.

Jaegerin was then bred to Ch. Brash Baer v. Pioneer, C.D. Only two puppies were the result, but Antren's Broadway Rhythm won both her majors (also with a Best of Opposite Sex over specials), her wins having been at Westchester Kennel Club (four points and Best of Opposite Sex) and the Colonial Rottweiler Club-supported Bucks County Kennel Club Show for five points. "Bonnie" is co-owned with Darryl and Dan Bologna.

Littermate Antren Bustin Loose, co-owned by Rosalie and Frank McCormick, was Best of Winners at the Wallkill Kennel Club and Westbury Kennel Association events.

Antren's third litter was sired by Am. and Can. Ch. Trifecta's Barbarian v. Murph, C.D., from Antren's All That Jazz, C.D., T.T.

Karen and Tony were instrumental in the formation of the Greater New York Rottweiler Club, where presently Karen is Secretary and Tony is President. Both Karen and Tony are Chief Testers for the American Temperament Test Society. Their two children share the family interest in dog shows and Rottweilers as well. Anthony and Cara are both active in Junior Showmanship. In three shows, Cara advanced to the Open Junior Handling Class, winning Best Junior on only her fourth appearance by defeating 23 other youngsters.

It is interesting to note that, as should be the case, the Antren Rottweilers are a hobby enjoyed, bringing pride and pleasure to each individual member of their family as well as to the family collectively.

BERGENHOF

Bergenhof Rottweilers are owned by Joan Harrison of Sandy, Utah, who had, in 1979, a most sad experience with her first pet-companion member of the breed. This puppy was diagnosed as having neuroaxonal dystrophy, and

Top: Kennrich's Top Gun, owned by Brenda Creek, at age 5 months winning First Place in the 3–6 Months Puppy Class at the 1988 National Capitol R.C. Specialty Match. Bred by Kennette and Richard Tabor, by Int. Ch. Amon vom Filmteich ex Ch. Radio Ranch's Casablanca Pia. *Middle:* Ch. Nelson v.h. Brabantpark, Dutch import, multiple Best-in-Show and Specialty winner. Owned by Powderhorn/ Wencrest Rottweilers, Inc. *Bottom:* Rassentreu Cayman v. Jano, C.D., T.T., is one of the definitive Rottweiler stars, owned by Bill and Lilly Lavender.

A very prestigious owner-handled win: Ch. Brinka von Ross, C.D., T.T., at age 23 months, takes Best of Opposite Sex at the A.R.C. Regional Specialty under judge Mrs. Joan Klem. Brinka is by Elko v.d. Nedermolen, SchH. III, ex Ch. Gundi von Ross. Owned by Karen and Harold Riddle, Jr., Fall Branch, TN.

had to be euthanized at age five months.

It was not until 1985 that Joan decided to try again with the purchase of her second Rottweiler, whose accomplishments following so unhappy a first experience utterly astounded her.

The second purchase was of a seven-week-old puppy bitch sired by American Rottweiler Club Bronze Producer, Best in Show Ch. Rhomark's Axel von Lerchenfeld,

U.D.T., ex Zimmer's Heidi von Kriegerhof, the latter a daughter of Ch. Rocky von Anderson and a granddaughter of Ch. Radio Ranch's Axel v. Notara, American Rottweiler Club Bronze and Gold Producers respectively. This youngster grew up to become Select Ch. Sophe von Bergenhof, C.D.

Inspired by Axel's outstanding obedience career, as well as success in the show ring, Joan started Sophe's obedience training at an early age, and at age 13 months she earned her Companion Dog Degree in three consecutive shows.

In 1987, before her second birthday, Sophe earned her championship in grand style. Handled by Dave Caulderwood, Sophe won three majors, going Best of Opposite Sex twice her first weekend in the ring. The following weekend she was awarded two Bests of Breed, finishing a month later with a fourth major.

In 1988, Sophe enjoyed a limited but successful specials career. Shown through only six months of competition by her friend and handler Ferris Hayes, she accumulated numerous Bests of Breed, Bests of Opposite Sex, and Group placements including the prestigious Group First. The highlight of Sophe's show career, however, came when she was chosen Best of Opposite Sex at the 1988 Rottweiler National Specialty in Oakland, California, under judge Robert J. Moore. Sophe made the A.R.C. Top Ten Bitches that year, and the Medallion Rottweiler Club Honor Roll.

In the summer of 1988, Sophe was bred to Best in Show Ch. Nelson von het Brabantpark, owned by Clara Hurley and Michael Grossman. That fall, Bergenhof's first litter was on the ground, consisting of 11 beautiful puppies—three females and eight males. A male from this litter is the

This handsome dog is Ch. Ai Jo's Bruin von Junge, pictured winning points towards his title at Greater Kingsport K.C. for owners, Chuck and Jan Freudenberg, Cordova, TN.

Top: Can., Bda. Ch. Gamegard's Dragonwyck Perry, son of Am., Can., and Int. Ch. Bronco v. Rauberfeld, SchH. III, F.H., from Gamegard's Black Britt, a British import. Bred by Victoria Weaver. Owner, Carlton Wilkinson. Photo courtesy of Felicia Luburich. *Bottom:* Ch. Blitz v.d. Donnereiche, a German import, pictured here at age 2 years. Bert Halsey is handling for owners David A. Gallo, M.D., and Barbara Hoard, Virginia Beach, VA.

A promising Alaskan youngster, Freedomfarms Asha Gold, by Am., Can. Ch. Bryloukis Great Expectations, C.D., ex Can. Ch. Simeberg's Fagen, at age 8 months. Owned by Katie and Pete Nolan, Anchorage, AK.

newest "star" at Bergenhof. Bergenhof's Gunther von Nelson is very promising and did well in his puppy kindergarten classes and tracking. Joan comments that she is very proud to say that all of the pups from this litter went to class and some are already tracking. This is the way to raise a Rottweiler!

Her owner's goal for Sophe is her C.D.X. degree. Since she is first and foremost a family companion, she will be specialed on a limited basis.

The future looks bright for Sophe and Gunther, who share their home with two Boxers. A second breeding is planned for Sophe in the future.

BIG COUNTRY

Big Country Rottweilers are owned by Johann Emedi in Warren, Michigan, who first became aware of the breed in 1970. It was not, however, until January 1978 that he acquired his first Rottie; then in early 1981 he decided that he would like one of show quality.

At a local dog show he had seen and been impressed by both the looks and the pedigree of a bitch who had attracted his attention. The proper contacts were made, and in due time Champion Olga von Gruenerwald had a ten-puppy litter. Johann's pick puppy came home to serve as foundation of what was to become Big Country Kennels.

Luther von Kruse was also acquired and then owner-handled to American and Canadian championship plus obedience degrees. "Sammy" as Luther is known to friends, was not used at stud until he had reached age five years, the principal reason being that Johann had not yet become interested in that phase of dog owning. Gradually all this changed, and his search began for a suitable bitch. Soon he had bought a female puppy from Edith Alphin, Altar's Rottweilers, that puppy maturing to become Am., Can. Ch. Altars Mingin Magic v. Amars, T.T. From Sammy and Magic, Johann kept two females and a male. They are Big Country Dakota's Bismark, Big Country Belinda, and Big Country Commotion. He needed one more son of his, and right about that time Jennifer Beban of Rosendorn Rottweilers asked about using Sam as the stud for one of her bitches.

Johann welcomed this opportunity, being an admirer of this breeder's successes. And so Rosendorn's Harmony, T.T., brought forth a Sam litter, from which Johann now owns Rosendorn's Negotiator, and Johann has his fingers crossed that this may become the best Rottie he has had.

Sam and Magic are the only two adult dogs now at Big Country. There are a few promising youngsters coming along though who are beginning to turn heads when they appear in the show ring.

Beyond breeding and showing his Rotties, Johann also belongs to the Great Lakes Rottweiler Club of Southern Michigan, and for the past few years he has served as president.

BIG SKY

Big Sky Rottweilers consist of one dog, but a very outstanding dog owned by Phyllis J. Clark. This dog is Am., Can. Ch. Cannon River Destroyer, C.D., T.T., known at home as "Chunk Edward."

He is sired by many titled Cannon River Oil Tanker, and in the tradition of his sire who is a living legend in the breed, he has already made a name for himself.

Destroyer won his majors in Chicago on the same weekend he took the last two legs of his C.D., which he earned in three consecutive shows. He also achieved his Canadian championship in one weekend. On that occasion he won Open Class three times; Winners Dog three times; Best of Breed all three days;

one Group First and two Group Seconds; and one Best in Show. The latter victory he won as a class dog at age two years.

He is also proving himself as a producer. His first puppy shown won his class the first time in the ring.

BLUEFOX

Bluefox Rottweilers are owned by Cheryl L. Kienast in Aurora, Colorado, where all of her Rotties live as house dogs and family

Top: Ch. Berit v. Alemannenhof, SchH. I, F.H., Z.T.P.R., a German import bitch, owned by Powderhorn/Wencrest Rottweilers. *Bottom:* Ch. Hans v.h. Brabantpark, Winners Dog, A.R.C. Specialty. A Dutch import owned by Powderhorn/Wencrest Rottweilers.

Top: Ch. Ebonstern Kali v. Abra, by Can. Ch. Life v. Tengen, SchH. III, ex Ebonstern Abra v. Lauffeuer. *Bottom:* Am., Can. Ch. Glynn's Luke von Imp, by Glynn's Fritz von Rodley ex Meagan Amity Bela. Owners, Larry and Karen Glynn.

companions. Cheryl acquired her first Rottweiler, Ch. V. Victor's Dame Brau v. Bruin, C.D., who is a granddaughter of Champion Bruin von Hungerbuhl, C.D.X. In 1984 as a young puppy, "Freya" was trained and shown to her championship by her owner and her friends, collecting Bests of Breed and several Best Opposites from the classes.

Freya's "A" litter produced four puppies by Eureka's Siegen Zur Kraftig, SchH. II, in 1987. Two males from that litter have been shown since they were 11 weeks old, first in fun matches and then at A.K.C. shows. "The Boys" have never taken less than a third and are usually first in their classes. They were shown twice in the Brace Class, the first time at the American Rottweiler Club Regional Specialty in Greeley, Colorado, which was held on their first birthday, and where they went on later in the day Best Working Dog Brace. "The Boys" are currently in training for a Schutzhund title while also being shown locally in the conformation ring.

Bluefox is proving its dedication to the preservation of the Rottweiler's spirit and working ability by following a very limited breeding program. All puppies are raised in the home with careful attention to proper socialization, and equally close attention is paid to matching the right puppy with the right owner. To that end, all puppies are aptitude tested at several weeks to facilitate placing the right puppy with the right owner. Any puppy which is deemed to be "companion quality" is sold on a spay/neuter contract only.

Bluefox puppy owners are encouraged to become involved in obedience, tracking, and carting, in addition to conformation showing. It is the hope of the owner that Bluefox puppies will continue to exhibit the characteristics that make this breed so special—courage, loyalty, and that indefinable "presence" that makes the Rottweiler unique.

Cheryl Kienast is a member of the American Rottweiler Club as well as the Hi Country Schutzhund Club and will be a founding member of the newly formed Mile High Rottweiler Club. Additionally, a group of Rottweiler owners have formed an informal "club" which they call the North Area Working Dogs. This group's purpose is to help one another in

the litters being produced by their dogs. These have consisted of truly beautiful puppies to the extent that choosing the best from among them is difficult. Their objective of raising Rottweilers of high quality and allowing no compromise in their standard is always adhered to diligently. It is their feeling that working and showing ability should both be main objectives when raising a Rottweiler.

Carat vom Aussee, German imported Rottweiler male, SchH. III, AD Z.T.P.R., V-rated is also show pointed. Vira von der Grurmannsheide is another with working titles and show conformation points.

Left: Graffin von Bayerland at Clarksville K.C., 1988. A daughter of Gero vom Koniggarten, SchH. I, ex Cora vom Schloss Lichtenneck, SchH. II. Owned by Doug and Cathy Nimmo.
Below: Head study of Am., Can., Mex. Ch. Quick von Siegerhaus, C.D., Z.T.P.R. Owned by Thomas and Carol Woodward. Photo by Mitchell.

all aspects of dog training—A.K.C. obedience, conformation handling, tracking, and, of course, Schutzhund training.

BORRASCO

Borrasco Rottweilers were established in 1986 by Rick and Teri Mutschler, who reside at Wimbledon, North Dakota. A long-time interest in the breed has led this couple, over the years, to study breeding and gather literature concerning the Rottweiler, with special emphasis on standards of the breed, pedigrees, etc. They did this to better prepare themselves to make a wise choice when the time came for them to join with others who already owned and were enjoying the breed.

Around 1986 they purchased their first Rottweiler, an 11-month-old male German import. They were delighted with the quality they saw in this dog, feeling that the German Rottweiler is a true family dog, a working dog and conformative as well. After owning him for a year, they knew that this was definitely "their" breed.

The Mutschlers have purchased all of their Rottweilers from Germany with one exception, a 100% German-bred dog from the Kruses.

The Mutschlers are pleased with

Above: Select Ch. Eischenwald's Basil v. Axel, C.D., with his family, Pat Derdivanis and Robert Baston of Oakland, CA. Below: Ch. Donar v.d. Hoeve Cor Unum, C.D., a Dutch import owned by Powderhorn/Wencrest Rottweilers, Inc.

BOULDER HOUSE

Boulder House Rottweilers are owned by W.B. Lavender and Patricia (Lilly) Lavender of Pioneertown, California. The theme at Boulder House would have to be patience, for that is what it has taken for the owners of this establishment to see it reach

their goals. According to the Lavenders, these goals include their personal big three—"exceptional temperament, typey conformation, and a sound body." Added to these goals should undoubtedly be selective breeding and placement, an on-going crusade for control of hip dysplasia, and a very high concern for public education regarding the breed itself.

After the first ten years of Rottweiler ownership and breeding, it can be said that the owners of Boulder House and its Rottweilers are actively involved in the process of striving for the maintenance of the breed and promotion of a good public image for the Rottweiler.

Never a large producer of puppies, Boulder House only breeds when most or all members of any planned litter have been spoken for in advance. The prospective owners are screened in depth and must wait a considerable length of time for their puppy. That pup, when taken home, will have been aptitude tested, conformation evaluated, thoroughly socialized, and, in the case of an older dog will have received some basic obedience training. The contract signed by the buyer insists on formal obedience training and a detailed lifestyle for the pup. Also, rebates are given for all American Kennel Club titles earned, including the full range of obedience degrees. The first year's membership in a code of ethics club of the buyer's choice is offered free.

Boulder House itself is an unusual kennel. Situated on 55 acres of California high desert, the buildings are set among giant boulders, some of which are actually within the various buildings and runs. It serves as the site of a unique activity each October when the Boulder House Rott Trot takes place. This event is a 5K run wherein each runner or walker must be accompanied by one or more Rotties.

Over the years the "Rott Trot"

Top left: Can., Mex. Ch. Leibgarde's "Heidi" vom Hochfeld, Am. T.T., Owners, M. and F. Mitchell. Photo by Callea.
Top right: Can. Ch. Simsberg's Fagan, by Ch. Trollegen's Benjamin ex Ch. Cita von Simsberg, at the first Alaskan S.K.C. Show. Owner, Donna Slownoski.
Middle left: Ch. Yden's Chase Manhattan, owned by Yvette M. Forest.
Middle right: Am., Can. Ch. Elka von Siegerhaus, Am., Can. C.D., is an A.R.C. Producer of Merit. Owners, Thom and Carol Woodward.
Bottom left: Ch. Von Hawthorne's Max Otto handled by Mae Piske for owner Alice Hahn.
Bottom right: Gina von Magdeberg, SchH. II, T.T. Co-owners, Bruce and Karen Billings.

Top: Chirlyn's Al E Gator, taking Reserve Winners Dog at Bryn Mawr in 1988. By Ch. Razdy's Akemo Grande, C.D., ex Ch. Darby's Solitaire von Meadow. Bred by Sheena R. Marchand; handled by Vicki L. Marchand; owned by Mary Ellen Thomas and J.M. Shinski.

Middle: HawkHaven Tiger Lilly belongs to Barbara Kellette, HawkHaven Rottweilers. She here is taking Best of Winners on the way towards championship.

Bottom: Ch. Zolti von Siegerhaus winning the 12–18 Months Class at the National Specialty in May, 1988. Owned by Thom and Carol Woodward.

has received national publicity and continues to grow in size, last year's event having found 81 Rotties competing. "Rott Trot" is dedicated to the furtherance of owner/dog activities where both have fun and can enjoy the companionship of other owners and their dogs without the stress and competitiveness of the usual more formal type of Rottweiler events.

Membership is maintained by the Lavenders in the American Rottweiler Club, the Rottweiler Discussion and Observation Group, the Medallion Rottweiler Club, and the Golden State Rottweiler Club. Bill Lavender is currently serving as a director for the Golden State Rottweiler Club.

Patricia Lavender, writing under her nickname of Lilly, is a nationally published author of articles concerning the Rottweiler breed. Professionals in the general field of newsletters for some 17 years, both Lavenders write very interesting and informative material for Rottweiler owners.

BRIARWOOD

Briarwood Rottweilers and Arabian horses are located at Lagrangeville, New York, where they are the combined hobbies of Martin Charlop and Lavonda Herring.

These folks have several very lovely bitches upon which they are basing their foundation stock for the Rottweilers, using the sensible procedure of breeding them to famed stud dogs of their choice whose lines are compatible with their own. It is working out nicely, judging by the quality of the young homebreds.

Patra Mastrangelo v. Foxcroft is the "senior brood bitch" here and is fast proving her excellence as a producer. Particularly, she has a young dog and bitch of very real promise to her credit: they are Von Petka's Briarwood Jack, by Ch. Arri von der Hembachbruke, the dog; and Gina Marie's Class Act, the bitch, a daughter of Ch. Altar's Gunner of Woodland.

Top: Janice Lynch with "Margot" at the end of one of their Rott Trot trips. *Bottom:* Ch. Garen's Baron Max v. Charm, C.D., T.T., a splendid Rottweiler and Registered Therapy Dog as well as a show champion, Obedience, and Temperament Test Dog. Owned by Gary F. and Karen L. Sims, St. Charles, MO.

Top: Ch. Simsberg's Gangster in September, 1987. A Top Ten Rottweiler in Canada for 1987 and 1988. Owned by Mary McGee and Cynthia Roney, Bryloukis Rottweilers. *Middle:* Select Ch. Sophe von Bergenshof, C.D., baits nicely for her handler, Ferris Hayes, as Janet Wilcox casts a judicial eye over this excellent bitch. Joan Harrison, owner, Sandy, UT. *Bottom:* Trollegen Freya von Simsberg, T.D., by Cyras von Leinetal ex Heidegruens Bekka, pictured taking a placement in the 12–18 Month Bitch Class when 14 months old. Owners, Susan Lyons and Maureen Wilkinson.

Class Act, in her turn bred to Ch. Marksman von Turick, C.D., is the dam of a bright young hopeful in the bitch Briarwood's Chantilly Lace; and the dog, Briarwood's Neko, is another impressive youngster.

Lavonda and Marty are truly enjoying working with their dogs, and have them all doing well in tracking and obedience. With a bit more maturity, we feel sure that they will be winning well in the conformation ring as well.

CAMAS VALLEY

Camas Valley Rottweilers of Springdale, Washington, reside on 60 wooded acres at the head of the Camas Valley which they share with their owners, Dan and Debby Kutz, and with the two Kutz children.

The foundation Rottweilers for this kennel were selected with the assistance of Ruth O'Brien, owner of the Gold Certificate (awarded to the sire of 50 or more champions) Ch. Rodsden's Ansel v. Brabant. From a breeding by Ansel from Duchess of Highland Park came Ch. Camas Valley Kaiser v. Kutz and Ch. Camas Valley Hildagard v. Kutz. This particular litter produced seven American champions, Mrs. Kutz tells us, and Duchess became a Top Producer for 1983 and 1984.

Hildagard's first breeding was to Ch. Eiko vom Schwaiger Wappen, C.D.X., SchH. III. This litter included Wilson's Treu Held Dillion, C.D., first in Novice B and second highest scoring dog in obedience at the 1986 ARC National Specialty; and Canadian Ch. Camas Valley Dickens v. Eiko, the Open Dog Class winner and Reserve Winners Dog at the Rottweiler Club of Canada's 13th National Specialty in 1988 and the Open Dog winner and Reserve Winners Dog at the American Rottweiler Club Regional Specialty that same year. Both of these are Rottweilers who contributed well to their breed.

Ryatti's Degan v. Camas Valley produced, in his first two litters,

Von Der Hess Brax v. Ryatti and Der Fruchtwald D.D. Bernhardt. Brax was 1987 and 1988 U.S.R.C. Youth Sieger and Most Beautiful Dog in Show. "Bernie" was Best of Winners at the 1988 Golden State Rottweiler Club Specialty and Winners Dog at the 1988 American Rottweiler Club Regional Specialty.

After that, Hilda was bred again, this time to American and Canadian Ch. Harras vom Sachsen, and produced Camas Valley Frenchtown Favour, the first Group winner for the Kutz's kennel.

Camas Valley's next addition was a puppy bitch sired by Ch. Eiko vom Schwaiger Wappen, C.D.X., SchH. III, ex Ch. Starkheims Catinka G. Roadway, who grew up to become Ch. Camas Valley Cassandra, who at ten months of age was sent to California to be shown by Patti Holt. She finished her American championship on her first birthday with points acquired in four majors. Patti and Cassy continued their winning ways with Bests of Breed over well-known specials.

Cassy culminated her career by winning Best of Opposite Sex at the Western Rottweiler Specialty in conjunction with Golden Gate Kennel Club in February, 1984, when only 15 months of age. Even though she was specialed during only three months of 1984, she earned sufficient points to become the American Rottweiler Club No. 8 Bitch for that year.

Ch. Camas Valley Cassandra was bred to Ch. Camas Valley Kaiser v. Kutz in 1986, from which she whelped a litter of three. Included among them were: Camas Valley Emerald Kutz, a major pointed bitch en route to championship; and Camas Valley Ruben Elexander, U.D., SchH. I. Ruben finished his obedience degrees in 11 shows and was the first Rottweiler from Camas Valley Kennels to receive the O.F.A. rating of "excellent."

Camas Valley Anna vom Ali, U.D.T., is now pointed towards her

Top: Can. Ch. Wyreglen's Archangel, owned by F. Mueller and C.E. MacPherson, is winning the Novice Dog Class at the Colonial R.C. Specialty in 1985. The judge is Mrs. Margaretta McIntyre, herself a famous Rottie breeder; the handler is Felicia Luberich of Srigo Kennels. *Middle:* New addition to Lakeview Rottweilers at Dawson Springs, KY: Concord's Tandem of Lakeview winning the Puppy Class at Crab Orchard K.C., owner-handled by Tonya Jones Oldham. *Bottom:* Am. Ch. Gretchen of Dugins Farms, bred and handled by Diane Johnston, owned by Robert K. Dugin and Erwin A. Dugin.

Ch. Wilderness Broud, owned by Linda Van Brunt, bred by JoAnn Harnish, Oakridge, OR. Winning Best of Breed at Cook Inlet K.C. in 1986.

Obedience Trial championship. Her name has been submitted for induction into the Medallion Rottweiler Club's Hall of Fame. Danamys Burley vom Frodo, Z.T.P.R., C.D., SchH. I; and Tonka, another working dog of distinction from Camas Valley, are two more belonging in this category.

Dan and Debby Kutz adhere to the Medallion Rottweiler Club Code of Ethics. Although young in their breeding program, they strive to breed the total Rottweiler with an emphasis on temperament and working aptitude as well as show type.

CANNON RIVER

Cannon River is a small kennel located about 50 miles from the Minneapolis/St. Paul area, at Faribault, Minnesota, where a 26-acre farm is home to these Rottweilers and their owners, George and Elfi Rice. Currently the Rotties there consist of three, plus one cat and two horses.

In speaking of the Rottweilers, one cannot too strongly emphasize the fact that this is a case of quality rather than quantity. It also illustrates the fact that one does not need a huge kennel establishment if one aims to breed winners, for among these three Rotties is Ch. Cannon River Oil Tanker, C.D., the Top Winning Rottweiler in the history of the breed who was bred by the Rices.

During his career as a show dog, Tanker has been 169 times Best of Breed; 62 times first in the Working Group; placed in the Working Group on 63 additional occasions, won 21 all-breed Bests in Show; plus twice Best in Specialty Show, including the American Rottweiler Club National Specialty.

By the spring of 1989, Tanker sired three champions, with several major-pointed sons and daughters also en route to their titles. There seems little question whether or not Tanker will become a Top Producer, as well as a top show dog. Tanker is a son of Ch. Rodsden's Berte v. Zeserwald, C.D.X., from Panda's Tugboat Annie, who is by Ch. Radio Ranch's Axel v. Notora.

Cannon River Showboat (by Am. and Can. Ch. Elessar's Caius of Ebonstern from Panda's Tugboat Annie), bred and owned by the Rices, is the producer of three champions to date, including a Best in Show winner (in Canada) plus several pointed sons and daughters. An accident kept this lovely bitch from the show ring (although she is pointed from the puppy classes), but she will make her mark as a top producer.

American and Canadian Ch. Cannon River Stowaway, Am. and Can. C.D., T.T., by Ch. Rodsden's Berte v. Zederwald, C.D.X., from Cannon River Showboat, was bred by Cannon River Rottweilers and is now owned by Mike Liberato. "Bravo" is a multi-Best of Breed winner and was awarded "Select" at the 1988 Medallion Specialty.

American and Canadian Ch. Cannon River Destroyer, C.D., T.T., is by Oil Tanker from Show Boat, bred by the Rices at Cannon River and owned by Phyllis Clark. "Chunk" is a Best in Show winner in Canada and has multiple Best of Breed wins and Group placements.

The Rices purchased their first Rottweiler in 1979, after long having been intrigued with the breed. It was Mrs. Rice who had recommended to her sister, when the latter had been looking for a family pet, that she consider a Rottweiler, and it was her dog, Ammi, who completely sold the Rices on the breed.

A four-and-a-half-year-old bitch, Ch. Gudrun of Graudstark, was the Rices' first Rottweiler. She had been purchased in co-ownership

Ch. Gentle Thor of Kinderfox, T.T., owned by Judith Koloski of Chatham Center, NY. Pictured winning Best of Breed under judge Marcia Foy at Newtown K.C., handled by Sheryl Hedrick. Despite limited showing, Thor was a top-winning Rottweiler in the Northeast in 1987 and 1988, and is highly esteemed by leading breeders.

Can. Ch. Wyreglen's Archibald, C.D., owned by F. Mueller and C.E. MacPherson, Uxbridge, Ont., Canada.

with a breeder from the Northwest. In those days, it was extremely difficult to find a good Rottweiler to purchase. Gudrun was bred to Ch. Radio Ranch's Axel v. Notara and produced one puppy, Panda's Tugboat Annie, who became the Rices' foundation dam and was the producer of Ch. Cannon River Oil Tanker, C.D.

From the beginning, George and Elfi Rice's goal has been to breed excellent Rottweilers, sound in mind and body, and although they rarely breed more than one litter a year, they are very proud of the many fine dogs they have produced—as indeed they should be!

CHIRLYN

Chirlyn Rottweilers, owned by Sheena R. Marchand of Stamford, Connecticut, although comparatively new to the breed, are already earning recognition in Rottie circles.

The foundation bitch here, Champion Darby's Solitaire von Meadow, was purchased on the advice of Sheena's handler-daughter, Vicki L. Marchand. "Shotzie," as she is affectionately known, was handled to her championship by Vicki within a year of acquisition.

When it became time to breed Shotzie, following careful evaluation, it was decided that Ch. Razdy's Akemo Grande, C.D., would be the stud to use. The results were two outstanding puppies, Chirlyn's Al E Gator and Chirlyn's Any Day Now. Both are started on their show careers, with both having major Reserves from the Puppy Class. Any, who is still owned by her breeder, has points from the Puppy Class.

In exaggerated anticipation of Shotzie's litter, Sheena decided that she couldn't wait and went out on her own. As "luck of the novice" would have it, she found a puppy bred by Pat Harms of Carteret, New Jersey. This was Stonehill's Eriskay, by Ch. Eiko vom Schwaiger Wappen, C.D.X., from Woodland's Dealer's Choice, who had a very exciting youthful career, completing her championship within five months of showing by the time she was 18 months of age.

Another young hopeful at this kennel is Stonehill's Constant Comment, also by Eiko but from Ch. Sigmund's Carbon Copy. She, too, was bred by Pat Harms.

COPPERDOT'S

Copperdot's Rottweilers are owned by Diana D. Gibson of Tinton Falls, New Jersey, who in 1984 changed her kennel prefix from Gibson's, which she had used since the early 1970s.

Diana had been introduced to her first Rottweiler by her former husband, as he owned a year-old Rottie bitch imported from Great Britain's Chesaia Kennels. The bitch was Plaissance Irma, known as "Bubbles," and she became Diana's foundation bitch. In fact, she made quite an impressive record as a producer of champions due in part to a meeting between the Gibsons and Mrs. Walton of Lyn Mar Acres fame. Mrs. Walton approved of Irma; as a result, Irma was bred to Mrs. Walton's famed Lyn Mar Acres Arras v. Kinta. This was the beginning of the Gibsons' breeding program.

Although Diana and her husband were not "into" dog shows, Peg Walton was, and she knew people who bought these puppies for the purpose of showing them. They did extremely well in the ring, and Irma was bred twice more to Arras and once to his son, Ch. Kokas K. Degan. Irma's total list of champions included such names as: Ch. Windmaker's Orlo Der Gremlin; Ch. Gibson's Kinta v. Sofienbusch; Ch. Beowulf Bonita of Saxe-Gotha; Ch. Lyn Mar Acres Cassie v. Amri; Ch. Beowulf Dragon Killer; Ch. Beowulf Gibson Girl; Ch. Gibson's Betti v. Bettl Buhl; Ch.

Top: Can. Ch. and O.T.Ch. Davinghof's Aqtar Terror Shai, T.D., who combines beauty so well with brains, here is winning a Group Third in conformation competition for Maasai Rottweilers, owned by Thelma Boyd, Alberta Beach, Alta., Canada. *Middle:* Rainhart's Kaiser von Helsing at his first show, age 8 months. Bred and handled by Diane Johnston, owned by Cheryl Sweeney. *Bottom:* Can. Ch. Simeberg's Gangster, by Am., Can. Ch. Trollegen's Frodo, C.D., ex Can Ch. Simeberg's Czarina. Pictured winning Best of Breed at the 1988 R.C. of Canada Specialty Show. Bryloukis Rottweilers.

Ch. Torburhop's Patton von Brawn, owned by Pamela Anderson.

Lyn Mar Acres Chessarras v. Amri; and Gibson's Rodsden von Bear, who was a C.D. and Diana's first Rottweiler. He was born in 1974.

The Gibsons bred very little and tried to keep their stock of high quality, always concentrating on temperament, as most of their dogs went where there were children. Diana grew to love the breed dearly, and comments that she probably will never be without one.

When the Gibsons separated and divided up their Rotties, Diana changed her kennel prefix to Copperdot's, due to the beautiful copper-colored spots above the dogs' eyes.

After meeting someone who encouraged her to show her dogs in the breed ring, Diana soon made her first show champion and then was really hooked. This was Ch. Copperdot's Best Gemini, who produced her own champions named Ch. Copperdot's Bo von Kohler and his littermate Copperdot's Bronze Medal, who has quite a few points towards the title. Their sire is Ch. Trifecta's Barbarian Murph, C.D.

DARAK

Darak Rottweilers, owned by Dale and Karen Innocenti of Hickory Hills, Illinois, are the home of a very famous dog who came to live with the Innocentis as a ten-month-old puppy, then grew up to become an outstanding winning and producing member of his breed.

This dog is Am., Can. Ch. Goldeiche Ara von Brader, Am., Can. C.D. He was handled exclusively from day one by his owner, Dale, and had completed his championship before reaching 18 months of age. His early honors include a Sweepstakes, a Best of Breed, and a Group placement. He had earned his C.D. degree by the time he was 20 months old, and won his first Best in Specialty Show at the 1987 Colonial Rottweiler Club Specialty at just two years of age. Little did Karen and Dale realize, however, that the fun had just begun. It was at this point that the kennel name, DARAK, was adopted.

Ara's good looks and great movement should have come as no surprise considering his parentage. His mother, Ch. Rodsden's Hella v. Forstwald, T.D., won the 1982 Colonial Rottweiler Club Sweepstakes, just four years before her son, Ara, did so. His grandsire, Ch. Rodsden's Kane v. Forstwald, C.D., was a multiple Best in Specialty Show winner including the 1984 Colonial Rottweiler Club Specialty just three years prior to Ara's coming East and doing it, too.

In 1988, Ara was honored to represent his sire, Ch. Eiko vom Schwaiger Wappen, C.D.X., SchH. III, when Eiko won the Stud Dog

Top:
Can. Ch.
Areneberg
Cryso Mau, by
Can. Ch. Life v.
Tengen, SchH.
III. Bred by
Keith and
Trudy Clark.
Owned by
Cheryl
Wheeler and
Becky Sumner.
Photo courtesy
of C. Wheeler.
Bottom:
Ch. Danny v.
Timmerman,
owned by
Powderhorn/
Wencrest
Rottweilers,
Inc.

Top: Ch. Garen's Benjamin Benning while still on the way to his title. Owned by Gary and Karen Sims, Garen's Rottweilers. *Bottom:* Ch. Srigo's Rainbow Wilderness, by Am., Can. Ch. Bronco v. Rauberfeld, SchH. III, F.H., from Srigo's Only By Magic. Owned by JoAnn Harnish.

Class at the American Rottweiler Club Specialty in July at age 11 years.

October, 1988, brought Ara his first all-breed Best in Show, his Canadian championship and Canadian C.D., and a Canadian Specialty win, all followed by a second American Best in Show at the end of the year. Ara closed 1988 with his third Specialty win in December, ranking him in the Top Ten among Rottweilers in the United States, all systems, and the

No. 1 Owner-Handled Rottweiler in the United States, all systems.

The year 1989 started off with still another (his third) Best in Show, All Breeds, and from the appearance of things, it should be smooth sailing for him through a bright future.

Not having bred a litter of their own with the DARAK prefix to date, Dale and Karen will undoubtedly be doing so before much longer. Meanwhile Ara has been used selectively on high-quality bitches, so he has several young major-pointed offspring coming along, including three Match-winning kids, a Sweepstakes-winning son, an American Rottweiler Club Specialty Best Puppy in Show daughter, and a Temperament Tested son.

Ara shares his home with housemates and travel companions and a couple of promising puppies.

DER FRUCHTWALD

Der Fruchtwald Rottweilers are located in Lemon Grove, California. "Der Fruchtwald," which translates as "fruit grove," seemed appropriate as an identification for the dogs owned by Janice M. Lynch. She acquired her first of the breed from Vivian Peters, owner of Vom Hochfeld Kennels at Alpine, California. Thereby began not only a happy breed association, but a lasting friendship as well with Ms. Peters, who has helped Janice tremendously in learning about the breed, and about good ethics and kennel practices.

This first puppy was an excellent buy—a beautiful bitch whom Janice named Vom Hochfeld Burley H Dehdra, by Buccola's Kodiak vom Duf (son of Ch. Starkheim Duf Morgen Carroll ex Uberra Shung) from Uberra Shung—a breeding which was repeated on more than one occasion. Uberra was a Top Ten Brood Bitch, Janice points out, due solely to these repeated breedings to "Duffy."

Dehdra became not only the

foundation bitch but also a successful producer in her own right. She is now semi-retired and is respected as an important part of the beginning at Der Fruchtwald. At age 13 months, she won a large class at the American Rottweiler Club Regional National Specialty in Bellevue, Washington, which was the beginning of the association of Patti Holt of Perris, California, as handler for Janice's show dogs—an appropriate choice as Patti had previously been the one to finish Dehdra's sire and several of his brothers and sisters.

When it came time to breed Dehdra for her first litter, Janice selected Patti Holt's stud dog, Ryatti's Degan v. Camas Valley, who is a son of Ch. Eiko vom Schwaiger Wappen, C.D.X. Degan and Dehdra were mated in October, 1987, with outstanding results.

From these puppies, Janice admired (and Patti was quick to second the motion) a male who is officially known as Der Fruchtwald DD Bernhardt. At age ten months, he entered his first dog show, in Arizona, where he was awarded Reserve Winners Dog. From that time on, he never stopped! First came a series of "Reserves," and then the points began coming, his first at age 13 months. He won his first five-point major just a few months later at the 1988 Golden State Rottweiler Club Specialty for Best of Winners in an entry of 121 Rottweilers. His second major, again five points, was at the American Rottweiler Club Regional in Woodlinville, Washington, in an entry of comparable size. All of these points were won from the Puppy and American-bred Classes.

Bernhardt has two litter sisters belonging to Barbara and Bill Baker in Riverside, California, who are Der Fruchtwald Barouka and Der Fruchtwald Bourafa, these also being handled by Patti Holt, with whom they are winning well. This litter also produced a gorgeous bitch, Der Fruchtwald DD Britta, who belongs to a San Diego

lady police officer; and a handsome dog owned in Chino, California, who is not being shown.

The Degan-Dehdra breeding was repeated in September, 1988. It turned out to be disappointing for Janice, who had wanted to keep a bitch puppy from it. Instead, she kept two males of exceptional promise, one of which she co-owns and campaigns with another fancier.

Dehdra's dam, Vom Rochfelt Celestial Charm, is in Janice's opinion one of the best bitches in all San Diego County. Thus when she learned that owner Vivian Peters bred her to a Nero son, Oleo vom Schmidall, SchH. III, owned by Eckhart Selquist in

Apache Hill's Peyote Odyssey at 14 months. Bred and owned by Irene F. Castillo, Apache Hill Rottweilers, Abilene, TX. By Ch. Tulakes Apollo ex Ch. Merrymoore's Pagan Ballyho, C.D.

Riverside, California, Janice promptly placed an order for the litter's pick bitch puppy. This is Vom Hochfeld Margot Vom Haus, who at two years old is well fulfilling her early promise. Throughout her puppy months, she was shown with great success, then pulled out for awhile in order for Patti to concentrate on finishing an Open Bitch entry in her charge. Janice has great plans for breeding Margot with Degan.

It is interesting to note that Janice with Margot has marched extensively in parades with the carting group of their Southwestern Rottweiler Club, and they travelled together to participate in the 5k "Rott Trot"

north of Palm Springs, California.

Other lovely Rottweilers owned by Janice Lynch include Der Fruchtwald Athea Mummler, a daughter of Timm vom Mummler, SchH. III, owned by Eckhart Selquist; and Vom Hochfeld Bridget, a Dieter daughter who is co-owned by Janice with Vivian Peters. She was born in 1986 and was Janice's pick of the litter. Athea has also whelped a litter by Harras vom Sachsen.

An arrival at Der Fruchtwald is a bitch puppy sired by Ch. Cannon River Oil Tanker. Her dam is by a Nero son, and she has placed in puppy classes at the start of her career.

Janice Lynch is a member of the

Timberline's Cat Dancing, by Ch. Merrymoore's Ric-O Shay ex Timberline's Earth Bare, C.D. Owned by Sara Winfield and Sharon Michael. Pictured taking a first point from the Bred-by-Exhibitor Class.

Top left: Ch. Von Gailingen's Chancellor, by Ch. Anka von Gailingen, C.D., ex Ch. Igor von Schauer. Owned by Mrs. Mishew Edgerton Smith.
Top right: Ch. Berit V. Alemannenhof, Sch I, FH, Z.T.P.R., owned by Powderhorn/ Wencrest Rottweilers, Inc.
Middle left: Am., Can. Ch. Ebonstern Morgan V. Musquaw, owned by Cheryl Wheeler.
Middle right: Von Gailingen's Lofty Ideals, C.D.
Bottom left: Ch. Anka Von Gailingen.
Bottom right: Ch. Hanni Vom Bakkes, owned by Dr. and Mrs. Jack Whitman.

Top: Am., Hol., and Belg. Ch. Oscar v.h. Brabantpark as the eighth Rottweiler in history to go Best in Show. Owned by Powderhorn/ Wencrest Rottweilers, Inc.
Middle: Best Brace in Show at Valdosta K.C. in 1984, Ch. RC's Eagle Jackson von Ursa and Ch. Springdale Inca Dove von Ursa II, littermates winning under judge Robert Moore. Owner-handler, R. Chriscoe.
Bottom: Ch. Nelson v.h. Brabantpark, Dutch import, on the day of his first Best in Show. Owned by Powderhorn/ Wencrest Rottweilers, Inc.

American Rottweiler Club and president of the Southwestern Rottweiler Club. This club's goals are compatible with her own—to improve the breed and to see that the Rottweiler remains the all-around animal it is intended to be, outstanding in show quality, temperament, and working ability.

DERDIVANIS-BASTON ROTTWEILERS

Although Pat Derdivanis is a relative newcomer to the Rottweiler world, Bob Baston has been an owner and fancier of the breed for more than 20 years. Both, however, are newcomers to the show world.

After diligently doing their homework, Bob and Pat became acquainted with the famous Best in Show Ch. Rhomarks Axel v. Larchenfeld, U.D.T., and his owners, Ken and Hildegard Griffin of Novato, California. Axel was the American Rottweiler Club Top Ten Dog in 1982 and 1983.

Through the Griffins, Pat and Bob, of Oakland, California, acquired their first Rottweiler in late 1983—a bitch named Elka von Axel who, as it turned out, did not like the show ring.

Two-and-a-half years later, with the Griffins' help, Bob selected another Axel puppy, Basil, as a pet and a companion for Elka—and what a pet he turned out to be!

By the time that Axel was six months old, his new owners realized that they had something special on their hands. At the urging of the Griffins and Robert Hanley, Axel's handler, they began to show Basil. Following in his sire's pawprints, he was always in the ribbons until he finished his championship under judge C. Seaver Smith in March, 1988, at age 26 months, with four majors—two of which were won from the American-bred Class. His show record for the remaining nine months of 1988 was still more impressive. American Rottweiler Club Select, 17 Bests of Breed, two Group Thirds, and a Group First.

He won two Bests of Breed in January, 1989, as well.

Basil's working abilities have not been overlooked either. He completed his C.D. in May, 1988, and was High Scoring Champion of Record at the National Specialty. He and Pat are now working on Basil's C.D.X. and plan to take on Utility and Tracking next.

Basil has sired two litters with Ch. Marin's Ilsa vom Astanwald ("Alex"). From the first litter of six, two dogs and one bitch are being actively shown. Himmelhoch's Albrecht v. Basil and Himmelhoch's Axel Borg v. Basil take turns winning their classes, the latter adding Reserve from a six to nine month Puppy Class. The bitch, Himmelhoch's Konigen v. Basil, has been shown only twice so far and has been in the ribbons both times. The most recent litter promises to have even more winners in the show ring. This is the start of a careful and limited breeding career for Basil.

Bob and Pat are constantly complimented on Basil's exceptional physical condition, which they feel is due to his good background and his daily five-mile walks with his family.

Basil is by Ch. Rhomarks Axel v. Lerchenfeld, U.D.T., ex Sierra Stars Bella v. Thurow.

DONNAJ

Donnaj Rottweilers in Woodstock, Vermont, have been among the most important in the breed, as those familiar with its earlier history as outlined in *The Book of the Rottweiler* and *The World of Rottweilers* are very much aware. For it is their owner, Jan (Mrs. Donald) Marshall, who enjoyed the triumph of owning the first Best in Show Rottweiler in the United States, Ch. Rodsden's Kato of Donnaj, C.D.X., T.D. This dog, owner-handled, won 80 times Best of Breed; 29 Working Group placements, and the Best in Show. In 1984, Kato's great-granddaughter, Ch. Pioneer's Beguiled, became the first Rottweiler bitch to win Best in

Show in the United States, carrying on the family tradition very handsomely.

Kato's successes were carried on as well by the second Rottweiler who came to Donnaj, the wonderful American and Canadian Ch. Donnaj Vermont Yankee of Paulus, C.D.X., T.D. Yankee won a notable array of Specialty Show and all breed honors, including Best in Show, and was in the Top Three of the breed based on Group wins over a four year period. "Yank" also earned the High in Trial, as had grandfather Kato before him, at the Colonial Rottweiler Specialty. Yank will long be remembered for his personality, character, and excellence, and also as a stud dog who sired more than 36 champions.

Ch. Clyde von Reishoff, by Ch. Alpha Alexandros G Broadway ex Ch. Ariel von Reishoff, is owned by Nadine Jaquez, Vone Dine Rottweilers, So. El Monte, CA. Handler, Jeannie Schuster.

Top left: Ch. Von Hottenstein's
Hubahubba, by Am., Can. Ch. Trifecta's
Barbarian v. Murph, C.D., ex Amber von
Hottenstein, winning Best of Breed, owner
handled, at 17 months. Bred and owned by
Nancy Reynolds, Von Hottenstein
Rottweilers.
Bottom left: Am., Can. Ch. Von Bruka
Indra v. Yden, Am., Can. C.D., T.T.,
winning Best of Opposite Sex at the
Westchester K.C. Dog Show, owner-
handled by Yvette M. Forest.
Top right: Ch. Von Hottenstein's Bear
Handed finishing her championship at age
19 months. Owner-handled by Nancy
Reynolds, Von Hottenstein Rottweilers,
West Chester, PA.

Top right: Ch. Von Gailingen's Finest Hour taking Best of Winners at Warrenton, VA, 1984. Owned by Ann Keyes and Catherine Thompson, Freehold, NJ.
Bottom right: Ch. Pioneer's Gainst All Odds, winning her first major at Greenwich K.C., breeder-owner-handled by Sheryl Hedrick, Hollis, NH.
Bottom left: Am., Can. Ch. Carado's Commander Cody, Am., Can. C.D., winning Best of Breed at age 6½ years, owner-handled by Suzanne Sosne. Co-owner Mike Sosne, Nouveau Kennels, Caro, MI.

Top: Ch. Merrymoore's Imp von Dorow taking Best of Breed at Clovis Portales K.C., Clovis, NM. Owned by Nancy C. Estes, Midland, TX. *Bottom:* Barlin's Abraxus winning a 3-point major at 11 months. Owned by Von Damien Rottweilers, Port Perry, Ont., Canada.

Chinguacousy Dog Fanciers' Association

There was a young hopeful born two weeks prior to Yankee's death who helped the Marshalls through the sadness of that loss. This was Donnaj Very Special, and we are glad to tell you that he did fulfill his promise and that he is a wonderful companion if not a top contender for breed and Group wins. For the latter, Jan is still looking for that elusive "dream dog." While looking for another Kato or Yankee, Jan has been doing some judging of Sweepstakes and she has recently received approval for her provisional as a Rottweiler judge. We know that she will be a popular and esteemed judge, as she has a great "eye" and knowledge to bring with her into the ring.

DOROH

Doroh Rottweilers in Clinton, Maryland, has been a kennel name registered with the American Kennel Club since 1978. Actually, the interest in Rottweilers of owner Dorothy O. Wade goes back to the 1960s.

It was in 1965 that Mrs. Wade obtained her first Rottweiler puppy. From 1965 through 1972, she owned and handled three Rottweilers to their championships: Ch. Pio v. Silahopp (German import); the notable import Ch. Dago v.d. Ammerquelle; and Ch. Erika v. Schauer.

Despite the fact that Dorothy Wade showed Dago sparingly in 1970, he ended the year as *Kennel Review's* No. 4 Rottweiler. Contributing to this standing, of course, was his Best of Breed, from the classes, at the Colonial Rottweiler Club Specialty in an entry of 60 Rottweilers, which was one of the largest Rottweiler entries at that time.

Following a few false starts in breeding, Mrs. Wade was extremely fortunate to become acquainted with John and Carol Epperly of Fairfax, Virginia, who owned Rodsden's Helsa v. Eberle, U.D. Helsa was the first dog ever trained by John, and they became the team to watch in the obedience rings. In 1973, Helsa received the *Dog World* Award for earning her C.D., C.D.X., and U.D. in nine months' time at 20 months of age. Helsa then became the American Rottweiler Club No. 1 Obedience Dog and *Front and Finish* (Shuman System) No. 1 Obedience Rottweiler and No. 6 All Working Breeds for 1974.

Dorothy Wade makes very special mention of the fact that she will be eternally grateful to John and Carol Epperly for having allowed her to lease Helsa for her "new beginning" in Rottweilers, for she truly feels that had it not been for this lovely bitch and what she produced in her only litter for this kennel, there might not have been a Doroh, proving the greatness of Helsa's impact.

Helsa was bred, for this litter, to Casper v. Partlow, a Dago son. The litter arrived in February, 1975. Among these puppies was Ch. Doroh's Enchantress v. Eberle (American Rottweiler Club Bronze Production Award and Medallion Rottweiler Club Honor Roll); Ch. Doroh's Escapade v. Eberle (American Rottweiler Club Producer of Merit); Doroh's Erinys v. Eberle, C.D., Am., Can. T.D. (American Rottweiler Club No. 1 Tracking Dog 1976, Medallion Rottweiler Club Honor Roll); and Doroh's Edra v. Eberle, C.D.

Following the birth of the above "E" litter, Dorothy Wade had the pleasure of showing Helsa to her championship. From this aforementioned solid foundation came these later Rottweilers: Ch. Doroh's Fantastic Serenade, Am. Can. C.D.X., American Rottweiler Club Silver Production Award, Medallion Rottweiler Club Hall of Fame; Ch. Doroh's Fantastic Demeter; Ch. Doroh's Grand Escapade, American Rottweiler Club Producer of Merit, Medallion Rottweiler Club Honor Roll; Doroh's Goniff v. Elenel, C.D.X.; Doroh's Gaylord v. Nosebag, C.D.; Ch. Doroh's Hess v. Hopp, Best in Sweepstakes, Colonial Rottweiler Club Specialty 1980; Ch. Doroh's Headliner, C.D., multiple Group placer; Doroh's Hellelujah Tulla, U.D.; Ch. Doroh's Janus Erdelied, C.D., multiple Group placer; Ch. Doroh's Just A Whim, Best of Opposite Sex Sweepstakes, Colonial Rottweiler Club Specialty 1981; Ch. Doroh's Jaegerin v. Noblehaus, C.D., T.T.; Ch. Doroh's Just Grand, the first bitch to win Best in Show at the American Specialty among numerous outstanding honors; Ch. Doroh's Kommand Performance; Ch. Doroh's MacLeod; Doroh's Manhattan Jasper, C.D.X., T.T.; Ch. Doroh's New Wave, C.D.; Doroh's

Orenda v. Arba, Am., Can. T.D., who earned T.D. at seven months and one week; and Ch. Doroh's Promises Promises.

In addition to the dogs listed above, there are several other fifth-generation homebreds who are halfway to their titles, plus some excellent sixth-generation youngsters who are showing notable promise.

Dorothy Wade also takes enormous pride in her daughter Veronica ("Ronnie") who, from the time she was 12 years old, not only successfully participated in Junior

Top: Stromhall Nayah, owned by Powderhorn/ Wencrest Rottweilers, Inc., is a granddaughter of "Fetz," who was exported to Australia by P/W. Nayah was Winners Bitch at the 1986 Medallion R.C. Specialty Show. *Bottom:* Ch. Gemstones Blitz Meister, T.T., by Ch. Rodsden's Berte v. Zederwald, C.D.X, from Eva Regnant of Gemstones, C.D. Owned by Karen and Harold Riddle, Jr. Owner-handled here by Karen to Best of Breed, November, 1988.

Top: **Best in Show and Best in Specialty winner, Am., Can. Ch. Mad River's Magnum von Worley, Top Ten U.S. 1986 and 1987. Owned by Dawn and Jim Worley, Newark, OH.** *Middle:* **Lieberswert Amber, C.D., T.T., a weight-pulling dog, won Strongest Dog of All Breeds at the Houston K.C. in 1987 and Highest Percentage Pull at the 1987 Am. R.C. National Specialty. Owned by Liebenswert Rottweilers, Alleyton, TX.** *Bottom:* **Shannon Coughlan, age 2 years, placing fourth in the Pee Wee Handling (9 competing), showing 6-month-old Can. Ch. Wyndhurst's vom Kaira.**

Showmanship competition but simultaneously showed a number of the Doroh dogs to their championships and obedience titles and some other exciting wins. Mrs. Wade comments that she wishes "more parents gave their children the opportunity to train and show their dogs in all aspects of the sport. What better way to showcase the calm, versatile and good-natured Rottweiler?"

EBONSTERN

Ebonstern Rottweilers are owned by Cheryl Wheeler in Mount Vernon, Washington, and are now in their sixth homebred generation.

It was in 1969, following a long search for "the right sort of dog," that Cheryl met her first Rottweiler and knew instantly that for her this was "the breed." It was a case of love at first sight, a love that has only strengthened through the years that she has owned Rotties. It took her three years to locate what she wanted to start a breeding program, as Rotties were not readily available at that period. Persistence paid off and eventually Cheryl Wheeler and Heidi's Molzberg Hella came together. This was in 1972.

Hella was the product of a half-brother to half-sister breeding with whose background Cheryl was familiar and liked. This enabled her to predict accurately the results of her linebreeding, and she has found that following this method with Hella and her son, Am. Ch. Ebonstern Cabo v. Klahnerhof, the soundness and quality have been reproduced with consistency. Hella's sire was Bautz v. Molzberg; her dam, Dralle v. Molzberg; both of them sired by Cuno v. Kronchen (Fetz v. Oelberg, SchH. II, ex Anka v. Siegerland, SchH. II). Bautz's dam was Centa v. Krainberg, a daughter of BSG. Int. Ch. Harras v. Sofienbusch. Dralle's dam Dojean's Adventurous Miss, daughter of Victor, was 1965's Top Rottweiler in Canada.

Hella's daughter, Ebonstern Bryt

Promis v. Heller, was sired by Ch. Rodsden's Hardecanute Brandy, C.D. (Ch. Bengo v. Westfalenpark, C.D., he by Harras, from Rodsden's Samantha, who was a daughter of Ch. Yritter v. Kursaal, ex Ch. Quelle v.d. Solitude).

Hella's son, Am., Can. Ch. Ebonstern Cabo v. Klahnrhof, was by Am., Mex. Ch. Jack v. Brabantpark. Cabo completed his American championship in ten shows with Bests of Breed over specials. He completed his Canadian title in three shows with three Bests of Breed in a short show circuit.

It was Bryt Promis and Cabo who formed the background from which the Ebonstern breeding program was developed. Although seldom permitted for use at public stud, Cabo, in only six litters, produced 26 title-holding Rottweilers, of which he and Bryt Promis provided the parentage for seven.

Because of these 26 title holders, they have been represented on the American Rottweiler Club Top Ten—as Group placing winners and as producers of champions.

"Missie's" total of 19 puppies earned 25 titles, and three of them were ranked in the Top Ten nationally. She is a Silver Production Award winner (American Rottweiler Club), lacking only three points to become a Gold Producer, which

Top: **Am., Can. Ch. Goldeiche Ara von Brader, Am., Can. C.D., with his owner-handler Dale Innocenti, winning Best in Show at Terre Haute K.C. under judge Louis Auslander.**
Middle: **Best in Show at the 1987 Colonial R.C. Specialty Show, Am., Can. Ch. Goldeiche Ara von Brader, Am., Can. C.D., is owner-handled by Dale Innocenti under judge Mrs. James Edward Clark.**
Bottom: **Two handsome bitches who share the same pedigree: Am., Can. Ch. Roma's Ultra von Siegerhaus, C.D., taking Winners Bitch for a 4-point major for Roberta Martin, while Vianca von Siegerhaus takes Reserve Winners for co-owners Bob and Shelly Velasco and Von Siegerhaus Kennels.**

Am., Can. Ch. Chena Wilderness at age 3½ years, the dam of Kobuk and daughter of Am., Can. Ch. Haserway's Rommel Victor ex Lady Ruger, C.D.X, U.D. Bred and owned by JoAnn Harnish, Oakridge, OR.

she will attain any time now, as several of her progeny are within a point or two of title.

It was Cabo and "Missie" who gave Ebonstern the third generation of the breeding program. Now their sons, Am., Can. Ch. Ebonstern Ivan v.d. Liebe and Ch. Ebonstern Olympus v.d. Liebe are proving that they, too, were Producers of Merit. In limited breeding these two dogs have provided some of Ebonstern's most successful show competitors. Their grandchildren, too, indicate that they will carry on the unbroken line.

Ch. Iolkos v. Dammerwald, C.D., was born in Germany and purchased by Cheryl Wheeler after

coming to America because she admired offspring from his earliest litters and because she felt he complemented the base line in the Ebonstern breeding program. Iolkos, Cheryl points out, had an outstanding topline, angulation, and smooth far-reaching action, all of which he maintained until his death in 1988 at 14 years of age.

Iolkos sired only two litters for Ebonstern, but in those litters he provided a very special gift in the form of Ch. Ebonstern Abra v. Lauffeuer. Abra is not only very special for herself, but for the puppies she has produced. This "out" line has combined beautifully with the Ebonstern base line to accomplish exactly what Cheryl had hoped would be the case.

Iolkos is the sire of Ch. Beaverbrook Alexis v. Iolkos, who is the dam and grand-dam of a number of outstanding winners for Beaverbrook Rottweilers. Although bred only a few times, Iolkos was given the American Rottweiler Club Silver Production Award.

Other Rotties purchased by Ebonstern to combine with their foundation stock include Ch. Gudrun of Graudstark. Gudrun's daughter, Ebonstern Megan v.d. Frau, C.D., is the dam of several champions when bred to the foundation line through Ch. Ebonstern Olympus v.d. Liebe. She was later co-owned by Elfi Rice of Cannon River Rottweilers and is grandmother of numerous Rotties at her kennels, too.

Lauffeuer Abbild was co-owned by Ebonstern with Debbie Gallegos of Lauffeuers Rottweilers. She was bred to Iolkos v. Dammerwald, C.D., as a result producing Ch. Ebonstern Abra v. Lauffeuer. Abra was then bred back to Ebonstern lines, producing some of the best youngsters currently starting out. Abbild was also bred to Ch. Trollegen's Frodo, C.D., producing Ch. Ebonstern Witch v. Lauffeuer and Am., Can. Ch. Ebonstern Warlock v. Lauffeuer, Am., Can. C.D., who was one of the most

Der Fruchtwald DD Bernhardt at age 17 months taking Winners Dog at the Golden State R.C. Specialty Show in May, 1988. Owned by Janice Lynch, Lemon Grove, CA.

consistent winners in the northwestern U.S. while being shown.

Can. Ch. Areneberg Cryso Mau was purchased from Keith and Trudy Clark of Langley, British Columbia. This one has 12 American championship points with both majors and has contributed well to the breeding program at Ebonstern by providing a line compatible for breeding back into the original lines of foundation stock.

Ebonstern Rottweilers maintain a network of co-ownership with sincere fanciers, in this way allowing others to enjoy some of their very special dogs, and vice-versa, which would never be sold outright. Thus a human "family" has been created which makes the dogs more fun through human friendship, the sharing of experiences and ideas, and the mutual dedication to quality Rottweilers. There may sometimes be as many as a dozen individuals included in the "family group." Cheryl Wheeler has found that it works out just fine, and after all, isn't any interest and success more rewarding when there are others to share the pleasure?

EINSAMSTADT

Einsamstadt Rottweilers, in Westfield, Massachusetts, first began around 1983, owned by Judith M. Sherman and Gary A. Ranney, with the purchase of an American-bred dog from an already established breeder.

Unhappily, their first two puppy bitches developed hip dysplasia and the male had eight missing teeth. This may well have been enough to turn new fanciers towards another breed. However, these folks handled their disappointment and decided to bring some foundation dogs from Germany on which to base their breeding program.

The primary goal at Einsamstadt became producing a high percentage of dogs free of hip problems, thus establishing and maintaining a reliable working line. As Judith remarks, "We have to be one of the lucky ones, as you will see."

The first importation was Fee von der Belmer Heide, a "pink-papered" bitch certified free of hip dysplasia from the A.D.R.K. Heide is in every way the No. 1 bitch in the kennel, treated with respect by all.

Next came the dog, Droll vom Waldwinkel, C.D., also bearing pink papers, H.D. free from the A.D.R.K. Heide was bred to Droll for the first Einsamstadt-bred litter, which resulted in six puppies, five of them males. All have passed their O.F.A. Three

males are working police dogs, one puppy died of parvovirus, one male is a dearly loved pet and the only bitch, Britta, is working on her Schutzhund and is also a registered therapy dog.

The next bitch added to the kennel, Radio Ranch Meg, had a first litter of four males, of which two have show careers. Mondbergs Jessie v. Beier is an American-bred bitch, purchased from Ruth Parker, who is working out successfully. Her first was sired by Droll and consisted of two bitch puppies, Cindy and Connie. The latter had a litter of her own and soon starts her show career. Their dam, Jessie, has since produced a "D" litter by Ch. Laddie von Meadow.

Then came Hannibal von Einsamstadt, who has indeed a very happy and interesting story to tell. This beautiful, high-quality Rottweiler was rescued by Judith and Gary, to quote Judith, "from someone's backyard where he had no housing protection from the weather; he was skinny, dirty, flea-ridden, and was just an ugly unwanted dog." The people had wanted a *mean* dog, and Hannibal, except for his name, is the most loving, tender dog one could meet, wanting only to please. Judith adds, "Thought went behind his breeding, but not to whom he went

as a puppy. I'll never say I have an eye for a dog, but there was just something about this one that said 'here I am' and so he came to Einsamstadt." Judith and Gary received their reward for their kindness and realization of Hannibal's unhappy situation when he turned out to be a born show dog, loving every moment in the ring. Kahlid Karriem took him to Westminster for them in 1988, and before the day had drawn to a close, Hannibal, in the Open Class for the very first time, had emerged Best of Winners.

After Westminster came several additional Best of Winners occasions, with his last three-point major garnered at Springfield, where he went on to Best of Breed—certainly a thoroughly satisfactory way in which to complete a championship. Now Hannibal is working on his C.D. and is in training for his T.D. He will return to the conformation ring as a special, and his first litter is by Jessie.

Hannibal goes back to some very distinguished bloodlines, with outstanding producers behind him including, on both sides, Ch. Kokas Ks Degan. Jessie is by Ch. Graudstark's Luger, C.D., from a daughter of Am., Can. Ch.

Mondberg's Dain v. Beier, Am., Bda. C.D., ex Ch. Mondberg's Belba Beier.

ELTON'S

Elton's Rottweilers are owned by Buck and Pat Elton of Granada Hills, California, who are fairly new to the ranks of Rottie breeders.

Their foundation bitch was Scirroco "Coso" Deja Vu, who was obtained from Pat Clark Hickman's famous Northwinds line. Coso is the daughter of Ch. Northwinds Jasmine and Ch. Ero van der Mauth, which makes her the granddaughter of the incomparable Ch. Northwinds Danka.

Coso was bred to Int. Ch. Rodsden's Njord v. Brabant, C.D., in 1982. Their first litter was used for working cattle dogs on the Elton's large cattle ranch, and they

Above: Janka v. Duracher Tobel, German import owned by Missy Taylor and Powderhorn/ Wencrest Rottweilers, Inc.
Left: Can., Mex. Ch. Leibgarde's "Heidi" vom Hochfeld, Am., Mex. T.T., going Winners Bitch and Best of Opposite Sex at Greater Sierra Vista K.C. Photo by Kohler. Owners, M. and F. Mitchell.

Top left: Am., Can. Ch. Windrock's Fanni von Richter, by Ch. Winterhawk's Chief Justice, U.D.T., ex Pinebrae's Britta Aus Dem Abend, C.D. Bred, owned and handled by Jane Justice. *Top right:* Can. Ch. Camas Valley Dickens v. Eiko was bred and owned by Dan and Debby Kutz. Dickens is by Ch. Eiko vom Schwaiger Wappen, C.D.X., SchH. III, ex Ch. Camas Valley Hildagard v. Kutz. Handler, Ingrid Linerud. *Below:* Ch. Clyde van Reishoff is proudly owned by Nadine Jaquez, Von Dine Rottweilers.

were magnificent herding dogs ranging as much as 20 miles daily.

Coso was next bred to a son of Njord which resulted in Elton's Northwind Ero, who obtained his American championship in Beverly Hills, California, in June, 1988, his Canadian championship in August, 1988, and his Mexican championship in 1989 at Mexicali, where he won a Group First and a Group Second on two consecutive days. Ero has sired 13 litters of

exceptional quality, and six of his sons and daughters are winning in the California show rings.

The Eltons acquired another handsome male from Pat Clark's "O" litter, Northwind Omni Cujo Elton, a son of Ch. Altar's Cujo vom Wald, C.D., ex Ch. Northwind's Juno granddaughter, Alexa vom Kranzusch. Buck and Pat have also added two new brood bitches to mate with their triple champion Ero.

EPIC

Epic Kennels started in 1977 with the purchase of the first Rottweiler of Bob and Rose Hogan of Chepachet, Rhode Island, a kennel prefix which soon became synonymous with quality in the breed. This first Rottweiler was Cyrus Max von Ragenbogan, C.D., who was Bob's first Rottie champion and his beginning in the obedience world. Shortly after that, a second addition, Von Bruka Alpine High, C.D., was purchased for Rose's obedience companionship.

It was not, however, until the purchase of their third Rottie, Ch. Donnaj Happy Hooker, that the kennel started attracting attention among the Hogans' fellow New England Rottie fans.

Happy Hooker was bred by Jan Marshall and Deborah Monague.

Owned by Bob Hogan, she became his first champion (winning both majors from the Puppy Class, which was quite an achievement in this breed during the early 1980s), an American Rottweiler Club Bronze Producer of Merit, the Foundation of Epic, and the producer of several championships including one International Champion and many obedience titled offspring. Rose Hogan says "We owe much credit to Jan Marshall and the Donnaj pedigree."

Ch. Epic's Adulteress, T.T., bred, owned and always handled by Bob Hogan, is a multiple producer of champions, obedience titlists, and A.T.T.S.-titled offspring, including a Therapy Dog International.

Epic's Burning Desire, C.D.X., was bred by Bob Hogan and Jan Marshall, owned by Pam Anderson and Mary Fielding. This is one of Epic's many obedience-titled progeny.

Ch. Epic's Dynamo, T.T., was bred by the Hogans, and is owned by Peter and Lisa Kaloostian. Handled by Bob Hogan, he is a many times Best of Breed winner, a Group winner, and a multiple Group-placing dog with numerous credits on his show record.

Ch. Epic's Divine Intervention, T.T., bred, owned and handled by Bob, is a product of the second generation of Epic breeding.

Top: **Ch. Tearsa von Siegerhaus, by Ch. Beaverbrook Eisen von Bruin ex Am., Can. Ch. Nemisis von Siegerhaus, owned by William and Pat Norton.**
Middle: **Am., Can., Mex. Ch. Quick von Siegerhaus, Am., Can. C.D., Z.T.P.R., T.T. Quick has received many enviable honors. He is a multiple Group winner and Group placer. Owners, Thom and Carol Woodward.**
Bottom: **Am., Can. Ch. Wilderness Kobuk v. Forstwald, bred and owned by JoAnn Harnish.**

Top: Ch. Winterhawk's Chief Justice, U.D.T., by Ch. Radio Ranch's X-tra Special ex Ch. Winterhawk's Cobe v. Bethel, owned by Jane Justice; alongside is Ch. Norbon's Nicole, in May, 1988, owned by Bonnie Rosenberg. *Middle:* Mrs. James Edward Clark judged the finals at the 1987 Colonial R.C. Specialty in conjunction with Bucks County K.C. Best of Breed went to Ch. Goldeiche Ara von Brader, C.D.; Best of Winners, Harley Hollow's Sherlock; and Best of Opposite Sex, Can. Ch. Select von Bruka Fiona, C.D. All three winners were sired by Ch. Eiko vom Schwaiger Wappen, C.D.X., SchH. III, Gold Producer. *Bottom:* Ch. Von Hawthorne's Solo Magnum-F takes Group placement under Richard Rennihan. Handler, R. Orseno; breeder-owner, A.J. Hahn.

The major-pointed Epic's Deidre Dahl, C.D., T.T., D.T., "Sophie" to her friends, is working on completion of her championship and C.D.X. titles and will continue to visit nursing homes, where her presence is always anticipated and helpful to the patients, in her spare time.

Bob Hogan was part of a memorable team during the early 1980s with Dr. and Mrs. Leo Minisce's Ch. Alina's Adelbear of Wesley, during which they won three all-breed Bests in Show and

numerous other honors in highly competitive New England events.

Bob Hogan held the position of president in 1987 and 1988 and vice president in 1986 of the American Rottweiler Club. He also served on various committees within this organization throughout ten years of active membership status.

Rose Hogan volunteers her spare time to the A.R.C. as membership renewal chairman, which she has been for the past few years. The membership has now grown from 900 to 1300 in just three years.

Although very active in showing their own dogs as well as those for clients from time to time, the Hogans make it a point to maintain their love and dedication for the Rottweiler breed as a hobby rather than as a business. They plot and plan their breeding programs methodically, always striving for the best in conformation, temperament, and healthy working Rottweilers. They believe in O.F.A., C.E.R.F., and V.W.D. testing to ensure the highest quality of health in the Epic breeding program.

EUPHORIA

Euphoria's Kennels are located in Cordova, Tennessee, where they are owned by Chuck and Jan Freudenberg. These folks have two handsome champion Rottweilers in whom they take pride and enjoyment. These are Ch. Aljo's Bruin von Junge and Can. Ch. Jimick's Ainabella.

The Freudenbergs also have some future breeding plans for their Rotties, we feel sure, as their enthusiasm is high for these dogs.

three-point major at Columbus late in 1988. Ingrid had her second litter in September, 1988, and passed away three months later at just six years of age.

The Jaynes are extremely proud of a young dog they own, Am., Can. Ch. Myran's Eon of Excalibur, who finished at 12 months of age, taking Breed and Group placement during the process. After finishing, Eon was out for awhile, but now will venture forth again under the handling of Vicki Fillinger.

Eon's litter brother is Ch. Myran's Excalibur, whom the Jaynes co-own with Mike and Pam Donley in Michigan.

EXCALIBUR

Excalibur Rottweilers belong to Brenda and John Jayne who live in Dayton, Ohio, and who acquired their first member of the breed in 1981.

Ch. Ingrid Von Krause was the Jaynes' first champion, and she also became a multiple breed winning female. She had her first litter when she was five years old, in which she produced Ch. Excalibur's Destiny's Revenge, who finished at age 14 months; and also Excalibur's Johan von Samons, who has started showing and took a

Top: Ch. Von Bruka's Fiona, taking Best of Breed at Delaware Water Gap in 1984 over her distinguished sire, Ch. Eiko v. Schwaiger Wappen, C.D.X., SchH. III, who took Best of Opposite Sex. Owners, Karen and Bruce Billings. *Middle:* Von Bruka Phina v. Gatekeeper, owned by Debbie McLellan, bred by the Billings, handled by Karen under Mike Conradt to a placement in the 1986 Colonial Sweepstakes. *Bottom:* Am., Can. Ch. Adlerberg's Aunka von Siegerhaus, No. 4 A.R.C. Bitch in 1985; No. 5 in 1986. Owners, C. and T. Woodward. Photo courtesy of Fox and Cook Photography.

Right: A.R.C. National Specialty in July, 1988. The mighty Eiko winning the Stud Dog Class with his multiple Best in Show son Ara, and his 1985 Specialty Winning daughter Fiona. This was one month prior to Eiko's death and likely the last exhibition portrait taken of him. *Below:* Wilderness Eastward Bronson, C.D., by Ch. Danny v. Timmerman ex Am., Can. Ch. The Chena Wilderness. Owned by Steve and Susan Hunt. Bred by JoAnn Harnish.

There is little doubt that the Jaynes have a special fondness for their very first Rottweiler of all, Ch. Mad Rivers Brenda's Bulltar. Of this one Brenda says "We never had much help with him, but we learned a lot and he is finished. He is a champion pet and has never been specialed."

FOXY'S ROTTWEILERS

Foxy's Rottweilers, formerly known as Von Fox, are owned by Maria and Marvin Fox of Philadelphia, Pennsylvania. They are the result of a lifetime of love and interest in animals. It has always been the Foxes' dream to own pure-bred dogs, but only when the time and conditions were right for them to do so. Thus it was with enormous enthusiasm that they finally brought home their first Rottweiler.

Their foundation bitch was Demon von Fox, C.D., born in October, 1979. Demon is a great-granddaughter of the breed's Top Producers: Ch. Amsel von Andan, C.D.; Ch. Lyn Mar Acres Arras v. Kinta; and Ch. Dago v.d. Ammerquelle.

Demon completed her C.D. in her first three obedience trials. She contributed to the breed by producing five A.K.C. title holders for her owners' kennel.

For Demon's first litter she was bred to Zum Verkauf's Eric Behalter, a.k.a. "Tank," owned by James Curran. Tank was sired by Zum Verkauf's Big Mac from Ch. Zum Verkauf's Little Bo Peep. This breeding produced Ch. Fraulein Gretchen von Fox, C.D., T.T. Ironically, Gretchen was sold but returned when the new owner was involved in a serious car accident.

Gretchen proved to be of outstanding quality. She began her show career by taking fourth place in the six to nine month Puppy Bitch Class at the 1983 Colonial Rottweiler Club Specialty Sweepstakes under judge Maureen Wilkinson. At 11 months on her first weekend of three shows, she received three blue ribbons, two Winners Bitch awards, one Best of Winners, and two Best of Opposite Sex awards.

Gretchen was not shown again until she had reached 20 months of age. She then made some good wins climaxed by the fact that she completed her championship undefeated in her final four shows on the way to the title. During her show career, she accumulated ten

Best of Opposite Sex awards. She earned her C.D. in July, 1985, finishing at the York County Kennel Club with 198.5 and Highest Scoring Rottweiler in Trial.

Another bitch from this litter was Tasha von Fiandra, C.D., T.T., owned by Barry and Lori Fiandra. Tasha completed her C.D. at the 1988 Kennel Club of Philadelphia Obedience Trial.

Demon's second litter was sired by Top Producer Ch. Bethel Farms Apollo. This breeding produced three outstanding offspring which include Fraulein Cinder Von Fox, C.D., T.T., VB, whose owners are Beth and Ron Cepil. She completed her obedience title at age 14 months in three straight shows.

Then there is Foxy's London Skylahr, C.D., owned by Mark and Eleanor London. Skylahr has distinguished himself as an extraordinary obedience worker. At the age of 15 months he went High Scoring Dog in Match. His first leg was earned at the 1985 Colonial Rottweiler Club Obedience Trial, where he placed third in Novice A. He also placed second with a score of 195 at the Greater Philadelphia Dog Fanciers' Association. From this same litter was Madchen Greta von Fox, owned by Ed and Ellen Towarnicki, who is championship pointed.

For Foxy's "C" litter, Gretchen was bred to Ch. Pandemonium's Ciastus, C.D.X., T.T. From this litter, born in January, 1986, the Foxes kept Foxy's Castaspell, C.D., who is pointed towards her championship. "Crista," as this bitch is called, completed her C.D. in her first three trials at age 15 months. From this same litter are: Foxy's Casey Can Do, C.D., T.T., owned by Jim and Kate Kendig, Jr.; Foxy's Catch A Falling Star; Foxy's Centurian; and Foxy's Cuddly Bear Von Heller.

Gretchen's second litter was by Am., Can. Ch. Donnaj Herr I Am C.D., T.T., owned by Bob and Rose Marie Hogan and Jan Marshall. This produced Foxy's litter of eight super puppies born in September,

BEST OF OPPOSITE
NORTH SHORE
KENNEL CLUB
1982
ASHBEY

1988. They are certain to display great promise.

All Foxy dogs are house dogs and part of the family. Their owners have no kennel or runs, and the puppies are raised with the family's two children.

The Foxes belong to the Colonial Rottweiler Club and the American Rottweiler Club. Their breeding program is aimed to produce top-quality Rottweilers with the versatility to excel in obedience as well as tracking. During ten years of involvement with the breed, the Foxes have bred only four litters, which have produced eight title holders. Their goal very clearly is quality rather than quantity.

FREYAN
Freyan Rottweilers, located in Lakeport, California, are owned by

Ch. Donnaj Happy Hooker, an A.R.C. Bronze Producer of Merit, was the third Rottie and first champion in the Robert Hogan household. Bred by Jan Marshall and Deborah Monague.

age of five months. "Mishka" is by Ch. Pandemonium's Ciastus, C.D., T.T., from Bergland Asha Adel v. Adja. In 1986, Mishka was bred to Am., Can., Mex. Ch. Quick von Siegerhaus, C.D., T.T., Z.T.P.R. The offspring of this litter are making their own names in the conformation and working rings. Freyan's Akayami, co-owned by Beth Simms of Middletown, California, has consistently been in the ribbons in limited showing and placed third in the Bred-by-Exhibitor Class at the 1988 American Rottweiler Club National Specialty in Oakland, California. "Akai" is currently dividing her time between conformation rings, polishing her C.D. work, and beginning Schutzhund training.

Freyan's Blatantly Brisis, owned by Gary and Char Shook of Corning, California, having acquired her C.D. and T.D. within a few months of each other, is now setting her sights on C.D.X. and T.D.X. Freyan's Bosch v. Siegerhaus is also concentrating on a Schutzhund degree while awaiting his turn in the breed ring. Freyan's Blythe v. Siegerhaus is currently in service as the loving companion and helper to wheelchair-bound Doug Nequette of Florence, Colorado.

"Mishka" herself, not to be outdone by her kids, is training for Schutzhund I, and plans to include C.D. and T.D. There will be a brief time out for "Mishka" somewhere along the way, as she will be taking a trip for breeding to Ch. Cannon River Oil Tanker, C.D. The offspring of this promising breeding will assist the goal of Freyan Rottweilers in producing a dog capable of excellence in both the show ring and in working capability. The slow maturing of this line permits the owners to participate in the working aspect of the breed as they await the "right moment" for entry into show competition.

Another bitch of Freyan's is Ch. Einman Lyric v. Rottdan   by Ch. Pandemonium's Faust out of

Rita McMahan, who has had the breed since about 1982. She had been a German Shepherd breeder for 15 years prior to that time.

As the last of her Shepherds grew older, Rita was unable to find a sound dog that could be competitive in the breed ring as well as the working ring. Having long admired the beauty and intelligence of the Rottweiler, she felt strongly that a member of this breed might fill both roles for her. She has never regretted having made this change in breeds, and feels that the dual roles lead to happier, healthier, better adjusted dogs.

The foundation bitch at Freyan is Ch. Einmin Immortelle v. Rottdan, acquired in 1983 at the

Bergland Asha Adel v. Adja. Lyric was acquired at age eight weeks during 1985, beginning her march towards championship with a four-point major her first time in the Open Class and finished 12 shows later by going Best of Breed over noted specials. During that time she also acquired seven points on Canadian championship. Lyric has plans for completion of her Canadian championship and further concentration on the working side of her career with Schutzhund work already under way.

GAREN'S ROTTWEILERS

Garen's Rottweilers are owned by Gary F. and Karen L. Sims in St. Charles, Missouri. The Simses purchased their first Rottweiler in 1978. This was the surviving puppy from a litter of seven. It was sadly necessary that he be euthanized at age seven months due to multiple physical deformities and health problems.

Their second Rottweiler was purchased in 1979, and preliminary hip x-rays at one year detected hip dysplasia. He was neutered but remained a member of the Sims family until the age of nine years, at which time they lost him to bloat. Due to his hip dysplasia, his breeder offered another puppy for conformation showing, which was the Sims's principal interest. They accepted the offer, but just a few weeks after they had this bitch, she was diagnosed as having parvovirus. After six weeks of extensive veterinary treatment, the breeder and the veterinarian convinced the Simses that she really should be euthanized as her condition only continued to deteriorate.

Determined to have a show dog, Gary and Karen spent the following several months phoning breeders all over the United States. They were put in touch with Jan Marshall just as she was about to visit and evaluate a marvelously bred new litter by her great winner, Am., Can. Ch. Donnaj Vermont Yankee of Paulus, C.D.X.,

T.T., from Rodsden's Belle, a littermate to Ch. Rodsden's Bruin v. Hungerbuhl, C.D.X. The Simses were impressed with this pedigree, so they described the qualities they were seeking in a bitch to Jan who promised to let them know if she found a puppy in that litter which would meet their criteria. A few weeks later, following discussion of the subject with Jan, Karen and Gary got in touch with the breeder of the litter who told them that they could have one of the "show potential" bitches. The breeder described two available bitches to them, then added that there was already a deposit on the pick bitch and that they would be notified when the person involved had reached a decision. Luck was

Ch. Pioneer's 'Gainst All Odds, shown winning a 4-point major at Middlesex County K.C. Sheryl Hedrick, breeder-owner-handler. By Ch. Noblehaus Beretta ex Pioneer's X-Rated Annie, C.D.

in the Simses favor as the other couple chose the larger, longer of the bitches while the one they wanted was smaller and more compact. So everyone was happy and arrangements were made for the puppy to travel from Boston to St. Louis as excess baggage with a gentleman on a business trip from the same company as the one where Karen works.

The puppy was named Garen's Fourth X A Charm. The "X" in her name is a multiplication symbol, therefore her name is read "Garen's Fourth Times A Charm," and she is called "Charli." Karen notes that once we have read of the disastrous results of their first

Above: Ch. Von Riddle's Gabriele v. Eisen, C.D., by Ch. Beaverbrook Eisen v. Bruin, T.T., ex Ch. Brinka von Ross, C.D., T.T., at age 17 months. Marcia Foy, judging. Laura Brewin is handling for Wilma and Max Williams and Karen Riddle. *Right:* Ch. True Lee's Dina v. Gunner, C.D., at age 22 months. Owned by Mrs. Denyse M. Adams, Frankfort, ME..

RJ's Azura von Bryloukis, by Am., Can. Ch. Bryloukis Great Expectations, C.D., ex RJ's Wilderness K.C., C.D. Bred and owned by Rhonda Nielson of Alaska.

Top: Ch. Von Riddle's Gabriele v. Eisen, C.D., T.T., pictured at age 14 months, placing at the 1988 Colonial Rottweiler Club Specialty. Owners, Wilma and Max Williams and Karen Riddle. *Bottom:* Can. Ch. Lowindy Flist von Ae, C.D., T.T., H.D., a son of Can., Am. Ch. Trollegen's Frodo ex Ch. Panamint Haunting Melody. This splendid dog received his points in 3 shows from the late "Tip" Tipton, Dr. Buris R. Boshell, and Robert Forsyth. Owner, Mrs. Barb Berard, My Valley Kennels, Calgary, Alta., Canada.

three starts at Rottweiler ownership we will understand how they arrived at this somewhat unusual name for this bitch!

Charli made her presence felt at numerous Rottie Specialty Shows. The first time she took Reserve Winners Bitch at the Medallion Rottweiler Club, then later at both Medallion and Colonial in Veterans and Brood Bitch Classes.

In 1985, Charli tied for second Top Producing Rottweiler Bitch. In 1988, she placed on the Medallion Rottweiler Club's Honor Roll. She had two litters sired by Ch. Birch Hill Minuteman, C.D. From them

she has three A.K.C. obedience degrees; one C.D.X.; one also working in Utility; and one VB working on Schutzhund degrees.

Charli's titled offspring are Ch. Garen's Baron Max v. Charm, C.D., T.T., Registered Therapy Dog, who was born in February, 1984. Max took first place in the American-bred Class at the 1985 Medallion Specialty, and went on to complete his championship owner-handled at age 19 months. He earned his C.D. in August, 1987, and is a multiple Best of Breed winner with Group placements. Max and Karen visit a local St. Louis Hospital and a local nursing home monthly, where Max volunteers as a therapy dog.

Ch. Garen's Baka v. Charm is a littermate to Max who has consistently placed in the Bred-by-Exhibitor Class at Rottweiler Specialty Shows. In November, 1988, she produced a litter sired by Ch. Ironwood's Cade which looked so promising that the breeding will be repeated.

Another littermate, Ch. Garen's Benjamin Benning, finished his championship at age 19 months and has won multiple Bests of Breed plus Group placement.

Garen's Christa von Zauber, C.D.X., has points towards A.K.C. championship and is working towards a U.D. Brandy v. Oberste, C.D., VH, is working on her Schutzhund degree and conformation title.

GOLDEICHE

Goldeiche Rottweilers (German for golden oak) began quietly in late 1981 with the purchase of a pet who became a loyal friend and companion to Ted W. Grisell in Cicero, Indiana. This dog instilled in Ted the strong desire for more Rottweilers—an affliction which seems to have infected most people who are actively involved.

A year and a half later an eight-week-old puppy bounced, growled and chewed his way into the family's heart at Golden Oak Farms. This delightful bundle was to become Ch. Rodsden's Cossack von Brader, C.D., the foundation sire for future generations of quality Rottweilers.

Cossack, Ted Grisell tells us, was an excellent example of breed type and was shown to numerous wins as a young dog by his friends Smokey Medieros and Michael Conradt. He was shown by owner-handler Ted Grisell. The last two years before retiring, Cossack had completed his C.D. shown by his teenage friend Beth Grisell.

Among his prestigious wins, Cossack was Best of Opposite Sex in the Colonial Rottweiler Sweepstakes at the Specialty in May, 1984. He was following in the footsteps of his mother, Ch. Rodsden's Hella v. Forstwald, T.D., who had been Best in Sweepstakes at the same Specialty in 1982. At the end of May, 1984, Cossack was Best of Winners at the American Rottweiler Club Specialty at the age of 13 months, going on to finish his championship owner-handled at age 14 months. Cossack has had an illustrious show career including Group winning and multiple Group placements, plus an Award of Merit at the 1988 Medallion Specialty.

Cossack's dam, Hella, moved to Goldeiche Rottweilers in the fall of 1984 and became the foundation bitch for this new kennel name in the Rottweiler world. She was bred to Ch. Eiko vom Schweiger Wappen, C.D.X., who was the sire of several Best in Show offspring.

Hella produced the dog destined to carry the Goldeiche name to new heights: Am., Can. Ch. Goldeiche Ara von Brader, Am., Can. C.D., who was born in April, 1985, and at the age of 13 months was Best in Sweepstakes at the Colonial Rottweiler Club Specialty and received a Select Award at the American Rottweiler Club Specialty a month later. Ara went on to win other Specialties and ultimately to win three all-breed Bests in Show by the age of four years.

Ara has always been shown and loved by his owner, Dale Innocenti. He is the first Rottweiler owned by Dale and his wife Karen, and they are now committed to developing more Best in Show prospects under their DARAK Rottweiler kennel name.

GRAUDSTARK

Graudstark Rottweilers are owned by Judy and Bill Johnson, who have recently relocated to Red Bank, New Jersey, from their former address of Oswego, Illinois.

The Johnsons, who were looking for a large dog to raise with their

Top: True Lee's Kaleigh's Gold, by Ch. Altar's Gunner of Woodland ex Ashby v. Foxcroft, C.D. Owned by Ann Adcock. *Bottom:* Ch. Olfa von Tengen, German import, by Int. Ch. Nero v. Schloss Rietheim, from Hedda von Tengen, I. Owners, J. Cary, B. Bedingfield, and S. Michael.

young growing family, purchased their first Rottweiler in 1964 through an ad which caught their eye in a Chicago newspaper. At this time, the breed was virtually unknown to the Johnsons. Their new male pup, eventually named Earl of Graudstark, became their first champion and his name became the Johnsons' kennel prefix which is now registered as "Graudstark."

In 1967, the first litter at the new kennel was whelped, producing the Johnsons' first homebred champion, Maude v. Graudstark, C.D.X. Now their title-holders are numerous, including Specialty winners at the Colonial and Medallion Specialty Shows, plus, while living in Venezuela, three Venezuelan champions.

The Johnsons are proud that their kennel produced foundation dogs (and most important, family friends) for Bethel Farms (Ch. Graudstark's Irma La Deuce, C.D.); Noblehaus (Ch. Graudstark's Luger); Pandemonium (Ch. Graudstark's Pandemonium and Ch. Quatro Tempo); Tulakes (Am., Can. Ch., Graudstark's Pegasus); and Von Staten (Ch. Graudstark's Rhapsody). They are also proud to have three generations of Graudstark dogs in the impressive pedigree of 21 times Best in Show winner Ch. Cannon River Oil Tanker, C.D.

Currently the Johnsons are showing a fifth-generation Graudstark dog, Joshua, a "Cassie" son.

Unless necessity dictates

Ch. Donnaj Music Man at 22 months. Handsome young dog owned by Pamela Anderson, Wilton Manors, FL.

WINNERS
CHESHIRE
KENNEL CLUB
AUG
1987
TATHAM PHOTO

Ch. Legend's Invocation finished championship with 3 majors. Owned by Lee Whittler, Legend Kennels, Woodstock VT.

otherwise, the Johnsons' own dogs are always family handled, since they feel that this is part of the fun. Much thought is given to the planning of each litter, which usually includes doing a complete five generation pedigree with two or three different studs, then studying and thinking out the pros and cons of each.

The Johnsons comment that "Rottweilers are riding the wave of popularity—something not all breeders and owners are pleased with. We agree—Rotties are *not* the dog for all people, but they are our dogs and we hope to continue producing the very best we can."

GLYNN'S IRISH RIDGE

Glynn's Irish Ridge Rottweilers are owned by Larry and Karen Glynn of Eyota, Minnesota,

formerly owners of German Shepherd Dogs and Dobermans. They were introduced to Rottweilers by Larry's brother Jim Glynn in California.

At the time of this meeting, Larry and Karen still had members of their earlier breeds; however, the Rottie made so deep an impression on them that it was decided that when the Shepherd and Dobe passed on, the Rottweiler would become their next breed. They especially liked the size of the Rotties and their keen intelligence.

In 1983 they purchased their first of their new breed, Meagan Amity Bela, followed by a second one—a male, Glynn's Fritz Von Rodney. These two became the beginning of their Rottweiler kennel.

From their first litter, the Glynns kept one puppy. He started in the

Top: Can. Ch. Raven von Rainhart, bred by Diane Johnston; owned by Rainhart Rottweilers, Greenbank, WA. *Bottom:* Am., Can., Mex. Ch. Quick von Siegerhaus, Am. C.D., Z.T.P.R., T.T., with daughter Ch. Zana von Siegerhaus, winning at the Golden Valley K.C. show over 121 Rotties in 1988.

show ring and earned one major when, unfortunately, his show career was ended by an accident.

In 1988 the Glynns finished their first champion, Glynn's Duke von Imp, who was breeder/owner-handled to his title in both the United States and Canada.

A while back, the Glynns decided that they would like to obtain something directly from Germany with which to work; thus a trip was made and numerous kennels visited for future replacements in their breeding program, as Fritz and Meagan were about to retire to strictly home life and relaxation. The result was the arrival of two "pink-papered" females, Carmen von Barensiek and Bessy vom Barensiek. This is where the kennel stands at present, with high hopes for the future owing to these German imports and Ch. Glynn's Luke vom Imp, the son of Fritz Von Rodney and Meagan Amity Bela, the latter bitch a granddaughter of Ch. Rodsden's Zarras v. Brabant, C.D.

GRUNHAUS

Grunhaus Rottweilers are owned by Charles and Danielle Green and are situated in Orinda, California. The first Rottie owned here, Am., Mex. Ch. Juno's Amanda Great Gretruda, C.D., finished entirely in California competition, doing so in three majors handled by her owner, Danielle, with a C.D. degree which included scores in the high 180s in three trials.

Born in April, 1977, Amanda was a daughter of Ch. Panamint Nobel v. Falkenberg, C.D., ex Trollegen's Bolinda. Greta's daughter, Ch. Grunhaus Eztrada, made all of her points to championship from the Bred-by-Exhibitor Class. Eztrada was by Ch. Elexi v.d. Gaarn ex Greta. Sadly, Eztrada died of gastric torsion in April, 1988.

Eztrada left a legacy of quality behind her in the form of three bitches that she produced, which are off to successful careers in the show ring. Bred to Ch. Rodsden's Berte v. Zederwald, C.D.X., for her first litter, she produced Grunhaus Harmony Marie and Grunhaus Havanna, both of whom fared well in strong classes at the 1988 American Rottweiler Club National Specialty. This was where Grunhaus Izadora, from the second Eztrada litter by Chardrick Yago, C.D., took Reserve Winners Bitch at age 13 months.

HAAKON ROTTWEILERS

Haakon Rottweilers, whose kennel is located in East Machias, Maine, with the winters spent at Providence, Rhode Island, are owned by two comparatively new

Top left: Can., Am. Ch. Wyreglen's Archangel, C.D., owner-handled by Caroline E. MacPherson. The late Kitty Drury is the judge.
Top right: Ch. Yempler von Siegerhaus, II. Owner, Von Siegerhaus Rottweilers of the Woodwards.
Middle: Can. Ch. Wyreglen's Archibald, C.D., owned by F. Meuller and C.E. MacPherson.
Bottom: Ben's Mercedes von Rainhart, bred by Diane Johnston, co-owned with Sandy Bowler.

but very dedicated Rottie fans, Paul and Judith Nelson.

The Nelsons, who say that they wish now they "had always been Rottie people," had the good fortune to acquire a puppy as their first Rottweiler, who grew up to become Am., Can. Ch. Haakon Moby von Reishoff and a Best in Show winner—this is surely starting out in a breed very well indeed.

Although they had always been dog people, the Nelsons, in the beginning, were not quite prepared for life with a very self-confident, young, and very "up" male Rottie. He taught them a great deal during the first year as they learned about getting him under control, and they learned that he wanted to work *with* them, not *for* them. Consistent and equal amounts of correction and love with the freedom to grow through new experiences and responsibility let him mature into the solid, dignified, friendly dog he has become. It was, the Nelsons remark, "an exhausting but rewarding experience."

Moby was not ready for the show ring until he had reached 20 months of age, when his owners entered him in eight shows. He finished his championship in five of these, taking breed over specials twice and once with a Group

placement. At that point, he was still a handful in the ring.

Taking a summer break paid off, as did working with him at his real home (the farm down east), and then into the ring he went again for his Canadian championship. Although somewhat awkwardly owner-handled, Moby, in four Canadian shows, took four Bests of Breed, first in two Working Groups, and a Best in Show.

By then it was realized that Moby, to do the winning he seemed capable of, needed an expert handler. Elizabeth Ann Coviello was selected for this task, as the Nelsons had admired her manner of presentation of Rotties in the ring. So well did this work out that Moby's record has grown considerably to at least a total of 17 times Best of Breed, four Group wins, and a Canadian and an American Best in Show. His future seems to be a bright one.

Moby is by Am., Can. Ch. Harras vom Sachsen (Dingo v. Schwaiger Wappen ex Carla vom Sachsen, SchH. I) from Ch. Ariel von Reishoff (Ch. Rocky von Anderson ex Ch. Gatstuberget's Huldra, C.D.).

HAUS TREZILIAN

Haus Trezilian Rottweilers belong to Douglas K. Loving who, since our *World of Rottweilers* for which he wrote an excellent chapter on Schutzhund work, has been located in the Pennsylvania area. We understand that he plans

Top: **Three handsome Rotties from Bluefox Kennels, owned by Cheryl Kienast: Ch. V. Victor's Dame Braus v.Bruin, C.D.; Bluefox Aaronhoff von Siegen; and Bluefox Abelman von Siegen.**
Middle: **Am., Can. Ch. Roma's Ultra von Siegerhaus, C.D., taking Best of Opposite Sex. Owner, Roma Rottweilers of the Martins of CA.**
Bottom: **Am., Can. Ch. Windcastle's von Scharnhass, by Am., Can. Ch. Donnaj Herr I Am, C.D., T.T., ex Am., Can. Ch. Gatstuberget's Katarina, T.T. Bred by the Kaufmanns; F. Cresci, handler.**

Ch. Radio Ranch's Bad Girl was bred by Pam Weller and M.K. Anderson. She is a daughter of Ch. Radio Ranch's Axel v. Notara ex Ch. Susan von Anderson. Handled by Darrell Hayes for owner Arthur Coia, Southwine Farms, Rehoboth, MA.

to move to California.

Although his affections are divided between his Rotties and the excellent American Staffordshire Terriers which he also owns, Doug will always be a staunch supporter of the Rotties with which he has been involved for a decent period of time.

Two of his favorite dogs are "Rommel," and Am., Can. Ch. Dina von der Brunnleithe, a German import sired by Citto v.d. Pinter, SchH. III, ex Anka vom Naabtalblick, SchH. I.

Dina was bred a while back to Am., Int. Ch. Santo vom Schwaiger Wappen and an outstanding young dog was produced, Ero vom Konigsadler, owned by J. Patrick Green.

HAWKHAVEN

HawkHaven Rottweilers are located in Crystal Lake, Illinois, 50 miles northwest of Chicago, where Barbara and George Kellett reside. The kennel began when its owners purchased a 100-year-old house on 12 acres where a multitude of hawks soared overhead. Hence the name, HawkHaven.

Shortly following the loss of their family companions, a 12-year-old Greyhound bitch, Ch. Kingsmark Slightly Scarlett, and their six-year-old red Dobe, a new dog was needed.

Since Barbara Kellett describes herself as one of those "fortunate people who needs to have a dog to live with," the search was on immediately with several breeds

Top: Can. Ch. Haramitas Kladie Son O'Garth, C.D., is a multiple Best of Breed winner and Group placer. Owner, Wyndhurst Kennels, Androssa, Alta., Canada. *Middle:* Ch. Timberline's Exquisite Gem, bred by Sharon Michael, owned by John and Judy McCormick, Gillette, WY. *Bottom:* Bda., Can. Ch. Wyreglen's Best of Both Worlds is sired by Am., Can., Int. Ch. Bronco v. Rauberfeld, SchH. III, F.H., Select, Bronze Producer, 1982 German Klubsieger.

under consideration until Barbara discovered Rottweilers at a dog show. This promptly answered the question as she made arrangements for the purchase of a lovely eight-week-old bitch puppy. This one she named HawkHaven's Thea, and she became the mother, grandmother and great-grandmother of all the beautiful HawkHaven bitches to follow.

Thea was bred to Rodsden's Strawlane Tyr, son of Ch. Axel von Brabant and Ch. Strawlane Abra. From this litter two bitches were kept, one being Ch. HawkHaven's Abbondanza, who finished her title in eight weeks at the age of 21 months. A male pup by Ch. Blitzkirk von HawkHaven was selected by Barbara's sister, Mrs. Bette Olson.

Thea's second litter was sired by Ch. Hasso vom Steigstraessle, C.D., and again two bitches were kept, HawkHaven's Ombre Rose and HawkHaven's Firstin May. In 1986, Firstin was bred to Ch. Von Brader's Eiger, producing three lovely girls. The first of these to finish was Ch. HawkHaven's Gretchel, who completed her title at the American Rottweiler Club Specialty in December, 1988, with a five-point major and Best of Opposite Sex. Second daughter, HawkHaven's Tiger Lily, took Reserve Bitch at the Medallion Rottweiler Club in June, 1988. The third beauty from this litter began her show career in 1989.

Another young bitch, HawkHaven's Madchen von Mione, is well on her way, needing a few remaining points. She is from a breeding of Weissenburg's Hamm (Ch. Birch Hill's Governor ex Ch. Weissenburg's Don't You Dare) and HawkHaven's Hermione, the latter one of the original two bitches from Thea's first litter.

Waiting to grow up and begin their careers are HawkHaven's Santo Domingo and his sister HawkHaven's Santa Catarina, from a breeding of Int., Am., Can. Ch. Santo vom Schwaiger Wappen, SchH. III, and Ch. HawkHaven's Abbondanza.

Barbara Kellett has based her breeding program on well-bred bitches from HawkHaven's Thea. Although Thea is not an outstanding conformation individual, she had the genes and great temperament to produce quality in her offspring. Her daughters' progeny are the proof of that theory, and Thea is lovingly referred to as "the goose that lays the golden eggs."

The Kelletts are members of the Medallion Rottweiler Club and have recently applied for membership in the American Rottweiler Club.

J-HAUS

J-Haus Rottweilers are owned by John and Janie Hayden of Speedway, Indiana, whose first Rottie was purchased, sight unseen, from Kimbertal Kennels after two years of reading and researching on the breed. John Hayden wanted to show his own dog, so hit the road with Kimbertal's Hoosier Max, making the dog an owner-handled champion at age 19 months who went on to win seven Bests of Breed and four Group placements, including two Group seconds.

The Haydens became members of the Hoosier Rottweiler Club in 1985, at which time they met Larry and Alice Lee of Franklin, Indiana. John and Janie fell in love with the Lees' multiple Best of Breed and Group-placing bitch named Kyra (Ch. Baroness Elka von Dealcrest, C.D.). They considered themselves privileged by having been able to purchase Kyra's first puppy bitch, which was the only bitch in this litter. From this event their breeding program started taking shape. Ch. Birchwood's Governor, C.D., now deceased, was the proud father of this puppy whom the Haydens named Laran's Andra von Mikon. She is mother-to-be with multiple Best of Breed wins including some top-ranked males. She, too, was owner-handled to her championship by John Hayden, and she has been ranked as high as No. 4 nationally, according to

Top: Srigo's Loaded For Bear is by the great Bronco from Srigo's Of Thee I Sing. Owner, Felicia Luberich. *Middle:* Ch. Merrymoore's Ric-O-Shay, C.D., winning first in the Working group at Cheyenne K.C. By Ch. Merrymoore's Zears Black ex Merrymoore's Imperial One. Photo courtesy of Sharon Michael, owner. *Bottom:* Rosendorn's Negotiator belongs to breeder Johann Emedi of Big Country Rottweilers, Warren, MI.

BEST OF
WINNERS
HOCKAMOCK
KENNEL CLUB
JULY
1986
THE STANDARD IMAGE
CHUCK TATHAM

WINNERS
LADIES
DOG CLUB
NOVEMBER
1986
JOHN ASHBEY

BEST OF
BREED OR VARIETY
CHESHIRE
KENNEL CLUB
AUG
1988
THE STANDARD IMAGE
CHUCK TATHAM

PLACING
OBEDIENCE
WOODSTOCK
DOG CLUB
JULY
1986
TATHAM PHOTO

Top: Ebonstern Libert v.d. Liebe, with 14 points including 2 majors. By Am., Can. Ch. Ebonstern Black Bart ex Ebonstern Bryt Promise. Cheryl Wheeler, owner.
Middle: Am., Can. Ch. Donnaj Very Special, C.D.X., T.T., pulling his cart. One of the outstanding Rottweilers owned by J. Marshall.
Bottom: Freyan's Blatantly Brisis, C.D., T.D., age 2 years. Owned by G. and C. Shook, Corning, CA.

Opposite top left: Pioneer's Miko v. Graz, C.D., at 16 months. Owned by Jim and Bobby Boyce, Kittery, NH. Earned C.D. at 11 months, his first major at 14 months (going through to Best of Breed over 5 specials from the American-bred Dog Class). Jim handles Miko.
Opposite top right: True Lee's Copper v. Gunner II, by Ch. Altar's Gunner of Woodland ex Ashby v. Foxcroft, C.D. taking the points at Ladies Dog Club in 1988. Handled by Elizabeth Coviello for Bob and Laura Condon.
Opposite bottom left: Ch. Pioneer's Maverick at 17 months, by Ch. Noblehaus Beretta ex Ch. Pioneer's Das Bedazzled, C.D., is pictured winning Best of Breed over 6 specials from the Bred-by-Exhibitor Class. "Bart" finished his championship with four majors, one from Puppy, two from Bred-by (Best of Breed), and one from Open. Bred and owned by Pioneer Rottweilers, S. Hedrick and V. Aceta.
Opposite bottom right: Pioneer's Gretchen v. Beretta, C.D.X., T.D., owned by P. and E. Shipman and S. Hedrick. Gretchen is a daughter of Ch. Noblehaus Beretta ex X-Rated Annie, C.D. She won Class placements and all three Novice legs and Open legs with enthusiastic Obedience work.

Top: **Powderhorn's Kier of Wencrest,** owned by Robin Bell and Powderhorn Rottweilers, Inc. *Middle:* **Ch. Jo Bea's Dallas von Duf,** owned by Jo-Bea's Rottweilers, Ontario, CA. Dallas is a daughter of Ch. Starkheim Duf Morgen Carroll ex Triple Oak Amber v. Mavinhaus. Breeders, Scarlet and John Saffer. *Bottom:* **Can. Ch. Srigo's Non Stop Magic,** by Am., Can., Int. Ch. Bronco v. Rauberfeld, SchH. III, F.H., Select, 1982 German Klubseiger, Bronze. Out of Srigo's Only By Magic, Felicia Luberich.

Jimeniz are new to the Rottweiler fancy but keenly enthusiastic and already the owners of two excellent champions.

Initially starting with a pet bitch, they had the good fortune of buying two puppies from good friends. These both have been shown to their championship, and the male, Ch. Misty Lakes Awol Kid, will be specialed and, in fact, is already a Best of Breed dog.

Awol's sister, Ch. Misty Lake's Afternoon D'Light, will be bred to Noblehaus Beretta, and Dr. and Mrs. Jimeniz look forward to the puppies with keen anticipation.

Awol and D'Light were bred by Ronnie and Elizabeth Greenman in Newtown, Connecticut. They are by Ch. Pandemonium's Laredo v. Blanka from the Marksman von Turick daughter, Diamond's Avatar.

Awol is proving a popular and excellent sire. One of his puppies is owned by Dr. and Mrs. Jimeniz, who have high hopes for her future.

KENNRICH ROTTWEILERS

Kennrich Rottweilers of Chesapeake, Virginia, are owned by Kennette and Richard Tabor. Kennette started in dogs in 1974 with Samoyeds, which she exhibited and bred for 13 years.

Rottweiler Quarterly magazine, despite limited showing.

J-Haus Rottweilers will continue to be a small family kennel dedicated to the breeding of O.F.A.-certified Rotties of excellent conformation and temperament. Andra's most recent litter was by Ch. Goldeiche's Ara von Brader, owned by Dale and Karen Innocenti of Chicago, who is a multiple Best in Show and Specialty Best in Show winner.

JIMENIZ

Located in Bridgewater, Connecticut, Dr. and Mrs. Eric

In 1983, Kennrich acquired their first Rottweiler and foundation bitch, a ten-week-old puppy named Ch. Radio Ranch's Casablanca Pia. She was sired by Ch. Radio Ranch's X-tra Special (a son of Ch. Radio Ranch's Axel v. Notara), and her dam is Centurian's Ivy League (a Ch. Astro vom Chrisstenbrad daughter). Kennrich acquired this puppy from Leslie Fulcher and Pamela Brown.

Pia was handled exclusively to her championship at the age of two years by Kennette. She finished easily with two three-point and two four-point majors and a Group Second from the Classes.

Kennrich bred their first litter of Rotties in 1985, and what a way to begin! With Ch. Radio Ranch's Casablanca Pia as the dam and an Austrian imported sire, Int. Ch. Amon vom Filmteich, SchH. III, FH, this litter produced Ch. Kennrich's Soaring Zena, who finished her championship when only one year old, after which she was shown to multiple Bests of Breed, Bests of Opposite Sex (including the American Rottweiler Club Region IV Specialty in 1988) and Group placements. She became the American Rottweiler Club's No. 2 Bitch for 1988. Zena is owned by Anne and Dennis McCormack. This litter also produced Kennrich's Playboy, pointed in limited showing, who will be quick to complete his championship title.

Two years later, in 1987, Pia produced a litter sired by the German import, Kimbo vom Siedlerpfas, SchH. I, the Winners Dog at the 1986 Colonial Rottweiler Club Specialty. This litter produced Philippine Ch. Kennrich's Arko of Radio Ranch, who finished title at age one year; and Kennrich's Arko v. Radio Ranch who almost has the Philippine title. Both of these dogs are owned by Jim Trillo of Manila, Philippines.

Kennrich Vic-Tory, from this same litter and owned by Kennrich, is just beginning his owner-handled show career and is

already pointed. Another male from this litter, Kennrich's Heir Apparent, won Best Puppy in Match at the National Capital Rottweiler Club Specialty Match. Still another, Kennrich's Romulus, is owned by police canine officer and trainer Gary Dayton and his wife. "Peppi" is ready for certification for Police Utility Dog, Police Tracking Dog, and the PSP certification (the German Police Dog classification). Romulus is the family's pet and companion and was trained by Gary as his training demonstration dog to compete in National Police Dog Trial events.

In 1988, the successful breeding of Pia to Amon was repeated and produced ten lovely, promising puppies. These youngsters are already doing quite well at matches and obedience matches.

Powderhorn's Yola of Wencrest owned by Katherine and Charles Laird and Powderhorn Rottweilers, Inc., Hollywood, CA.

Above: Apache Hill's Ana v. Harrel, C.D., taking Winners Bitch at 1988 A.R.C. National Specialty. Owners, Jacques Harrell and Irene F. Castillo.
Below: Am., Can. Ch. Gipfel's Bourbon Breeze, C.D.X., is the foundation Rottie owned by Dr. and Mrs. Karl W. Rice.

Kennrich kept a striking male, Kennrich Gold Strike, and has high hopes for him.

All dogs owned by Kennrich are owner-handled. Kennrich also teaches show-handling training classes.

KERNECHT

Kernecht Rottweilers, located in Lebanon, New Jersey, are owned by Haidar and Erika Beqaj, who are continuing to do well with their homebreds. Probably one of the more unusual "success stories" we have heard is Mrs. Beqaj's account of a bitch puppy of hers named Molly, who, we are quite certain, has the distinction of being the only Rottweiler to have been raised by a Yorkshire Terrier!

It seems that Molly was the sixth pup born in her litter, and she was rather small. She started out O.K. for a few hours, then stopped feeding, and Mrs. Beqaj thought there was no hope for her. As it turned out, her mouth was too small to enable her to feed normally from her dam. A friend who had helped with the whelping was determined that she would try to rear the puppy, so she took her home, where she started feeding her by dropper. Then, as the puppy's strength gradually improved, she put her on her Yorkshire bitch who had just weaned a litter of her own. This did the trick, starting a gradual weight gain for Molly, and soon she had grown sufficiently to return home to her own dam and littermates. Molly grew up to become a champion, to the amazement of her co-breeders, Kernecht and Von Stolzenfels Rottweilers. At only 16 months of age, never before having been in the conformation ring, she took Second in the Open Class and Reserve Winners Bitch in the tough competition at the Colonial Rottweiler Club Specialty, carrying on in the tradition of her sire, Ch. Ursus von Stolzenfels, C.D., who in the 1984 Colonial Rottweiler Club Specialty Show, had gone Winners

Dog and Best of Winners at 19 months.

The following month, Molly went on to second placement in Open Class at the Medallion Specialty under German judge Dieter Hoffmann, who critiqued her, emphasizing her "powerful head, excellent topline and outstanding gait." This just goes to show you that a mouse *can* look at a lion—or a Yorkshire Terrier at a Rottweiler—with a happy ending.

Ch. Bulli's Molly von Stolzenfels has to her credit a couple of Best of Breed and Best of Opposite Sex wins in very limited showing.

KHETAQUA

Khetaqua Rottweilers in Center Ossipee, New Hampshire, are owned by Priscilla Drake Qua, who purchased her first Rottie in 1984. Since then she has acquired several with which she was disappointed, leading her to search further for the type and quality she wanted to own and raise.

Now she feels that her foundation stock is a solid base from which to build, as her current dogs consist of Altar's Arabesk vom Freyr, True-Lee Heika of Khetaqua, and Southwind Dempsey of True-Lee. Arabesk has produced quality puppies in her first two litters, thus the future now looks bright for this young kennel.

Top: Cara DiCicco placing Best in Junior Showmanship at Penn Ridge K.C. in 1988 with Noblehaus Hi-Voltage v. Antren, owned by Antren Rottweilers, Lynbrook, NY.
Middle: Ch. Garen's Baka v. Charm, owned by Gary and Karen Sims.
Bottom: Tri-Lee's Cavalier Rauber and Tri-Lee's Champagne, littermates, pictured each winning first points on championship at Moberly, MO, in 1986. Owner-handlers, Don and Norma White; judge, R. William Taylor.

Top: Ch. Mad Rivers Brenda's Bolltar was bred by Dorothy Davis and is owned by Brenda and John Jayne. *Middle:* Blackthorns von Buckley taking Best Puppy at the Seminole R.C. Bred, owned and handled by Ann Sims Bayles. Sired by Ch. Little Bit of Cash ex Max von Lott Anna. *Bottom:* Ch. Roxer's Rhiannon, C.D., by Am., Can. Ch. Rodsden's Vinegar Joe, C.D.X., T.D., ex Ellsbeth von School, C.D. Bred and owned by Ann and William Scholl, Roxer Rottweilers, Kingston, IL.

with the fact that these two ferocious-sounding dogs were behind a partly opened screen door and could have come bounding out at any given time but did nothing beyond warning her that she had come close enough to their domain that she immediately knew this was the breed for her—especially since they also had the short tail and coat she had already decided would be requisites for her future dogs.

It was not too difficult, on this basis, to convince her husband that she really *needed* a Rottie to protect their home in the country

KOSTLICH-VON URSA ROTTWEILERS

Kostlich-Von Ursa Rottweilers, A.K.C. registered, began from a long-time love of dogs. Since she can recall, Rebecca L. Chriscoe of Micanopy, Florida, had dogs of the Shepherd type. But when she became a homemaker, she quickly made the discovery that a dog with a shorter coat and tail would be much nicer for a house pet.

Rebecca went one day to see some horses, which is when her first encounter with Rottweilers took place. So impressed was she

and that her old Shepherd could train the youngster to the family ways if she could obtain one before long. The difficult part was *locating* the available Rottie puppy. This was in 1970.

Several of the Rottweilers she found turned out not to be the dog she had wanted. Then things took a turn for the better when a puppy called Ursula was purchased and grew to become Ch. Ursula, SchH. II. It was for her that the suffix Von Ursa was selected as identification for the Chriscoe Rottweilers, and later on, when registering the kennel name with A.K.C., she added "Kostlich," which means "exquisite," to the Von Ursa for identification of her dogs.

In 1977, Rebecca purchased a three-month-old bitch who became foundation for a highly successful breeding program. She became Ch. RC's Gator Bel von Meadow, T.T., a Top Producer for many years, and believed to be the Top Producing Rottweiler Bitch in the United States with 18 American Kennel Club champions of record to her credit.

Gator was the dam of Ch. RC's Magnum Force von Ursa, T.T., the American Rottweiler Club Bitch of

the Year for 1981. That same year, another of Gator's daughters was rated as No. 4 Bitch. Gator was bred by Donna Wormser, sired by Ch. Radio Ranch's Notara ex Bella of Limehouse.

Many of the Kostlich-Von Ursa Rotties have become foundation blood of new Rottweiler Kennels and have gone on to become Top Producers in their own right.

LAKEVIEW

Lakeview Rottweilers are a fairly new kennel located in Dawson Springs, Kentucky, where they are owned by Tonya Jones

Oldham. Judging by the enthusiasm of Tonya and her husband Don Jones, these dogs would seem headed for a bright future in both the show and obedience rings.

A good deal of Tonya's life as a youngster was spent in training and showing quarterhorses, in which field she was both well known and respected. In 1986, however, she gave it all up when she solely dedicated herself to searching for the best bloodlines that she could acquire as foundation stock for her new project—breeding Rottweilers.

Top: Can. Ch. Xcel Rambo De Chafard as a handsome and most promising young campaigner in July, 1988, placing second in the Working Group at Chateauquay Valley K.C. Handled by Denis Fafard for breeder-owner Sylvia Fafard, St. Eulalie, Que., Canada. *Middle:* This impressively titled Rottweiler is Am., Can., Dom., Ven., Bha., Bda., So.Am., P.R., Int. Ch. America's Miss Demeanor, pictured winning Group first in Puerto Rico. Owner, Powsell Rottweilers. *Bottom:* Xcalibur De Chafard, 10-month pointed puppy by Can. Ch. Wyreglen's Archimage ex Can. Ch. Dakrajou De Forte Brise. Bred by S. Fafard, owned by P. Tourignant.

Epic's Burning Desire, C.D.X., one of the Zornhaus Rottweilers owned by Pamela Anderson, Wilton Manors, FL.

During the same year, she purchased a splendid stud dog, Denel's Instigator v. Eisen, a son of Ch. Beaverbrook Eisen v. Bruin, the 1986 Medallion Rottweiler Club Specialty winner and sire of the No. 1 Bitch among Rottweilers in 1988. Instigator seemed ideal in temperament and pedigree, having nine Top Producers in the first three generations.

Adam's Abi-Bel von Ursa, a robust, masculine bitch who already had championship points, was next purchased as Tonya's first selection of a bitch for breeding. Abi-Bel is a Ch. RC's Falcon von Ursa daughter and a granddaughter of Ch. RC's Gator Bel von Meadow, the No. 1 Producing Bitch in the history of the breed. Abi-Bel's pedigree also has nine Top Producers in the first three generations.

In the fall of 1986, Tonya also acquired Lyndal's Cindy Vondez, a perky, well-structured bitch sired by Ch. Concord's Alexia vom Schultz. In the first two generations of Cindy's pedigree are some famed names, including the American Rottweiler Club Gold Producer Ch. Welkerhaus Rommel, U.D., and American Rottweiler Club Bronze Producing Dam, Concord's Special Edition.

The final selection to round out the foundation stock from which Lakeview Rottweilers would proceed was Shikara von Dular, a powerful, well-defined bitch sired by Ch. RC's Jackson von Ursa. Shikara's dam was Tanja von Marchenwald, a German import who had been selected by Friedrich Berger, A.D.R.K. Head Breed Warden for 17 years. Unfortunately, she was unable to be shown due to an accident.

With this stock established, Tonya started her breeding program on a once-per-year-per-bitch basis, with a watchful eye on quality and great attention to temperament, conformation, and intelligence. All puppies here are hand-raised in Tonya's home until age three weeks, after which time they are introduced to Lakeview's recently built kennel and its new facilities. It is Tonya's desire to see all of her young puppies, who are Medallion Rottweiler Club-nominated, owner-trained and handled by their purchasers. Thus she places emphasis on the great pleasure to be enjoyed in this manner. New owners thus are always encouraged to attend obedience and conformation classes.

One of the most impressive and largest Lakeview litters thus far has consisted of 16 puppies from Cindy Vondez and sired by a German import, Brando vom Dattelner Hof, SchH. II, FH, a son of Igor vom Kastanienbau, SchH. III, FH. Tonya chose to keep a female, TJ's Tasha of Lakeview, from this litter, to bring the Brando bloodlines strongly into her breeding program. At the age of ten months, Tasha has already earned two Reserve Winners awards in the show ring, been Winners Bitch and Best of Opposite Sex owner-handled from the Puppy Class; and has won the 1988 Medallion Rottweiler Club Sweepstakes nine to twelve month Puppy Bitch Class in Miami, Florida.

LANGHOFFEN

Langhoffen Rottweilers are owned by Coco Steinford in Veradale, Washington, whose goal is to breed a performance Rottweiler who is sound in mind and body, with proper working structure as well as correct temperament and drive.

With those qualities foremost in mind, Coco purchased a lovely sound bitch in 1979 from Mrs. May Kalbas. This was Haus Kalbas Delight, who became the foundation bitch for Langhoffen Rotties. Delight was a daughter of Ch. Starkrest's Polo R from a German import, Ch. Happy v. Dammerwald. She was shown only sparingly, but gained championship points before retiring to the whelping box for Langhoffen's "C" litter.

This "C" litter was sired by Lonkeena v. Norwald, and among others produced Langhoffen's Camber, who gained championship points, a C.D., C.D.X., and a T.D. She had many class placements and numerous High Scoring Rottweiler in Trial awards, as well as High Scoring Working Dog in Trial awards. She is a member of the Medallion Rottweiler Club Honor Roll, was trained and handled by her breeder-owner, and produced Langhoffen's "D" and "E" litters.

The "D" litter was sired by Dan Amy's Burley von Frodo. From this litter came Langhoffen's Dream, C.D.; Langhoffen's Daja, C.D.; and Langhoffen's Dixi, SchH. I. These girls all did well, but special performance credit goes to Dixi, who was owned, trained and titled

by Wayne Curry.

Langhoffen's "E" litter, again from Camber, was sired by Am., Can. Ch. Alpha Alexandros G. Roadway. These puppies included Langhoffen's Eick, VB, SchH. III, I.P.O. III, F.H., U.D.T.; Langhoffen's Esse, C.D.X., H.I.C.; and Langhoffen's Envy.

By age 18 months, Eick had earned his SchH. I, SchH. II, and SchH. III. He went on to earn his F.H. and an I.P.O. III. In 1988, he earned a C.D., C.D.X., U.D., and T.D. in less than 12 months, for which he was presented with *The Dog World* Canine Distinction Award. All the above titles were gained before Eick had reached his third birthday, and it is believed that Eick is the youngest Rottweiler in the history of the

This Rottweiler is Judge John von Baron, owned and dearly loved by Judy M. Sample of Bakersfield, CA. Judge has already earned his C.D. and works towards C.D.X. He also started his conformation with some nice wins.

Top: Ch. Camas Valley Hildagard v. Kutz, beautiful bitch title-holder, owned by Dan and Debby Kutz. *Middle:* Am., Mex. Ch. Juno's Amanda Great Gertruda, C.D., the first Rottweiler owned by Charles and Danielle Green, Grunhaus Rottweilers, Orinda, CA. *Bottom:* Von Worley's Divine Miss M, Am., Can. C.D., is by Am., Can. Ch. Mad River's Magnum von Worley. Owners, Dawn and Jim Worley.

Langhoffen's "F" litter, by Am., Can. Ch. Alpha Alexandros G. Roadway from Langhoffen's Dream, C.D., produced Langhoffen's Fax and Langhoffen's Flax, C.D.

Fax is owned and trained by Glen Stephenson, and at age 13 months is prepared for his SchH. I. Flax is co-owned and trained by Steve Severson, and together they have earned a C.D. in three consecutive shows. At the age of ten months, he went High Scoring Rottweiler and High Scoring Working Dog.

Langhoffen's "G" litter, by Ch. Endikai von Edelhart, C.D., from Langhoffen's Envy, produced Langhoffen's Grete and Langhoffen's Garet. At age six months, the Langhoffen "G-Men" reside in Schutzhund and show homes. Grete is owned by Rachel Murray while Garet lives with his breeder.

The latest addition to the Langhoffen gang is the lovely Timm vom Mummler, SchH. III, daughter of Jeneck's Roxi.

Coco Steinford is involved with all facets of Rottweiler ownership. She is a member of the American Rottweiler Club, the Medallion Rottweiler Club, the United States Rottweiler Club, the United Schutzhund Clubs of America,

breed to have obtained all ten of these titles, very definitely an outstanding performance. Eick is breeder/owner-trained and handled.

Esse is co-owned, trained, and campaigned by Sandy Peppers Phillips. In 1988, she earned 140 Delaney points, competing in Novice B and Open A. She was ranked in the Top Ten Obedience Rottweilers for 1988.

Envy is currently being shown in conformation classes, owner-handled, and has several championship points.

The famous Ch. Panzer von Krenkel following an important win in Guatemala. Handled by Fileberto Auxiella for owners Carlos and Wanda Bonilla.

D.V.G. America, Tri-State Schutzhund Association, and the Spokane Training Club.

Coco comments: "To establish a successful breeding program, you must find the best handlers to prove one's dogs. During the past several years, I have been fortunate enough to place promising young dogs with excellent handlers. I am grateful for their support and assistance."

LATIMERE

Latimere Rottweilers, owned by Jan Latimer in Dickinson, Texas, have been breeding since the early 1980s. Jan takes pleasure in many aspects of Rottweiler ownership, ranging from breeding and showing,

obedience, taking part in local parades, and generally proving what a great all-around breed the Rottweiler can be.

Top Rottie at this kennel is Ch. Big Oaks High Class v. Brenna, Therapy Dog, who is now eight years old and has friends by the dozen in her home area. One could not find a better ambassador for the breed than this lovely bitch who participates fully in her family's interests and activities.

LEGEND

Legend Rottweilers are owned by Lee Whittier in Woodstock, Vermont. This is the home of the famous American and Canadian Ch. Marksman von Turick, C.D.

Although he campaigned on a somewhat limited basis, he has made a notable record in competition, particularly in the eastern part of the country, during his career.

Marksman started to attract attention to his quality when, at age 15 months in 1982, he took Best of Opposite Sex in Sweepstakes at the Colonial Rottweiler Club Specialty and then completed his championship three short months later. Since then, his list of honors is admirable. Starting with high ratings in the *Canine Chronicle* and Routledge Systems beginning in

April, 1983, Marksman held his own throughout the next few years.

In 1986, Marksman became a member of the American Rottweiler Club Hall of Fame. In 1987, he was No. 1 Rottweiler in the *Rottweiler Xpress* System. Probably the best award of all, in addition to his show honors, he was recipient of the American Rottweiler Club Producer of Merit.

All of Marksman's wins were made with his co-owner, co-breeder handling. This marvelous dog belongs to K. Kaiser and Jan Whittier, who will surely be enjoying success with his descendants.

LEIBGARDE

Leibgarde Rottweilers, owned by Michael and Faith Mitchell, are in Santee, California, which is located in San Diego County. Their first Rottweiler, East Spring vom Hochfeld, was purchased from Vivian Peters as a family pet and protection dog, since Mike worked many nights away from home as a highway patrol officer. "Spring" has been the grandlady and guardian of all the Mitchell household, including the new puppy arrivals ever since.

Later on, the conformation ring entered their lives and has been in their hearts ever since. Both Mike

Top: Windwalker's Willsden's Annie, C.D., took a 4-point major at Asheville in July, 1988, handled by owner, James S. Bryan, Columbia, SC. *Bottom left:* Senda Kim De Chafard, 1-year-old and pointed, is by Can. Ch. Darkajous De Forte Brise. Bred by Sylvia Fafard. Owned by Suzanne LeTarte. *Bottom right:* At age 5 months, Ch. Laran's Andra vom Mikon winning Best in Match at the Hoosier R.C., owner-handled by John Hayden. Daughters Jessica and Jill proudly look on.

Top left: Ch. Altar's Gunner of Woodland, owned by Arthur Coia. Handled by Darrel L. Hayes. This handsome dog has multiple wins and Group placements to his credit. *Top right:* Am., Can. Ch. Big Timbers Sweetest Taboo, owned by Nancy Schoenbeck. By Ch. Birch Hills Quincy ex Ch. Future Farms Lucy-D, Taboo was bred by Craig Ames, Big Timber Rottweilers. *Bottom:* Ch. Srigo's Rainbow Wilderness taking a 5-point major to finish at the A.R.C. Region V Specialty in 1988. Owner, JoAnn Harnish.

and Faith have learned to handle their own dogs and show other dogs professionally as they travel across the United States, Canada, and Mexico. Mike is also a dog show photographer and specializes in photographing Rottweiler Specialty Shows and Matches. In 1988, he was the official photographer for the American Rottweiler Club National Specialty in Oakland, California.

The foundation for Leibgarde was the bitch, Can., Mex. Ch. Leibgarde's Heidi vom Hochfeld, A.T.T., M.T.T., who has had an outstanding show career. In 1986, at age 13 months, Heidi went Winners Bitch at the Rottweiler Club of Canada National Specialty in Vancouver, British Columbia. Two months later, at age 15 months, Heidi went Best of Winners at the Kachina Kennel Club in Phoenix, Arizona, thus taking her first four-point major here in the United States.

Of the many accomplishments to Heidi's credit, there have been none more noteworthy and exciting than those on the 1987 International Show Circuit in Tijuana, Mexico. The four-day F.C.I.-sanctioned event was stiffly competitive as several of the Top Ten A.K.C. Rottweilers competed. Heidi returned home from there

with three International points, a Mexican championship; two Bests of Breed and one Best of Opposite Sex. Topping it all off, she had completed her Temperament Test requirements.

Heidi was bred to Am., Can., Mex. Ch. Quick von Siegerland, C.D., Z.T.P.R. II. Together they produced a very promising litter. At 13 months, her daughter, Leibgarde's Fireball Kassie, twice earned Reserve Winners Bitch. Heidi and Kassie are currently working on their obedience and Tracking Dog Degrees.

WINNERS

TUXEDO PARK
KENNEL CLUB
988   DAVE ASHBEY

Ch. Epic's Divine Intervention, T.T., bred, owned and handled by Rose Hogan, Epic Kennels. A second-generation Epic!

As members of the Golden State, Medallion, and Southwestern Rottweiler Clubs, the Mitchells share a commitment to a code of ethics. Faith served as president of the Southwestern (1987-1988) and Mike as 1989-1990 president.

LIEBENSWERT

Liebenswert Rottweilers in Alleyton, Texas, belong to Patricia J. Storer, who was first attracted to the dogs when she learned, following intensive research of the subject, that this territorial breed excelled in working qualifications, including the ability to herd and drive livestock. The tough Brangus blood of the commercial cattle

raised on her ranch necessitated a breed of dog that would not back down from a bluff, would hold its own against a non-bluffing mother cow, and would have the intelligence to "get the heck out of there" when that course was appropriate. Pat Storer's concern over a dog suitable for her purposes was brought about by the breeding of conformation, performance, and racing quarterhorses for more than 20 years.

Once the decision that the dog was to be a Rottweiler had been reached, Pat searched the country to find a pup from a place where Rottweilers were currently working cattle. Finally, "Gumbo" was selected, brought home, and later became a foundation for Liebenswert Kennels. Gumbo far exceeded even the highest expectations which had preceded her arrival by becoming a champion, Utility Dog, and valued, loving member of the ranch and household.

In many ways, Gumbo was one of a kind, although she faithfully passed along her desirable characteristics to her offspring. All of her progeny have excelled in herding instincts and temperament; many of them have gone on to achieve championships and both obedience and working degrees. Included in these are: Can. Ch. Liebenswert Abner; Am., Can. Ch. Liebenswert Vater Abraham, C.D.; Ch. Liebenswert Cafe Ole, C.D.; Liebenswert Amber, C.D. (A.K.C. pointed); Weight Pull Dog, Liebenswert Count v. Robinwalk, SchH. III; Liebenswert Celestia Star, C.D.X.; and Liebenswert Cakes Baby, C.D. Most of the above named, and others also, have T.T.s and H.I.C.s.

Since the beginning, Liebenswert bitches have been bred to champions or other studs of particular merit. The kennel has become noted for superior temperament—"gentleness without sacrificing character." Patricia Storer believes that a Rottweiler must be bred first of all to have a "livable temperament and character," and that it is the breeder's responsibility to test all litters for signs of weakness, over-aggression, high suspicion, as well as for certain potential instincts and abilities. After testing many litters, Pat sees strong value in these tests, as most often they enable her to predict and guide

owned by Linda and Bill Michels in Whitmore Lake, Michigan, who acquired their first Rottweiler in 1978 with the help of Pat Hickman Clark of Northwinds fame. This was an eight-week-old Dutch import who became Can. Ch. Astor, C.D., T.T. Astor was sired by Astor von Landgraben, SchH. III, F.H., who has sired many top working

Powderhorn's Raven of Wencrest, owned by Carol and Nicky Meyer.

clients to proper conditioning and nurturing of each individual puppy. "Liebenswert" means "worthy of love," and all litters are bred as if they were being kept by Pat herself, which she frequently ends up doing anyway.

LINDENWOOD
Lindenwood Rottweilers are

and conformation dogs in Germany, including the famous International Champion Ives Eulenspiegel, SchH. III.

As a show dog, young Astor started out with a bang at age 18 months. He was exhibited five times in Canada, taking Best of Breed on all five occasions and twice over specials, gaining his

Can. Ch. Northwind's Inka, the latter from the highly successful Ch. Igor von Schauer ex Am., Can. Ch. Northwind's Danka, Am., Can. C.D., breeding. The puppy grew up to become Am., Can. Ch. Bola von Meyerhoff, C.D., T.T., who was the foundation bitch for Lindenwood Rottweilers and a multi-Best of Breed winner in both the United States and Canada.

During 1981, Bola was bred to Champion Rodsden's Kane v. Forstwald, C.D., which was linebreeding on the Northwind's "D" litter. From this came Ch. Lindenwood's Anaconda, C.D., T.T., who finished with three majors and had several Best of Opposite Sex wins over specials.

The three bitch puppies from that Lindenwood "A" litter were shown at the 1982 Colonial Rottweiler Club Specialty with considerable success in both the Specialty itself and in the Sweepstakes. This was Bola's only litter.

In 1982, the Michels acquired a 17-month-old bitch from the famous Ch. Rodsden's Kane v. Forstwald, C.D., ex Ch. Rodsden's Roma von Brabant breeding, who became Ch. Rodsden's Heika v. Forstwald, C.D., VB, T.T. Heika finished her championship with four majors, then was bred to Ch. Gasto vom Liebersbacherhof, C.D.X., T.D., SchH. I, for the first time in 1983 and for the second time in 1984. This produced the Lindenwood's "B" litter and Rodsden's Lindenwood "L" litter, respectively.

The "B" litter included Ch. Lindenwood's Bouncer, C.D., T.T.; Ch. Lindenwood's Blixen, T.T.; and Ch. Lindenwood's Bitternight Bear, T.T. The Michels kept Bouncer, who is making his mark as a sire with Specialty placing and A.K.C.-titled offspring.

The "L" litter produced Ch. Rodsden's Lindenwood Liesl (Best Female Puppy, 1985 Medallion Rottweiler Club Futurity), Can. Ch. Rodsden's Lindenwood Lamia, Am., Can. C.D.X., VC, T.T.; and Rodsden's Leo of Lindenwood,

Canadian title owner-handled by Linda Michels. He earned his American and Canadian C.D. degrees in three shows each. He was x-rayed shortly thereafter and was unfortunately found to have hip dysplasia. He was then neutered and never shown again in conformation in the United States. "Thor," as he is known to friends, lives the good life of the family pet, including having his own wading pool.

The Michels, in 1979, acquired an eight-week-old bitch puppy from Ruth Meyer in Canada. This youngster was sired by Top Producer Am., Can. Ch. Ero von der Maoth, Am., Can. C.D., T.T., from

C.D., who has 13 points towards his A.K.C. championship including three majors.

In addition to Bouncer, Lindenwood has Windwalkers Alex The Great, C.D., T.T. (Ch. Mirko vom Steinkopf, C.D.X., SchH. III, I.P.O. III, FH), from Ch. Rodsden's Heika v. Forstwald, C.D., VB, T.T., who is just starting to show in conformation and is ready for a SchH. II and C.D.X.

Also at Lindenwood are four promising puppies. First is Barhaus Cain of Lindenwood (Am., Can. Ch. Ara von Brader, Am., Can. C.D., ex Ch. Weissenburg's Joker's Wild),who did well at Specialties as a puppy and is working for his obedience and Schutzhund degrees and will eventually go to the conformation ring. Second is Lindenwood Freddi von Been, C.D. (Ch. Lindenwood's Bouncer, C.D., T.T., ex Ch. Bonnie Jo von Beenen, C.D.), also successful in the puppy classes at the Colonial and Medallion Specialties and awaiting full maturity. Next, Lindenwood Charli of Mikon (Am., Can. Ch. Weissenburg's Field Marshall ex Ch. Lindenwood's Blixen, T.T.) and Lindenwood Axxa von Blauen Tor (Ch. Lindenwood's Bouncer, C.D., T.T., ex Iron Maiden vom Wint Haus). Axxa and Charli made their debuts at the 1989 Specialties. Charli is from a one-puppy litter and is co-bred and co-owned by Linda Michels and Deborah Conradt of Mikon Rottweilers.

The Michels enjoy obedience, tracking, Schutzhund, conformation, and the relatively new sport of French Ring. They put a premium on quality in temperament as well as type and soundness. They have also become closely involved with Temperament Testing of puppies and adults.

LITTLE FLOWER

Little Flower Kennels, owned by Mr. and Mrs. Frank Fiorella at Boxford, Massachusetts, are continuing on their planned breeding program for World Competition. Champion Rodsden's

Pandora v. Forstwald's pups are winning in the American Specialties and, having completed their American championships, a few will add to their laurels by trying for further honors in Canada, the Dominican Republic, Mexico and Puerto Rico.

The kennel's grand dam, International Ch. Green Mtn's Flora, C.D., is proceeding with her fantastic career. She has added some titles to her list, defeating tough competition from Germany and elsewhere around the world. Flora attained the Grand Peruvian Champion title and World Champion for 1988 a couple of weeks past her eighth birthday. Her list of titles follows: American, Dominican, Canadian, Puerto

Ch. Doroh's Promises Promises, 5th generation homebred, owner-handled to championship by Anita Sisney. Breeder, co-owner, Dorothy A. Wade.

Top: At the Coos K.C. in 1985, Winner's Bitch Grunhaus Eztrada, age 4 years; Reserve Winners Bitch, Grunhaus Germain. These bitches are littermates bred and owned by Danielle Greene. *Middle:* Ch. Laran's Andra vom Mikon winning Best of Breed. Owner, John and Janie Hayden. Breeders, Larry and Alice Lee. *Bottom:* Ch. Pioneer's Das Bedazzled, C.D., at home in Hollis, NH, taking Winners Bitch at 1985 A.R.C. National Specialty. Completed title in 11 shows. Bred and owned by Virginia Aceti and Sheryl Hedrick.

Rican, Mexican, Champion of the Americas (for four years), South American, International, Peruvian Grand Champion, F.C.I. World Champion for 1988, Mexican T.D., Mexican T.T., American C.D., Dominican C.D., *Dog World* award winner, Best Foreign Dog in Show in Puerto Rico, and the Medallion Rottweiler Club Hall of Fame. All this, and she is still planning more. Flora was bred in the U.S. by Tony Attalla at Green Mountain Kennels.

Frank tells us that "with the combined help of Rodsden in the United States and Brabantpark Kennels in the Netherlands," Little Flower has been able to import one of Europe's great dogs, International Ch. Barto v.t. Straotje, I.P.O. III, who came to America during 1988 as the most titled Rottweiler in Europe at that time. To these titles, Canadian and American championships were added, plus American T.D. The Fiorellas are highly elated at having this magnificent dog, and hopes are high not only for his own future success but for his progeny's following through in the tradition of their sire. He was bred by Ton and Wil Emmers.

LYONS

Sue Lyons of Mariposa, California, has been active in the Rottweiler breed since 1976. She is involved with all types of Rottie activity including training for obedience and working abilities and handling some exciting Rottweilers to prestigious victories in the show ring.

As co-owner with Maureen Wilkinson of Trollegen's Freya von Simebert, T.D., Susan was delighted at the 1988 National Specialty with Freya's accomplishments of achieving her tracking title along with some good placements in the conformation classes. More success took place at Golden State Rottweiler Specialty, and both Sue and Freya are working on further honors for the future.

Freya is by Cyras von Leinetel,

SchH. III, ex Can. Ch. Heidergruens Bekka, Can. C.D.X., and was bred by Marie Kanera and M. Wilkinson.

The handsome male, Ch. Trollegen Bacchus von Simeberg, T.D., is another Rottweiler owned by Susan Lyons who is doing quite well for her. He too was bred by Marie Kanera and Maureen Wilkinson, and is by Oleo vom Haus Schmidgall, SchH. III, I.P.O. III, ex Can. Ch. Heidergruens Bekka, Can. C.D.X.

MERRYMOORE

Merrymoore Rottweilers in Duluth, Georgia, have been widely respected in Rottie circles over a very long period of time. As the owner herself, Mrs. John W. Moore, Jr., is quick to comment: "It is difficult to say when Merrymoore Kennels actually began. Both my husband and I attended the University of Georgia, where we became engaged. Both of us were dog lovers, and I was not at all surprised when he gave me a Cocker Spaniel bitch as an engagement present. She went everywhere with us, including on our honeymoon. A few years later our son and daughter led us to our first Toy Poodle."

Mrs. Moore was also training and showing horses, which meant lots of time spent grooming, on both the Poodles and the horses. This is a good way to study a dog's anatomy, and it also involved a lot of work and family time. One day as they were preparing both horses and dogs for show, one of the children said, "Aren't we a merry bunch of Moores," and the kennel name was born.

Next, thanks to their son, the Moores added a Doberman. Mrs. Moore has always been interested in genetics as applied to breeding dogs, and she is fascinated with the challenge of producing bloodlines that will reproduce to a standard while still holding working ability and proper temperament.

This type of breeding is *serious* breeding, which requires both linebreeding and inbreeding as well as doing some outcrossing for

specific traits or features. It also requires room to keep entire litters until maturity, which is why Mrs. Moore's husband refers to Merrymoore as "a hobby that got completely out of hand."

While studying the background of the Dobermans, Mrs. Moore occasionally would run across some mention of "the Rottweiler dog," which she never had seen at that time. Both Moores became intrigued with the breed and tried to obtain additional information about it. But in 1962, information on the Rottweiler breed was sparse at best.

Following months of research, Mrs. Moore located and imported a puppy bitch. This was Cora v.d. Grurmannsheide. She became a birthday gift to Mrs. Moore and the Merrymoore foundation in Rottweilers. Cora became known at home as "Hilda," due to her papers with the registered name not

Timberline's Pennybrooke taking the points at South Jersey K.C. in October, 1987. Henry Stoecker judging. Owned by Timberline Rottweilers.

Top: Multiple Best in Show and Best in Specialty winner, Ch. Von Brader's Eiger, Award of Merit 1988. Best of Breed and Group IV, Westminster K.C. 1989. Owners, Frank and Mary Brader; handlers, Brian and Cindy Meyers. *Middle right:* Kimbo vom Siedlerphad, SchH. I, taking Best of Winners. Owned by Radio Ranch, Chesapeake, VA. *Middle left:* Best in Show, Am., Can. Ch. Haakon Moby von Reishoff, owner-handled by Judith Nelson. Owner, P. and J. Nelson, Providence, RI. *Bottom:* Ch. Radio Ranch's Kilroy Is Here! at age 18 months, taking points towards title for Radio Ranch Kennels.

arriving until some weeks after her arrival.

In the entire metropolitan Atlanta area, there were only five or six Rottweilers. But one of them was Ch. Georg of Rodsden; he became the sire of Merrymoore's first litter. The Moores kept a male, Ch. Merrymoore's Chug-A-Lug, for their son, and a bitch, Ch. Merrymoore's Behexed, for their daughter. The only other pup from this litter to have ever been shown was Ch. Hillgrove's Cora, owner-handled all the way.

Mrs. Moore had now started to

visit kennels all over the East and Midwest in order to acquire knowledge and to see dogs that might fit into a breeding program which she was beginning. One of the people she visited was Herman Heid, and from his Von der Heid Kennel she purchased Merrymoore's Mico von Hohenreissach. He was used twice for breeding to Behexed, which produced Merrymoore's Fleur de Lis, and to Hilda, which really gave Merrymoore the strong depth it was seeking in Ch. Merrymoore's Grand Desire, Ch. Gamboling Girl,

Ch. Gift of Glory, and Ch. Gay Spirit. This "G" litter also produced Merrymoore's Gladiator, who was kicked by a horse, suffered a broken leg, and consequently was never shown. Even so, he contributed greatly to the line by producing Ch. Merrymoore's Zears Black among others.

Zears Black, called "Rocky," produced a number of champions and dogs with obedience degrees. His titled offspring include Mrs.

Top right: Ch. Cannon River Oil Tanker, C.D., on one of his record-breaking Best in Show successes; here at the Coulee K.C. in 1985. George and Elfi Rice, breeder-owners.
Top left: Ch. V. Victor's Dame Brau v. Bruin, C.D., the first Rottweiler which Cheryl Kienast ever owned.
Middle: Can. Ch. Liebenswert Abner, winning points towards his title. Owned by Liebenswert Rottweilers, Patricia J. Storer, Alleyton, TX.
Bottom right: Am., Can. Ch. Von Worley's Alexander, Am., Can. C.D., with breeder-owner-handler, Dawn Worley. Jim and Dawn Worley, Newark, OH.
Bottom left: Best in Specialty, Select, Am., Can. Ch. Obstgartens Countess Oraya, owned by Jerry and Deanna Warkentin, Dinuba, CA.

Irene Castillo's Pagan Ballyhoo, C.D.

At about the same time, the Moores had the good fortune to acquire a bitch, Wonne Bulloides, who through breeding back into the old Panamint line, carried the ability to produce a few tailless puppies in her litter. From her, the Moores produced three champions, including the well-known and

for specific purpose, that the Merrymoore breeding program continues today.

The Moores are always striving for "the perfect Rottweiler," as their feeling is that gait is of utmost importance. The Rottweiler is a working dog that cannot function correctly in the work for which he was originally developed with an improper gait. A perfectly

Der Fruchtwald Bernhardt at age 17 months winning a 5-point major with Best of Winners at the Golden State R.C. Show, May, 1988. Owned by Janice Lynch, Lemon Grove, CA.

influential Ch. Merrymoore's Invincible, a dog who throughout his life was a strong contributing stud in the kennel and who passed on the tailless trait in a limited way to future generations.

The Moores took their Behexed to the lovely German import, Ch. Dino von der Kurmark, C.D., to produce Ch. Merrymoore's Xorcist. It is from a careful combination of the above bloodlines, with inclusion of an occasional outcross

proportioned head and body are both absolute *musts* if one is to have a *good* representation of the breed. Temperament is of vital consideration in any breeding program. What the breeders want to see is a confident, outgoing dog—not one who loves the world necessarily—nor one with a sharp disposition; rather, a dog that can be easily trained to handle any situation in the manner that the owner wants it to be handled.

This famous bitch is Can., Am. Ch. Carado's Satin Classic, by Ch. Ebony Acres Yankee Alliance ex Carado's Satin Sydney. She has held her position as No. 1 Rottweiler Bitch in Canada since 1986, and holds strong into the 1990s. Bred by Carol Kravets, owned by Suzanne and Mike Sosne, Caro, MI.

Merrymoore Kennels is over 25 years old and has been exclusively in Rottweilers since 1966. During this time, the Moores have produced approximately 35 Rottweilers who have become A.K.C. champions. Mrs. Moore is not quite sure of the number of Merrymoores who have won obedience degrees, but she does know that one of them, Merrymoore's Jupiter, C.D., in 1978 won the American Rottweiler Club's first place in obedience.

MURRAY'S ROTTWEILERS

Murray's Rottweilers are owned by Kenneth T. Murphy of Murfreesboro, Tennessee, the home of a handsome winning Rottie male, Ch. Von Hawthorne's Murray.

This dog was born in April, 1985, sired by Ch. Rangarr's A Sultan (Ch. Rodsden's Bruin v. Hungerbuhl ex Ch. Haserway's Fine Hildegarde) ex Von Hawthorne's Magna F, C.D. (Ch. Radio Ranch's Axel v. Notara ex Ch. Fritzi T. von Hawthorne).

Top: Von Riddle's Yvette v. Eisen, age 19 months, taking Winners Bitch from the Bred-by-Exhibitor Class under judge Mrs. Robert Forsyth. Yvette was bred and is owned by the Riddles. *Bottom:* Ch. Von Hottenstein's Hubahubba, by Am., Can. Ch. Trifecta's Barbarian v. Murph, C.D., ex Amber von Hottenstein. Owner-bred by Nancy Reynolds; handled by Alan Levine.

He is a multiple Group winner with additional frequent placements in strong Working breed competition. He placed No. 7 in the American Rottweiler Club ratings in 1987, with only half a year's showing. By the end of 1988, he was rated No. 4.

A beautifully dispositioned dog who loves children and adults, this Rottweiler is another who brings tremendous pleasure to his family.

NOBLEHAUS

When we left the Noblehaus Kennels in our review of them for

The World of Rottweilers, it was with Patricia and Mark Schwartz expressing hopes and expectations for the future of some of the youngsters at their West Nyack, New York, establishment.

To update this history is to pay tribute to one of these youngsters, now American and Canadian Ch. Noblehaus Explorer, T.T., who is a son of Am., Can. Ch. Birch Hill's Governor ex Ch. Noblehaus Ain't Misbehavin'.

This young dog has become a Best in Specialty Show and Multi-Group winner, Best of Breed at Westminster along the way, and in 1988 became America's No. 1 Rottweiler, in the process of which he defeated more Rottweilers in one year than any Rottweiler in like time in the history of the breed. Julia Uris of Westport, Connecticut, is co-owner of Explorer with the Schwartzes.

Considering the quality of this young dog, and the pedigree standing behind him, we feel very safe in saying that by the time the next new Rottie book comes out, it will be Explorer progeny who will be carrying the banner for this kennel.

NORDIKE

Nordike Rottweilers are owned by Norma Dikeman of Westfield, N.Y., whose introduction to the breed took place at a horse show where a friend had brought her puppy to socialize. Norma was immediately impressed with the appearance of this pup, plus his outgoing attitude towards strangers. At that time, Norma's six kids all were competing in 4-H endeavors, ranging from cattle, horses, chickens, purebred Duroc hogs, and the myriad of things offered in handicrafts. Norma herself was a 4-H leader. That was not her time to pursue a hobby of her own, but she promised herself that Rottweilers would be a project to consider when her turn came.

Being allergic to all of the animals, hay, etc., finally led to Norma developing emphysema. When all the kids grew up and left home, it was obvious that Norma was unable to continue farming, so they sold out and Norma bought a Rottweiler. It was her first, a seven-week-old puppy. This puppy was to become Scharf Elko von Regenbogen, T.T., VB, Am., Can. C.D.X.

At the beginning, Norma had to enlist her husband's aid at obedience classes because this fireball of a puppy was more than her lungs could keep up with. As time went along and she became more adept, the dog became more inclined to want to please her, and she took over the training.

Norma had never expected to be able to go into the ring herself with the dog, her intention having been to do the training and then hire someone to show in both breed and obedience. The first match she attended was such a thrill that she literally giggled all the way home. Watching beginners on lead, she thought "I can do that," so she gathered together her courage and entered. As she says, "I will never forget the feeling of being able to show my own dog. Maybe not in breed—but as it turns out, I can show in breed if there is not much running involved." However, Norma is not always successful in the ring due to feeling out of breath at crucial times. But in obedience, she can show successfully, and absolutely loves doing so, spending five days a week at one class or another, and seven days a week training.

In 1985, the Dikemans acquired their second Rottweiler. Norma was not sure that she could manage the two of them, but this was a bitch who needed a home, and Norma promptly fell in love. Thus Can. Ch. Rodsden's Lindenwood Lamita, T.T., VB, Am., Can. C.D.X., as she was to become, joined the family. She was seven months old at the time, and as Norma Dikeman says, "As you can see, I *was* able to have two dogs. In fact, some of the Canadian points were actually won with me on the other end of the lead."

During this time, the Dikemans formed a therapy group to perform at nursing homes, psychiatric centers, day care centers, and schools. This is as much fun as the shows, and to them, far more rewarding. The dogs love the attention and are unbelievably intelligent about the acceptance of unusual behavior from their audience. Rottweilers love to show off and play tricks on their people, or at least Norma's do; and here is the ideal place to do so without getting into trouble.

It was not the Dikemans' intention to breed, but they had

Top: Canada's No. 1 Rottweiler for 1987: Can. Ch. Rotterre's Bardolph Buckenberg is winning Best in Show at Muskoka District K.C. Owner, J. Jacqueline Stephenson. *Bottom:* Ch. Timberhaven Star Buck taking Best of Breed for the second consecutive year at the Mission Dog Show, B.C., Canada. Owner, Alouette Rottweilers, Pitt Meadows, B.C.

GROUP 3RD
BUTLER COUNTY
KENNEL CLUB INC
KLEIN   MAY 1987

Above: Ch. Powderhorn's Clu of Wencrest owned by Angie Grimalsi and Powderhorn/ Wencrest Rottweilers. *Right:* Can. Ch. Windcastle's Morning Magic, by Ch. Razdy's Akemo Grande, C.D., ex Am., Can. Ch. Gatstuberget's Katarina, T.T. Owners, Carolyn and Bert Kauffmann, Windcastle Rottweilers.

and Deb Conradt, who are going to take care of the showing in the breed ring while Norma handles obedience. At this point they are in the training stages, but it looks as though this will be a very competitive dog indeed. Norma comments on how smart a pup he is and that you can really see him think before doing what he is asked.

Norma Dikeman (as she puts it "to keep me busy and out of trouble") became the Colonial Rottweiler Club's newsletter editor, along with Julie and Sue Grupp, in 1986. It comes out every two months.

At present, Norma is directing her energies towards herding, and they have a Herding Instinct Test scheduled for the near future. She also is a great fan of the American Temperament Test Society and she is a Certified Tester.

NOUVEAU

Nouveau Kennels in Caro, Michigan, came into existence during June, 1986, and is presently comprised of three Rottweilers, two Basset Hounds, and a Smooth Fox Terrier.

Of the Rotties, some familiar names make their homes with the Sosnes. American and Canadian

their first litter of Rottweilers in the summer of 1988. It turned out great. Norma had a beautiful bunch of pups and found terrific homes for them. It also gave her a whole lot more to worry about. Luckily their owners are so conscientious that Norma worries only a *little* about them, now.

In 1989, a second litter was born. There were some splendid homes all lined up for the pups, and Norma kept one for herself this time.

The acquisition of Birch Hill's Checkmate Mikon, a Governor son from his last litter, gave another little "push" to keep away the debilitating aspects of emphysema. This dog has the potential of being a worthy son of his sire. Norma Dikeman co-owns him with Mike

Ch. Carado's Commander Cody, Am., Can. C.D., earned his C.D. both in the United States and Canada in the fall of 1987, and still is shown occasionally, as he loves being in the ring.

Am., Can. Ch. Carado's Satin Classic, known as "Casey," continues in her winning ways. She has been the No. 1 Rottweiler bitch in Canada since 1986. Also in 1986, she was the No. 3 Rottweiler and a multiple Group winner. She was No. 6 Rottie bitch in the United States for 1987, and was in the Top Five of the Breed in Canada for 1988.

The Sosnes' newest addition in Rottweilers is Can. Ch. Carado's Sudden Impact, nicknamed "Crash," who was born in August, 1987 and had attained his Canadian championship at age 11 months. He is now preparing his campaign for American championship.

OBSTGARTEN

Obstgarten Rottweilers are owned by Jerry and Deanna Warkentin who live near the small farming community of Dinuba, California, where they farm 60 acres of deciduous fruit trees.

As it became apparent that even country living was safer with the companionship of a good dog, the Warkentins began raising German

Shepherds for obedience and protection in 1974. Many of their puppies found homes with local fruit growers who needed dependable yard dogs and area guards for their farms and ranches.

Soundness and working ability have always been of major importance to the Warkentins. When they finally met their first Rottweiler it was "love at first sight." After inspecting a number of litters, a puppy bitch was chosen and came to live at the farm. At that time the kennel name "Obstgarten," which means "orchard" or "fruit garden," was added, and the new puppy was named "Tressa," which means "bearing the harvest." A few weeks later, a Ch. Alpha Alexandros G. Roadway son named Ali's Orion von Obstgarten joined Tressa. The original intention was that they would be protection dogs, but a

Left: Antren Rottweilers had a big day at the 1988 Buck County K.C. Show. Antren's Anything Goes takes Best of Winners, handled by Karen Di Cicco. *Below:* Ch. Powderhorn's Xmas of Wencrest, C.D., a multi-Group placer owned by Jody and Peter Mirabella and Powderhorn/ Wencrest Rottweilers, Inc.

Top right: Ch. Blackwood's Bete von Dorow, C.D., T.D., taking Best of Opposite Sex over specials for a major en route to championship Owner-handled by Dave and Ellen Mintura.

Top left: Can. Ch. Rodsden's Abbatab of Stepshire, T.T., the first Rottie owned by J. J. Stephenson and the foundation of the Rotterre Kennels. She is by Am., Can. Ch. Rodsden's Elko Kastenienbaum, C.D.X., T.D., Can. C.D., from Ch. Rodsden's Red Pepper.

chance attendance by the Warkentins at a local dog show set them on a different course.

Tressa eventually produced two fine litters sired by Ch. Rhomarks Axel v. Lerchenfeld, U.D.T. Obstgartens Alexander has at least ten points with a Best of Opposite Sex and a Best of Breed over specials, owner-handled. His younger brother, Obstgartens Bravo v. Axel, is waiting for his turn in the show ring.

Jerry and Deanna believe that "Ori" exemplifies true Rottweiler character. He was trained in obedience, fully protection trained, and shown in conformation all at the same time. He participated in all of these activities with zest and enthusiasm. Because of his smaller size, about 98 pounds, he was never seriously pushed in conformation until it was apparent that he was producing some marvelous puppies. He had won five points with one major in only a few shows at the time of his accidental and untimely death at age five-and-a-half years. His legacy is some outstanding progeny.

The Warkentins' Ori daughter, Best in Specialty Show, Select American and Canadian Ch. Obstgartens Countess Oraya, finished her American and

Canadian championship prior to her second birthday. She was a Select winner at the American Rottweiler Club National Specialty in Oakland, California, in May, 1988, and she was Best of Breed at the American Rottweiler Club Region II Specialty followed by a Group Second in January, 1989. She completed 1988 as the No. 3 bitch in the American Rottweiler Club standings.

Several Axel daughters were also bred to Ori, and the Warkentins' own bitch, Tressa, produced a litter by him prior to his death. Many of these puppies are of excellent promise and will be shown.

"Owning, working and loving these incredible animals is reward in itself," says Deanna, "but the terrific people we have met and the friendships we have formed are as precious as this remarkable handiwork of Mother Nature, the Rottweiler."

PANAMINT

Panamint Rottweilers are among the longest established kennels for the breed in the United States. Barbara Hoard, the founder-owner, acquired her first in 1948.

This was Zada's Zanda, bred by Nancy and Andrew Cooper. He was purchased for Barbara by Noel

Jones, an important pioneer Rottie fancier and handler on the Pacific Coast during the period of the 1940s. A male, Zuke, was also acquired by Barbara from the first litter bred by Noel Jones.

Barbara has been active and consistently in touch with the Rottweiler world over the years, sometimes more so than others, but she has never lost interest in the breed at any time. Dogs have been always, and will continue to be, an important part of Barbara Hoard's life.

Barbara had moved to a different area between my first and my second Rottweiler books, thus I was unable to get in touch with her while working on *The World of Rottweilers*. We tried again with a note for *this* book, and this time, to my delight, it was received. So here we are to tell you what is currently taking place at this famed kennel. Panamint and Barbara Hoard are now in Virginia Beach, Virginia, where Panamint is jointly owned by Barbara Hoard and David Gallo, M.D.

Dr. Gallo made Barbara an offer to enter into this arrangement, bringing herself and the dogs to Virginia, which she accepted. At this point, Dr. and Mrs. Gallo are deciding on whether or not they wish to advance in the dog fancy or just enjoy the Rotties in a more leisurely manner.

Recently, Barbara lost two of her older Rotties, which is always a heartbreak, but she does still have some of her own Panamint stock and is planning to breed one of her younger homebreds.

Both Dr. and Mrs. Gallo and Barbara herself are awed at the thought of having an 11th generation of Panamint home-breds in their midst. The Gallos have some outstanding representatives of most prestigious bloodlines. One cannot help but contemplate the quality brought together by the merging of the original Panamint with Dr. Gallo's splendid dogs.

Barbara is an outstanding judge who loves her work and is constantly in demand for assignments. She will have the opportunity of accepting these assignments more frequently in the future, something to which she looks forward.

PANZERN

Panzern Rottweilers are located in the rural community of Stephenville, Texas, where they are doing their share to create good public relations for the breed. Prior to 1984, this area could boast only one Rottie. But in the spring

Bottom right: **Two of Mike and Suzanne Sosne's handsome Rotties winning Best of Breed and Best Puppy in Breed in Canada in 1988: Am., Can. Ch. Carada's Satin Classic and Can. Ch. Carada's Sudden Impact. Nouveau Kennels.**
Bottom left: **Catalina von Dorow, age 16 months, Medallion R.C. Grand Prize Futurity Winner, 1988. By Am., Can. Ch. Rodsden's Berte v. Zederwald, C.D.X., from Ch. Merrymoore's Imp von Dorow. Owned by Bob and Anne Simulcik.**

of that year, Pansy Roberts and Sharon Wood, a mother-daughter team, began their initial attempts to research the Rottweiler. What began as the nucleus of an idea, the purchasing of one sound bitch companion for home protection, has since developed into a dual home kennel operation. Pansy and Sharon have built extensions onto their homes, specially designed Rottie rooms, in order to raise their Rottweilers in a family environment. Education was the name of the game during those first 18 months. Every Rottweiler book available found its way to the shelves of Pansy and Sharon's library. With the determination to breed responsibly, the search began for a stud dog for Gretchen Mein Liebe, C.D., whom they had selected as foundation bitch. The search ended when Am., Can. Ch. Rodsdens Berte v. Zederwald, C.D.X., owned by Lew Olson, moved to Texas.

While looking at the progeny of Berte, the mother-daughter duo fell in love with a four-month-old puppy named "Beau," who was by Berte from Ch. Excalibur's B Apache War Song, C.D. They subsequently purchased the youngster and innocently assumed the task of show conformation training. One week later Beau had

earned Best Puppy in Sweepstakes at an Abilene, Texas, fun match and "the bug had bitten."

Beau, officially American Kennel Club and States Kennel Club Ch. Apache Hill's Make My Day, C.D., finished his A.K.C. championship at 12 months of age, compiling three majors and a Best of Breed from the Puppy Classes. He acquired his Companion Dog degree in three consecutive trials, going from breed conformation ring to obedience ring and back to the Group ring with great aplomb. In 1987, Beau brought home 35 Bests of Breed and 17 Group placements, including four Group Ones. As the youngest dog in the Top Ten, Beau ranked fourth in the Routledge System and fifth in the American Rottweiler Club System. In 1988, he officially added the States Kennel Club Rottweiler Champion of this recently formed organization.

Meanwhile, the "A" litter of December, 1986, (Gretchen Mien Liebe, C.D., and Ch. Rodsdens Berte v. Zederwald, C.D.X.) was making itself known. Passing their second birthday, six of the eight were x-rayed and issued O.F.A. numbers. One of the eight littermates is presently a "support dog" for a nonambulatory young woman. A second has begun

Schutzhund training. Four are being successfully shown in the conformation ring with class wins.

Panzern's Ayla Mein Geschenk, owned by Panzern Rottweilers, has earned Winners Bitch, Best of Winners, and Best of Opposite Sex several times while gaining two majors and ten points. Panzern's Arri Oil Patch Blu, owner-handled by Clara Coker of Briaroaks Rottweilers, has achieved nine points with one major and twice Best of Breed over specials.

The "B" litter arrived in January, 1988, (Berte and Gretchen again as the parents), consisting of one male and one female puppy. Following the example of her older brothers and sisters, Panzern's Bell of Arcosanti (with 14 entries in the Puppy Classes) acquired 12 blue ribbons, one Reserve Winners, one Winners Bitch award, a Best of Winners, and a Best of Opposite Sex, all owner-handled.

Placing emphasis on working ability and temperament as well as conformation, Pansy Roberts and Sharon Wood have continued with obedience, Schutzhund, and public education appearances. Their Rottweilers perform demonstrations for the public schools and Girl Scouts, with information about the breed being distributed through these appearances and television

Gamegard's Femme Fatale, by Srigo's Loaded For Bear, C.D., taking Winners Bitch for a major under judge Mrs. Muriel Freeman in 1988. Owned by Srigo Rottweilers, East Brunswick, NJ.

Foxy's Castaspell, C.D., by Ch. Pandemonium's Ciastus, C.D.X., T.T., ex Ch. Fraulein Gretchen von Fox, C.D., T.T. This is the third generation of Fox Rottweilers. Owners, Maria, Marvin and Beth S. Fox, Philadelphia, PA.

interviews (Station KNCT, Killeen, Texas). Their plans for the future include an upcoming "C" litter and the training of their recently imported German puppy bitch, Cleo v. Der Schoppenheide (Arras vom Hertner Wappen ex Gina vom Anselhof).

PEPPERHAUS

Pepperhaus Rottweilers are owned by Sandy Peppers Phillips and are located in Fallon, Nevada. Sandy has had a lifetime interest in dogs, dating as far back as 1969 when she, at the age of 13, trained and titled her first dog, a Boxer. The interest in training grew and several different breeds followed,

but it was in 1980 that she had the good fortune to meet Rita Welker, owner of Welkerhauser Kennels. From that day on, the Rottweiler became first breed in Sandy's heart.

In July, 1981, Sandy purchased from Rita her first Rottweiler, a grandson of Welkerhaus Rommel, U.D., out of Gibson's Welkerhaus Hulk, C.D.X., ex Ch. Welkerhaus Anna von Rommel, C.D. The puppy became Welkerhaus Early Edition, U.D., who trained Sandy in the ways of Rottweilers. They became a team. He was, and still is, quite the show dog who loves crowds and applause. He averaged 195–198 throughout his career, and in 1986, No. 1 American Rottweiler Club Open Dog, No. 2 in the Schuman System, and No. 5 in the Delany System. In 1986, he was in the Top Ten American Rottweiler Club Open Dog, and No. 4 in the Schuman System. Now retired, he plays with his owners' four kids and keeps an eye on Sandy as she trains other dogs—making sure, no doubt, that she is remembering his lessons.

In 1982, Sandy purchased a bitch puppy from Barbara Dellinger. This one was out of Ch. Welkerhaus Boaz von Barken, C.D., and Gretchen vom Schwitzgebel, who was to become Barkens Welkerhaus Star, C.D.X. A steady worker, Star obtained her titles easily but preferred staying home watching TV with the kids rather than attending dog shows. Star was bred in 1985 to Am., Can. Ch. Arenenberg Astro Warrior, SchH. II, FH, C.D., T.D. This breeding produced only three puppies, one of which died at three months. The surviving two went on to become Pepperhaus Arco von Warstar, C.D.X., T.D.X., and Pepperhaus A-Turbo von Warstar, C.D.X., T.D.X. Turbo currently is working towards his U.D. title with owner Virginia Bordwell of Astoria, Oregon. Virginia has taught Turbo an array of tricks, including balancing balls on his nose and clearing off the table after lunch.

Arco, owned by the Phillips

family themselves, is pointed and needs one leg to complete U.D. Degree. He has been featured on Portland, Oregon's "TV 6 News" in a special "Can Guard Dogs Be Family Dogs?" presentation. He was High in Trail at the American Rottweiler Club Region Specialty. He is the American Rottweiler Club No. 1 Novice Dog and No. 5 in the Delany System. He loves kids and accompanies Sandy to school, where he helps teach responsible pet dog ownership.

Star was again bred to Warrior in 1986, producing four puppies: Pepperhaus Black Brat, Pepperhaus Batlstar Jeunstd, C.D., owned by Nick Phillips; Pepperhaus Best Ace, C.D., H.I.C., owned by Lynn Heimbuch of Eatonville, Washington; and Pepperhaus Black Guy, C.D., H.I.C., owned by Sheryl Fuller of Reno, Nevada.

In 1985, Pepperhaus purchased Am., Can. Ch. Fraulein Anka von Ascothaus, Can. U.D., from Bill and Jennifer Rhodes. Anka is by Ch. Trollegens Frodo, C.D., from Ch. Gamecards Ninette. In 1986, she completed her American U.D. in four shows, always in the ribbons, making the 1986 American Rottweiler Club Top Ten Open and Utility Dog. She earned her T.D. in one try that same year.

In 1987, Anka was bred again to Am., Can. Ch. Arenenberg Astro Warrior, SchH. II, FH, C.D., T.D., producing four puppies. One of these, a fine working bitch named Pepperhaus Country Cache, C.D., T.D., is owned by Dave and Ellen Minturn of Los Alamos, New Mexico.

Anka is the dam of two American-Canadian champions and several obedience-titled offspring. Over ten years old, she is still going strong, winning the Veterans Class at the 1989 American Rottweiler Club National Specialty with a score of 191. She is a popular therapy dog, too, visiting the local convalescent center and schools on a regular basis.

Langhoffens Essem, by Ch. Alpha Alexandros G. Roadway ex Langhoffens Camber, C.D.X., T.D., came to Pepperhaus under a co-ownership between Steinford, her breeder, and Sandy Peppers Phillips. Esse has a super working temperament and earned her C.D. in five showings. She placed first or second each day and is always High Scoring Rottie and Working Group dog. She is currently in training for her U.D., T.D., and SchH. I. She is also a registered therapy dog with a bag full of tricks!

The newest additions at Pepperhaus are two very promising bitch puppies, one from breeder Pat Storer and one from breeder Joann Harnish.

Ch. Kostlich Beretta von Ursa, handled by Lee Ann Stagg under judge Mrs. Bernard Freeman for owner Paul Roy Girouard. Bred by Kostlich-Von Ursa Rottweilers, Rebecca L. Chriscoe, Micanopy, FL.

Since 1984, when Sandy put a C.D. on her first Rottweiler, she has put 14 obedience titles on eight Rotties. Her dogs have been in the Top Ten Obedience Rottweilers (all systems) for several years.

History in the making: Radio Ranch's Ch. Arri von der Hembackbruckem, SchH. III, F.H., a multi-Specialty winner, taking Winners Dog under Barbara Hoard Dillon, handled by Joe Hedl for Radio Ranch.

Sandy has been a member of the American Rottweiler Club since 1981. She is training director of *Good Dog Obedience School*, and president and editor for Sierra Rottweiler Owners. A member of the Willamette Rottweiler Club, Northwest Rottweiler Fanciers, and Schutzhund U.S.A., she is also Churchill County's 4-H Dog Club Leader, working with 25 kids on responsible pet ownership, showing and therapy dog work. Sandy and her husband Nick hope to start a Schutzhund club in the Reno area in the future.

PIONEER

Pioneer Rottweilers in Hollis, New Hampshire, are owned by Virginia Aceti and Sheryl Hedrick. In 1978, after 18 years of breeding Welsh ponies and exhibiting show hunters and three-day event horses, they acquired their first Rottweiler, a 12-week-old daughter of famed Am., Can. Ch. Donnaj Vermont Yankee of Paulus, C.D.X.

As recalled from our previous book, *The World of Rottweilers*, this bitch grew up to become Ch. Robil Marta von Donnaj, the foundation bitch at Pioneer Kennels, who produced five A.K.C. champions and seven obedience-titled offspring. She was the *Kennel Review* System Top Producing Rottweiler Dam in 1984, and is a member of the Medallion Rottweiler Club Honor Roll.

Known as "Brick," this bitch has to her credit the very significant accomplishment of having produced Ch. Pioneer's Beguiled, sired by Ch. Graudstark's Luger, C.D., T.T., the first Rottweiler bitch as well as the breeder/owner-handled Rottweiler of either sex to achieve Best in Show honors in all-breed competition. In limited showing as a special during only two years of competition, she attained 47 Bests of Opposite Sex, 17 Bests of Breed, three Working Group first prizes, two Group seconds, a Group fourth, and a Best in Show.

Her other wins of particular importance include Best of Opposite Sex at the A.K.C. Centennial Show in 1984 and Best of Opposite Sex at the 1985 American Rottweiler Club Region III Specialty. Her dam was also at the latter event, winner of the Veterans Class and of the Brood Bitch Class with Beguiled and another daughter as her progeny.

Like her dam, Beguiled is a member of the Medallion Rottweiler Club Hall of Fame. She was ranked nationally No. 7 bitch in 1984 and 1985 and was the only bitch ranked in the top 20 American Rottweiler Club Group System for 1984.

Beguiled is the dam of two Specialty-winning champion daughters, both sired by Ch. Birch Hill's Governor, C.D. One of these, Ch. Pioneer's Image of Evrmor, C.D., co-owned by Janna Morgan and Sheryl Hedrick, went Winners Bitch at the 1987 Colonial Rottweiler Club Specialty, handled by her breeder Sheryl Hedrick. She finished her championship with three majors including a Best of Opposite Sex over specials; and the other, Ch. Pioneer's Ingar von Krahn, co-owned with Christine Senter, finished with prestigious wins including Winners Bitch at the Colonial Rottweiler Club Supported Trenton Kennel Club event over 70 class bitches.

Beguiled's last and final litter, sired by the Dutch import Ch. Nelson v. Brabantpark has allowed her to retire to "queen of the household" at Pioneer.

A highlight for Pioneer Kennels was the selection of Beguiled and her half-sister Bedazzled to represent the breed in the official A.K.C. video on Rottweilers.

Beguiled's litter brother, Ch. Brash Baer von Pioneer, C.D., co-owned with Kathy Galotti, is a multiple Best of Breed winner, Group placer, and is making his mark as a producer. In just six litters, his progeny include four champions, six Specialty winners, and three other pointed offspring.

The other Brick daughter living at Pioneer is Ch. Pioneer's Das Bedazzled, C.D., sired by Am., Can. Ch. Bronco vom Rauberfeld, SchH. III, FH, who became a champion in just 11 shows, breeder/owner-handled by Sheryl Hedrick. She, too, has done especially well in outstanding competition. Her successes include Winners Bitch at the 1985 American Rottweiler Club National Specialty from the Bred-by-Exhibitor Class at age 18 months, Winners Bitch, Best of Winners, and Best of Opposite Sex over leading specials for a five-point major at the Colonial

Rottweiler Club Supported Ladies Dog Club event.

Bedazzled's first litter by Am., Can. Ch. Marksman von Turick, C.D., produced Bda. Ch. Pioneer's Jasmin and Am., Col. Ch. Pioneer's Jared of Legend, who finished with Best of Winners at the American Rottweiler Club Region I Specialty, owner-handled by Lee Whittier. He now belongs to Juan Andres and Inga Jaramillo of Medallin, Colombia, and is working towards his International championship.

Bedazzled's second litter was sired by Ch. Noblehaus Beretta. This litter included Ch. Pioneer's Maverick, who finished breeder/owner-handled by Sheryl with four majors, and is the first of their homebred dogs to be retained at Pioneer as a stud dog.

Ch. Southwinds Oden of True Lee winning the Working Group at just over 11 months age, handled by Darrell Hayes for owner Zoila Truesdale.

179

Ch. Srigo's Eagle All Over, by Ch. Eiko v. Schwaiger Wappen ex Ch. Srigo's Heart of Gold. He is the sire of Ch. Windyknobs Mein Ulrica and Ch. Amelia Erhardt. Ms. Felicia E.H. Luberich, Srigo Rottweilers.

Another promising dog from the "M" litter is Pioneer's Miko v. Graz, C.D., co-owned with Jim and Bobbie Boyce, who earned his C.D. at age 11 months, then at 14 months won Best of Breed from the American-bred Class, owner-handled by Jim, over an entry which included five specials. Miko is now working towards his C.D.X. and will be returning to the breed ring now that he is over two years old and more mature.

A litter sister to Miko, Pioneer's Mystique, owned by Richard and Robin Roncoroni, is another off to a good start in Puppy Classes and will be shown seriously along with three other handsome bitches from this same litter.

The third champion bitch currently in residence at Pioneer is Ch. Pioneer's 'Gainst All Odds,

by Ch. Noblehaus Beretta from Pioneer's X-Rated Annie, C.D., co-bred by Cheryl Corbett and Sheryl Hedrick. This was a recovered "parvo puppy" who went along purely for the ride to the 1986 Colonial Specialty—her very first show—where she wound up Best of Opposite Sex to Best in Sweepstakes at a mere 14 months. Breeder/owner-handled to her championship by Sheryl, "Urchin" finished with three majors including one for five points at the Colonial Supported Ladies Dog Club show.

Pioneer's Gretchen v. Beretta, C.D.X., T.D., co-owned with Philip and Emilie Shipman; Pioneer's Native Son, owned by Dr. Gerard De Leo; and some 11-month-old puppies from Ch. Pioneer's Ingar von Krahn by a little-known Dutch import—Int. Ch. Ruben, BHP 1, WS 1988 (Peru)—are all "young hopefuls" who show great promise for carrying on the Pioneer tradition.

In total, Pioneer Rottweilers have bred ten A.K.C. champions, one Bermuda champion, 11 obedience title holders, and six Specialty winners, all but one of which have been breeder/owner-handled. Sheryl is now a professional handler.

There are no kennels at Pioneer; all of the dogs live in the house and are part of Virginia and Sheryl's daily lives. All puppies are whelped and raised in the home, well socialized, and Temperament Tested. Prospective owners are interviewed at length to assure placement into the proper family environment for each puppy.

POWDERHORN/WENCREST

Powderhorn/Wencrest Rottweilers, Inc., is owned by Mrs. Clara Hurley and Michael S. Grossman, aficionados of the breed since 1966. As the history of Powderhorn/Wencrest has been covered in *The World of Rottweilers*, the following is a summary of their activities since 1985.

In 1982 in Bad Dyenhausen, Germany, Mrs. Hurley had been

elected as the second president of the International Federation of Rottweiler Friends. Her duties encompassed the presentation of the Sixth Conference of the Federation, held for the first time in the United States in 1985. The I.F.R., born in 1968 in Essen, lectures related to the breeding, training, raising, problems, solutions, and testing of our Rottweilers. This 1985 conference was a tremendous success with delegates and friends from at least ten countries assembled. The conference was held in Valley

Noblehaus Hi-Voltage v. Antron taking First in 6–9 Month Puppy Bitch Class, Bucks County K.C., May, 1988. Owner-handled by Karen DiCicco for Antren Rottweilers.

Germany, is an organization for the avowed purpose of having a tri-annual meeting of delegates from each country in the world, with a sizable Rottweiler population.

Delegates and interested breed observers from all over the world attend these meetings to listen to

Forge, Pennsylvania. In addition to the lectures and official meeting mid-week, the weekend prior to the opening provided the opportunity for visitors to attend the Colonial Rottweiler Club Specialty and the weekend following, the American Rottweiler Club's (host club to the conference) National Specialty.

Within the kennel things have been active and busy too. The present sire of eminence is Ch. Nelson v.h. Brabantpark, imported from Holland and closely related to the great sires of the past—Ch. Oscar v.h. Brabantpark, Ch. Quanto of Brabantpark, and Ch. Donar v.d. Hoeve Cor Unum, C.D. Nelson arrived at Powderhorn/Wencrest in December, 1987, finished his championship with alacrity, was a Top Ten Rottweiler in 1988, and is his owners' second Best in Show. Nelson has two Bests in Show, is a multi-Group winner, American Rottweiler Club Specialty winner and was the No. 1 Rottweiler in the country for 1989.

Another outstanding Brabantpark male, Hans v.h. Brabantpark, came to Powderhorn/Wencrest in 1986. Hans also finished his championship quickly, was a Top Ten Rottweiler in 1987, and a multi-Group placer in addition to helping his owners maintain the bloodlines which over the years have worked so well for them.

A 1985 import from Germany, Mirko v. Sofienbusch; Powderhorn's Fido of Wencrest (an Oscar son); Ch. Powderhorn Kapt of Wencrest, C.D., T.T. (a Quanto son); and Ch. Powderhorn's Xmas of Wencrest, C.D. (a Donar son) have all been important assets to the Powderhorn/Wencrest stud group.

In April, 1985, the bitch Stromhall Nayah arrived at Powderhorn/Wencrest from Australia. Nayah is a granddaughter of the first American Rottweiler exported to Australia, Powderhorn's Fetz of Wencrest (an Oscar son). The importation of this lovely bitch gave Powderhorn/Wencrest the opportunity not only to continue its linebreeding, but also to incorporate a very strong Australian line into the program.

A Dutch bitch, Lada v.h. Land v. Sittard, came in 1986 in co-ownership to Anita Owen and Powderhorn/Wencrest. Lada became a champion with ease and also earned her C.D. degree. As a Quanto granddaughter, she is enabling her owners to continue their linebreeding program without its becoming too tight. Powderhorn's Gewl of Wencrest, Powderhorn's Que of Wencrest, Powderhorn's Wyve of Wencrest; and Powderhorn's Yola of Wencrest were also added as brood bitches.

Powderhorn/Wencrest remains firmly committed to the use of only O.F.A.-certified sires and dams. Mrs. Hurley's Powderhorn Press continues to seek out titles in other languages for translation and publication for the English-speaking Rottweiler fanciers.

POWSELL

Powsell Rottweilers are owned by Deborah Moneque in Lake Worth, Florida. The kennel started originally in 1968 with Shetland Sheepdogs, the name having been derived from her husband's name *Pow*ell and her son's name Rus*sell*. Powell saw Ch. Rodsden's Kato v. Donnaj, C.D., and it was he who caused that gentleman to fall in love with the Rottie breed.

A lot of time went into the search for a top-quality show male, as it seemed almost impossible to find

Can. Ch. Janlynn's Quasar taking a Group placement at Chataqua Canine Club in 1988. Owned by Mr. and Mrs. D.G. Flury, Saskatoon, Canada.

what they wanted. Then the decision was reached to purchase Can. Ch. Northwind's Helga in 1975 and to attempt to breed that dog they so wanted. Helga was co-owned by the Moneques and Jan Marshall, a distinguished lady of the Rottweiler world who turns out to be Deborah's aunt!

Jan helped to set the breeding standard for Powsell. The Powsell lines were established on Kato and Am., Can. Ch. Donnaj Vermont Yankee of Paulus, C.D.X. They really worked hard for soundness and good movement with strong toplines. The Moneques wanted good type and good temperament.

Helga finished her American championship after only seven times in the ring. She also went Best of Breed twice from the classes. She was handled to her title by her owner, Powell Moneque.

Helga provided Powsell's foundation, and, bred to Yankee, the established goals were reached quickly. Helga produced champions with two Best in Show winners in one litter. The latter were Ch. Donnaj Green Mountain Boy and Int., Best in Show, Am., Can., Bda. Ch. Powsell's Song of Deborah. Green Mountain Boy acquired 300 Bests of Breed, 100 Group placings, and was No. 1 Rottweiler in 1982 and 1983.

In the early days, the Moneques travelled to the shows as a family in a motor home. Then their daughter Michelle arrived and they went to the New England circuit and to Canada, which started the new family on their interesting travels. At the time, they had no idea that they would become so caught up in showing, even to the extent of taking on foreign countries.

Powsell's Dorca, a Yankee daughter, was added to the family, along with several other lovely and correctly bred bitches. They will be stand-bys for when the original foundation bitch is ready for retirement.

Daughter Michelle, meanwhile, is going into dogs and is proving to

be a very adept junior handler. She finished her first champion at only nine years of age.

RADIO RANCH

Radio Ranch Rottweilers were established in 1969 by Pamela Crump Brown (who then was Pamela Weller) in Chesapeake, Virginia, with a simple goal in mind—to breed the best possible Rottweilers, using the best bloodlines available and a willingness to spend money and time necessary to meet these goals.

Pamela's first purchase was a three-year-old male, Zander of Rafter, who was an outstanding dog who finished his championship undefeated.

Next came two more foundation dogs: a male puppy, Rodsden's Nomad; and a two-year-old female, Ch. Kuhlwald's Tara of Ronlyn. Nomad received both majors from the Puppy Class and finished his championship at age 19 months. Tara finished undefeated, an especially remarkable feat considering she had whelped a litter of pups seven weeks earlier.

Tara unfortunately produced only nine live puppies during her lifetime. However, these pups made quite an impact on the breed. The most famous of them were Ch. Radio Ranch's Annamingle (a top

Black Orpheus von Dorow, age 13 months, by Am., Can. Ch. Rodsden's Berte v. Zederwald, C.D.X., from Merrymoore's Imp von Dorow. A handsome young homebred owned by Nancy C. Estes, Von Dorow Rottweilers, Midland, TX.

winner and a top producer); Ch. Radio Ranch's Kilroy Is Here!; Ch. Radio Ranch's Karma; Ch. Radio Ranch's Kari On (a Top Producer); Radio Ranch's Afra v. Notara (Top Producer and a foundation bitch for Concord Kennels), and Tara's most famous offspring of them all, the incomparable Ch. Radio Ranch's Axel v. Notara, who made a tremendous contribution to the breed.

Axel, I am proud to say, was the "cover dog" on my first book about Rotties, *The Book of the Rottweiler*. He was a top winner for two years (his successes included Best of Breed at Westminster and Maryland Kennel Clubs, the latter under German judge and breed warden Willi Faussner).

The most important contribution to the breed made by Axel was that of Top Producer. As the sire of more than 50 champions, he is the All-Time Top Producer in the history of the breed, an especially notable fact since Axel was only bred to an average of four bitches a year! Today Radio Ranch uses several Axel sons, daughters and grandchildren in their breeding program.

Other important dogs in Radio Ranch's current breeding program include the German import, Ch. Arri von der Hembachbruche, SchH. III, FH. Arri earned the Korüng in Germany, which is the highest breed survey—it is passed by only a few Rotties. He was, as well, SchH. III 13 times, and always rated outstanding in courage.

Arri finished his championship by winning two Specialties, including the American Rottweiler Club event, where he was the first dog in their history to go over all the male champions from the classes (the entry for this Specialty was 300). Arri is a full brother to International Ch. Dingo vom Schwaiger Wappen, SchH. III, the second most titled Rottweiler in his time. Arri is also making his mark on the breed as a top producer.

There is also International Ch. Amon vom Filmtick, SchH. III, I.P.O. III, FH III, Austrian Sieger and Austrian Youth Sieger; Kimbo vom Siedlerpfad, SchH. I, German import, a Specialty winner; Alf vom Harderwald, SchH. III, German import; and Ch. Radio Ranch's Timochen.

Radio Ranch plans to continue breeding a few select litters each year and selling some puppies to those who appreciate the time and effort that goes into breeding quality animals. The present owners at Radio Ranch are Pamela Crump Brown and Jennifer Hughes.

RAINHART

Rainhart Rottweilers are owned

Ch. Radio Ranch's Timochen, taking points towards title at North Shore K.C. 1984. Owned by Radio Ranch Rottweilers, Chesapeake, VA.

by Diane Johnston in Greenbank, Washington. Ms. Johnston has bred, owned, and shown numerous handsome Rotties.

REED'S ROTTWEILERS/VON LUKEGAROO

Von Lukegaroo is the identification which Betty and John N. Reed of Black Forest, Colorado, use for their Rotties, which are dearly loved as well as proudly owned.

Betty tells us that their first important wins were made in 1988 with a handsome male which actually started life as a "bottle baby," raised on a formula which Betty and her veterinarian concocted. He was three days old when Betty realized that it would be her job to get him off to a good start in life. Now as a strapping mature dog, he is stepping into the Winners Circle with points and a Specialty Reserve Winners to his credit. Just think of the added pleasure it must give her to watch this splendid young dog start his show career with the realization that, had it not been for her care and diligence, this might not have happened.

This dog is Duke von Lukegaroo, by Duke Wylie ex Marta von Kreigerhof, and his Specialty Reserve award came at the American Rottweiler Club 1988 Region VI Annual event.

"Lukey," as he is known to his friends, is also meeting with success as a sire through a daughter named "Tosca." She has a number of good wins in puppy competition and now that she is moving into American-bred has yet to be defeated.

Although they conduct only a limited breeding program, the Reeds endeavor to breed only sound and excellent dogs. All show prospect puppies are fully guaranteed in writing. A bonus is offered by the breeders in the form of a rebate on the original price to new owners gaining either American Rottweiler Club and/or foreign titles on show prospect dogs purchased at this kennel. This

is an excellent way to ascertain the likelihood of showing what the breeder has hoped to see finish! Pet-quality puppies are guaranteed for health and hips, then sold with a spay or neuter clause in the contract.

Betty Reed comments on the deep respect with which she and her husband regard Rottweilers, and adds that she hopes one day their small kennel will become well known for its dedication to this wonderful breed.

RICE

Donna and Karl Rice of Longview, Texas, purchased their first Rottweiler during the early 1980s from Denise Cribbins. A most handsome bitch who grew up to become Am., Can. Ch. Gipfel's Bourbon Breeze, C.D.X., Am., Can. C.D. Breeze is a daughter of Int., Am. Ch. Van Tieleman's Cisco, C.D., and of Gatstuberget's Hexa, C.D.

Windcastle's Special Blend, sired by B.I.S., Select, Ch. Goldeich's Ara von Brader, C.D., ex Am., Can. Ch. Gatstuberget's Katrina, T.T., winning the 9–12 Months Sweepstakes Class at the 19th Annual G.S.R.C. Specialty under judge Jan Marshall. Owners, Carolyn and Bert Kaufmann.

Above: Antren's All That Jazz gained third leg on C.D. with score of 192.5. Karen DiCicco, owner-handler.
Below: Ch. Von Bruka Nadia, U.D., gaining points towards her title at Holyoke K.C. in 1987. Owned by Von Bruka Rottweilers.

Above: The great Ch. Eiko vom Schwaiger Wappen, C.D.X., SchH. III, Gold Sire. Owner-handled by Bruce Billings, Von Bruka Rottweilers, Needham, MA.
Below: Gambl'r Pitboss von Helken, age 11 months, handled by Chris Hellmann, age 10 years.

Top: Ch. Lindenwood's Blixen, T.T., was bred by Bill and Linda Michels. Lindenwood Rottweilers, Whitemore Lake, MI. Photo by John Ashbey. *Bottom:* Ch. Rodsden's Helsa v. Eberlem, U.D., foundation bitch at Doroh Rottweilers®. Owner-trained by John and Carol Epperly. Helsa won *Dog World* award for earning C.D., C.D.X., and U.D. degrees in less than 9-months time, at age 20 months. Handler, D. Wade.

When it came time to breed Breeze, the Rices elected to send her to the great Int., Am. Ch. Mirko vom Steinkopf, C.D.X., SchH. III, I.P.O. III, FH, Registered Therapy Dog. A wise choice, indeed, for this litter produced Ch. Bourbon's Anvil von Mirko, C.D., Registered Therapy Dog, who has brought tremendous pleasure to his owners.

ROCK-SOLID

Rock-Solid Rottweilers are owned by Barbara Kiefer of Baldwin Park, California, and are headed by the well known and widely admired obedience "star" Way-Mar's Rocky Raccoon, U.D., T.T.

Rocky is a son of Ch. Roger's Summer Thunder ex Ch. and OTCh. Way-Mar's Disco Dawg.

Rocky's obedience accomplishments include eight times High in Trial, each one from advanced classes. Currently he has 42 obedience trial championship points, and will soon, like his dam, be sporting this title, too. In 1985, Rocky was No. 4 Novice Dog among all-breeds in northern California. In 1987, he was No. 3 Open Dog among all breeds in southern California. A true ambassador of good will for his breed, Rocky has

an outgoing personality and quickly makes friends with all people he meets.

Although she has concentrated mainly on obedience work, Barbara *does* have conformation points on Rocky.

The next litter at Rock-Solid Rottweilers is from Barbara Kiefer's bitch Bog Oaks Affirmative Action (Int. Ch. Santo vom Schwaiger Wappen, SchH. III, ex Ch. High Class v. Brenna). These puppies should be highlighted with excellent workability and temperament.

ROMA ROTTS

The owners of the Roma Rottweilers, Gary and Roberta Martin of Chico, California, became interested in the breed during 1980 when they wanted a dog that had intelligence, a desire to work, and a protective nature towards its family. In other words, the ideal breed for them was the Rottweiler.

It was not until 1983 that they acquired their first Rottie, and were lucky in that choice, as he became Am., Can. Ch. Roberta's Buddy De Pattiz, Am. C.D.X., T.D., and Can. C.D.X. Buddy finished his championship from the American-bred Class with three majors. While being shown in conformation, he also attained his Companion Dog degree and the Tracking Dog title the first time out. In both the C.D. and C.D.X. work he consistently scored in the 190s with numerous placements. Buddy is now busy working towards the T.D.X., U.D., and Schutzhund titles.

The Martins also have at their home Nacht Music von Siegerhaus, Am., Can. C.D. She is a daughter of Am., Can. Ch. Trollegen's Frodo, C.D. (American Rottweiler Club Gold Sire), by Ch. Kyna vom Odenwald, C.D. (American Rottweiler Club Silver Dam). "Raven," as she is known, came to the Martins when she was three years old.

Raven had been bred by her co-owners (with the Martins), Thom

Am., Col. Ch. Pioneer's Jared v. Legend finishing his championship with Best of Winners at the A.R.C. Regional Specialty in 1987. Owners, Juan Andres and Inga Jaramille, Medallion, Colombia, South America.

BEST OF
WINNERS
NORTH SHORE
KENNEL CLUB
NOVEMBER
1988
JOHN ASHBEY

Epic's Deidre Dahl, C.D., T.T., T.D.I (Therapy Dog International, Certified), owned by Ed and Ellen Somerford.

and Carol Woodward (Von Siegerhaus Rottweilers), to Am., Can., Mex. Ch. Quick von Siegerhaus, Z.T.P.R., American Rottweiler Club T.T. From the litter, the Martins kept a female who is now Am., Can. Ch. Roma's Ultra von Siegerhaus, C.D.

Ultra finished her American championship at age 26 months. She was owner-handled to all of her titles, and is now concentrating on her working for the near future. Her first litter was born in January, 1989. This was a very special and exciting litter as she was bred to Ch. Best in Show Int., Am. Ch. Mirko vom Steinkopf, SchH. III, FH, I.P.O. III, C.D.X., Registered Therapy Dog, American Rottweiler Club Producer of Merit,

owned by Mr. and Mrs. Richard Wayburn (Waxel Rottweilers in South Carolina). From this Mirko-Ultra litter, the Martins kept two dog puppies, Roma's Ultra Adtude A'justr and Roma's Ultimate TNT v. Mirko.

ROXER

Roxer Boxers in Kingston, Illinois, are owned by Ann and Bill Scholl. Ann originally was a Boxer exhibitor, and her husband wanted "his" dog. He had been impressed by a Rottie bitch, Ch. Rodsden's Lady Luck, C.D., owned by the Voorhes family. So the Scholls ended up with a Rottweiler of their own, Ellsbeth von Scholl, C.D., whom they bred to Am., Can. Ch. Rodsden's Vinegar Joe, C.D.X.,

Can. Ch. Roma Star von Stolzenfels, owned by Jan and Danny Bougton. Bred by Jack Ellman, Augusta, MI.

When the time came that the Scholls decided to add a male to their household, they felt quite fortunate in being able to have the help of June and Ray Severs (Jayarr Rottweilers) and Beverlee and Marvin Smith (Weissenburg Rottweilers). They are most happy to have Ch. Weissenburg's Lucifer v. Roxer, who took points the first time shown and completed title when he was two years of age with three majors. Only one week after finishing his championship, Lucifer won the Group at Park Shore Kennel Club, and currently he is working on earning his C.D. and on cart pulling. The Scholls take enormous pride in the fact that Lucifer is a son of Ch. Mirko vom Steinkopf, SchH. III, I.P.O., FH, C.D.X., T.D., Therapy Dog.

SRIGO

Srigo Rottweilers, owned by Ms. Felicia E.H. Luberich, in East Brunswick, New Jersey, have been a hallmark for quality in the breed since the late 1940s. Champion after champion has been raised here. Rottweilers bearing this identification are among the best known in the world. Felicia is a respected breeder known for good dogs and high quality both in her homebreds and in her imports. We salute her as a true dog lady who thoroughly understands quality and sportsmanship.

We have told the Srigo story in detail in both *The Book of the Rottweiler* and *The World of Rottweilers*, and will now bring our readers up to date on what has been taking place with Srigo and Felicia.

Until recently, Felicia was in the same old kennel help situation which seems to plague all of us who own multiple dogs. Any kind of help is extremely difficult to find. Luckily, Felicia now has two excellent helpers and she hopes to get out to more shows.

The wonderful "Bronco," Am., Can., Int. Ch. Bronco v. Rauberfeld, SchH. III, FH, passed on in January, 1989. He left about a dozen champions in the United

T.D., owned by June and Ray Severs. Today, only Rottweilers reside at Roxer Kennels, as Ann quickly grew to love this breed best of all.

A bitch was kept from the first litter, and it is she who became Ch. Roxer's Rhiannon, C.D., continuing to take Winners Bitch at the 1986 Medallion Rottweiler Club Specialty. En route to her obedience degree, Rhia was High Scoring Rottweiler at Kishwaukee Kennel Club in 1987. Rhia's pedigree includes the bitch who first impressed Bill Scholl, Ch. Rodsden's Lady Luck, C.D. Rhia's offspring have already won titles in conformation, obedience, and tracking.

States and another dozen in Canada.

Additionally, there are the same number of obedience degrees on his progeny in each country. He also has two Bermudian champions, including a Best in Show winner.

Bronco consistently produced high-quality offspring with splendid temperament and outstanding movement. He outdid himself at the 1985 American Rottweiler Club National Specialty where there were more winners sired by him than by any other dog in the country. The awards for which they accounted included many in both the Specialty and the Sweepstakes. This sort of day gladdens the heart of any breeder or the owner of such a sire!

There are four Bronco daughters at Srigo, in addition to a daughter of BS, CS, WS, ES Nero v. Schloss Reitheim, SchH. III, HD-Gekort, the top-winning Rottweiler in Europe in his time.

Felicia's latest lovely winner is Ch. Srigo's Rainbow Wilderness who belongs to Joann Harnish. This bitch finished with three five-point majors, the last as Winners Bitch at the Region V Specialty of the American Rottweiler Club.

Felicia also has Bronco sons and daughters in obedience along with some from Karol and Nero descent that will give a good account of themselves in the future. One of these is from her Nero daughter, Srigo's On The Wings Of A Dove, and one by her brother, Srigo's On Dangerous Ground. A son of Karol, Srigo's Point Blank, is also a SchH. I.

As Felicia has not been showing, most of her best dogs are not titled. Since most people won't take the time and trouble to do what is necessary to make a dog a winner, Felicia is not anxious to let her promising young ones go. Too many people look upon a dog as a replaceable commodity and do not realize that a quality dog is not replaceable. In all too many hands it is wasted. Felicia's immediate plans are to continue to breed

quality Rottweilers. She will be breeding Srigo's Her Diamonds Glitter, C.D., to Srigo's Secret Weapon, who is ready for his C.D.X. "No thoughtful Rottweiler owner does jumping work in show weight" is Felicia's comment on this. Then she will breed Gamegards Diamond Lil, Srigo's Dove, and Wyreglen's Burning Desire to Ch. Srigo's Eagle All Over.

Currently Felicia is looking for a male to buy or lease from outside bloodlines. Now that Bronco is gone she must look for a suitable dog. It has been suggested that she look for another Bronco. But Felicia is wise enough to know that anyone who has once been so fortunate as to have a dog of Bronco's stature never can find a replacement, for they are truly "one of a kind."

Junior Handler Marianne Coviello winning a strong Junior Showmanship Class at Eastern Dog Club in November, 1988, with Bob and Laura Condon's Ch. Altar's Gunner of Woodland.

SUREMAC

Suremac Rottweilers are owned by Anne and Dennis McCormack of Lebanon, New Jersey. They are a small kennel which was unlucky with their first Rottweiler, who did not turn out to be of the show quality for which they had hoped. They did, however, put a C.D. on

No. 8 A.R.C. Bitch for 1984, Ch. Camas Valley Cassandra, here taking Best of Opposite Sex at the Golden Gate K.C. in 1984.

her, and it was their love for this Rottie that made them anxious to get more involved with the breed.

The Rottie that made her mark in the ring for the McCormacks is Ch. Kennrich's Soaring Zena, whom they purchased from the Kennrich Kennels in August, 1985. Zena quickly made up her championship, which she

completed just prior to her second birthday, taking a five-point and a four-point major at age 18 months under Mrs. Joan Klem and Marjorie J. Knapp.

Zena was specialed occasionally during 1987 and throughout all of 1988, handled by Walter Kuberski. She is a multiple Best of Breed winner with numerous Group placements. She culminated her year of specialing with Best of Opposite Sex at the American Rottweiler Club Specialty in Miami on December 9, 1988, at the Fort Lauderdale event on December 10, 1988, at Greater Miami on December 11, 1988. All of these shows had more than 70 bitches in competition.

Born in June, 1985, Zena is a daughter of Int. Ch. Amon vom Filmteich, SchH. III, F.C.I. Her dam is Ch. Radio Ranch's Casablanca Pia. In addition to her show successes, Zena is a Rottie of wonderful temperament and personality who gives tremendous pleasure to her family.

TIMBERLINE

Timberline Rottweilers are owned by Sharon Michael-Carlin who lives in Sheridan, Wyoming. Having grown up on a cattle ranch in southern Montana, Sharon has been associated with animals all her life, but did not become seriously interested in showing dogs until after her daughter had started a dog project in 4-H.

It was during the summer of 1977 that Sharon purchased her first Rottweiler, Timberline's Loki, C.D. She was the first of Sharon's Rottweilers to win points in the breed ring for her and was also her first obedience-titled dog with a placement in Novice A on her way to a C.D. title. A stifle injury forcibly retired her from the shows and obedience rings, but she has remained Sharon's personal companion for over 11 years.

The second of Sharon's Rottweilers was purchased in 1978 from Shelley Moore and the Merrymoore Kennels in Atlanta, Georgia. This one became Ch.

Merrymoore's Ric-O-Shay, C.D. He finished his championship in Denver, Colorado, in 1981 by going Best of Breed from the classes and then continued on to take a Group Four. He was often owner-handled as a class dog, but usually shown by Sharon Cook as a special, although he was never sent out with any handler. To the best of Sharon's knowledge, Ric-O-Shay was the first Wyoming-owned Rottweiler to complete his championship. He was in the Top 20 listing in 1981 and 1982 and was the sire of the first litter of Rottweiler puppies whelped in Wyoming.

A breeding to Timberline's Loki to produce   Timberline's Earth Bare, C.D., a bitch who was co-owned with Traci Belmain. Earth was pointed out of the Puppy Classes, had her C.D. before becoming 11 months of age, but tragically lost a leg to a gunshot wound shortly before her C.D.X. competition. However, Earth did recover and went on to produce Timberline's Cat Dancing, a bitch who was the first Rottweiler to be nominated for the Ken-L-Ration Hero Dog Awards, in which she became one of the five finalists in 1987.

A major-pointed O.F.A.-certified Rottweiler purchase but turned out to be a disappointment as a producer. Then it was decided to return to Merrymoore Kennels for a bitch puppy in 1980. This puppy was Merrymoore's Diablique who earned her first points out of Novice by going Winners Bitch over major-pointed open bitches. She was later co-owned with Doug and Laura Carpenter, then of Casper, Wyoming, and at age five years took points owner-handled by Laura at Laura's first dog show.

Diablique's last litter, for which she was bred to the German import, Hasso von Hennekamp, was her most successful. In this litter, she produced the bitch Ch. Timberline's Pennybrooke, owned by Doug and Laura Carpenter, who has been a very successful specials bitch since completing her title by taking Winners Bitch at the 1988

Top: Ch. Zolti von Siegerhaus pictured going Best of Breed from the classes for Thom and Carol Woodward under judge Mrs. Jane Forsyth. *Middle:* A bright young star at Nouveau Rottweilers, Can. Ch. Carado's Sudden Impact was born on August 10, 1987, and attained his Canadian championship at age 11 months. Owners, the Sosnes of Caro, MI. *Bottom:* Ch. Rodsden's Lindenwood Liesl won Best Puppy Bitch in the Medallion R.C. Futurity her first time in the ring at age 9 months. Owners, Elaine E. DeVol and Linda Michels.

Top: Langhoffen's Eike and handler Coco Steinford. Langhoffen's Esse and handler Sandy Peppers. Littermates bred by Coco who completed their C.D. degrees on the same day! *Bottom:* Am., Can. Ch. Carado's Mighty Quinn, T.T., taking a 4-point major along the way. Owner-handled by Peggy Cojocar, Lexington, KY. Bred by Carole Kravets, Windsor, Ont., Canada.

Westminster Kennel Club Dog Show. Also from this litter is Timberline's Flandry Sackett, co-owned with Gary Walton. This is the only other puppy that has been shown from this litter, and he was pointed from the Bred-by-Exhibitor Class his first weekend out.

The loss of Ric-O-Shay as a breeding dog at an early age was a tremendous setback to the Timberline program, which has taken at least several years to overcome. Sharon's efforts to breed to outside studs were relatively unsuccessful in one way or another, as two breedings did not produce litters, and the three litters that did materialize were not the quality she demands.

It was at about this same period that parvovirus first began, and for several years breeding was extremely limited. Time considerations and the problem of parvo (prior to the development of the very effective vaccine) caused the majority of the Timberlines to be placed with co-owners. Sharon chose, for the time being, to keep only the older dogs which she was actively showing or working.

Diablique was placed with the Carpenters due to this decision, and this has become one of the most successful human-canine

relationships Sharon has known in dogs.

The bitch that Sharon actually considers to be the real foundation of Timberline's present breeding program is Merrymoore's Pride and Joy, purchased in 1985 from Merrymoore Kennels. She is a Ch. Zears Black daughter, a full-sister of Irene Castillo's highly successful special, Ch. Merrymoore's Pagan Ballyhoo. This bitch, bred to Hasso von Hennekamp, has produced Ch. Timberline's Exquisite Gem, owned by John and Judy McCormick, who finished by going Best of Opposite Sex for a five-point major at the Astrodome Show in 1988. She has since taken Best of Opposite Sex at the 1988 Region VI Specialty, owner-handled. She has been shown nine times as a special at all-breed shows, and has seven Best of Opposite Sex and two Best of Breed awards from these occasions.

Between 1980 and 1985, Timberline added three puppy purchases, two adult bitches, leased a male from Merrymoore Kennels, and purchased a bitch from another owner. Partly due to the parvo situation and to the loss of the stud which she had planned to use, Sharon was unable to continue with the breeding

program as originally anticipated. In 1984, she had the good fortune to locate two excellent German imports, a daughter and a son of Int. Ch. Nero von Schloss Reitheim, SchH. III, FH.

Ch. Olfa von Tengen was purchased in May, 1984, co-owned with Stacy Lowe of Lafayette, Louisiana, and was shown first on a seven-show circuit in June, where she was never less than Reserve Winners Bitch. Shortly after that, it was unfortunately discovered that her A.D.R.K. papers were missing a required signature and it was three years before she could be registered with A.K.C. In 1987, transferred to the A.K.C. Registry, she went out for the first time in three years and went Best of Breed both days. Now co-owned with Janet Cary and Bill Bedingfield, Olfa finished her championship in February, 1989, at the Seattle Kennel Club with a five-point major.

In the fall of 1984, a Nero son out of Int. Ch. Olfa von Hennekamp, SchH. I, was located in Canada and was imported early the following year. The two Merrymoore bitches were bred to this dog with exciting results in the form of some extremely handsome puppies.

The latest additions to Sharon's

breeding program are a young dog, Agitato von Dorow, bred by Nancy Estes of Midland, Texas, and Solveig's Yankee von Manree, co-owned with Stacy Lowe.

TOBANT

When Sherri Page Bozant purchased her first two pet Rottweilers during the early 1970s, she had not the slightest idea or intention of becoming so involved with showing dogs, much less learning how to handle, exhibit, or breed. Her prior involvement with dogs had always been strictly with pets. However, her great-aunt and great-uncle raised show Boxers, and Sherri's dad had raised field Beagles; but still they were kept as pets.

ToBant Kennels, as it is known today, began in Houston, Texas, as the result of Sherri's having been constantly harrassed by a breeder and exhibitor friend to join an all-breed obedience club. It was here that this new world of show dogs opened up to her.

Quickly Sherri discovered that there was much to know and to understand, and through her friend she chose her course of action. She attended numerous shows (at which there were very few Rottweilers in attendance at that time and many, many classes). She

Top: Tara von Siegerhaus, C.D., by Ch. Beaverbrook Eisen von Bruin ex Am., Can. Ch. Nemisis von Siegerhaus, C.D. Owned by Michael and Patti Owens. *Bottom:* Winning the Working Group in July, 1987, at Evelyn Kenney Kennel and Obedience Trial is Can. Ch. Heidegruen's Dauntless Frisco, C.D., age 3 years. Owned by Montclaire Rottweilers, Will and Cathy Wankel, Calgary, Alb., Canada.

BEST OF
BREED
SARATOGA
KENNEL CLUB
1988
JOHN ASHBEY

Am., Can. Ch. Nobelhaus Explorer, T.T., famous multi-Group and Specialty winner pictured taking Best of Breed en route to a Group victory under judge Marcia Foy at Saratoga K.C. in 1988.

It was at this point that Sherri became really serious about learning to handle. She travelled with several friends who were handlers, gaining valuable training and experience. Now she has pointed and finished several jobs of various breeds, and has come to truly love the sport. However, she adds, her first love will always be the Rotties.

At the American Rottweiler Club Specialty Match in Winston-Salem, N.C., Sherri's daughter Amy made her Junior Showmanship debut with Ander. As she left the ring clutching her ribbon, she informed her mother that she would like a Rottweiler of her own to train and show, a wish that came true several years later.

In late 1979, Sherri acquired a co-ownership on a lovely bitch from Southwood's breeding, Efie v. Lohauser, who quickly completed her championship (daughter of Ch. Assy v. Lohauserholz and Southwoods Iric vom Dahl), then shared Amy with Ander in the Junior Showmanship ring.

With these two lovely animals and Amy's rapidly growing handling ability, she soon graduated from Novice to the Open Class in her first six shows. Soon after she repeated her request for a dog of her own to train and show.

Sherri decided to breed Ander to Efie, which produced ToBant's Helka, and Amy's wish came true. She was given a co-ownership to a dog of her own. Amy was responsible for all of Helka's care, feeding, grooming, and training—a true bonding relationship developed between them.

Helka's striking looks and Amy's excellent handling really came together in 1983 and 1984. During the first of those years, Amy handled Helka to a second place win in the Open Senior Juniors Class and their big triumph of the day—Winners Bitch at the Medallion Rottweiler Club Specialty. Amy, 13 years old at the time, finished her dog that day under breeder-judge Dan Canino. Sherri says, "It was a very proud

also contacted breeders and decided on her first show puppy.

Under the helpful guidance of the folks at Rodsden's Kennels, Sherri learned about breed clubs, code of ethics, etc., and joined the Medallion Rottweiler Club. She also purchased her first show dog, Ander, who was to become Am., Can. Ch. Rodsdens Ander v.j. Brabant, Best of Opposite Sex at the 1974 Canadian Rottweiler Club Specialty Show. He is now in the Medallion Rottweiler Club Hall of Fame and is an American Rottweiler Club Bronze Sire. Ander was owner-handled to his championship wins and multiple Best of Breed placements. Sherri did use Tom Glassford occasionally as a Group handler, and Tom did an excellent job of presentation.

day for ToBant, as we had bred them both."

Amy and Helka continued on together not only to multiple Best of Opposite Sex wins at all-breed shows but also to Best Junior Handler. Amy also placed, with Helka, in the American Rottweiler Club Top Ten for three consecutive years.

In early 1980, ToBant had another addition to its canine family, Fancy, by Ander from Shearwater Texas Sunshine. She became Ch. Tobant's Fancy Girl, of L.R., and was a very lovely bitch. In 1981, from the nine-to-twelve-month Bitch Class, she took Best of Opposite Sex at the Medallion Rottweiler Club Sweepstakes, her first time in the ring. She later completed championship with all majors.

Efie was bred for a second time to Ch. Furst von Liebersbacherhof which produced Am., Can. Ch. ToBant Iza Winner. "Moosie," as she is known to her friends, now resides with Craig Ames of Big Timber Kennels.

Recent additions at ToBant Kennels include ToBant's Honey Bun, who was pointed at age 13 months and co-owned by Debbie Whelan; ToBant's Iza Toot Sweet; and the little "kids," Grant and Scarlet (by Best in Show Ch. Nelson v.h. Brabantpark) from Fancy's daughter.

TRI-LEE

Tri-Lee Rottweilers are owned by Norma "Pat" L. White at Solon, Iowa. The Whites have been in Rottweilers since 1978, when they purchased their first bitch as a companion for Norma, with no intention of ever showing her.

However, this bitch attracted much attention by her good looks and excellent conformation, and friends were constantly urging that her owners at least try her out in the show ring. They finally did so, and their friends were proven right. Soon after, she had become Ch. Tri-Lee's Dark Gypsy. The Whites do breed an occasional litter, and one of their big thrills

was when a bitch they bred and owned went Winners from the American-bred Class at the 1987 American Rottweiler Club National Specialty. This splendid bitch became Ch. Tri-Lee's Champagne.

The Whites show their Rotties in both conformation and obedience, thoroughly enjoying everything that has to do with their breed and their dogs. They are members of several Rottweiler Clubs including the American Rottweiler Club and Medallion Rottweiler Club. Their goal is to continue breeding on a

Top: Am., Can. Ch. Ebonstern's Warlock v. Lauffeur, Am., Can. C.D. Photo courtesy of Cheryl Wheeler who co-owns Warlock with Gary and Shirley Stiles. *Bottom:* Ch. Zana von Siegerhaus taking points en route to the title at Two Cities K.C. in October, 1988. Owners, Thom and Carol Woodward, Corning, CA.

Ch. Xemplar von Siegerhaus II, owned by Thom and Carol Woodward.

very selective basis in order to participate and see their wonderful breed improve and prosper.

TROSTHEIM ROTTWEILERS

Sharon Alkus of Santa Clarita, California, is the owner of Trostheim Rottweilers, having started her lifetime commitment to dogs as a 14-year-old 4-H youngster, raising and training puppies for the blind. In addition to this having been a wonderful working experience, it also gave her a clear insight into the usefulness of a working dog, especially when its full potential has been developed.

Additionally, this after-school hobby took Sharon to dog shows with her German Shepherd puppies; at one show she had her first meeting with a Rottweiler, and made her decision that one day the Rottie would be her breed.

Fifteen years later, Sharon purchased her first Rottweiler brood bitch, Strudel von Trostheim, from Betty and Bill Carroll and started regularly attending the local dog shows. Rottweilers have brought her the satisfaction of meeting many new friends who share a mutual interest in the breed. She also collects Rottweiler pictures and graphics. The kennel name of "Trostheim" loosely translates, "place in trust."

At one of these early dog shows, Sharon met Cynthia Campbell and her charge, Ch. Harras vom Sachsen, son of Dingo v. Schwaiger Wappen, SchH. III, and Carla vom Sachsen, SchH. I. A permanent friendship followed, as did four Harras litters.

Sharon chose Harras not only because of his spectacular record but for his dominance as a sire, which added up to what she wanted for her bitches. She admired the good toplines of his progeny, his line, size, strong bone, dark color, dark eyes, high set ears, and, of course, his supreme temperament.

Ryatti's Degen v. Camas Valley is another stud dog who Sharon has used successfully. This son of Ch. Eiko vom Schwaiger Wappen, C.D.X., SchH. III, ex Ch. Camas Valley Hildegard v. Kutz, has sired two Trostheim litters to date, one with Strudel. This produced Dirk von Trostheim, who won his Puppy Class at age four months, rated in 1988.

Trostheim's second litter with Degen was from Thatcher von Trostheim (Harras-Strudel) in 1985. It produced five dogs and two bitches.

Sharon's foundation bitch, Strudel, is by Ch. Starkheim Duf Morgan Carroll, C.D., ex Wheelhorse Fanny Fox. Each of her Harras litters has included winners, with Thatcher von Trostheim from the 1985 litter. She won Best Puppy at the American Rottweiler Club in 1986 from judge Ed Biven, and First in Sweepstakes six to nine months from judge Judi Wilson at the Garden State Rottweiler Club in 1986, along with a number of other firsts to her credit.

Damien von Trostheim, from the

1986 litter, won 12–18 Month Dogs at the National and has twice been V-rated by German judges. KC's Heike von Trostheim (1987 litter) was rated V-2 at her first show and received a virtually faultless review. She is now being shown towards her championship.

Sharon comments on the consistency of her litters, with which she is especially pleased. The fourth litter, most likely the last for Strudel, was born in February, 1989: three girls and three boys. From the look of them, she feels that success definitely will be in their future.

With Sharon Alkus, the Rottweilers are definitely a hobby, but a serious one. She limits herself two litters a year and keeps one or two show dogs. Her sister, Sue Lieurance, and her good friends Lori and Casey Ballwey, help her to continue her breeding program.

Important to Sharon's success and pleasure with her Rotties is the fact that her husband Michael is an outstanding photographer who contributes professional pictures for herself and her friends and obviously shares her love of the breed.

TRUE LEE

True Lee Rottweilers are in Revere, Massachusetts, where they are owned, loved, and greatly enjoyed by Lee McKenney. This kennel identification was selected as Lee had always wanted a Rottweiler, having had Collies and Boxers without the success of breeding a champion. Through this period, she was repeatedly saying that she would be, and was, and still is, truly happy with the Rottweiler breed. She used the word *truly* so frequently in connection with the Rotties that it seemed only natural, considering also her first name being Lee, that she adopt the kennel name True Lee.

Lee's foundation bitch is Ashby v. Foxcroft, C.D., a daughter of Ch. Eiko v. Schwaiger Wappen, C.D.X., SchH. III, an American Rottweiler

Club Gold Producer. "Margo" herself is an American Rottweiler Club Producer of Merit and a member of the Medallion Rottweiler Club Honor Roll. She was purchased with the understanding that Lee wanted a breedable bitch and might show her if she could. She was the runt in the litter, and Lee says that she little understood what she was buying at the time.

Fate has a way of playing games, and Lee almost lost Margo at ten months to parvovirus. She wrote a story about this and won a "finalist" position in the 1988 *Rottweiler Quarterly.* Then, as Margo was getting better, she was

Ch. Epic's Adultress, T.T., bred, owned and handled by Bob Hogan. Sired by Am., Can. Ch. Birch Hill's Governor, C.D., T.T., ex Ch. Donnaj Happy Hooker.

Ch. Iada v.h. Land v. Sittard, C.D., a Dutch import bitch, owned by Tita Owen.

hit by a truck in front of her home in a freak accident. The fact that she survived the accident and did not lose her eye or her sight, as the vet had feared might happen, was indeed a miracle. But fate obviously had better things in mind for Margo!

The stud dog selected for Margo's first litter was Von Bruka Arabis (a litter brother to the dam of Select Champion Von Bruka Fiona, C.D.). She produced a bitch, True Lee's Minuette, who was 1984 Best Puppy in the New England Rottweiler Club Match Show under judge Anthony Attala. She was only six-and-a-half weeks of age at the time, and died four weeks later from parvovirus. Being very inexperienced in Rotties, Lee had sold the remainder of the litter as

pets, so it was not until two years later, when she saw them as mature dogs, that she realized that quality had been produced in that first litter. Had it not been for the fact that Von Bruka Arabis was killed by a car before that litter was eight weeks old, Lee would have repeated the breeding.

Thus for Margo's second family, she was bred to Ch. Altar's Gunner of Woodland, a son of Ch. Radio Ranch's Axel v. Notara, American Rottweiler Club Gold Producer, and of Ch. Gudrun von Anderson, an American Rottweiler Club Silver Producer. After seeing the first Gunner/Margo litter, Lee has bred the two of them three more times. The puppies have carried an amazing consistency in type and quality which have been a delight to her.

Their first litter produced Am., Can. Ch. True Lee's Dina v. Gunner, Am., Can. C.D., and True Lee's Djana v. Gunner, C.D. Four puppies from the original eight were lost due to parvovirus by the time the litter was seven months old. The second litter produced a male who won the Working Group as an 11-month-old puppy and who placed in a Working Group the next day. He was Southwind's Oden of True Lee. That same litter also produced True Lee's Kaleigh's Gold; True Lee Traum v. Gunner, C.D.; Southwind Dempsey of True Lee; True Lee's Heika of Khetaqua (the foundation stock for Priscilla Qua's Khetaqua Kennels in New Hampshire); and Lee McKenney's very own True Lee Majestic, C.D.

The next litter brought forth True Lee Chelsea v. Gunner, Am., Can. C.D., who was Best Puppy at the 1987 New England Rottweiler Fanciers' Match under breeder-judge Ellen Walls, who drew an entry in excess of 70. Chelsea is pointed in both the United States and Canada.

True Lee Copper v. Gunner, T.T., is another who won a big New England Match show in 1988 judged by Dorothy Wade. He is halfway to his title. True Lee Cody v. Gunner is the male of the litter who

PLACING
OBEDIENCE
COLONIAL ROTTWEILER
CLUB SPECIALTY
1987
ASHBEY

A proud trio at the 1987 Colonial R.C. Specialty Show: Fred Mueller and Caroline MacPherson with their Can. Ch. Fairvalley's Latin Lottie, C.D.X., T.D., Am. C.D.

possesses exciting potential and is a Junior Showmanship dog who seems destined to shine in the obedience ring.

The fourth and last litter from these same two parents consisted of two male puppies, Special Cause and Special Issue. Margo's next litter was by Ch. Pioneer's Mavericka, a fine dog owned by Sheryl Hedrick.

Lee McKenney's dogs are raised and live in the house and sleep in the beds. True Lee is not just a kennel, it's a home.

VON BRADER

Von Brader Rottweilers are owned by Frank and Mary Brader at Downers Grove, Illinois. Frank Brader has been an employee of Brookfield Zoo, near Chicago, Illinois, for the past 21 years. He is Senior Lead Keeper/Trainer in the Children's Zoo and has trained baby elephants, llamas, pigs, goats, mules, as well as dogs, for the Animals in Action program.

Frank and Mary began their Rottweiler kennel in 1978 with a beautiful puppy bitch from Birch Hill's Kennel. Her name is Am., Can. Ch. Birch Hill's Nanna v. Brader, T.D. She is in the Medallion Rottweiler Club Hall of Fame and was Best of Opposite Sex at the 1983 Medallion Specialty. She was also a 1986 Top Producer and a 1986 Medallion Rottweiler Specialty No. 1 Brood Bitch.

Shortly thereafter, the Braders acquired another bitch who became Ch. Rodsden's Hella v. Forstwald, T.D., Medallion Rottweiler Club Honor Roll. In 1982, Hella was the Reserve Winners Bitch at the Colonial Rottweiler Specialty and Winners Bitch at the Medallion Rottweiler Specialty.

Since then, Frank and Mary have produced many champions, obedience-titled dogs, and two multiple Best in Show and Specialty winners.

The Von Braders' "E" litter, by Eiko from Nanna, has produced their best dog to date, the Best in Show and Specialty Best in Show-winning Ch. Von Brader's Eiger, Medallion Rottweiler Club Hall of Fame; Top Ten for 1987 and 1988. He has been a seven-time Best in Show winner, which includes the 1988 Best in Specialty Show at the Colonial Rottweiler Club Specialty. Added to all this, in 1989 Eiger won Best of Breed and fourth in the Working Group at the Westminster Kennel Club's prestigious event in Madison Square Garden, New York City.

The Braders' latest achievement has been their "I" litter, out of Best in Show and Best in Specialty Show Ch. Birch Hill's Governor,

C.D., and Ch. Von Brader's Elsa (Eiger's littermate), which produced Von Brader's Icelander. At age 13 months, "Ice" went Best of Winners at the 1988 Colonial Rottweiler Club Specialty while Eiger went Best of Breed—certainly a real field day!

Frank and Mary have always believed in researching pedigrees and having long as well as short term goals. Frank conducts classes in obedience and conformation to help instruct and motivate newcomers in the breed. Both he and Mary are extremely grateful to Jane Wiedel of Birch Hill's Rottweilers for giving them their start, not only with Nanna but also by being an informative and wonderful friend. The Braders also extend their deepest gratitude to Brian and Cindy Meyer, their handlers, who have helped them to succeed in the show ring.

VON BRUKA

Von Bruka Rottweilers is the name used by Bruce and Karen Billings of Needham, Massachusetts, for the identification of their dogs and kennel. Their initial interest in the breed began as a result of a Rottweiler male coming to their boarding kennel, Canine College, Inc., to be trained by Bruce. This impressive Rottweiler made such a favorable representation of the breed that the Billings resolved to acquire one of the dogs for themselves. Following one full year of searching and inquiring, they purchased their first Rottweiler in 1976. This was Von Bruka Shasta, U.D., Can., Bra. C.D.

Shasta was ranked in the top five in obedience over three consecutive years. She received multiple all-breed High in Trial awards, and her first leg in utility was in 1985. Shasta was shown to 22 conformation points in the Breed Classes, including one major, but never made up that second major which would have brought her the title of champion.

Shasta was the Billings's foundation bitch. She was, as well, their friend who paved the way for them in the Rottweiler world. She passed away in 1988, and is deeply missed by those who loved her.

It was decided to add a male Rottweiler to the family at Von Bruka, which turned out to be no simple matter. The Billings wound up buying, neutering, and placing in pet homes several very nice males which, due to hips, bite, etc., were obviously suitable only as pets, not breeders. Then "Flyer" was acquired, Ch. Georgian Court Flying High, C.D.X.

Flyer became Reserve Winners Dog at the very first American Rottweiler Club Specialty Show; got his first two C.D.X. legs in his first two shows; and then "the nightmare of the show grounds" began! Flyer blew 16 straight trials and finally finished his C.D.X. with a first place and was retired. The Billings say about him, "He taught us more about correcting a ringwise dog than any dog of any breed we have trained."

Flyer and Shasta produced the

first Von Bruka Rottweiler litter, from which the pick bitch was placed with a dear friend. This was Von Bruka Alpha Girl, who was eventually bred to Eiko and produced her only litter before she was killed in an auto accident. From Flyer's second breeding came Ch. Von Bruka Brutus, U.D., T.D.X.

In October, 1981, Bruce Billings decided on the spur of the moment to travel to West Germany for the Working Sieger Championships. He made reservations, then came home and mentioned casually to Karen that, "I would really like to go to this big show in Germany." She said, "You should go sometime," which surely made it lots easier for him to tell her that he would be leaving the next day!

In Germany, Bruce found himself at the airport in Frankfurt not speaking one word of German nor knowing where he was going. He attended the Schutzhund Championship in a cold, driving rain. But it was well worthwhile for he saw many great dogs and became acquainted with numerous people, some of whom had dogs for sale. Quickly he learned when they said that "I have a good dog for America," it actually meant that "He is no good for Germany."

Bruce was shown "coyote after

Above: Ch. Doroh's Just Grand, T.D., Owned by Junior Handler Veronica Wade. Bred by Dorothy A. Wade, Doroh Rottweilers. *Below:* Ch. Camas Valley Kaiser v. Kutz, by, Ch. Rodsdens Ansel v. Brabant ex Dutchess of Highland Park. Owned by Dan and Debby Kutz, Springdale, WA.

coyote," and after driving hundreds of miles between stops, he was truly disappointed. These breeders certainly knew a good dog but hoped someone would buy the dogs they wanted to get rid of!

Finally he was down to the final three days of his two-week trip. He found himself at the home of Xaver Meixner in Nuremberg, the owner of the Schwaiger Wappen Rottweilers. Herr Meixner spoke no English, but he and Bruce managed between them to communicate. He had none and knew of no good dogs for sale and, adding to Bruce's feeling of discouragement, he had a large drag bag packed full of letters from people all over the world wanting to buy a dog from him.

That night Bruce went to supper with Mr. and Mrs. Meixner and their friend who acted as translator. Next day Bruce travelled with Herr Meixner to his Schutzhund Club, where they continued their conversation about Rottweilers and training. Finally, late in the day, Herr Meixner said to Bruce, "I do know of one dog for you. His name is Eiko vom Schwaiger Wappen!" He made the calls for Bruce to drive that night to look at Eiko, as he was leaving the next morning for America.

Bruce drove north, arriving at the home of Burghart Scheller late that night. Eiko was so impressive, a very proud and confident four-and-a-half year old male with a Schutzhund I degree and V-rating in conformation. Bruce worked Eiko on his bite, taking him outside and standing under a dim little light on a pole. He could hear Eiko barking furiously and he could hear the dog's feet pounding on the pavement as he ran at Bruce, but Bruce could not actually see the dog in the dark until he was on him. Eiko bit full and powerfully, unaffected by the stick hitting him. Bruce knew right then that Eiko was to become his dog. He left shortly thereafter, bringing Eiko to his new home in America.

Within days of arriving home, Eiko was x-rayed and bred to Von Bruka Alpha Girl. From Eiko's very first breeding in America came Select Ch. Von Bruka Fiona, C.D., the 1985 American Rottweiler Club National Specialty winner, handled always by Karen Billings. At the Colonial Specialty, she was chosen Best of Opposite Sex three years consecutively.

In 1987, Rotties sired by Eiko took Best of Breed, Best of Opposite Sex and Best of Winners among many other placements on

Bottom left: Ch. Kimbertal's Hoosier Max, C.D., pictured winning Best of Breed and Group placement. This is a multiple Best of Breed and Group-placing dog who was owner-handled to the title. Owners, John and Janie Hayden . *Bottom right:* Powsell's Athena taking a 5-point major at age 18 months. Athena is a daughter of Ch. Degan's Talta von Meadow ex Relhaus Fauna v. Sunnyside. Bred by Deborah Moneque, who co-owns with Linda Vanderlaan.

that exciting, highly competitive Rottweiler weekend.

Eiko completed his championship in about a year, handled by Walter Kurberski of Englishtown, New Jersey, and was trained and handled by Bruce Billings to his C.D., C.D.X., SchH. II and SchH. III degrees.

A Gold Producer of Merit, Eiko's progeny are fast putting him in the All-Time Top Producing role among Rottweilers. He has two sons of exceptional merit, both being multiple Best in Show winners. These are Can., Am. Select Ch. Goldeiche Ara von Brader, C.D., and Select Ch. von Brader Eiger.

Eiko died in August, 1988. This sad event marked the loss of a great Rottweiler, and of a good friend and companion. His marvelous influence on the breed in America will continue to be felt down through coming generations. One can only feel that if Bruce Billings had not made that trip to Germany, and had he not stuck to it until he found the dog he wanted, the loss to the breed here would have been inestimable.

Select Ch. Fiona has produced three fine litters, the first sired by Ch. Arri vom Hambackbrucke, SchH. III, from which Ken and Janet Benson in Connecticut have Ch. Von Bruka Nadia, U.D. For her second litter, Fiona was shipped to West Germany to be bred to Int. Ch. Osco vom Schwaiger Wappen, SchH. III. The five show puppies from this litter all have received O.F.A. numbers and four already have titles. For her third breeding, Fiona again went overseas, this time to Holland, where she was bred to Int. Ch. Sieger of the Netherlands Duuck v.d. Nedermolen, SchH. III. The Billings have kept a very promising male from this litter and their daughter, Robin, who works with horses and trains dogs, has a very promising young female, Von Bruka Venturous Ayla.

Over the years, Bruce and Karen have imported numerous Rotties from Europe, including the only

A.D.R.K. Klub Siegerin to come to America, Babette vom Magdeberg, SchH. I. Her daughter by A.D.R.K. Klub Sieger Dingo vom Schwaiger Wappen, SchH. III, lives with the Billings. She has her SchH. II, winning both titles at American Rottweiler Club National Specialties, going High Scoring Schutzhund I and II, trained and handled by Bruce.

During 1988, Bruce and Karen travelled to Italy, having the opportunity to bring back the pick male and female from a repeat breeding of A.D.R.K. Siegerin Int. Ch. Yvonne vom Margraferland, SchH. III, bred to Bulli vom Bayerland, SchH. III. The two previous litters from this combination were exceptional,

Ch. Stone Hill Eriskay, by Ch. Eiko vom Schwaiger Wappen, C.D.X., from Woodland's Dealer's Choice. Bred by Patricia Harms, Stone Hill Rottweilers. Handled by Vicki L. Marchand for owner Sheena R. Marchand, Chirlyn Rottweilers, Stamford, CN.

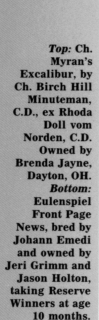

thus the Billings felt themselves extremely fortunate at having this privilege. Yvonne Richards, breeder of the litter, and her wonderful dogs made the Billings' visit to Italy very memorable. The two pups who came to America with their new owners are continuing to look exceptionally handsome.

With the new imports and the fourth generation of Von Bruka's breeding program going for them, the Billings are looking forward to the future, which they hope will

give them many more years of producing sound, beautiful working Rottweilers.

As frosting on the cake, the Billings' oldest son, Bruce Jr., has now graduated from college and is working full time at the kennel training. The youngest son, Douglas, is helping out and working with the dogs at home. So it would seem that there will be this generation to carry on Von Bruka's success in the future.

VON DINE

Von Dine Rottweilers are owned by Nadine Jaquez and located in South El Monte, California. The "head man" here is the handsome dog, Ch. Clyde von Reishoff, who, in limited showing, was in the Top Ten National Rankings for the breed in 1986, 1987, and 1988. Clyde has numerous Bests of Breed to his credit as well as Group placements.

Ms. Jaquez has some promising young dogs coming along by Clyde, including Jondine's Ain't MisBehavin', whose dam is Rodan von Warlock.

VON DOROW

Von Dorow Rottweilers are owned by Nancy C. Estes of Midland, Texas. Her foundation bitch was Merrymoore's Imp von Dorow, purchased from Shelly Moore as a nine-week-old puppy in 1981.

Imp grew up to become Ch. Merrymoore's Imp von Dorow, T.T., and American Rottweiler Club Top Ten Bitch for 1984 and 1985. She was two years old, winning 16 Bests of Breed, one Group placement, and Best of Opposite Sex on 38 occasions. To date, Imp has 12 points towards the American Rottweiler Club Bronze Producer Award and four towards the Medallion Rottweiler Club Honor Roll. With several of her progeny expected to gain championships, obedience, or Schutzhund titles, Imp should meet the requirements for both awards in a short time.

Imp was lost, as is too often the case with a favorite pet, much too soon. She died of lymphosarcoma in 1988 at seven-and-a-half years of age. She left as her legacy not only an impressive show record but also three very consistent litters of typey, good-tempered, sound puppies. She will be remembered as a lovely companion and friend as well as an exceptional brood bitch.

Imp's first litter was by Am., Can. Ch. Tulake's Apollo. All of the "A" litter puppies were given musical terms for names. Of the five surviving members of this litter, only one of them, Agitato von Dorow, is in a show home, with Sharon Michael of Timberline in Sheridan, Wyoming. "Agi" is expected to finish his championship along with earning his C.D.

Von Dorow's "B" litter and "C" litters were both sired by Am., Can. Ch. Rodsden's Berte v. Zederwald, C.D.X., out of Imp. This is a "loose linebreeding" with Berte, a top winner and producer, as he and Imp are of similar and complementary type. Both litters produced consistent good quality. There are nine in the "B" litter, all with the "Black" prefix, and eight in the "C" litter, all with names of islands.

Fortunately, Imp's offspring do not share her distaste for obedience—after three "busts" Imp was retired from that activity. She made up for it in her kids, however, as they include to date one C.D.X. with a leg on his U.D., three with C.D. legs, and one (Bete Noire von Dorow) currently in training for Schutzhund, owner-handled. Ms. Estes plans to try to go for Bete Noire's C.D. before he starts his SchH. I. Several others from the "B" and "C" litters are also working towards obedience degrees.

Although Imp, fortunately, did not pass on her ineptitude for obedience, many of her offspring do have her showy personality. She has produced to date one American and Canadian Champion, Black Maria von Dorow, and one American Champion,

Blackwood's Bete von Dorow, whose wins were all owner-handled. This includes a Best of Breed and a Group placement from the classes over specials. Imp is also the dam of two consecutive Medallion Rottweiler Club Grand Prize Futurity winners: Black

Orpheus von Dorow (1987), Cataline von Dorow (1988), and the 1987 American Rottweiler Club's Best of Opposite Sex Sweepstakes winner, Jack. Six of her offspring are pointed, two with majors.

A second generation "D" Von Dorow litter is in planning, sired by Barry von Lohlein, SchH. III, FH. The same bitch from Imp's "C" litter will be bred again to her half brother, Agi, to further set type.

Can. Ch. Wyreglen's Dancing Shadow, owned by F. Mueller and C. MacPherson, Wyreglen Rottweilers.

Can. Ch. Wyreglen's Dancing Shadow, born October, 1987, completing title at Credit Valley K.C. in 1988. Owned by F. Mueller and C.E. MacPherson, Uxbridge, Ontario.

VON EVMAN

Von Evman Rottweilers at Land O'Lakes, Florida, are owned by two of the most dedicated of Rottie fanciers, Manson and Eve Johnson, who devote an amazing amount of time and dedication to the breed, both here and in Germany.

Ever since his high school days, Manson Johnson admired Rottweilers, and it was back in 1971 when he purchased one, after a hard time finding any of the breed available. There was a minimum number of breeders of the big black dogs which were to become so popular, and, needless to say, the dogs were not readily accessible, as advertisements for the breed were so few and far between.

Persistence won out, and Manson did manage to find his first Rottweiler. The breeder did all the things which a responsible breeder should do, such as demanding letters of reference from the Johnsons' vet and from Manson's parents. Manson mowed lawns to pay for his dog. This dog was a best friend and source of enormous pleasure to him for the years they were together.

When this dog died, there was never a moment's hesitation. Manson and Eve agreed that they needed another Rottweiler and searched in the manner usually considered correct for making a wise and sensible canine purchase. This time there were zillions of ads listing, in glowing terms, breeders to buy from and puppies of excellence. The Johnsons studied books with care, read everything they could find on the subject, then called a widely known kennel and bought a male. He was adorable and they loved him. Thus the shock was almost unbearable when several months later he was found to be dysplastic. Unfortunately, this was a situation widely shared at that period of time, at least so it seems from hearing and reading the number of similar instances.

The amount paid for the puppy was bad enough, but the disappointment and concern for the dog were even worse. Though he had a written guarantee, Manson gave little consideration to making a claim on it, and besides he had grown fond of the dog. So he placed it for a fair price in a pet home, then set about the business of finding himself a female. He decided on one who was a year old. Again disappointment, as this bitch also failed her O.F.A.

In his studies of the breed, Manson became well aware of the A.D.R.K. (German Rottweiler Club) and its careful guardianship of breeding operations. It seemed to Eve and Manson that a puppy who had come from a litter whose parents must pass a Breed Suitability Test might have a bit more going for it. Germany is where he and Eve turned for their next dog and where they have acquired their Rottweilers since. Eve and Manson have developed a warm rapport with the German Rottweiler Fancy, and they have brought together a kennel of outstanding bloodlines and individuals from that country. The Von Evman Kennel has become a collection of Rottweilers who have distinguished themselves both in Germany and in the U.S. in the strongest manner of true working dogs. Manson completed another triumphant visit there with many pleasant achievements to savor.

The Rottweilers at Von Evman include Amboss vom Konigssiek, whose formidable list of credits include SchH. III, I.P.O. III, FH, A.D., H.D., Korüng plus multiple V-1 Winners in conformation credits. His sire is Amboss vom Siebertal, SchH. III, I.P.O. III, FH, AS-Gekort. His dam is Lucy von Hohenhameln, SchH. I, Z.T.P.R., H.D.

Gretel von der Silberdistel, SchH. III, I.P.O. II, A.D., H.D., Korüng is a multiple V-1 winner in conformation, the V-1 winner of the Gebrauchshundklasse at the prestigious Klubsieger show five years in a row—certainly an achievement of honor! Gretel is by Dazi vom Rauschenberg, SchH. III, FH, A.D., H.D.-Gekort. Dolly von der Silberdistel, SchH. I, A.D., H.D.-Gekort is her dam, a bitch renowned as a top producer.

Then there is Janny von der Gruberheide, daughter of the renowned Nero. Janka and Jenny von der Silberdistel are two pink-papered bitches for whom the Johnsons expect great futures. There is also Sita vom Schwaiger Wappen, a worthy bitch.

The Johnsons are members of the A.D.R.K., the United States Rottweiler Club, and the American Rottweiler Club. They enormously enjoy the pleasure of seeing their dogs in competition at the German shows, and thus attend them with regularity.

As a gesture of friendship, the Johnsons have designed and presented a rotating trophy known

as the American-German United Friendship Trophy in an effort to serve as a bond between Germans and Americans.

VON GAILINGEN

Von Gailingen Rottweilers, owned by Mrs. Catherine M. Thompson in Freehold, New Jersey, are long established and noted for quality. The following discussion is an update of developments which have taken place there since *The World of Rottweilers* went to press several years back.

Sadly, 1987 was a disastrous year at Von Gailingen with the loss of those two wonderful homebreds who achieved fantastic honors and recognition, Dark Delight in January and Dassie in July. To make matters worse, the lovely Ch. Arras v. Hasenkamp ex Dassie

Ch. Powderhorn's Kapt of Wencrest, C.D., T.T. Owned by Jim and Sue Johnson and Powderhorn/ Wencrest Rottweilers, Inc.

daughter, Von Gailingen's Lofty Ideal, C.D., died in April at only two-and-a-half years of age. Lofty Ideals (Lindsey) was Winners Bitch at the American Rottweiler Club Region I Specialty in September, 1985. Fortunately not all was lost, as Lindsey was the dam of the Von Gailingen "M" litter.

Am., Can. Ch. Marksman von Turick, C.D., winning Best of Breed at Tuxedo Park in 1985. Lee Whittier, owner.

Carrying on in the family tradition are the dog Von Gailingen's Matinee Idol (Rudi) and the bitch Von Gailingen's Made To Order (Taylor). They are linebred on Ch. Anka von Gailingen, being sired by a Chancellor son and out of a Dassie daughter. Rudi was Best in Sweepstakes at the 1988 American Rottweiler Club National Specialty in Oakland, California, after which he needed only a major to finish and add champion to his name. He was just three points short of Canadian championship, too. Both Rudi and Taylor achieved their American and Canadian C.D. degrees prior to 18 months of age.

Mrs. Thompson remains active in obedience, being a licensed judge for Novice Classes. She is past training director and current president of the Bayshore Companion Dog Club. Serving the Rottweiler, she was two-term president of the American Rottweiler Club and was active on the board of directors for an additional six years.

Cathy was instrumental in formulating the American Rottweiler Club's system for production awards and continues to keep all necessary records for them. She is also the club's statistician for the Annual Top Ten Awards.

Currently Mrs. Thompson chairs the Standard Revision Committee. In 1988, Mrs. Thompson received approval from the American Kennel Club to judge Rottweilers.

VON GAMPP

Von Gampp Rottweilers, owned by Paula L. Gampp at Reddick, Florida, are recognized as a leading bloodstock source of the Eulenspiegel lines of which we wrote so extensively in *The Book of the Rottweiler*. The kennels are located in Ocala, Florida, on 150 acres of a working buffalo ranch, coupled with show Arabian horses in the paddocks. It is within this verdant environment that Paula Gampp, a serious breeder of Rottweilers for more than 18 years, trains her mature dogs and temperament tests her puppies for suitability to work cattle, track successfully, be in harmony with other livestock, and serve man effectively.

Having a deep interest in Schutzhund training, and realizing the utter importance of using proven Schutzhund III dogs in tight linebreeding, Von Gampp offer top show pups for *predictable* extreme type and *predictable* working abilities, particularly through the Int. Ch. Ives Eulenspiegel, SchH. III, sons Int. Ch. Nero vom Schloss Rietheim and Dingo vom Schwaiger Wappen.

Realizing that the cornerstone of any successful breeding program is quality, tightly linebred bitches,

Von Gampp Rottweilers feature the essence of Rottweiler type. The Nero granddaughter, Elkee vom Meadow, two-time Reserve Winners Bitch at Rottweiler Specialties, is among these. Additionally, Ursula vom Gampp, a two-year-old sired by the German import Lex vom Mummler, SchH. III, moves the breeding program forward through her outstanding working and tracking abilities.

Paula Gampp's Igor vom Kastanienbaum granddaughters, Abba vom Gampp and her sister Anna von Gampp, further set type by breeding to the Sanjo son, Geuger vom Gampp, who is a very rich, robust and promising show male of excellent temperament. A puppy bitch sired by a Nero son from a Nero daughter will enter the program.

Previously, in the early 1970s, Paula Gampp exclusively trained and showed Ch. Krueger vom Odenwald, U.D.T., SchH. III, to multiple Bests of Breed. She also permits a matron brood bitch, Czirka vom Haus Kalbas, 13 years of age, to continue to pen and work cattle for her. This bitch is probably the last living granddaughter in the United States of Ch. Harras von Sofienbusch.

Believing in the merits of the working Rottweiler, with a long-range commitment to the breed

BEST OF
WINNERS

WESTMINSTER
KENNEL CLUB

1988
JOHN ASHBEY

Hannible von Einsamstadt taking Best of Winners at Westminster K.C. 1988, his first time in the Open Class. Kahlid Karriem is handling this fine dog for Einsamstadt Kennels.

Ch. Merrymoore's Pagan Ballyhoo, C.D., (by Ch. Merymoore's Zears Black ex Merrymoore's Doodlette) pictured with his owner-handler, Mrs. Irene Castillo, Abilene, TX.

and a breeding program clearly defined and in place, Paula Gampp hopes that Von Gampp Rottweilers will be at the pinnacle of performance in future generations. This seems probable since the puppies are "bred to pass it on," having that Nero look with sound temperaments and correct conformation through judicious selection.

VON GRUENERWALD

Von Gruenerwald Rottweilers, at Colorado Springs, Colorado, are owned by Dorothea Gruenerwald. We are happy to say that she wrote a wonderful chapter for this book telling of her memories and opinions of what has taken place in this breed between April, 1959, when she and her husband Bill

attended their first dog show, the Chicago International, and now.

Bill Gruenerwald lost no time in finding the five-month-old female puppy that was their first Rottweiler, since which time their enthusiasm for Rottweilers has never waned.

Dorothea has not bred a litter since 1985, and she sold her eight-acre kennel and farmhouse in 1986. Since she and Bill lived about six miles from this kennel property, it was always difficult during the 15 years which she owned the kennel to manage and resolve all the problems, and I am sure that she has not missed the constant problems that are always associated with that part of our "doggy" lives. Even so, she notes that very likely she would do it all over again.

The Gruenerwalds now have two pet Rottweilers at home, and Dorothea has been concentrating on judging matches and stewarding in prospect of obtaining her American Kennel Club judging approval.

VON HANDA

Von Handa Rottweilers are owned by Michael and Rosemarie Kennedy of Centereach, New York.

The Kennedys' first Rottie was a very nice bitch who, for reasons of health, was spayed. The second was a male, purchased at ten months of age, who turned out to have hip dysplasia and therefore could not be bred. He is now a great and dearly loved pet whom his owners "would not trade for anything."

Luck took a turn for the better when the Kennedys acquired their third Rottie, a male who is Ch. Buster's Zeke von Scuilla, from their friends, Fran and Ric Scuilla. Zeke's show career highlights include his fourth ring appearance, at age seven months, when he took Best of Winners. He also had seven Reserves from the puppy classes. After that he was held back for a while to mature, then resumed his career at age 19 months, immediately gaining a five-point major and taking Best of Breed over top specials at Monticello in March, 1988, finishing within a month. As a special in limited showing, he has to his credit eight Bests of Breed and a Best of Opposite Sex. Zeke now is semi-retired but will be selectively specialed upon occasion. Zeke was trained and handled exclusively by his friend Khalid A. Karriem.

The Kennedys are starting their breeding program with what they feel are two splendid bitches. The first of these is a German import, Hanni von der Siegquelle. Second is Eida von der Einstamstadt, an American bred from two German imports. Hanni has been bred for a second time to Ch. Schultz v. Watch-Haus. Eida was bred to Ch. Cisco Huter. The first Hanni breeding produced two nice bitches which began to show in 1989.

The Kennedys' breeding goals are to better the breed and also to preserve it. Because of the recent popularity, a decline of quality is almost certain to follow. Their personal ambition? To breed a Best in Show dog, which we truly wish for these enthusiastic fanciers.

VON HAWTHORNE

Von Hawthorne Rottweilers came into existence in December, 1973, when Alice Hahn of Evanston, Illinois, went to Starkrest Kennel to pick up her young bitch Fritzi and Fritzi's dam Tara. Kennel owner William Stark said of Fritzi, "This bitch should be shown." Fritzi was sired by Ch. Starkrest Polo-R, owned by William Stark and his wife, Mildred.

Five months later Fritzi entered the ring for the first time, winning a four-point major under the late Mrs. Winifred Heckman. Fritzi was soon well under way to championship and had 11 Bests of Opposite Sex awards collected along the way—several of them while she still was in the classes. She also earned a C.D. degree during the same period. A beautiful bitch with large head and

Above: Ch. Powderhorn's Lars of Wencrest, owned by Alice and Ben Beckler and Powderhorn/Wencrest Rottweilers, Inc.
Below: Ch. Fraulein Gretchen von Fox, C.D., T.T., daughter of Zum Verkauf's Eric Behalter ex Demon von Fox, C.D. Gretchen here is taking Best of Opposite Sex to Best of Breed at 1985 Camden County K.C. Owners, Marvin and Maria Fox.

Bottom left:
Radio Ranch's
Big Bertha,
handled by Bert
Halsey at 1988
Chesapeake
K.C. of
Maryland Dog
Show, taking
points towards
her title for
owner David
Gallo, M.D.
Bottom right:
Ch. Srigo's
Rainbow
Wilderness, by
Am., Can., Int.
Ch. Bronco v.
Rauberfeld,
SchH. III, F.H.,
BPA, ex Srigo's
Only By Magic,
W.B., 5 points,
A.R.C. Region V
Specialty.
Bonnie Van
Dervort,
handler.

bone, she loved to show and walked with an air of greatness.

Fritzi's littermate, owned by Radio Ranch, was none other than George Anderson, top producer of champions 1977–1978. Fritzi and George Anderson were two of a litter of four from Alice Hahn's Tara von Hawthorne.

Fritzi was bred twice to Westminster Best of Breed dog, Ch. Radio Ranch's Axel v. Notara, producing two champions from the first litter. Her second litter proved even more productive: three bitches pointed, one of them a top scorer in obedience, plus the only male in the litter, appropriately named Solo Magnum. Handled by Richard Orseno, Solo became an important Group dog in 1982 and 1983.

In two generations, Von Hawthorne produced four champions plus four pointed dogs, including George Anderson with a Best of Opposite Sex at the Medallion Rottweiler Club Specialty and a strong Group System rating in 1982 and 1983.

Fritzi's offspring seemed determined to do their dam one better. Von Hawthorne's Magna-F, C.D., bred to Ch. Rangarr's A. Sultan Rachmanov, owned by Lance Murdock, produced Ch. Von

Hawthorne's Murray, who fared conspicuously well in the rating systems.

Maggie's littermate, Von Hawthorne's Chiba-F, also bred to the same sire, produced two males who became the absolute apples of Alice Hahn's eye. A few years earlier, Ch. Solo Magnum had been the first male Alice kept. Now she was ready for another. That puppy became Ch. Von Hawthorne's Max Otto-C, a champion at 19 months, a "Top Ten" in 1986 and 1987, and multiple Group winner in 1988.

Max Otto's littermate, Ch. Von Hawthorne's Brutus-C, became a champion at 21 months but then was not campaigned. Both dogs were handled to their championship by Richard and B.J. Orseno, whose handling of Rottweilers goes back to when Richard became only the second handler to earn a Rottweiler Best in Show in the United States.

The fourth generation Von Hawthorne champion, Max Otto-D, like his littermate Ch. Brutus-C and his half-brother Ch. Murray-M, has an exceptional Rottweiler temperament—friendly and loving, yet impossible to intimidate. The size of Max Otto's head is awesome, and his stature displays extraordinary strength, according

to his owner. At 26 inches tall and 140 pounds, he is considered by Alice Hahn to be everything the breed was meant to be. Max Otto passes on to his progeny the air of importance of being a Rottweiler.

Every Von Hawthorne Rottweiler is a direct descendant, through the female line, from the original Tara. Through selective breeding, Alice has maintained even improved, the head, the bone, the size, and especially the temperament of the breed.

VON HOTTENSTEIN

Von Hottenstein Rottweilers, located in West Chester, Pennsylvania, are owned by Nancy Reynolds. She chose to identify her Rotties with her paternal grandmother, a lady by that name of German descent.

With no previous background or experience with dogs, Ms. Reynolds felt the need to do as much studying as possible prior to her purchase of her first Rottweiler. Over a period of more than a year she attended all possible dog shows, traveling the eastern part of the country as far south as Florida, to see, visit, and discuss the breed of her choice before making a decision.

A puppy finally was chosen, in the summer of 1981, from a very uniform litter which had the "look" that Nancy Reynolds had come to admire and a pedigree to match the quality. At seven weeks old, that puppy was named "Muppy" and became part of the Reynolds' household. While still in the Puppy Class, she began her show career by taking Reserve Winners Bitch at a four-point major event, and it was not long until she became Ch. Von Hottenstein's Bear Handed, at the age of 19 months. Muppy was bred by Diana Gibson in New Jersey. Behind her are the bloodlines of Ch. Lyn Mar Acres Arras v. Kinta and Ch. Kokas K's Degen von Burga, C.D., T.D., both holders of American Rottweiler Club Top Production Awards as "Gold" sires; and Plaisance Irma, also a top

producer of champions, who was an English bitch.

Once Muppy gained her championship, Ms. Reynolds became interested in acquiring another puppy from the same dam, Gibson's Bubbles v.d. Best, but instead had the privilege of co-owning Bubbles herself. Bubbles, who was by Ch. Kokas K's Degen von Burga, C.D., T.D., from Plaisance Irma, had her last litter at Von Hottenstein Kennels. Ms. Reynolds had selected Ch. Arras vom Hasenkamp to be sire of these puppies. Arras is an American Rottweiler Club "Bronze" sire.

The puppies from this litter were excellent, but unfortunately few of them were ever shown. One of the puppies won first place in the Puppy Bitch Sweepstakes, nine to twelve month bitches, at the Colonial Rottweiler Club Specialty in 1985. A sister, Ch. Copperdot's Best Gemini, is owned by Diana Gibson.

Leibgarde's Fireball Kassie, at age 13 months, going Reserve Winners Bitch at the Silver Bay K.C. Show under judge Milton Walker. Owned by Michael and Faith Mitchell. Photo by Bergman.

Gamegard's First Impression, by Srigo's Loaded For Bear, taking Best of Winners at Southern Maryland K.C. in 1988. Srigo Rottweilers, Ms. F.E.H. Luberich.

Muppy herself produced three litters, two of which were sired by Am., Can. Ch. Donnaj Herr I Am, C.D., T.T., and one by Ch. Alina's Adelbear of Wesley, both of whom were sired by the famed Gold Sire, Am., Can. Ch. Donnaj Vermont Yankee of Paulus, C.D.X., T.T. There are four champions to date among those by Herr I Am: Ch. Von Hottenstein's Alli Baba, a multiple Best of Breed winner and Group placer; Ch. Von Hottenstein's A Dare, who won first place in the 12–15 month Puppy Bitch Sweepstakes at Colonial Rottweiler Club Specialty in 1985; Ch. Von Hottenstein's Angel; and Ch. Von Hottenstein's Fandango, ranked No. 2 Bitch, American

Rottweiler Club System, for 1988. Von Hottenstein's Free Spirit and Von Hottenstein's Above All are both major-pointed. Muppy's fifth champion to date is Ch. Von Hottenstein's Charisma, sired by Adelbear. Muppy is now eligible for the American Rottweiler Club Bronze Production Award.

Now Muppy's daughters and half-sister (Von Hottenstein's The Boss) are taking over where Muppy herself left off. They are producing some youngsters of exceptional merit. The Boss has a major-pointed son and daughter, plus a son who won the nine to twelve month Puppy Dog Class at the Colonial Rottweiler Club 1988 Specialty. Ch. Von Hottenstein's A Dare has three offspring pointed towards their championships and one with a C.D. degree. Von Hottenstein's Checkmate has a major-pointed son and another who has done well in the puppy classes. Amber von Hottenstein has two pointed daughters and a son, Ch. Von Hottenstein's Hubahubba, sired by Am., Can. Ch. Trifecta's Barbarian Murph, C.D. (by Gold Sire Ch. Eiko von Schwaiger Wappen, SchH. III, C.D.X.).

Hubahubba earned his championship in four weekends and at age 17 months, after which he made it big on his first weekend out as a special, when owner-handled he won Best of Breed at an American Rottweiler Club Regional, sponsored by the Eastern Great Lakes Rottweiler Club. Before he turned two, he became a multiple Best of Breed and Group placer, making his future look bright.

Ms. Reynolds' belief is that Rottweilers need plenty of individual attention and should not live solely in a kennel environment. Out of this belief came several co-ownerships with other fanciers which enable the dogs to live a quality pet lifestyle yet still be shown and used in a breeding program.

All Von Hottenstein puppies are home-whelped and home-raised, temperament tested, and thoroughly evaluated prior to being sold into other homes.

VON RIDDLE

Von Riddle Rottweilers are owned by Karen and Harold Riddle of Falls Branch, Tennessee, who purchased their first Rottie, as a pet, in 1982. That eight-week-old bundle of joy became Schultz von Riddle, C.D. The Riddles became interested in showing through obedience training. From that point on, the whole snowball effect of "Rottweiler fever" set in.

In December, 1984, the Riddles bought their foundation bitch, who became Ch. Brinka von Ross, C.D., T.T., as a ten-week-old puppy. Brinka is out of Elko v.d. Nedermolen, SchH. III, and Ch. Gundi von Ross. She finished her championship at the age of 22 months. Her first time out as a special, she won Best of Opposite Sex at an American Rottweiler Club Regional Specialty under judge Mrs. Joan Klem.

Brinka was a lovely show bitch and a beautiful producer. Her first litter was sired by Ch. Beaverbrook Eisin v. Bruin, T.T. Von Riddle's first homebred champion, Ch. Von Riddle's Gabriele v. Eisen, T.T., came from that litter and is owned by Wilma and Max Williams and Karen Riddle. She gained her

championship at age 29 months and earned her Companion Dog degree at age 23 months. The Riddles own two other pointed bitches from this litter.

Von Riddle is extremely proud of Brinka's first place Brood Bitch wins at Specialty shows with her young daughters, including first place Brood Bitch at the 1987 American Rottweiler Club Regional Specialty, the 1988 Colonial Rottweiler Club Specialty, and the 1988 Medallion Rottweiler Club Specialty. Brinka's second litter is doing well in the show ring. These youngsters are sired by Ch. Gemstones Blitz Meister, T.T. So pleased were the Riddles with this litter that they repeated the breeding.

The Riddles especially take pride in their male, Ch. Gemstones Blitz Meister, T.T., whom they bought at one year after seeing him at the 1986 Medallion Rottweiler

Above: Am., Can. Ch. Windcastle California Kid, by Am., Can. Ch. Donnaj Herr I Am, C.D., T.T., ex Am., Can. Ch. Gatstuberget's Katarina, T.T. Owned by C. and B. Kaufmann. *Left:* Can. Ch. Heidegren's Celib, C.D., at age 2 years. By Ch. Trollegen's Benjamin ex Ch. Northwind's Jewel, C.D. Handled by Shannon Smith; bred by Sheila O'Brien.

Ch. Trollegen Bacchus von Simsberg, T.D., owned by Susan Lyons, Mariposa, CA.

Club Specialty Show. As a puppy, Blitz "stole the show," taking Best Junior Dog and Best of Opposite Sex to the Grand Prize Futurity Winner. Then in the regular classes, from nine to twelve months

Ch. Trollegen Bacchus von Simsberg, T.D., owned by Susan Lyons, Mariposa, CA.

Puppy, he went on to Winners Dog and Best of Winners. The crowd really cheered him on, making it a thrill to watch. Karen notes, "I did not realize that three weeks later I would be lucky enough to own him!"

Blitz is by Ch. Rodsden's Berte v. Zederwald, C.D.X., from Eva Regnant of Gemstones, C.D. He finished his championship, owner-

handled, at age 14 months, and since then has won multiple Bests of Breed and Group placements. At the 1988 Medallion, Blitz won an Award of Merit. Now the Riddles are hoping that he will follow in his sire's footsteps as a great producer. Blitz's loving personality and temperament have made him the Riddles' house dog.

Being comparative newcomers to the breed, the Riddles strive to breed quality dogs. Karen is a member of the Medallion Rottweiler Club and the Rottweiler Club of Knoxville. She and Harold are grateful to Brinka's breeder, Kelly Ross, and to Blitz's breeder, James Lynch, for allowing them to own these wonderful Rottweilers.

The Riddles are already well on the right track as breeders, judging by Karen's statement that they believe a beautiful quality bitch to be the key to a breeding program! How true that is!

The Riddles love their dogs and strive to place their puppies in good homes. Karen's high point of the year, so far as showing dogs is concerned, is the thrill of showing at the various Annual Specialties.

VON SIEGERHAUS

Von Siegerhaus Rottweilers are owned by Thomas and Carol Woodward of Corning, California. Carol Woodward has loved the breed ever since 1963, but it was not until she married Thom in 1972 that they became involved in showing and breeding.

The first Von Siegerhaus litter was born in 1979. Since then the kennel has had a dog qualified for the Top Ten Awards of one type or another nearly every year. The Woodwards have almost always owner-handled their dogs, something which they enjoy doing to this day.

The foundation bitch, Ch. Kyna vom Odenwald, C.D., 13 years young, has the remarkable record of producing eight American champions, six Canadian champions, twelve C.D.s, (two who earned the C.D.X. degree), and one Tracking Dog. This qualified her

Can. Ch. Rotterre Breezy Brae by Ch. Gasto vom Liebersbacherhof, C.D.X., T.D., SchH. I, ex Can. Ch. Rodsden Abbatab of Stepshire, T.T. Breezy is owned by J. Jacqueline Stephenson, Rottere Rottweilers®, Shelburne, Ont., Canada.

for both the *Canine Chronicle* and the *Kennel Review* System's Top Producing Awards. She also qualifies for the Medallion Rottweiler Club's Hall of Fame and the American Rottweiler Club's Silver Production Award. She was Top Ten in Obedience, American Rottweiler Club, in 1977.

Kyna is also the granddam of Von Siegerhaus's Senior Stud Dog, Am., Can., Mex. Ch. Quick von Siegerhaus, Z.T.P.R., Am., Can. C.D., whose credits include: the *Dog World* Award of Canine Distinction; *Canine Chronicle*'s Top Ten Award, 1987–1988; Routledge System Top Ten, 1987; No. 7 Rottweiler in Canada, 1986 (breed points); and No. 3 overall Rottweiler in Canada, 1987. Quick is a Group winner and a Group placer many times over and has now retired from the show ring to pursue his Schutzhund degrees and his C.D.X. He is at the same time making way for his sons and daughters to prove themselves in the show ring. At the youthful age of five years, Quick had ten champion progeny (and numerous ones with working titles) to his credit.

Along with Quick, there are three "junior studs" at Von Siegerhaus. Am., Can. Ch. Oden von Siegerhaus, T.D. (a son of Ch. Trollegen's Frodo, C.D., American Rottweiler Club Gold Producer, ex Ch. Kyna vom Odenwald, C.D.,

219

Can. Ch. and OTCh. Davinghoe's Aqtar Terror Shai, T.D., was born in November, 1984. Bred by Ingrid Paul, handled by Debbie Van Meer, owned by Thelma Boyd, Maasai Rottweilers, Alberta Beach, Alta., Canada.

American Rottweiler Club Silver Producer), is among the latter. There is also Ch. Zolti von Siegerhaus, a Quick son from two-time American Rottweiler Club Top Ten Bitch, Am., Can. Ch. Kitty von Kodiak, Am., Can. C.D., SchH. I; and Amos von Siegerhaus, a Quick son from two-time Top Ten Bitch, Am., Can. Ch. Adlerberg's Aunka von Siegerhaus. The dams of both "Zoltie" and "Amos" have been multi-Group placers. The strength of pedigree is obvious in these young studs.

Von Siegerhaus has always enjoyed a reputation for excellence in its bitches, as proven by the fact that the kennel has had a Top Ten Bitch from 1984 through 1987, the only four years that they have campaigned one. The latest

campaigning bitch is the Quick daughter Ch. Zana von Siegerhaus. This kennel has been responsible for over 35 Rottie championships, more than 30 with Working degrees.

VON STOLZENFELS

Von Stolzenfels Rottweilers are owned by Jack and Dr. Evelyn Ellman at Augusta, Michigan. This is another very well-established kennel of long duration.

The ownership and limited breeding program at Von Stolzenfels can lay claim to 22 American champions, one Canadian champion, 29 dogs with American and/or Canadian C.D. degrees; two C.D.X. dogs; two U.D. dogs; 12 American and/or Canadian T.D. dogs; one T.D.X. dog; and several dogs with one of the following titles: VB, A.D., SchH. I; and Z.T.P.R. Further, all dogs bred by the Ellmans are tested for T.T. (Temperament Test) and have passed. Of course, there are many titled dogs today which are either bred out of dams bred by the Ellmans or sired by one of their stud dogs.

One of the above-mentioned titles is owned by Ch. Bandetta von Stolzenfels, U.D.T. This is a record to which the Ellmans point with pride, especially since they breed relatively few litters and their foremost requirement for puppy placements is a qualified home where the pup will be trained in basic obedience. If such a home later becomes a show home, then that is icing on the cake.

Dr. Ellman has been a member of the A.D.R.K. (German Rottweiler Club) for several decades and has received the Club's gold membership pin. It is therefore not surprising that she based her breeding program on the selection and importation of an A.D.R.K. bitch, Ch. Cosi vom Steigstrassle.

Ch. Dolf Fuller von Stolzenfels, C.D., was the resident stud at the Ellmans for many years. He lived to be over 12 and never lost his absolute perfection of topline and iron nerves. He was a wonderful, treasured dog who is dearly missed. There is a very large and quite widespread Von Stolzenfels "family" that never loses touch with Evelyn, nor she with them. One of the things that makes this lady so special is her true *interest* in her dogs—not just the great ones but each and every one that she has owned and raised. It is to her enormous credit that she has so many true and close friends which have grown through the sale or purchase of a puppy. In no way does Evelyn hand over a puppy to someone and then forget about it. The purchasers know that they can always "call home" for help or advice. The Ellmans like to know how each dog is doing and to keep in touch with it. Pictures are a delight, as are notes and progress reports throughout the dog's entire lifetime. This is what I consider to be a truly dedicated breeder: one who cares about dogs, to whom "out of sight" is never out of mind!

VON WORLEY

Two very keen Rottweiler enthusiasts own the Von Worley Kennels, located in Newark, Ohio. They started out in Dobermans during 1968, then in 1981 acquired their first Rottie, Abigail, as a puppy from the Mad River Kennels owned by Dorothy and Kenny Davis. So pleased were the Worleys with "Abby" that the next year a male was purchased by them also from Kenny Davis. It was a good move on their part, as the second pup was destined to become Best in Show and multiple Best in Specialty Show, Am., Can. Ch. Mad River's Magnum von Worley. Magnum was ranked in the Top Ten for 1986 and 1987. He was a truly thrilling dog to show or to watch in the ring, as to him the show ring was Disneyland.

In 1986, Magnum went Best in Show, keeping up the proud tradition begun when his great-great-grandsire Kato (Am., Can. Ch. Rodsden's Kato v. Donnaj, C.D.X., T.D.) took the first Best in Show ever taken by a Rottweiler in the United States, and continued

Top: A head study of Ch. Hans v.h. Brabantpark, 1987 Top Ten Rottweiler, multiple Group placer, Best of Opposite Sex Golden State R.C. Specialty. Owner, Powderhorn/ Wencrest Rottweilers, Inc. *Bottom:* Vanlare's Standing Ovation is co-owned by Connie J. and Robert M. Weir with Lori and Greg Benkiser, Vanlare's Kennel.

by Kato's son Ch. Donnaj Vermont Yankee v. Paulus, who followed in the pawprints of Kato. It was the grandson of Yankee, Magnum, who introduced the Worleys to the thrill of owning a Best in Show winner. In fact, many exciting victories were provided by Magnum during his show career, which lasted over a period of five-and-a-half years prior to his retirement in December, 1987.

Born in March, 1982, Magnum completed his championship owner-handled with three straight majors at age 13 months. During his show career in the United States and Canada, he brought home Best

Top: Kiesler von Stolzenfels, Am., Can. T.D., at age 1 year. Owned by Walter Wernig, Middleton, MA. By Ch. Imor's Bulli von Stolzenfels ex Herta Vicka Stolzenfels, C.D. Bred by Jack P. and Dr. Evelyn Ellman, Augusta, MI.
Bottom: Ch. Robil's Marta von Dannaj winning Best of Breed at Windham County K.C., handled by Bill Burrell for owners Virginia Aceti and Sheryl Hedrick.

Opposite top left: Pastel portrait done by Sharon Michael Carlin of Ch. Timberline's Exquisite Gem. Sharon owns the Timberline Rottweilers at Sheridan, WY.
Opposite bottom left: Ch. Heidegren's Dauntless Frisco, C.D., in January, 1989, paws planted firmly on a bale of hay. Owned by Will and Cathy Wankel, Calgary, Alta., Canada.
Opposite top right: Ch. Winkler's Adam von Ursa was bred by Rebecca L. Chriscoe and is owned by Alice and Greg Winkler.
Opposite bottom right: Wilma and Max Williams and Karen Riddle owned by Ch. Von Riddle's Gabriele v. Eisen, C.D., T.T., by Ch. Beaverbrook Eisen v. Bruin ex Ch. Brinka von Ross, C.D., T.T.

Xenda Kim De Charfard, by Can. Ch. Wyreglen's Archimage ex Can. Ch. Darkajou De Forte Brise. Bred by Sylvia Fafard, owned by Suzanna Fafard.

of Breed on close to 100 occasions, took Best in Specialty at the Ontario Canadian Sovereign Rottweiler Club's Specialty in October, 1985, and again in October, 1987. He was the winner of the American Rottweiler Club Specialty Show in December, 1988, under Dr. Q. LeHam. While still a youngster, he was the American Rottweiler Club Sweepstakes winner of the 12–18 month class in Cincinnati in 1983.

Magnum was Best in Show, all breeds, in Springfield, Ohio, in October, 1986, in an entry of 1399 dogs. In 1986, he was ranked No. 6 for all Rottweilers despite an extremely limited showing (the Worleys show in Ohio and only a few nearby states), and in 1987 he ranked No. 9 in the U.S. Group systems.

Heidi, a daughter of Magnum's from his first litter, was shown. She finished both her American and her Canadian championships in July, 1987, at age two years. On the way to doing so, she was Best of Winners at the Sovereign Rottweiler Specialty in Canada under judge Muriel Freeman and Best of Opposite Sex on numerous occasions over top specials in the United States.

Another Magnum daughter, owned and shown by the Worleys,

completed her American and Canadian Companion Dog degrees by age 18 months. She has at least seven points towards her A.K.C. championship, including a five-point major. She was Best Junior Puppy Bitch at the A.R.C. Regional Sweepstakes in December, 1987.

Am., Can. Champion Von Worley's Alexander is a homebred from the Worleys' own bitch, Mad Rivers Abigail Diana. His sire is Am., Can. Ch. Zarras v. Brabant, Am., Can. C.D.

Born in March, 1984, Alexander was breeder/owner-handled with a record including numerous Bests of Breed in the U.S. and Canada, Group placements in both countries, C.D. degrees in three shows apiece in the U.S. and Canada, and was Best in Sweepstakes at the Western Pennsylvania Rottweiler Specialty at age 14 months.

Alexander was shown very infrequently during 1986 and 1987 due to his owners' showing of Magnum. In 1988 he won a splendid assortment of Bests of Breed and Group placements, including about a dozen Bests of Breed in entries totaling between 50–60 Rotties. Many authorities describe him as "a breeder's dog." For the future, the Worleys are keeping a close watch on a beautiful Magnum granddaughter, Von Worley's Divine Miss M, who completed her Am., Can. C.D. by 18 months of age and by 20 months was halfway through to her American championship.

WEIR

Connie J. and Robert M. Weir of Kennesaw, Georgia, are the owners of Ch. Von Helmer's Red Wolf, who is a son of the German import, Ch. Artus v. Adelshof, SchH. III, he by Ch. Ilo Eulenspiegel, SchH. III, FH, H.D., from Sage Croft's Hetty v. Herta (Am., Can. Ch. Hasso v. Steigstrassle ex Am., Can. Ch. Rodsden's Vixen v. Hungerbuhl, C.D.X.).

Red was Best of Winners at the Medallion Rottweiler Club Specialty in June, 1988, went on to complete his title with ease, and brought home several Best of Breed awards. He has also been shown a bit in Canada and should attain his title there as well. Red is also obedience trained and looks forward to gaining a C.D.

The Weirs also co-own a handsome bitch, Vanlare's Standing Ovation, with Lori and Greg Benkiser. This bitch and Red share the Weir household, where they are much loved and enjoy life as "just dogs" in their large fenced backyard where they have lots of time to play and relax.

Standing Ovation is by Ch. Pomac's Always A Cinch, C.D. (Ch. Bulli v. Meyerhoff ex Ch. Hallmark's The Sting) ex Ch. Inner Sanctum Oh Jezebel, C.D. Certainly the Weirs have some important bloodlines on which to start a breeding program.

WHITHAUS

Whithaus Rottweilers of Ponte Vedra Beach, Florida, are owned and loved by Dr. and Mrs. Jack Whitman. They are the proud owners of Ch. Hanni vom Bakkes, who was shown while quite young in Germany and received obvious recognition while attaining her V-2 rating and SchH. I degree before being exported to the United States.

Upon arrival in the U.S., this lovely two-year-old bitch was immediately put on the Florida circuit with handler Wendy Wolforth, and she swept through to her championship within 30 days.

Ch. Trollegen's Bacchus von Simsberg, T.D., winning Best of Breed at Chico Dog Fanciers, CA, October, 1988. Owned by Susan Lyons, Mariposa, CA.

Wyndhurst's Dark Ches, C.D., is major-pointed for owners Guy Trahan and Susan Lock.

After proving herself in the specials ring, where she was Best of Breed and Best of Opposite Sex on a satisfactory number of occasions, she put aside her show career briefly in order to be bred to the celebrated Int. and Am. Ch. Mirko von Steinkopf, SchH. III, C.D.X., and Therapy Dog.

As the foundation bitch at Whithaus, Hanni is a proven producer of proper breed type and temperament. Her breeding to this late great sire produced 11 puppies of significant quality. One such puppy was retained to be the future flag-bearer of the line. This pup's name is now Ch. Alfa vom Whithaus, and despite two unfortunate accidents as a puppy,

each of which might have terminated a future show career, she had a try at show competition and was so successful that at only 17 months she completed her title under Mrs. Bernard Freeman. She took not only the points in the classes but went on to Best of Breed that day followed by, as frosting on the cake, a second-place award in the Working Group at Tampa. The Whitmans feel that "Alfie" is the epitome of the true German standard of the breed, as are her sire and dam. This breeding was carefully researched and chosen on the premise that it was a heavy linebreeding effort and a very compatible connection, doubling up on the Int. Ch. Ives Eulenspiegel line which has produced so many Top Producing Rottweilers, both past and present.

The first litter, referred to as the "A" litter, in addition to Alfa, produced Anka vom Whithaus owned by Marilyn and John Brennen, of Fort Pierce, Florida. They are currently in competition on show circuits. Anka's fondness for the show ring and her winning attitude have already put her in the spotlight. An International Championship is planned for her. Arko vom Whithaus, the only male in the litter, is ready for a Tracking degree and Schutzhund I.

Others from this litter have been shown in U.S. Rottweiler Club German Style Conformation and Schutzhund Trials. They have placed in conformation consistently, and three others have continued their Schutzhund training and are headed towards Working degrees like Alfa. Mrs. Whitman notes that, as a result of complications resulting in the delayed registration of these puppies, some had been placed in loving homes as pets and were subsequently neutered, preventing their competing for championship honors.

Hanni's second breeding was to Int. Ch. Santo vom Schwaiger Wappen, whose offspring have accounted for numerous titles. This time ten puppies resulted (five males and five females), all appearing uniform in structure and type. Nine of these went into show homes where they will also be trained for Schutzhund. These pups all show significant quality. They have already done their bit in Match Shows and prepare for full-scale show careers. One bitch among these, Burga vom Whithaus, is in Hawaii, where she is owned by Robert Petrucci. She has three winning appearances at point shows, handled by her owner. Robert is President of two Schutzhund clubs on the islands. Burga has been raised in a working environment and has as much drive as any of the males competing in Hawaii.

Also produced in this "B" litter was Brock vom Whithaus, an outstanding male, owned by Cheryl Koepp in St. Croix, Minnesota. He has been used as a demonstration dog for Temperament Testing at Working Dog Seminars and has been accepted with open arms in the two Schutzhund Working Clubs, one of which was a U.S.A. German Shepherd Dog Club until Brock proved his worth and thus was accepted as a star performer. Despite the limited experience of his owner-handler in breed competition, Brock went to the American Rottweiler Club Regional in Chicago and the all-breed event there, winning both classes on this first time out.

The Whitmans retained a male from this "B" litter who had somehow been passed over when the puppies were being selected for new homes. His name is Barry vom Whithaus, and judging by the success of his early ring appearances he, along with Brock, will make a very positive contribution to the breed. Berrie vom Whithaus is another lovely littermate, a male of identical type and temperament. Michelle Amaroux of Washington State has had him in Schutzhund training and also has plans to show him in conformation.

The five bitches in the "B" litter all have won top honors at the

matches and have placed consistently in the point shows. Their owners plan with confidence to continue their show careers.

Because it is not a large commercial venture, the Whitmans' breeding program has been designed around their needs as conscientious breeders. They carefully place puppies with individuals who know and understand the important bloodlines represented in these pedigrees.

WILDERNESS

Wilderness Rottweilers are owned by JoAnn Harnish and are now located at Oakridge, Oregon. The promising youngsters of which we wrote in *The World of Rottweilers* have now grown and matured into fine representatives of the breed. Many of their offspring have earned obedience titles and championships in the United States and Canada.

The Wilderness Rottweilers started out in Alaska, when JoAnn was JoAnn H. Turner. The foundation bitch, Lady Ruger, went on to earn her C.D.X. and various other breed titles. The only bitch from her first litter, Ch. The Chena

Ch. Heiko, C.D., a son of Ch. Czarina von Stolzenfels, C.D., was bred by Jack P. and Dr. Evelyn M. Ellman, Von Stolzenfels Rottweilers. Owner, Ammersberg Kennels.

Top: Pepperhaus Country Cache, C.D., T.D., age 1 year, by Am., Can. Ch. Arenenberg Astro Warrior, SchH. II, F.H., C.D., T.D., from Am., Can. U.D.T., AD, T.D.I. Owned by Dave and Ellen Minturn, Los Alamos, NM. Bred by Pepperhaus Rottweilers. *Bottom:* Arko vom Whithaus in January, 1988, age 14 months. Owned by Helen Gaily of Orlando, FL. Arko is a son of the great Mirko and is Schutzhund trained. Photo courtesy of the Whitmans.

Wilderness, has added a Canadian championship to her American one and is working on her C.D. title.

Chena's brother, Ch. Wilderness Proud, owned and owner-handled by Linda Van Brunt, finished his championship on his second birthday and is currently ranked in Alaska as No. 1 Rottweiler. A third dog from this litter, Ch. Wilderness Black Turk, owned by Mark and Silvia Whaley, finished his championship in February, 1989, after taking a couple of years off while his family moved to Utah.

Lady Ruger's second litter, by Ch. Starkheim Duf Morgan Carroll, produced two C.D. bitches, R.J.'s Wilderness K.C., C.D., and Connie's Wilderness Ursa, C.D., who is also pointed towards conformation championship. Both have proven to be excellent producers.

Chena's first litter, sired by Ch. Rodsden's Tristan v. Forstwalk, C.D., T.D., produced Am., Can. Ch. Wilderness Kobuk v. Forstwald, who in his very first shows won nine to twelve month dogs at the American Rottweiler Club Region V Specialty Sweepstakes, handled by his breeder-owner.

Kobuk went on to finish his American Rottweiler Club championship easily at age 23 months, and then his Canadian

championship a year later, taking several Group placements. Kobuk is a consistent Best of Breed winner in Oregon but was pulled from the ring in 1989 to concentrate on his Schutzhund training. A re-breeding of Chena to Tristan is also planned.

A promising male from Chena's second litter, sired by Ch. Danny von Timmerman, is Wilderness Eastward Bronson, C.D., owned by Steve and Susan Hunt. Bronson has accumulated seven points, including a major towards his championship, earned his C.D. degree, and is also in Schutzhund training.

Am., Can. Ch. Way-Mar's Brooks Dawg von Jas, C.D., went on to finish her American championship with three five-point majors; her Canadian championship with a Group Second; and earn her C.D. She is currently working on her C.D.X. Brooks was acquired from Wayne and Jo Sohlman as an eight-week-old puppy because of her top working and conformation pedigree. Sired by Ch. Bratiana's Rommel von Laurich, U.D., out of Ch. and OTCH Way-Mar's Disco Dawg, Brooks has lived up to both her conformation and obedience heritage, and has produced well. In her first litter, by Ch. Wilderness Broud, came several nice dogs,

including Wilderness Damon v. Sampson, owned by Sharon Richey. Also, Wilderness Kobuk Yogi Bear, owned by Bill and Sheri Harris, has started with some strong Puppy wins to his credit. This one is among several promising youngsters from Brooks' third litter. This breeding will be repeated.

Selected for his outstanding working ability as well as conformation quality, Ch. Rodsden's Quito of Wylan, C.D.X., T.D.X., B.H., SchH. II, FH, was the sire of Brooks' fourth litter.

Ch. Srigo's Rainbow Wilderness was added to Wilderness Rottweilers as an eight-week-old puppy in 1984, acquired from Srigo Kennels, selected for this kennel's long-standing record for excellence. Sired by Am., Can. Ch. Bronco vom Rauberfeld, SchH. III, FH, out of Srigo's Only By Magic, "Ruby" finished her championship in style with four majors, earning her second five points to finish at the 1988 American Rottweiler Club Region V Specialty in Woodlinville, Washington. She has been bred to Kobuk.

Another bitch added to Wilderness in 1986, Damarot's Beretta Von Grave, T.D., sired by Belg. Ch. Grave Kapenborgh, SchH.

I, C.D., out of Heimgard's Adel Eisen Damm, C.D., passed her Tracking Test on her first attempt, owner trained and handled. Breeding to Kobuk is planned for her future.

Wilderness Rottweilers, although a small kennel, continue to produce quality dogs; they are excited over the up and coming litters and the continued success of their older dogs.

WILLSDEN

Willsden Rottweilers belong to James S. Bryan of Columbia, South Carolina. Mr. Bryan has owned Rottweilers since 1978, when he obtained a co-ownership of Ch. Edwards Brandy Caroline, who was five-and-a-half years old at that time. Brandy Caroline was later bred to Best in Show, Best in Specialty Show, multi-Group winning Am., Can. Ch. Donnaj Vermont Yankee v. Paulus, C.D.X., T.T. Brandy enjoyed a long life, as she lived to become 13½ years of age.

As a stud dog for its foundation bitches, Willsden currently uses the famed K.S., Int. Ch. Mirko von Steinkopf, C.D.X., FH, I.P.O. III, SchH. III, Registered Therapy Dog, whose numerous titles also include membership in the Medallion Rottweiler Club Hall of Fame,

American Rottweiler Club Silver Sire, plus numerous other titles and honors. Owner Jim Bryan notes with pride that there are now in his kennel two youngsters and two grandchildren of Mirko. They include a dynamic bitch puppy who was whelped in 1985 by Mirko ex Ch. Rodsden's Heika v. Forstwald, C.D., T.T., VH, Medallion Rottweiler Club Hall of Fame, bred by Jim and Roxanna McGovern (Windwalker Rottweilers) in New York. This pup became Windwalker's Willsden's Ande, C.D., who earned her first leg at 13 months after a run-off the first time out. She is also major-pointed, owner-handled. These points came just three days following her return from California where she was bred to

V-1 Oleo vom Haus Schmidgall, I.P.O. III, SchH. III. This litter was planned for its linebreeding on E.S., Int. Ch. Ives Eulenspiegel, SchH. III. James has kept one dog, Willsden's Jace Anden; and one bitch, Willsden's Cande Anden. They "just looked too good to part with."

Before Ande was bred, though, James had the opportunity to co-lease Ch. Weissenburg's Fury with Revera Wayburn, Mirko's owner. This bitch is by Am., Can. Ch. Birch Hill's Governor, Am., Can. C.D., ex Am., Can. Ch. Weissenburg's Don't-U-Dare. Both are in the Hall of Fame. Fury was leased from Marvin and Beverly Smith of Arkansas.

Fury was of course bred to Mirko, with James hoping for another foundation bitch like Ande. As fate would have it, they got six males, of which James kept one anyway because, again, it "just looked too good." This young dog is now Willsden's Joseph v. Mirkury, and he has tremendous potential. Very loving like his sire, he has already started Schutzhund training.

WINDCASTLE

Windcastle Rottweilers of Arroya Grande, California, became a reality after several years of research and intensive study when Carolyn and Bert Kaufmann acquired a puppy, Gatstuberget's Katarina, from Margareta McIntyre. "Kookie" was given to Mrs. Kaufmann as a birthday present by her husband, with the intention that the puppy would be a companion. Because of Katarina's intelligence, willingness to please, and excellent conformation, it was decided that she should be shown.

After becoming an American champion, Katarina was shown to her Canadian championship by her owner. With temperament as prime importance, a search was made for a potential stud dog of quality to whom she could be bred. So it was that, in 1983, Katarina was bred to Am., Can. Ch. Donnaj Herr I Am,

Can. Ch. Wyndhurst's Bond Apollo, a multiple Best of Breed winner and Group placer, owned by Randy and Roberta Shaw, Alta, Canada.

C.D., T.T., producing 12 puppies.

From this litter, there were two rated O.F.A. "excellent" and nine rated "good." Two of the males, Am., Can. Ch. Windcastle's California Kid ("Bulli") and Am., Can. Ch. Windcastle's X-tra Special, T.T. ("Rocky"), have remained together in the Kaufmann household as their owners' companions. Windcastle's Contessa, C.D., T.T., and Windcastle's Donnerkopf Gust, C.D., are also from this litter.

Because of the temperament and quality of the dogs from the first litter, the breeding was repeated. Am., Can. Ch. Windcastle's von Scharnhost ("Sam") resulted from this second breeding. Sam was originally a companion to an older couple who, because of a change in residence, returned him to Windcastle, where he was shown to his championship.

To broaden their base and at the same time maintain quality and substance for future breedings, Katarina was then bred to Ch. Razdy's Akemo Grande, C.D. Of the eight puppies whelped, a typey bitch, Canadian Ch. Windcastle's Morning Magic, was kept by the breeders and was bred to Best in Show, Best in Specialty Show Am., Can. Ch. Goldieche Ara von Brader, using the fresh-cooled shipped-

semen method. Litter brother Windcastle's Valentino, co-owned by Debbie and Leo Gravelle and Debbie and John Stafford, was Grand Sweepstakes Winner at the Golden State Rottweiler Club Specialty in June, 1988.

Katarina was bred to Ara in June, 1987, producing one bitch, Windcastle's Special Blend, who is presently in the conformation ring. She was Best in Match at the Medallion Rottweiler Club's Fall 1988 Best of Breed Match.

All dogs at Windcastle are house dogs. Bulli and Rocky are inseparable as their owners' constant companions and guardians of the ranch at Arroyo Grande, California. The search goes on for Rottweilers which, when bred to Windcastle bitches, will improve the breed.

Above: Janlynn's Onyx taking Best of Opposite Sex (and Best of Winners) at Saskatoon K.C. Janlynn Rottweilers are owned by Mr. and Mrs. D.G. Flury, Sask., Canada.
Left: Can. Ch. Wolfsanger's Ashburg, C.D., was the foundation bitch of Prairiesky Rottweilers, owned by Mrs. Corinne Walker.

Can. Ch. Wyndhurst's von Kaira is a multiple Puppy Group winner and the youngest Rottie to have earned a championship. Owners, Wyndhurst Kennels.

WINDROCK

Windrock Rottweilers are owned by C.M. and Jane Justice of Ypsilanti, Michigan. The kennel is the result of a lifelong interest in dogs and a family who owned and operated a large boarding and training kennel in Michigan.

Jane's father, Paul Dawson, was a field trial judge and handler specializing in Brittanys. As a child, most of Jane's weekends were spent on the road traveling to field trials in the Midwest with her father.

In 1978, Jane and her husband obtained their first Rottweiler, a pet bitch purchased for obedience. She became Mar-Jan's Windrock Roxie, Am., Can. C.D.X., T.D., and a member of the Medallion Rottweiler Club Honor Roll. She is still going strong. It was not until 1983 that the Justices became involved in conformation breeding and showing of Rotties. At that time, they purchased a male puppy from Nancy Back in Germantown, Maryland. He was sired by Ch. Radio Ranch's X-tra Special out of Ch. Winterhawk's Cobi v. Bethal. Although he too was purchased for obedience, it did not take his owners long to be bitten by the "bug"—conformation competition. "Rosco," as they called him, became the Justices first champion, Am., Can. Ch., OTCH Winterland's Chief Justice, U.D.T., Can. T.D.

Justice finished his championship with all majors. He has multiple Best of Breed wins and Group placements. He is a member of the Medallion Rottweiler Club Hall of Fame and was American Rottweiler Club Top Ten Obedience Dog for 1986. The Justices enjoy training and handling their own dogs.

The first litter was not bred at Windrock until 1985. It was sired by Chief Justice from Pinebrae's Brita Aus dem Asend, Am., Can. C.D., who was a daughter of Ch. Donnaj Vermont Yankee of Paulus, C.D.X. From this litter two bitch puppies were kept, Am., Can. Ch. Windrock's Fanni von Richter and Am., Can. Ch. Windrock's Flora von Richter, T.D.

Fanni was bred to Can. Ch. Goldeiche Brick v. Mikon, C.D.X., (Ch. Birch Hill's Governor ex Ch. Rodsden's Hella v. Forstwald), resulting in nine puppies which show lots of promise. Hopes are especially high for a male and a female that the Justices are keeping, Windrock's Ollie von Richter and Windrock's Sophia von Richter. Both have some nice match wins and have started working careers, Ollie in tracking and Sophie in ring sport.

Flora is now awaiting the birth of her first litter, also sired by Can. Ch. Brick v. Mikon, C.D.X. She will then resume her Schutzhund training.

The Justices are proud to say that they have personally earned 24 titles on their dogs so far in conformation, obedience and tracking–not to mention the hardworking people who are out earning titles on Windrock puppies and those dogs sired by Rosco out of some very nice bitches.

Rosco is now retired from conformation showing, although he will be very actively working on his SchH. I and FH. He still races in Flyball competition and competes in Agility and Grand Prix-style racing and is always in the ribbons when he attends these events.

WINDWALKER

Windwalker Rottweilers are owned by James William McGovern of Port Crane, New York. Mr. McGovern started out in Rotties

with an experience which might well have discouraged a less dedicated fancier.

The McGoverns leased the lovely bitch, Ch. Rodsden's Heika v. Forstwald, from Linda P. and William L. Michels for their first litter, to which they looked forward with keen anticipation. The sire of the puppies was the many-titled Ch. Mirko vom Steinkopf.

When the eight puppies in that litter were three days old, their tails were docked, and the veterinarian examined Heika. He pronounced everything fine, and optimism was high. But that very night, due to an unusually fast and virulent organism, Heika died of septicemia.

Canada's No. 1 Rottweiler for 1987. Best in Show, Best in Specialty, Can., Bda. Ch. Rotterre Bardolph Buckenberg, T.T., is a member of the Sovereign R.C. Honour Roll and the Medallion R.C. Honor Roll. Owner, J. Jacqueline Stephenson.

Am., Can. Ch. Bryloukis Great Expectations, C.D.; Freedom Farms Asha Gold; Wilderness Heir of Freedom; and Can. Ch. Simsberg's Fagan prepare for a super Rottie ride. Photo courtesy of Katie Nolan, Anchorage, AK.

Thus the eight orphans were left for Jim and Roxanna McGovern to raise by hand. Some novice breeders would have immediately panicked, but not the McGoverns. Despite the fact that both worked full time (fortunately in this case on different shifts), they still managed to keep every one of the puppies alive and healthy. They even chose to bottle-feed rather than tube-feed, since they felt that the sucking reflex was important. Today seven of these eight puppies are titled (the untitled one lost a hip socket in a car accident but is still a happy, healthy pet), and there are more titles still to come.

Such a happy ending is a great credit to the McGoverns; they rose so competently to the emergency and stuck so faithfully to a schedule which must sometimes have seemed a trying one. They must take pride in the success of these babies, and I must say that they are folks who this author thinks of as being truly dog people!

Not in the least discouraged by any of this, the McGoverns since have had a "B" and a "C" litter, both of them high-quality and most promising.

YDEN

Yden Rottweilers are owned by Yvette M. Howard of New Ipswich, New Hampshire, where presently two Rottie bitches share the home with their owners and three small children.

Yden's first Rottweiler and foundation bitch was purchased as a puppy from Von Bruka Kennels. She was the only bitch in that litter. Owner-handled, she became Am., Can. Ch. Von Bruka Indra v. Yden, Am., Can. C.D., T.T. She was sired by Top Producer and Gold Sire Ch. Eiko vom Schwaiger Wappen, C.D.X., SchH. III, out of the lovely German bitch, Gundy vom Luckshof, Z.T.P.R.

"Indy" started her show career at age eight months with a Best in Match over adults at the 1983 Colonial Rottweiler Club Specialty Match. The highlights of her career are: at the 1984 Colonial Rottweiler Club Specialty Show, first in a large American-bred Class; at the 1984 Silver Anniversary event of the Medallion Rottweiler Club, first in the 12–18 months Junior Bitch Class; first prize and Winners Bitch over 125 bitches in competition under judge Mrs. Tineke Boltjes of the Netherlands. She completed her championship at the Ladies Dog Club, a Colonial Rottweiler Club-supported entry, with a Best of Winners for a four-point major. The following weekend, as a special, she went Best of Breed and on to a Group Four.

Indy was also the American Rottweiler Club Regional Specialty Best of Opposite Sex, followed the next day by Best of Opposite Sex at Westchester Kennel Club. At the 1987 Colonial Specialty, she was winner of the Brood Bitch Class and earned the first leg of her C.D. with a third in Novice. With interruptions due to motherhood for both Indra and her owner, she was only specialed on a limited basis, and her obedience title was delayed. But she always bounced back and achieved multiple breed wins, Bests of Opposite Sex, and another Group placement along with the completion of her C.D. degree in four shows. In the last leg she earned first place in Novice A at the 1988 Colonial Rottweiler Specialty.

Indra next achieved both championship and C.D. in Canada in just three days. She is a Producer of Merit and the dam of Specialty winners.

Yden's first litter was from Indra and sired by Ch. Bronko vom Rauberfeld, SchH. III. This litter produced three puppies, one of them Yden's Morgen, C.D., who, sad to report, died of parvovirus right at the beginning of a promising career.

In the second litter, Yden combined German and American lines with the objective of producing offspring with strong working ability plus sound conformation qualities. The stud selected was Ch. Brash Baer von Pioneer, C.D., who is the son of Ch. Graudstarks Lugar, C.D., T.T., Medallion Rottweiler Club Hall of Fame; the dam was a Ch. Donnaj Vermont Yankee daughter, Ch. Robil Marta v. Donnaj, dam of Best in Show Ch. Pioneer's Beguilded. Baron O.J. Von Yden has become a numerously titled obedience dog, who finished his C.D.X. in three consecutive trials with three first

placements, these having included the 1988 Colonial Rottweiler Club Specialty and the 1988 American Rottweiler Club National. O.J. has consistently earned placements of Highest Scoring Rottweiler in Trial and was ranked as No. 4 nationally in the combined Open A and Open B classes.

O.J.'s littermates are Bda. Ch. Pioneer's Bounder v. Yden and Ch. Yden's Blithe Spirit. The former, owned by Jerome Simons, a resident of Bermuda, completed his title in Bermuda within three

Top: Denel's Instigator v. Eisen, age 2 years, by Ch. Beaverbrook Eisen v. Bruin ex Denel's Limited Edition. Tonya Jones Oldham, owner, Lakeview Rottweilers. *Bottom left:* Ch. Doroh's Just Grand, T.D., owned by Veronica Wade and D.A. Wade, Clinton, MD. *Bottom right:* A Just Grand head study—a very grand Rottie.

Roma Rottweiler's famous "Buddy" here finishing his Canadian C.D. and taking First in Class while doing so. Smiling Robert Martin accepts award as Buddy maintains his dignity.

days by taking Best of Breed at the 1987 Bermuda Rottweiler Club Specialty after some good wins in the United States. The latter, Blithe Spirit, has had an exciting show career which found her a champion with three majors, including two consecutive Bests of Breed from the classes over Specials and Winners Bitch at the A.R.C. Regional in Tennessee for five points. She is owned by Sandra A. Moses, Adler Rock Rottweilers.

The "C" and "D" litters are doing well in competition. Yden's second generation will carry on nicely in the family tradition.

ZOLTY

Although a new kennel of the breed, Zolty Rottweilers, owned by Bob Csolti, are off to a flying start

with their notable bitch, Am., Can. Ch. Kitty von Kodiak, Am., Can. C.D., SchH. I.

Located in Chico, California, Zolty is justly proud of the fact that Kitty was a Top Ten Bitch in the American Rottweiler Club System for 1987–1988. She was Best in Specialty Show at the American Rottweiler Club Regional in 1988 in Region V, and she has multi-Best of Breed and Group successes to her credit.

Kitty is eligible for the Medallion Rottweiler Club Honor Roll in 1989 and the Medallion Rottweiler Club Hall of Fame in 1991. Additionally, she has one leg on her C.D.X. and is going for her Schutzhund II and will continue, hopefully, to gain her Utility and Schutzhund III degrees.

Kitty's first breeding to Am., Can., Mex. Ch. Quick von Siegerhaus, Am., Can. C.D., has produced three champions and two others who are pointed towards their titles.

The Csoltis had been working and showing different breeds of dog since the late 1970s, in search of one that could do all forms of working as well as succeed in the show ring. Their first Rottweiler was Kitty, whom they acquired in 1984 and who proved that this is the breed which meets all their requirements. With her bench show, obedience, and Schutzhund titles, Kitty more than fills the bill as the dog they were seeking.

ZORNHAUS

Zornhaus Rottweilers are owned by Pamela Zorn Anderson, who is a highly successful and extremely talented naturalist artist. The kennels have been established since the mid-1970s, located in Wilton Manors, Florida.

Top bitch among these Rotties and the favorite in her owner's affections will always be Ch. Katryn The Great von Ursa. She had a highly successful show career, earned her C.D. at 11 months, and produced some very notable puppies. Sadly, Katryn had to be put to sleep in her owner's

NEW CD

arms at age 11 years, as she was suffering from spinal arthritis.

Pamela Anderson has remained consistent in her breeding program, continuing to cross the Ch. Donnaj line descended from Jan Marshall's Yankee. She tells us quite proudly that she has gained a reputation of being one from which buying a dog is difficult, as those doing so are required to complete an obedience course with their dog. This requirement and the soundness of her dogs have both made a steady list of wonderful homes seeking them. She breeds only when looking for a new show dog for herself and is most particular about to whom the others will be entrusted.

To improve knowledge of the breed, Pamela has been involved with numerous testing of new vaccines on her litters, congenital tracking on hips, and nutrition. Also, working with some leading veterinarians across the country, it has been possible to help other breeders with pre-, post- and neo-natal problems. As she says, "We all know there is a vast knowledge pool out there, but unfortunately not enough breeders are willing to share the wealth."

Some of the current "stars" at Zornhaus include Zornhaus Ex Zacht, C.D., pointed towards a conformation title; Epic's Burning Desire, C.D.X., pointed, with several high scoring awards (bred by Bob and Rose Hogan); and Ch. Donnaj Music Man, bred by Jan Marshall. There are also several other splendid young dogs who are in the ring now earning points for titles.

ROTTWEILERS IN ALASKA

Freedomfarms Rottweilers came about by accident, according to Katie Nolan who, with her husband, Pete, owns this excellent establishment which is dedicated to Rottweilers in Anchorage, Alaska.

Katie was looking for a large purebred dog with short hair and no tail when she was introduced to her neighbor's Rottweiler. Katie

contacted the breeder, Cynthia Ronay, of Bryloukis Rottweilers in British Columbia, Canada, inquiring about a "pet quality" female. A twist of fate brought her a dog destined to become Am., Can. Ch. Bryloukis Great Expectations, C.D.

A late-maturing dog like his sire, Select Am., Can. Ch. Don-Ari's Harras, "Tank" finished at three years with three five-point majors. Circumstances in Alaska do not make training and showing easy, with only eight American Kennel Club shows plus an additional four trials per year. Majors are few and far between in most breeds, and "clusters" are encouraged, to take advantage of long drives and difficult weather conditions. When

Ch. Double C's Ajib taking Best of Winners under noted authority Mrs. Muriel Freeman, while en route to his championship back in 1984. Owned by Arthur Coia and handled by Darrell L. Hayes. Ajib is a son of Ch. Lyndhausens Alpha Sunrise ex Ch. Kanine Alerts Double C's Basha.

Above: Christmas 1987: the Von Bruka Rottweilers out with their sleds in the snow. Owners, Bruce and Karen Billings. *Below:* Am., Can. Ch. Ebonstern's Ivan v.d. Liebe, by Cabo from Bryt Promise, is another on the Top Producer list. Owner, Cheryl Wheeler.

an Alaskan dog makes any Top Ten list, it's a real accomplishment. To finish, as Tank did, with back-to-back majors, is practically unheard of in Alaska.

An experimental breeding produced Doubledee's Alternate Choice, who became a multiple Best of Breed and Group place winner, and Katie Nolan was "hooked."

Husband Pete Nolan brought home a puppy bitch from JoAnn Harnish's Wilderness Kennel. That pup, Wilderness Heir of Freedom (Int. Ch. Arras Zur Spielmannsaus, SchH. III, ex Am., Can. Ch. The Chena Wilderness, C.D.) did quite well in her breed classes, winning both days at the last cluster, and completed the first leg of her C.D. on that same weekend. Only in Alaska, Katie ruefully remarks, would it be necessary to wait four months for her next trial.

Meanwhile, Tank produced a second litter with RJ's Wilderness K.C., C.D. (Ch. Starkheim Duf Morgan Carroll ex Lady Ruger, C.D.X., VB) which resulted in several excellent offspring. This litter included RJ's Bear Mountain Ace, a multiple Best of Breed and Group winner both in Alaska and in limited showing elsewhere; and Axel von Trume and RJ's Azura von Bryloukis, both of whom displayed outstanding obedience and conformation potential.

Tank's third breeding, to Panamint Polar Delight, C.D. (Ch. Donar von der Neckarstroom ex Von Chrisstenbrade Desire) again produced some winning offspring, including Glacier Valley Flying Ebony, pointed from the puppy classes, and Glacier Valley Man 'O War, who is being groomed to fill his dad's shoes.

Again going back to Wilderness, Tank's next breeding was to Connie's Wilderness von Ursa, C.D. ("Connie's" is owned by Connie Thomas), a littermate to K.C. This smaller litter produced several more winners, including Connie's Rana von Ursa, who is undefeated from the Puppy Classes and has taken several Winners Bitch and Reserve Winners Bitch awards from there. Rana also won Best of Opposite Sex from the Bred-by-Exhibitor Class at age 15 months.

Noticing too many dogs in the breed ring who were not proving working ability, Katie saw to it that Tank gained his C.D., trained for his C.D.X., and between trials started working on his Schutzhund title. Tank is well on his way

towards a tracking title and enjoys the protection phase immensely. He was Temperament Tested, scoring 32 out of a possible 33 points; is used throughout the local school district's animal education program in grades kindergarten to sixth; and pulls a racing-type dog sled full of neighborhood kids for wintertime fun.

Pete and Katie were aching for their kennel name on an offspring, so returning to Canada they purchased one of that nation's top winning bitches, Can. Ch. Simebergs Fagan (Am., Can. Ch. Trollegen's Benjamin ex Ch. Cita vom Simeberg) from the Simebergs' well-known "F" litter. Tank and Fagan, very compatible genetically, produced Freedomfarm's "A" litter. A tragedy left but one surviving puppy, Freedomfarms Asha Gold, so named because she was raised by a Golden Retriever, Ch. Kinsha's Flight to Rush Hill. A second breeding is planned.

Meanwhile, Fagan is looking for those elusive majors to finish her American championship. She took Best of Opposite Sex and Best of Winners with one of the first five-point majors seen in the state since Tank finished in 1986.

There are advantages to be found in living in an isolated area. On her first major show circuit *outside* (i.e., away from Alaska), Katie was struck by the incredible, wide variety of type seen in the breed ring. Alaska's more limited gene pool narrows that variety, and the overall excellence of the breed is, she feels, quite good. Also, with such experienced breeders as Sheila Carter of Sheilarae's Rottweilers and JoAnn Harnish of Wilderness (now located in Oregon), the standard of excellence was set. With several conscientious new breeders such as Rhonda Nielson of RJ's, Connie Thomas of Connie's, Sandy Potter of Tealaske, Adrianne Schaeffer of Glacier Valley, and Merle Page of Black Watch, the Rottweiler's future in Alaska is most promising.

Katie feels strongly that the top

Alaskan show Rotties must be able to work and to produce working temperaments in their offspring, and she is committed towards working titles as well as conformation on all her offspring and breeding stock. Her "A" litter pup, Asha, is currently in early training for a Schutzhund degree. Trainer Roman Bratslavsky says of Asha, "This young bitch shows an

Above: The Scholls' Ch. Weissenburg Lucifer v. Roxer and Ch. Roxer's Rhiannon, C.D. *Below:* Von Gailengen's "M" littermates at age 7 months: Miller Time, Match Point, Matinee Idol, and Made To Order. Bred and owned by C.M. Thompson.

Right: Von Gailengen's Made to Order, Am., Can. C.D.C.M. Thompson, owner. *Below:* EPA Hekili Ino von Riva, C.D., windsurfs with owner Nancy Blackeney in Makakilo, HI.

excellent blend of prey and defense drives, with a tremendous desire to work. Her strong fighting drive and enthusiasm, combined with her good conformation, create a dog which can be trained for virtually anything. Once you've owned a dog like her, you won't settle for anything less."

Looking to the future, Freedomfarms plan to continue their breeding program, emphasizing the Canadian and American bloodlines which they feel are superior to the rest of the world's.

ROTTWEILERS IN HAWAII

Probably one of the first Rottweilers seen in Hawaii was imported from the U.S. mainland as a puppy during the 1960s and sold to George and Wanda Brenner. This puppy was Rodsden's Kaiser v.d. Harque, and he was the only Rottweiler shown in Hawaii at that time. Exhibited on only two occasions, he took a Group Second on one of them. The Brenners got several more Rottweilers following Kaiser, these from George Williams, who imported breeding stock from England.

During the early 1970s, Ralph and Thora Martin imported a male from Australia. "Rome," as he was called, became the first Rottweiler to earn a C.D.X. in Hawaii. He was bred by Mrs. Maureen Wilkinson and was by Ch. Jaheriss Drummer Boy ex Jaheriss Arzolle. A multiple Best of Breed and Group placer, he was the first Rottie to go Group First in Hawaii, the No. 3 ranked Working Dog in 1978, and the No. 1 Working Dog in 1979.

Ch. Stablemates Diamond Bear (Ch. Rodsden's Rough Diamond ex Ch. Trollegens Bear) and Ch. Cybele J. von Goldenwest (Ch. Sussis Jens ex Fairvalleys Allouette Humbug) were the first and second female Rottweilers to finish championship in Hawaii. Bear was not only Hawaii's first female champion Rottweiler but also the first bitch to go over two male specials for Best of Breed.

Ch. Combo J. von Goldenwest, C.D. (same sire and dam as Ch. Cybele J.), was the first imported American champion Rottweiler to come to Hawaii. He became the first recognized home protection Rottweiler in the state.

Ralph and Thora Martin were the pioneers who started the Rottweiler off in show and obedience in Hawaii. Thora trained and exhibited many of her dogs herself in the breed ring and in the obedience ring. Ralph wanted to show the public that a woman is capable of handling a big, powerful dog of this type.

The mid-1970s also saw Peter Kamakawiwoole import a dog and a bitch from Pat Lanz's Borgvaale Kennel in England. The male was Borgvaale Vigilant Ekaika, C.D.X., (Jentris Gerontius ex Borgvaale Bonita) and the bitch was Borgvaale Black Tulip C.D., (Jentris Kyrie ex Borgvaale Bonita); thus they were half-brother and half-sister. Peter was very active in obedience with his dogs, and did extremely well training and handling them himself. Richelle Uyeda got a bitch from Peter's breeding of his two Rottweilers. Konia's Danica von

Lanz, C.D., T.D., became the first and remains the only Rottweiler to earn a tracking degree in Hawaii.

The late 1970s and early 1980s saw the importation of numerous Rotties from Australia to Hawaii. The dogs principally came from the Heatherglen, Auslese and Rotvel Kennels in Australia. The advantage of bringing dogs in from Australia versus the United States mainland was that there was no quarantine restriction for dogs coming from the rabies-free areas such as Australia, New Zealand, and the United Kingdom.

The mid-1980s was the beginning of a massive importation of Rottweilers to Hawaii. Jill Oder-Nakache imported numerous dogs from England (Upend Kennels),

Above: **Florentina von Stolzenfels, bred by Jack and Dr. Evelyn M. Ellman, is owned by Dr. Brent Bailey.** *Left:* **Can. Ch. Damien's A Sly Guy, C.D., and the future Can. Ch. Barlin's Abraxus von Damien (at 6 months) are representative of the type and quality that sets apart Mike and Irene Jackman's kennel in Port Perry, Ont., Canada.**

Germany, and the U.S. mainland (von Meadow, Big Oaks, Jenecks Kennels). Others imported from Majorhousen, Stablemate, Trollegen, Sanron, vom Haus Schmidgall, and Rassentreu lines.

Richelle Uyeda imported a bitch puppy from Thora Hart of Ridgerunner Rottweilers in California. She is Ch. Ridgerunners Rowdy Roma, U.D., also known as "Inga." She is from Am., Can. Ch. Trollegens Benjamin ex Trollegens Mittens. Inga is a multiple Best of Breed winner, a Group placer, the only Rottweiler to earn a U.D. in Hawaii, as well as the only champion U.D. Rottweiler in Hawaii. She was awarded the American Rottweiler Club's No. 8 Rottweiler in Obedience for 1985. Inga is a great goodwill ambassador for the breed as she

participates in obedience, scent/hurdle relay, and Flyball demonstrations at elementary schools, fairs, childrens hospitals and nursing homes.

Kathy Crumpton has imported several dogs from the mainland. Ch. Miss Ellie von Meadow, C.D., T.D. (Ch. Donnaj Vermont Yankee of Paulus ex Ch. Minnelli von Meadow), was brought over in whelp following breeding to Int. Ch. Ingo vom Steinkopf, SchH. II, C.D. Miss Ellie was the No. 1 Rottweiler in the State of Hawaii for 1985. Ch. Asta von Rika, C.D. (Lex vom Mummler ex Prinzess vom Meadow) finished her championship in Hawaii and was the No. 1 Rottweiler there for 1984. Many dogs from Kathy's breeding can be seen in the ring today.

Eleanor Hinton imported several dogs from Germany, including Jupp vom Hagdeberg (Anton vom Heim ex Babette vom Magdeberg), Dina von Fusse de Angelberg (Basko vom Willgensteiner Land ex Assy vom der Teichmuhle), and Heidi vom Bergenhaus (Brando vom Haus Neubrand ex Molli vom Hause Haegele). Mrs. Hinton had several litters and took some of her dogs with her when she moved to Australia.

Bruce Mau was a big importer of dogs from the mainland and Germany. His Ch. Bucmars Apollo Regere (Ch. Radio Ranch's X-tra Special ex Ebony Acres Onyx Amber) and Ch. Anro's Gold Hanna (Ch. Krugaran von Meadow ex Allegra von Meadow) both finished their championships in Hawaii. Ch. Anro's Hawaiian Angel (Ch. Krugaran von Meadow ex Allegra von Meadow) not only finished her championship but was a multiple Best of Breed and Group placer as well. She was Hawaii's No. 1 Rottweiler for 1987. Maureen Wilkinson (Trollegen) and Thora Hart (Ridgerunner) found a beautiful male for Bruce on the mainland, Ch. Simeberg's Gambler (Ch. Trollegens Frodo ex Ch. Simeberg's Czarina), who finished his championship in Hawaii, was a Multiple Best of Breed and Group

Turning the tables, this puppy at the 1988 National Specialty is obviously enjoying being taken for a sled ride. Photo by C.M. Thompson.

placer and was Hawaii's No. 1 Rottweiler for 1986. Another import was Ridgerunner Aint Misbehavin (Achat vom Daemmerwald ex Trollegens Mitten) from Thora Hart. Bruce imported several bitches from Germany, too, and his most recent import is a male, Urban Eulenspiegel (Elko vom Hohenhamelin ex Laska von Schwaiger Wappen).

Garry and Marcia Fross originally started off with Australian stock but later imported several dogs from the mainland. They are Trinity's Bravo v. Liebenswert (Ch. Mirko vom Steinkopf ex Ch. Trinity Danke v. Dachmar, C.D.X.) and Altar's Frani of Alastar (Ch. Altar's Gaither vom Axel ex Bruins Aja v. Edgewater Iris). These folks and their Rotties are active both in obedience and conformation.

Lia Mesquit imported several dogs of Dedeaux breeding when she moved to Hawaii with her family from the mainland. Her Ch. Rivy's Samson de Dedeaux (Plato's Noesis ex Dedeaux's Grace) finished his championship and consistently placed in the Group to earn Hawaii's No. 1 Rottweiler for 1988, No. 3 Top Working Dog for 1988, and No. 7 All-Breed for 1988. Sam is handled by Mrs. Sue Cates.

Tom and Nancy Blakeney, as well as Daniel Chock, are all very active in obedience with their Rottweilers. The Blakeneys' Epa Ino von Rika, C.D., (Axel's Magic von Meadow, C.D., ex Mis Ellie von Meadow, C.D., T.D.) and Daniel Chock's Miki 'ala Tyler Ross are both working in Open towards their C.D.X. degrees.

These are just a few of the people in Hawaii committed to preserving the Rottie as a working breed, protecting the Rottweiler through the efforts of a Code of Ethics Rottweiler Club, and educating as many people as possible about the Rottweiler.

Dog fanciers in Hawaii are faced with a special handicap: there are very few shows and obedience trials available for them to enter.

There are only four licensed all-breed shows offered throughout the year on the island of Oahu, where 90% of the dog fanciers reside. There are also four all-breed shows offered on the island of Hawaii that involve shipping the dogs by air to the outer island and locating lodgings that will accept dogs, which is almost impossible. There are only six licensed obedience trials offered per year on Oahu and four on Hawaii. Only three tracking tests and one T.D.X. test are available per year in the state, all on Oahu.

ROTTWEILERS IN PUERTO RICO

Carlos and Wanda Bonilla are Rottweiler enthusiasts whose dogs have brought fame and admiration

Merrymoore's Herr Memphis, as a puppy, becomes a Valentine's Day card for his owners, Earl M. Capellen, III, and Ron Briggs, Birmingham, AL.

Gina Marie's Class Act by Ch. Altar's Gunner of Woodland ex Patra Matrangel v. Foxcroft. Owners, L. Herring and M. Charlop.

to their kennel, located at Cagues, Puerto Rico. This is the home of an especially noted winner, Am., P.R., S.A., Guatemalan, Venezuelan and Int. Ch. Panzer von Krenkel.

Panzer was born in 1982 of royal lineage, being a son of WSG Brando vom Hause Neubrand, SchH. III, ex Mollie vom Hause Haegele, a daughter of BSG, Int. Ch. Benno vom Allgaeuer Torm, SchH. III. Panzer's pedigree shows him to be descended from some of the most highly esteemed Rottweilers of all time.

In the show ring, along with his numerous titles, Panzer accumulated the first place award in 20 Variety Groups, and was second place on five occasions. He was Best Visiting Dog when shown in Venezuela. He has competed in the United States at Westminster, and he has been seen by most of the important judges throughout the United States and South America. The Bonillas also are

owners of a very outstanding bitch, Venezuelan and Dominican Republic Ch. Beine von Steinbeckland, who should prove a tremendous asset to this kennel both in the show ring and as a producer.

Enthusiasm is high over Brando von Bergtanna-n-Bau, who looks to have a bright future. He is by Panzer and certainly seems destined to follow in the pawprints of his sire.

Puerto Rico is the only place in the world where it is possible to attain championship honors under both the American Kennel Club and the Fédération Cynologique Internationale at the same time, owing to the fact that these leading governing bodies both are recognized there. Thus it is a tremendously popular place for both North and South Americans to show dogs, which leads to some especially keen competition in the rings.

Top right: Ch. Janendorf Sensation, C.D., by Brabantsia Raiko ex Colbrae Candace. Owners, the Van Helvoorts.
Bottom right: Pioneer's Pine Island Ransom at 8 months, by Int. Ch. Ruben BGP I (a Danish import) ex Ch. Pioneer's Ingar von Krahn. Bred by Sheryl Hedrick and Christine Senter; owned by Ed Zwilling, Gerry Arth, and Sheryl Hedrick, Cleveland, OH.
Bottom left: Aust. Ch. Heroden Betty in April, 1989, by Guiding Flame (U.K. import) ex Rossvalley Marika. Owners, the Van Helvoorts of Gidgegannup, Western Australia.

American Rottweiler Club
PRODUCTION AWARDS

These awards are open to all Rottweilers, living or dead, that have distinguished themselves by their American-titled offspring. As production points accumulate, the individual sire or dam may receive the next higher award.

To be eligible for any award, a Rottweiler must meet the following four (4) requirements:

1. have produced at least one AKC Champion of Record
2. have produced at least one advanced obedience-titled pup (CDX, TDX, SchH I)
3. have produced at least three (3) titled offspring
4. have met the point requirements.

Bronze Production Award		*Silver Production Award*		*Gold Production Award*	
Males	25 points	Males	50 points	Males	75 points
Females	15 points	Females	30 points	Females	45 points

Production points are calculated as follows:

AKC Champion	3 points
AKC CD	1 point
AKC CDX	2 points (3 total points, CD & CDX)
AKC UD	3 points (6 total points, CD & CDX & UD)
AKC TD	1 point
AKC TDX	2 points (3 total points, TD & TDX)
AKC OTCH	3 points (9 total pts. CD & CDX & UD & OTCH)
SchH I	2 points
SchH II	2 points (4 total points, I & II)
SchH III	2 points (6 total points, I & II & III)
FH	2 points

Application for these awards may be sent to either Cathy Thompson or Mildred Bailey. The application must contain the name of the dog/bitch, breeder, owner, owner's address and phone number. It must also contain the names and titles of the offspring. In order to verify the titles, the application must also contain either the issue of the Awards magazine in which the title was published or a photocopy of the title certificate. Schutzhund titles must be verified by a photocopy of the certificate, scorebook, or the page of the USA or DVG America magazines in which the score was published.

If you are having trouble verifying the offspring, please contact either Cathy or Mildred for assistance.

SEND INFORMATION TO:

Cathy Thompson
RD #2, Box 384
Freehold, NJ 07728

Mildred Bailey
9130 W Marshall
Glendale, AZ 85305

American Rottweiler Club
PRODUCTION AWARDS
as of May, 1988

Gold Sires (75 or more points)

CH BIRCH HILL'S GOVERNOR, CD	23 CH, 1 CDX, 13 CD, 2 TD	87
CH DIETER VOM KONIGSBERG, CD	18 CH, 1 UD, 7 CDX, 23 CD, 2 TDX, 4 TD	114
CH DONNAJ VT YANKEE OF PAULUS, CDX	42 CH, 2 UD, 1 CDX, 29 CD, 2 TD	172
CH DUX VOM HUNGERBUHL, SchH1	39 CH, 1 UD, 4 CDX, 15 CD, 2 TD	152
CH EIKO VOM SCHWAIGER WAPPEN, CDX, SchH3	30 CH, 5 CDX, 30 CD, 5 TD, 1 SchH1	142
CH FALCO VAN HET BRABANTPARK	25 CH, 2 UD, 4 CDX, 15 CD, 2 TDX, 1 TD, 1 SchH3	127
CH GASTO VOM LIEBERBACHERHOF, CDX, TD	16 CH, 3 CDX, 19 CD, 1 TD	76
CH IGOR VON SCHAUER	24 CH, 1 OTCH, 5 CD, 1 TD, 1 SchH1	89
CH JACK VOM EMSTAL, CD, SchH1	17 CH, 3 CDX, 14 CD, 2 TD	76
CH KOKAS K'S DEGEN VON BURGA, CD, TD	21 CH, 4 UD, 1 CDX, 5 CD, 1 TD	96
CH LYN-MAR ACRES ARRAS V KINTA	20 CH, 1 UD, 2 CDX, 7 CD, 1 TD	80
CH MCCOY VON MEADOW, CD	18 CH, 2 CDX, 14 CD, 2 TD	76
CH PANAMINT OTSO V KRAEWEL, UD	10 CH, 3 UD, 4 CDX, 6 CD, 6 TD, 1 SchH3, 1 SchH2, 1 FH	84
CH RADIO RANCH'S AXEL V NOTARA	52 CH, 1 UD, 16 CD, 2 TD	180
CH RODSDEN'S ANSEL V BRABANT	48 CH, 11 CD, 1 TD, 1 SchH1	159
CH RODSDEN'S BRUIN V HUNGERBUHL, CDX	50 CH, 2 UD, 3 CDX, 28 CD, 8 TD, 2 TDX	213
CH RODSDEN'S ELKO KASTANIENBAUM, CDX, TD	31 CH, 7 CDX, 29 CD, 8 TD, 1 TDX, 1 SchH3	160
CH RODSDEN'S KANE V FORSTWALD, CD	22 CH, 2 CDX, 25 CD, 5 TD, 1 SchH2	106
CH RODSDEN'S KLUGE V D HARQUE, CD	33 CH, 3 UD, 3 CDX, 18 CD, 4 TD, 1 SchH2	152
CH TROLLEGEN'S FABLE	15 CH, 1 UD, 3 CDX, 16 CD	76
CH TROLLEGEN'S FRODO, CD	25 CH, 2 UD, 3 CDX, 16 CD, 2 TD	114
CH WELKERHAUS ROMMEL, UD	17 CH, 2 CDX, 19 CD, 1 TD	77

Gold Dams (45 or more points)

CH ANKA VON GAILINGEN	10 CH, 2 UD, 1 CDX, 5 CD, 2 TD	52
CH RC'S GATOR BEL VON MEADOW	17 CH, 1 CDX	54
CH RODSDEN'S GYPSY	7 CH, 3 UD, 1 CDX, 4 CD, 3 TD	49
CH RODSDEN'S LADY LUCK, CD	12 CH, 1 UD, 2 CD, 1 TD, 1 SchH2	49
CH V GAILINGEN'S WELKERHAUS CIA, CD	9 CH, 1 CDX, 12 CD, 1 TD	45

Silver Sires (50 to 74 points)

CH ASTRO VOM CHRISSENBRAD	13 CH, 1 CDX, 5 CD, 1 SchH3	53
CH AXEL VOM SCHWANENSCHLAG	17 CH, 3 CDX, 3 CD, 1 TD	64
CH BRATIANA'S GUS DE MICHAELA	13 CH, 2 UD, 8 CD	59
CH BIRCH HILL'S HASSO MANTEUFFEL, CDX, TD	6 CH, 1 UD, 2 CDX, 14 CD, 6 TD	50
CH BIRCH HILL MINUTEMAN, CD	16 CH, 14 CD, 1 TDX, 2 TD	67
CH CENTURION'S CHE VON DER BARR	13 CH, 1 UD, 1 CDX, 7 CD, 2 TD	57
CH GRAUDSTARK'S PEGASUS	15 CH, 1 CDX, 5 CD	53
CH HINTZ VON MICHELSBURG	15 CH, 1 CDX, 4 CD	52
CH NICK VON SILAHOPP	13 CH, 3 CDX, 6 CD	54
CH MIRKO VOM STEINKOPF, SchH3, FH, IPO3, CDX	12 CH, 1 CDX, 13 CD, 1 TD	52
CH NORTHWIND'S KAISER OF MALLAM	11 CH, 3 CDX, 8 CD, 1 SchH2	54
CH PANAMINT SENECA CHIEF	16 CH, 1 UD, 1 CDX, 6 CD	63
CH REX OF OLD ACRES	14 CH, 1 CDX, 6 CD	51
CH RODSDEN'S AXEL V H BRABANT	16 CH, 2 CDX, 10 CD, 1 TD	65
CH RODSDEN'S BERTE V ZEDERWALD, CDX	13 CH, 2 CDX, 17 CD, 1 TD	63
CH RODSDEN'S ZARRAS V BRABANT, CD	11 CH, 1 CDX, 17 CD	53
CH SRIGO'S ZARRAS V KURTZ	9 CH, 2 UD, 2 CDX, 5 CD, 2 TD	52
CH STARKREST'S POLO R	19 CH, 1 UD, 10 CD, 1 TD	74

Silver Dams (30 to 44 points)

CH AMSEL VON ANDAN, CD	9 CH, 1 UD, 1 CDX, 2 CD
CH ASTA VOM FORSTWALD, CD	7 CH, 1 UD, 1 CDX, 5 CD, 1 TDX
CH BRADY HASERWAY V HAUS KALBAS	12 CH, 1 CDX, 4 CD
CIRCE V GERTRUDENSHOF, CD	10 CH, 1 CDX, 4 CD
CH COSI VON STEIGSTRASSLE	6 CH, 1 UD, 4 CD, 3 TD
CH DOROH'S FANTASTIC SERENADE, CDX	4 CH, 1 UD, 2 CDX, 7 CD, 2 TD
EBONSTERN BRYT PROMIS V HELLER	8 CH, 1 UD, 3 CD, 1 TDX, 1 SchH2, 1 FH
CH FREEGER'S INGELA, CDX	6 CH, 1 UD, 3 CDX, 2 CD, 1 TD
CH GUNDI V REICHENBACHLE	8 CH, 1 CDX, 5 CD, 2 TD
CH KYNA VOM ODENWALD	8 CH, 2 CDX, 10 CD, 1 TD
CH NORTHWIND'S DANKA, CD	12 CH, 3 CD, 1 TD, 1 SchH1
PANAMINT DAGNA VD EICHEN	5 CH, 3 CDX, 7 CD, 1 TD
CH PANAMINT JOLLE VD EICHEN, CD	9 CH, 1 UD, 8 CD
CH PANAMINT SAPHIR V RHEINTAL, CDX, TD	2 CH, 1 UD, 2 CDX, 2 CD, 4 TD, 1 SchH3, 1 FH
CH PANAMINT SHASTA SAGE	7 CH, 2 CDX, 1 CD, 2 TD
CH RODSDEN'S BIRCH HILL BESS, CD, TD	7 CH, 1 CDX, 4 CD, 2 TD
CH RODSDEN'S BIRCH HILL HANNA, CDX, TD	6 CH, 3 CDX, 6 CD, 3 TD
CH RODSDEN'S BRUNNHILDE	6 CH, 1 UD, 1 CDX, 3 CD, 1 TD, 1 TDX, 1 SchH3
CH RODSDEN'S GAY LADY, TD	8 CH, 2 CDX, 3 CD, 2 TDX, 2 TD
WYVONIE VAN HET BRABANTPARK, CD, TD	4 CH, 1 UD, 1 CDX, 4 CD, 1 TDX, 1 TD, 1 SchH3, 1 FH

Bronze Sires (25 to 49 points)

CH ALPHA ALEXANDROS G BOADWAY	3 CH, 2 CDX, 12 CD, 2 TD, 1 SchH3, 1 FH
CH ARRAS VOM HASENKAMP	10 CH, 2 CDX, 10 CD, 1 TD, 1 SchH1
CH ARRI VON DER HEMBACHBRUCKE, SchH3, FH	5 CH, 1 CDX, 7 CD
CH BETHEL FARM'S APOLLO	10 CH, 1 UD, 1 CDX, 8 CD
CH BRONCO VON RAUBERFELD, SchH3, FH	8 CH, 1 CDX, 7 CD
CH BURLEY VON MORGEN CARROLL, CD	9 CH, 1 CDX, 3 CD
CH CARO VOM ZIMMERPLATZ	11 CH, 1 CDX, 6 CD, 2 TD
CH D'ARTAGNAN OF CANIDOM, CD	5 CH, 1 UD, 1 CDX, 2 CD
CH DONAR VON DER NECKARSTROOM	8 CH, 1 UD, 1 CDX, 5 CD, 1 TD
CH DON JUAN, UD	6 CH, 2 CDX, 5 CD
CH DONNAJ CRUSADER	9 CH, 3 CDX, 7 CD, 1 TD
CH DONNAJ GREEN MOUNTAIN BOY	8 CH, 1 CDX, 3 CD
CH ELEXI VON DER GAARN	7 CH, 1 UD, 4 CD, 1 TD
CH EPPO DON DER KEIZERSLANDEN, CDX	5 CH, 2 CDX, 10 CD, 2 TDX, 1 FH
CH FALK VOM KURSAAL, SchH1	11 CH, 1 CDX, 2 CD, 1 TD
CH GATSTUBERGET'S ESKIL JARL, CD	4 CH, 3 CDX, 5 CD, 1 TD
CH GROLL VOM HAUS SCHOTTROY, CD	5 CH, 1 UD, 10 CD, 1 TD
CH HASERWAY'S POLO BEAR C, CD	4 CH, 1 UD, 1 CDX, 9 CD, 1 TD
CH IOLKOS VOM DAMMERWALD, CD	6 CH, 1 CDX, 7 CD
CH JULIAS FRANS, CDX	7 CH, 1 OTCH, 1 CDX, 5, CD
CH MASON VOM ODENWALD, CDX	4 CH, 4 CDX, 22 CD
CH NORTHWIND'S DONAR OF RODSDEN	7 CH, 1 UD, 6 CD
CH PANAMINT NOBLE V FALKENBERG, CD	6 CH, 2 CDX, 2 CD, 1 TD
CH RADIO RANCH'S X-TRA SPECIAL	9 CH, 1 UD, 1 CDX, 8 CD, 1 TD
CH RHOMARK'S AXEL V LERCHENFELD, UDT	6 CH, 3 CDX, 5 CD, 3 TD
CH ROCKY VON ANDERSON	5 CH, 1 UD, 9 CD
CH RODSDEN'S ANDER VH BRABANT	12 CH, 1 CDX, 6 CD
CH RODSDEN'S DUKE DU TRIER	10 CH, 1 UD, 1 CDX, 4 CD, 1 TD

CH RODSDEN'S GORO V SOFIENBUSCH, UDT	7 CH, 1 UD, 1 CDX, 2 CD
CH RODSDEN'S HEIKO	6 CH, 2 CDX, 6 CD
CH RODSDEN'S ROUGH DIAMOND	7 CH, 1 CDX, 2 CD, 1 TD
CH RODSDEN'S TRISTAN V FORSTWALD, CD, TD	7 CH, 11 CD, 1 SchH1
CH TROLLEGEN'S BENJAMIN	7 CH, 1 UD, 2 CDX, 4 CD
CH UWE VOM KURSAAL	8 CH, 1 UD, 4 CD
CH VAN TIELEMAN'S CISCO, CD	7 CH, 4 CDX, 4 CD, 2 TD
CH WOTAN VOM KASTANIENBAUM, SchH3	4 CH, 1 UD, 2 CDX, 6 CD, 1 TD

Bronze Dams (15 to 29 points)

CH BEOWULF'S GIBSON GIRL	5 CH, 1 CDX
CH BIRCH HILL'S MAGNUM OPUS, CD	4 CH, 1 CDX, 4 CD
CH BRAV VON ANDAN	4 CH, 1 CDX
CH BRITZ VON ANDAN	3 CH, 1 OTCH, 1 CDX, 1 CD
CATJA VOM FRIEDRICHSBERG	4 CH, 1 UD, 2 CD
CH CEDAR KNOLL'S ALEXIS	6 CH, 5 CD, 1 SchH1
CH CHELSEA DE MICHAELA, CD	4 CH, 1 UD, 3 CD, 1 TD
CONCORD'S SPECIAL EDITION	7 CH, 1 CDX, 4 CD
CH DACHMAR'S ADAH VD BARENHOF, UDT, SchH2	4 CH, 2 CDX, 2 CD, 2 TD, 1 SchH1
CH DARRA MICHAELA VON STOLZENFELS, CD	3 CH, 1 CDX, 4 CD, 1 TDX, 1 TD
CH DELPHI BITT AMAX	3 CH, 1 UD, 1 CDX, 5 CD
CH DE RIEMER'S HROTSVITHA, CD	2 CH, 2 CDX, 3 CD, 1 TDX, 2 TD
CH DONNAJ HAPPY HOOKER	3 CH, 2 CDX, 2 CD
CH DONNAJ HIGH CLASS	5 CH, 1 UD, 1 CD
CH DOROH'S ENCHANTRESS V EBERLE, CD	4 CH, 1 UD, 1 CDX, 1 CD
CH DUKE'S OWN LADY BIANCA, CDX	2 CH, 2 CDX, 6 CD
CH ELOISE V GRUENERWALD	6 CH, 1 CDX, 1 CD
CH FREEGER'S JUNO, CD	5 CH, 1 CDX, 2 CD
CH GATSTUBERGET'S ASA V KLEINHOLZ, CD	4 CH, 1 UD, 1 CDX, 3 CD
CH GATSTUBERGET GISELLE GAMINE	2 CH, 1 CDX, 7 CD, 1 TD
CH GATSTUBERGET'S HEXA, CD	4 CH, 3 CD, 1 TD, 1 SchH3
CH GINA VON INGENHOF, CD	3 CH, 1 CDX, 3 CD
GRAUDSTARK'S QUATRO TEMPO	4 CH, 1 CDX
CH GUDRUN VON ANDERSON	6 CH, 1 CDX
GUNDA VON INGENHOF	3 CH, 1 UD, 2 CD, 1 TD
CH JACQUELINE DA BRATIANA, CD	6 CH, 1 CDX, 5 CD, 1 TD
CH JAY-SAN'S MEISTER ZUCKER BAR, CD, TD	3 CH, 1 UD, 3 CD
CH MARGARITA VON MEADOW, CD	3 CH, 1 OTCH, 2 CD
CH MERRYMOORE'S ULTIMATUM	5 CH, 1 CDX
CH NOBLEHAUS AIN'T MISBEHAVIN	7 CH, 1 CDX
CH PANAMINT LINDE V RHEINTAL, CD	2 CH, 2 CDX, 2 CD, 2 TD, 1 SchH2
CH PANAMINT RANI V D SANDHAUFFEN, CD	4 CH, 1 UD, 1 CDX, 1 CD, 1 TD
CH PANAMINT RIGHT BRIGHT, CD	4 CH, 1 CDX, 2 CD
CH QUELLE VON DER SOLITUDE, CD	7 CH, 1 CDX, 2 CD, 1 TD
CH ROJA'S A GUMBO FILE', UD	2 CH, 1 CDX, 5 CD, 1 SchH2
CH RODSDEN'S FROLICH BURGA, CD, TD	5 CH, 1 CDX, 5 CD, 1 TD
CH RODSDEN'S HEIKA V FORSTWALD, CD	4 CH, 1 CDX, 3 CD
CH TANA VOM ODENWALD	3 CH, 3 CDX, 7 CD
CH VANGARD'S KELSEY, CD	4 CH, 1 CDX

Right: A lovely head study of the Specialty-winning bitch Ch. Pioneer's Image of Evrmor, C.D., owned by Janna Morgan, Aurora, CA. *Bottom:* Ebonstern Yonada v. Musquaw (by Olympus ex Megan) at a stock trial. Photo courtesy of Cheryl Wheeler.

The Rottweiler in Great Britain

The history of the Rottweiler in Great Britain dates back to the occasion when a very famous and well-respected fancier of many breeds of dog, Mrs. Thelma Gray, making one of her frequent visits to a German Sieger Show, found her attention being attracted away from the Alsatians (the breed she had come to watch) and toward a number of big black dogs in a line on the benches. It was love at first sight, as Mrs. Gray was little short of fascinated by what she saw. She admired every inch—from the clean-cut conformation to the sensible, chunky heads and the friendly, kindly, and intelligent expressions. She thought the coats ideal, the color striking. Then and there, the Rotties gained a new friend.

Coincidentally, at about this same time, Thelma Gray received a small legacy from a distant relative. How better to enjoy it than by bringing this breed home for an introduction to Great Britain?

So it was in 1936 that Thelma made her first Rottweiler purchase, a bitch she admired tremendously by the name of Diana v.d. Amalienburg, SchH. I. Thrilled at having ownership of her, Thelma could hardly wait for her quarantine period to be done with.

But we all know about the "best laid plans of mice and men," and although she did so reluctantly, Thelma finally agreed to sell this bitch to a most eager and persistent lady who *also* thought her something special, Mrs. Simmons from Newbury, who added her own kennel prefix, Crowsteps, to Diana's name. Mrs. Gray had pondered long and hard prior to parting with Diana, but did so for the sensible reason that she was anxious to popularize the breed in Great Britain and that this could be best accomplished by encouraging more people to become owners.

Thus it was that Thelma Gray made her second Rottie purchase, this time another bitch, three years old, Enne v. Pfalzgau, who had been bred by Herr Weinmann and was sired by Dago v. Stadweiher.

A consistent winner in Germany, Enne had many awards, including first, and ratings of excellent to her credit. Thelma, however, was not truly delighted with her head, and was disappointed when Enne quite consistently passed this trait along to her offspring. She did have other features to recommend her, though, such as good body conformation, a gentle disposition, and particularly brilliant coloring of glossy black highlighted by

> "She admired every inch—from the clean-cut conformation to the sensible, chunky heads and the friendly, kindly, and intelligent expressions."

Top: Black Velvet von Dorow, a homebred owned by Nancy E. Estes, Von Dorow Rottweilers. *Middle:* Ch. Mink Hollow's Briana, C.D., and Ch. Heidegruen's Dauntless Frisco, C.D., are owned by Montclaire Rottweilers, Wil and Cathy Wankel, Calgary, Alta., Canada. *Bottom:* Merrymoore's Bounty Hunter, by Hasso vom Wildberger Schloss III ex Merrymoore's Moment In Time, is a handsome young male owned by Mrs. John W. Moore, Jr., Duluth, GA.

bright copper.

By a strange coincidence of circumstances, this bitch was also sold prior to coming out of her quarantine when a lady named Miss Paton saw her and promptly asked to purchase her. Thelma agreed just prior to the arrival of Enne's litter (born in quarantine, sired by Sieger Ido v. Kohlerwald, SchH. I, to whom Enne had been bred prior to departing from Germany). Sadly, those were the days of raging distemper—before all the modern preventative measures we now take for granted.

Of course, the puppies contracted it at the quarantine kennel and were lost, except for two, who were in bad shape and having seizures; they were not really expected to survive. Poor Miss Paton was, to say the least, distracted by the situation, and phoned Thelma to ask if she would take the two sick puppies and try to save them, in which case Miss Paton would give them to her. One would personally have to recall how it was during times of the great "distemper scourges" to know how Mrs. Gray must have felt at the thought of

bringing those sick puppies near her dogs at home. But she could not turn her back on them, so a complete isolation area was prepared and Thelma went to get them. One was so sick that it died almost immediately. The other Thelma succeeded in nursing back to good health and was named Anna from Rozavel. This bitch matured into a first-class worker, and her expertise in the trials helped to convert numerous spectators into Rottweiler lovers and owners.

Anna was trained by Mr. R.

Montgomery. Her career was a bright one which included many prizes and the C.D. degree. She fared well in conformation competition, and her successes there included Best of Breed at Crufts in 1939. Mrs. Gray has been quoted as not having considered Anna by any means a terrific show

report that Anna was given as a pet to the serviceman with whom a great mutual devotion existed. Having been born in 1936, she was considered too old to breed; but even if she wasn't, there was no stud dog around so far as anyone knew.

Following the sale of Enne,

Beautiful British-bred Rottweilers at the kennel of Violet Slade in England.

bitch. However, she must have felt well rewarded for her kindness in working so hard to save Anna's life when the dog was but a sick pup.

When World War II hostilities began, Anna went to war dogs, and so far as is known, she was the only Rottweiler left in England when the War ended. We like stories with happy endings, so we are glad to

Thelma Gray applied to the German Rottweiler Club for a good bitch and a young dog. As a result, Asta von Norden (by Bruno v.d. Burghalde ex Alma, bred by Herr Rohm) and Arnold v.d. Eichener Ruine (also sired by Bruno but from Bella v. Kaltental) arrived in England.

Arnold was a splendid dog and

Ch. Powderhorn's Lars of Wencrest, owned by Alice and Ben Beckler and Powderhorn/Wencrest Rottweilers, Inc.

Vefa von Kohlerwald Z.T.P.R. (sired by Arno v. Zehnthof ex Aga von Lederberg) was the last of Thelma Gray's importations, and she has been quoted as saying she was also the best. A big winner on the Continent, she did notable winning in Great Britain, too. Sadly she was involved in another quarantine tragedy, as she had been bred before leaving Germany and lost the entire litter of ten puppies.

The first breed class for Rottweilers in the U.K. was at Crufts in 1937. About eight of them turned out, Arnold taking Best of Breed and Enne Best of Opposite Sex, a clean sweep for Rozavel's entries. In 1938, Vefa was Best of Breed at Crufts.

During 1937 and 1938, classes for Rottweilers were included in an increasing number of show schedules, among them Cheltenham in 1938, where the judge was the very knowledgeable Herr Kammerer from Czechoslovakia. His selection for Best of Breed was Arnold.

The last pre-World War II import was a lovely young dog for Miss Homan. He was Benno von Kohlerwald, and had only just come through quarantine when war was declared. Benno was loaned to the Air Force, where he made out well, but it seemed impossible for him to readjust to civilian life.

Miss Paton married during the War, and thus went out of dogs. Mrs. Simmons died. The dogs Mrs. Gray had placed with a woman in Ireland "for the duration" (i.e. until they could safely return to England) simply disappeared and were never found.

The post-war story of Rottweilers in Great Britain cannot exactly be said to have picked up immediately at the end of hostilities, as this is not the case. For one reason or another, virtually none of the pre-war Rotties were left, and it was not necessary to pick up the pieces but rather to start entirely anew. Captain Roy Smith, who eventually

widely admired by those knowledgeable regarding type and quality in the breed. Arriving in England at age five months, he missed any opportunity of competing in Germany, where his admirers felt he should easily have become a *sieger*. Thelma did considerable winning with him in conformation and obedience, but she was sad to find that going through quarantine at his age had an adverse effect on his temperament. He never fully recovered from the trauma of the lonely confined siege of the quarantine. He was finally put down and the entire experience made Mrs. Gray resolve never again to put a puppy of that age through quarantine.

moved to Australia and in so doing helped with the establishment of Rottweilers there, is the person who in 1953 imported Berny v. Weyher and Ajax v. Fuhrenkamp, a dog and a bitch, purchased for the purpose of breeding to one another. Capt. Smith (Frederick Roy Smith, called Roy) was then a young officer in the Royal Corps of Veterinary Surgeons who grew tremendously interested in Rottweilers. As soon as he was settled with a veterinary practice in Romsey, he started importing dogs on which to build a kennel of his own.

Ajax was a nice enough dog, but we have read that Berny was a disappointment, as she was long-coated and not of much value as a matron for breeding. Lotte v. Oesterberg came next and was eventually bred to Ajax. She had real quality herself, but unfortunately was not a great producer, as she gave Capt. Smith just two male puppies. These were Rintelna the Aigeuner and Rintelna the Adjutant; almost immediately there were inquiries about them for stud dogs, which Capt. Smith would not permit as they were lacking the quality he hoped for, and he preferred that they did not perpetuate themselves for that reason.

Lotte did not produce what one would call a real litter until June, 1958, from which one dog was kept in England which was very much needed, as Ajax was then getting along in years. This dog became Rintelna the Bombadier and he was owned by Mrs. MacPhail. We have heard that he was a dog with much to offer, short backed and closely knit, of medium size and outstanding movement.

During this span of time, Rottweilers were acquiring a new enthusiast in one Mrs. Joanna Chadwick. She too made some importations, a dog and a bitch from the famed Eulenspiegel Kennel of Marianne Bruns (this kennel was extensively detailed in *The Book of the Rottweiler*). The bitch Quinta Eulenspiegel was the

first to arrive. She came out of quarantine extremely cowhocked, and thus was another disappointment. The dog, Rudi Eulenspiegel of Mallion, followed quite triumphantly, however, as he was a regal and beautiful dog of tremendous disposition who truly contributed to the progress of Rotties in Great Britain. Actually Quinta turned out better than originally expected despite the cowhocks. She produced six litters from 1956–1960 with seven to ten pups in each. Her "black" litters ("A," "B," "D," and "F") were sired by Rudi and her "C" litter was by Ajax.

Ch. Von Hottenstein's Charisma, by Ch. Alina's Adelbear of Wesley ex Ch. Von Hottenstein's Bear Handed. Bred by Nancy Reynolds, owned by Louis and Tammy Michnick.

Right: Cayman von Dorow, bred by Nancy C. Estes, owned by Mary Jo York, Elgin, TX. *Below:* Panzern's Ayla Mein Geschenk, handled by Jeanenne Thompson, taking Winners Bitch, Best of Winners and Best of Opposite Sex at Abilene K.C., for breeder-owners, Pansy Roberts and Sharon Wood.

This is the historical point when serious thought began about "where do we go from here?" Obviously the breed needed to be popularized to become more widely known and appreciated. The problem then looming was that a large majority of those who had selected Rottweilers as their breed did so because they admired the dogs as workers and as family pets, with little or no thought given to them as show prospects. Thus there was little temptation to show the breed and less desire to exploit it. Among those who were shown at this period were the Mallion "A" litter which started out well. Mrs. Maud Wait owned Adonis, who did well until a road accident ended

his career (later this lady was in the limelight as the handler of WT. Ch. Bruin). Abelard "Metropolitan Police Dog Abelard," was one of those dogs recommended for the Black Knight Police Dog Award, presented by Lady Mannings. Alberich went to Miss Maureen Cole. Adda was selected by Mrs. Stella Gawthorp, by whom she was trained and shown. Anne went to Mrs. Joan and Dr. Penny Wheacroft. The latter two Rottie bitches were eventually bred.

The "Black" litter, born six months later, was just average, and none of these were shown or used for breeding.

After this litter, Quinta took a year's rest and then produced the litter which included WT. Ch. Bruin of Mallion in October, 1957. Bruin was a truly great dog with notable ring successes to his credit. Brunnhilde of Mallion was also in this litter, going to Newcastle where she was with the late Mr. and Mrs. Joe Garland. Brunnhilde was campaigned extensively and successfully at the shows. There were also others of note in this litter.

Quinta was mated to Ajax. v. Fuhrenkamp in 1958. There were nine in this litter, all of good quality. Another important Rottie event that year was the birth of

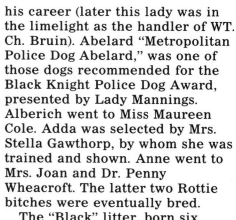

Rintelna the Bomber.

It was at the close of the 1950s that a Rottweiler won the breed's first Best in Show at a British event. This was at an Open Show where Mrs. Wait had presented Bruin, and excitement was at a high pitch as the top award was made by Mr. Bill Siggers. So tremendous was the enthusiasm brought about by this big win that it was decided the time had come to organize a Rottweiler Specialty club, founder-members for which were quick to volunteer. Permission was sought and granted by the Kennel Club of Great Britain.

The year 1960 saw Rottweilers for the first time included with their own breed classification at Crufts. It was arranged that the initial meeting for the formation of a new breed club take place there, which it did following the breed judging by Mrs. Winnie Barber.

At the founding meeting for the Rottweiler Club, Capt. Roy Smith became chairman; Mrs. Wait the secretary; and Mrs. MacPhail the treasurer. Mrs. Thelma Gray, who had done so much for the breed in the earliest days, when she brought in the first importations from Germany, became president.

Around this time, several new litters brought some excellent new competition into the ring. That well-known producer Quinta scored again in her final litter, which included the lovely Erich of Mallion, the first male C.C. winner in the breed in England. He followed in the pawprints of Bruin (after the latter's retirement as the result of an injury), becoming the Top-Winning Dog of the 1960s. He was owned by Miss Eve Cook.

Coming to present-day Rottweilers in Great Britain, a most distinguished kennel, founded during the 1960s and still going strong, is Potterspride, owned by Violet E. Slade at Saffronwalden in Essex. All of the dogs here originate from Eng. Ch. Prince Gelert of Bhaluk, who was born in August of 1972, was Top Dog of the breed in England in

1975, and the winner of a dozen or so Challenge Certificates. Sired by Ch. Gamegards Bulli v.d. Waldachquelle, Gelert brought in some of the finest of the early lines. Ch. Casses Lass of Potterspride is another who played an important role in the foundation stock of this kennel.

Violet Slade has been breeding Rottweilers so successfully for more than 20 years that, as she says, "we are, I suppose, the top kennel now in the U.K." All of the Rotties live as kennel and house dogs, thus never more than two litters a year are born there.

Ch. Apache Hill's Make My Day, C.D., owner-handled by Sharon Wood, co-owned by Pansy Roberts, Panzern Rottweilers, Stephenville, TX.

Top left: Elkee vom Meadow in front, and her son Geiger vom Gampp, age 6 months, in rear. Paula Gampp, breeder-owner. *Top right:* Ch. Ebonstern Olympus v.d. Liebe (Am., Can. Ch. Ebonstern Cabo v. Klabernorn ex Ebonstern Bryt Promise), owner, Cheryl Wheeler.

THE KENNEL CLUB OF GREAT BRITAIN STANDARD FOR THE ROTTWEILER

General Appearance—Above average size, stalwart dog. Correctly proportioned, compact and powerful form, permitting great strength, manoeuvrability and endurance.

Characteristics—Appearance displays boldness and courage. Self-assured and fearless. Calm gaze should indicate good humour.

Temperament—Good natured, not nervous, aggressive or vicious, courageous, biddable, with natural guarding instincts.

Head and Skull—Head medium length, skull broad between ears. Forehead moderately arched as seen from side. Occipital bone well developed but not conspicuous. Cheeks well boned and muscled but not prominent. Skin on head not loose, although it may form a moderate wrinkle when attentive. Muzzle fairly deep with topline level, and length of muzzle in relation to distance from well-defined stop to occiput to be as 2 to 3. Nose well developed with proportionately large nostrils, always black.

Eyes—Medium size, almond shaped, dark brown in colour, light eye undesirable, eyelids close fitting.

Ears—Pendant, small in proportion rather than large, set high and wide apart, lying flat and close to cheek.

Mouth—Teeth strong, complete dentition with scissor bite, i.e., upper teeth closely overlapping the lower teeth and set square to the jaws. Flews black and firm, falling gradually away towards corners of mouth, which do not protrude excessively.

Neck—Of fair length, strong, round and very muscular. Slightly arched, free from throatiness.

Forequarters—Shoulders well laid back, long and sloping, elbows well let down, but not loose. Legs straight, muscular, with plenty of bone and substance. Pasterns sloping slightly forward.

Body—Chest roomy, broad and deep with well sprung ribs. Depth of brisket will not be more, and not much less than 50% of shoulder height. Back straight, strong and not too long; ratio of shoulder height to length of body should be as 9 is to 10, loins short, strong and deep, flanks not tucked up. Croup of proportionate length, and broad, very slightly sloping.

Hindquarters—Upper thigh not too short, broad and strongly muscled. Lower thigh well muscled at top, strong and sinewy below. Stifles fairly well bent. Hocks well angulated without exaggeration, metatarsals not completely vertical. Strength and soundness of hock highly desirable.

Feet—Strong, round and compact with toes well arched. Hind feet somewhat longer than front. Pads very hard, toenails short, dark and strong. Rear dewclaws removed.

Tail—Normally carried horizontally, but slightly above horizontal when dog is alert. Customarily docked at first joint, it is strong and not set too low.

Gait/Movement—Conveys an impression of supple strength, endurance and purpose. While back remains firm and stable there is a powerful hindthrust and good stride. First and foremost,

movement should be harmonious, positive and unrestricted.

Coat—Consists of top coat and undercoat. Top coat is of medium length, coarse and flat. Undercoat, essential on the neck and thighs, should not show through top coat. Hair may also be a little longer on the back of the forelegs and breechings. Long or excessively wavy coat highly undesirable.

Colour—Black with clearly defined markings as follows: a spot over each eye, on cheeks, as a strip around each side of muzzle, but not on bridge of nose, on throat, two clear triangles on either side of the breast bone, on forelegs from carpus downward to toes, on inside

of rear legs from hock to toes, but not completely eliminating black from back of legs, under tail. Colour of markings from rich tan to mahogany and should not exceed 10% of body colour. White marking is highly undesirable. Black pencil markings on toes are desirable. Undercoat is grey, fawn, or black.

Size—Dogs height at shoulder between 63–69 cm (25–27 in). Bitches between 58–63.5 cm (23–25 in). Height should always be considered in relation to general appearance.

Faults—Any departure from the foregoing points should be considered a fault and the seriousness with which the fault should be regarded should be in exact proportion to its degree.

Note—Male animals should have two apparently normal testicles fully descended into the scrotum.

Top: **Bete Noir von Dorow, bred and owned by Nancy Estes; co-owner, Linda Herrscher.** *Middle:* **Ch. Doroh's Just Grand, T.D., alongside Ch. Doroh's Grand Escapade. Owners, Dorothy and Veronica Wade.** *Bottom:* **Snapped informally, Ch. Vom Helmer's Red Wolf owned by Connie and Robert Weir.**

Rottweilers in Canada

We have learned that Rottweilers were being bred in Canada as long ago as the 1950s—only by very few people, however. It was not until the 1970s that the breed truly started coming into its own there.

One of the breeders of the 1950s was Marilyn Bell, kennel identification "Glockenhof," by whom Glockenhof Crystal was sold to become a foundation bitch at Taylor Kennels, located in Grande Prairie, Texas.

Karl Eggebrecht was influential in the breed's early Canadian days through Winterland Kennels in Calgary. One especially outstanding dog from there has a descendant still making history, Winterland's Enno, C.D., having among his descendants his notable grandson, Can. Ch. and OTCh Kyladie's Kismet Kato, who belongs to Bernie and Perry Eitzen of Karoo Kennels.

The majority of Rottweiler breeders who are still participating in the Canadian Rottweiler world are those who started during that very busy period, the 1970s. One of these is Northwinds, which contributed tremendously to the quality and advancement of the breed. The owner of Northwinds, Patricia Hickman Clark of Ottawa, was the founding president of the Canadian

Rottweiler Club and a charter member of the American Rottweiler Club. This remarkable kennel started in 1963 with the purchase of Northwind's Tina from Dr. and Mrs. D.S. Masland of Carlisle, Pennsylvania. Tina was by Der Vis vom Weyerhof ex Katharina's Adorn of Townsview. Not only had Tina been destined to become the foundation bitch at Northwinds but she holds a special niche in history as one of the great early bitches who helped establish Rottweiler quality both in Canada and in the United States. This was through three of her famed offspring, Northwind's Darras, Danka, and Donar.

Northwind's Darras (not to be confused with Barras) did for Canada what Barras and Donar did for the United States. To Darras goes credit for the establishment of Don-Ari and Fairvalley Kennels in Canada, while Donar was influential in the United States at Rodsden. Danka, meanwhile, contributed well to *both* sides of the border.

Although she had only four litters during her lifetime, Tina produced in these litters four American champions, three Am., Can. champions, 14 Canadian champions, and four Rotties holding Obedience degrees.

Opposite: Can. Ch. Fairvalley's Latin Lottie, C.D.X., T.D., Am. C.D., a member of the Sovereign R.C. Hall of Fame in Canada. Owned by F. Mueller and C.E. MacPherson, Uxbridge, Ont., Canada.

Wyreglen's Clancy and Caroline Price Holman making a blue-ribbon win at the Specialty, London, Ont., 1987. Photo courtesy of F. Mueller and C.E. MacPherson.

Danka, Deena, Della, Darras, and Donar remained at Northwinds to set a solid foundation for future generations of breeding. Eventually Danka and Della took over Tina's former position as head foundation brood bitch there.

Della, who succumbed to cancer while still little more than a youngster, produced only one litter, a carefully planned breeding by Rodsden's Goro von Sofienbusch. She became the first Canadian-bred bitch to earn a Working Group placement, and she was the dam of Gage, Gina and Gino, three who gained championship titles in keen competition.

Danka, as her dam had done, produced four litters prior to retirement in 1978. Danka's first litter was by Jan Marshall's noted Ch. Rodsden's Kato v. Donnaj, and this, the "H" litter at Northwind, was to be followed by Danka with "I," "J," and "K" litters sired by Igor v. Schauer ("I" and "J") and Ero von der Mauth ("K"), respectively. The total of 29 puppies in these four litters led to 14 Canadian champions, 23 American champions, nine Obedience degrees and two SchH. I degrees.

Other kennels, breeders, and dogs who have shared in creating the success of Canadian Rottweilers include Heidegruen

Kennels at Irricana, purchasers of Can. Ch. Northwind's Jewel, C.D., from the East. Jewel in her turn produced Can. Ch. Heidegruen's Bekka, C.D.X., a bitch whose career was brilliant in both conformation and obedience. She was owned by Dave Haddon.

Can. Ch. Heidegruen's Dauntless Frisco went on to become 1987's No. 2 Canadian Rottweiler, another of those whose earned fame was well deserved.

Firsts are always interesting, thus we salute Canadian Ch. Rinteln a the Dragoon on not only being a winner of Specialty Shows but on having been the first Canadian-bred all-breed Best in Show Rottweiler in Canada. Pat Johnson and Jim Schwartz were the breeders of this celebrated dog who hailed from Winnipeg.

Wherever notable progress is taking place within a breed, one can be sure that a worthy Specialty Club is at work. The Rottweiler Club of Canada is such an organization. This splendid association was founded in the mid-1970s, and in July, 1988 held its 13th Specialty.

The Fraser Valley Rottweiler Club is also a busy organization, this one hosting an Annual Sieger Show under A.D.R.K. sanction each year. It is, we understand, customary to have an A.D.R.K. judge to officiate at these events, which include numerous special features of an educational nature, both beneficial and educational to those participating. Usually two days are given over to seminar discussions, Schutzhund training, working practices, breeding principles and so on—very much in the style of the European A.D.R.K. Specialty events.

Another notable Canadian Specialty Club of Rottweilers is the Sovereign Rottweiler Club of Ontario, which also holds exciting, keenly contested Specialties and educational seminars.

Numerous breeders in all parts of Canada are now making proud records with dogs of outstanding quality, working ability and intelligence. The kennel stories on the following pages present a quite clear picture of the progress being made; they are presented here with pride.

ALOUETTE

Alouette Rottweilers are owned by Sue Thiessen and Joe Balasa at Pitt Meadows Farm near Vancouver, British Columbia. Their association with the breed started in 1980, when Sue and Joe were crossing the Faser River on a

Top: Ch. Timberhaven Star Buck and Ch. Contessa Christina of Alouette in Vancouver, Canada. *Bottom:* Father and daughter victory for Alouette Kennels. Star Buck and Yazees Dutchess of Alouette.

Ch. Lindenwood's Blixen, T.T., is one of the outstanding Rottweilers bred by Linda and Bill Michels, Whitmore Lake, MI.

ferry and noticed two majestic Rottie puppies sitting in the back of a pick-up truck.

Neither Sue nor Joe at this time had ever previously seen a Rottweiler, but one meeting was all it took to convince them that this was the ideal dog to have on their ten-acre farm.

It took more than a year before a puppy bitch was located that instantly conquered this couple's hearts. J.B.'s Black Phantom Kaluha finally arrived at the farm and met the numerous pigs, birds, and three Dobermans already there. In true Rottweiler fashion, she lost no time in taking over the management of the estate.

Kaluha, initially purchased to be a pet, later became the foundation bitch of Alouette Rottweilers.

Although Kaluha's parents were never shown, she comes from such grandparents as Can. Ch. Jeheriss Drummer Boy, and one of her great-grandparents is Bulli vom Hungerbuhl.

In 1984, Kaluha entered the show ring, and by October of that year she became a Canadian champion with five- and four-point majors to her credit along the way.

In 1983, a young male Rottweiler had joined Kaluha at the farm. Panzer's Jolly Boy, through an accidental breeding, sired Kaluha's first litter. By a strange quirk of fate, on the very day that this litter was born, Panzer's Jolly Boy was accidentally killed. He left behind an impressive legacy, however, of 11 puppies, which included Can. Ch. Contessa Christina of Alouette and Can. Ch. Edward von Donovan, plus several others who are within a point or two of championship.

At the end of June, 1985, a male was purchased from Timberhaven Kennels. This male, Can. Ch. Timberhaven Star Buck, sired by Am., Can. Ch. Don Ari's Harras from Can. Ch. Koskemo Flashy Terra, grew up to become a very magnificent member of the breed.

Meanwhile, in both 1985 and 1986, Kaluha was bred to Can., Am. Ch. Don Ari's Harras. Several of the litter are very close to finishing.

Star Buck has proven a most valuable addition to Alouette Kennels. He finished his championship at less than two years of age, winning 12 Bests of Breed in 12 shows and placing 11 times in Groups that year. This made him sixth in the Top Dogs All Breeds, and he was again in all-breeds for 1986 in Canada. He also was rated "4" by respected German Rottweiler judge Willie Hedke. In 1987, "Bucky" placed eighth in Top Rottweilers in Canada. He now totals more than 30 times Best of Breed and more than 15 Group placements. Star Buck's list of champions also keeps on growing, and now includes some lovely ones.

The history of Alouette

1988 at the American Rottweiler National Specialty, on this occasion from the Veterans Class. In addition, Harras is a multiple Best in Show winner in Canada and a multiple Group placer in the United States. As frosting on the cake, this splendid dog has been owner-handled exclusively to all his wins.

Many of Harras's offspring are prominent winners. His granddaughter, D'Armistice Brunna, was Youth Siegerin at the United States Rottweiler Club, under judge Willie Hedtke, and at the Fraser Valley Rottweiler Club in 1988.

D'Armistice is a very small

Left: Bryloukis Just The Beginning, Black Swan's Abraham, and Ch. Simsberg's Gangster at the Canadian National Specialty (1988). Owner, Bryloukis Rottweilers, Campbell, B.C. *Below:* Top Ten for 1986, A.R.C. System, Am., Can. Ch. Harras vom Sachsen, owned by Cynthia Campbell, Stablemate Kennels.

Rottweilers is short in time, but since 1981, when the foundation bitch arrived, until this time, they have produced seven Canadian champions and an equal number pointed and close to title, as well as having acquired and raised one of Canada's leading male Rottweilers.

D'ARMISTICE

D'Armistice Rottweilers are owned by Marlin Easton at Mission, British Columbia, where one of the All-Time Top Rottweilers in Canada is to be found: Best in Show, Best in Specialty Show, Can. and Am. Ch. Don-Ari's Harras.

Harras has a formidable list of credits on his record, including such honors as No. 1 Rottweiler in Canada in 1983, No. 5 Working Dog in Canada in 1984, No. 1 Rottweiler and No. 11 Working Dog in Canada for 1985. He was triple V-1 rated at the Canadian Sieger show under A.D.R.K. rules with A.D.R.K. judges in 1985 (Herr Freiburg), 1986 (Willie Hedtke), and 1987 (Herr Altpeter). Harras also was a Winners and Best of Breed at the American Rottweiler Club Specialty in 1986 in an entry of 250, making him the only Canadian dog to have accomplished Best of Breed from the classes at the American National. He went Best of Breed for the second time in

Ch. Concord Midnite Gambl'r Boy, C.D., with Amie L. Hellmann, making a nice win for Hellmann Kennels, Robstown, TX.

hobby kennel with a limited breeding program. Marlin tries to stick closely to the basics, looking for the old established bloodlines, mostly German, or the Rottweilers descended from them.

Harras is strongly linebred to the great Harras von Sofienbusch. What a proud moment it was for Marlin to see this young Harras's name engraved below that of his grandsire, Ch. Donnaj Vt. Yankee of Paulus, for Best of Breed on the American Rottweiler National Specialty Trophy. One is indeed blessed to own a dog of Harras's caliber and to enjoy the privilege of starting a kennel on such an outstanding foundation.

BRYLOUKIS ROTTWEILERS

In 1974, Cynthia Roney of Bryloukis Rottweilers (permanently registered with the Canadian Kennel Club), Campbell River, British Columbia, was introduced to her first Rottweilers by Maureen Wilkinson of Trollegen's Rottweilers.

In 1975, Cynthia obtained her first Rottweiler, a bitch, Trollegen's Faith, from Maureen. While Faith was never shown, she was impeccably bred, sired by Ch. Dux v. Hungerbuhl, SchH. I, and out of Can. Ch. Jaheriss Baaca, C.D. When Faith was bred to Trollegen's Demon, she produced Am., Can. Ch. Bryloukis Alexander, a Group winning and placing dog who went on to be No. 1 Rottweiler in Canada in 1980 and No. 2 in 1981. Faith's only other litter, sired by Am. Ch. Trollegen's Ammon,

Top: Can. Ch. Bravamar's Buccaneer and Ch. Bravamar's Brittany, owned by Bravamar Rottweilers, Mary Coughlan, Stony Plain, Alta., Canada.
Bottom: Bobbie Whitman comments on this head study of Barry vom Whithaus, "This head is the perfect culmination of the finest breeding selection we have made."

of male offspring, it has been difficult to retain suitable bitches of her own breeding to carry on with. The good bitch Ch. Eltre Christel aus Kiros, at the time owned by Trollegen's Rottweilers, was leased and bred to Alex. This litter included Ch. Bryloukis The One And Only, C.D.X., who in turn produced titled offspring for her owner, Margaret Cumming of Tolfield, Alberta; and Ch. Bryloukis Front Runner, T.D., owned by Marilyn Linegar of Surrey, British Columbia.

In 1986, a partnership was entered into with Mary McGee of Pt. Alberni, British Columbia. Mary is responsible for all the kennel's showing.

Above: **Windwalker's Alex The Great, C.D., T.T., was bred by James William McGovern and is owned by the Michels.** *Right:* **Ch. Clyde von Reishoff proudly wears one of his many Best of Breed award ribbons. Owned by Nadine Jaquez, Von Dine Rottweilers.**

produced Ch. Bryloukis Evil's Guardian Ninja and the excellent working dog Bryloukis Extra Special, C.D.X.

An Alex daughter, Bryloukis Dynasty, when bred to Am., Can. Ch. Don-Ari's Harras, produced Am., Can. Ch. Bryloukis Great Expectations, C.D. This dog is owned by Kate and Peter Nolan of Anchorage, Alaska. "Yank," as he is known, was the Top Rottweiler in Alaska in 1987 and 1988, and in 1989 was campaigned extensively in the lower 48 states.

Cynthia has always been very partial to the Dux v. Hungerbuhl lines for both type and temperament. As her own bitches seem to produce a preponderance

In 1987, an imported bitch, Ch. Hillcrest Samantha, was purchased. Samantha is from English bloodlines, and in two very small litters she has produced some promising conformation and working dogs. Bryloukis Just The Beginning, owned by the Nortons in Victoria, British Columbia, was major pointed as a puppy and is presently working towards a Schutzhund title. Bryloukis Kristoff's Chief and Bryloukis Kool Gangster also look like they will have promising futures in the show ring. Also in the present breeding program is Ch. Grizzly Bear's Atreyu, a beautiful Alex daughter from his last breeding. Her first pups are showing great promise in the conformation ring.

The present star of the kennel is Ch. Simeberg's Gangster, purchased from Simebergs Rottweilers, Langley, British Columbia, as an eight-week-old pup. Gangster is a son of Am. and Can. Ch. Trollegen's Frodo and a grandson of Dux von Hungerbuhl. His show credits include a Best Puppy in Show at ten months of age, championship at 12 months, and multiple Group wins and placements. He was Best of Breed and Best Stud Dog at the 1988 Canadian Specialty and also Best Stud Dog in Show at the Victoria Centennial Show in 1988. He is reproducing his quality and fantastic disposition in his offspring. Bryloukis Rottweilers have always been a very small kennel consisting only of house dogs and engaging in very limited breeding to ensure proper homes for all the puppies bred. They are proud of the fact that, with very few dogs competing, between 1982 and 1987 they have been included in the Top Ten Rottweiler Club of Canada's Breeders four times.

While the Bryloukis kennel has produced many dogs which have obtained conformation championships, obedience and tracking titles, Mary and Cynthia believe that the strength of their breeding program lies in the temperament of all their dogs, who are living happy, productive lives as family companions and model canine citizens.

BRYSON

Bryson Rottweilers are owned by Sonja and Bryan Bridgeman of Omenee, Ontario, Canada. This

kennel selected its bloodlines on those of German imports. Currently, Prince Rupert v. Konigsberg is standing at stud at Bryson. He is a son of Cliff v.d. Moosheide of Konigsberg Kennels, who was sired by the great dog Bandit vom Geirersberg, SchH. III.

To quote a phrase from horse breeders, Bryan notes that: "Your

"Breezy" viewing the countryside. Can. Ch. Rotterre Breezy Brae, from Roterre Kennels' famed "B" litter. J. Jacqueline Stephenson, owner, Shelburne, Ont., Canada.

Ch. Lindenwood Bitternight Bear, T.T., winning Best of Breed at the Canadian R.C. Supported Show, K.C. of Buffalo. Bred by Linda and Bill Michels; owned by Joe and Karen Millard; handled by Tim Conradt.

fame is in your studs, but your wealth is in your bitches." (A quote probably less true among dog breeders.) Bryson Kennels have been truly selective in this respect, thus enjoying the unequalled pleasure of producing dogs that please both their customers and the critical eye of the dog show judges.

CARADO

Carado Rottweilers are a small kennel, permanently registered with the Canadian Kennel Club, and owned by Carol Kravets. They are located in Windsor, Ontario, on the border of Detroit, Michigan, thus easily accessible to both Canada and the United States. The kennel was established in 1972.

Carol started in Dobermans, producing three champions in that breed prior to becoming interested in the Rotties in 1975. As a Rottweiler breeder, she adheres to the standard which, along with type and show quality, also produces great family dogs.

It was in 1980 that Carol acquired Inga von Tannenwald, T.T., a daughter of Ch. Radio Ranch's Axel v. Notara (All-Time Top Producing Rottweiler) out of Ch. Rue De Rennes. Inga produced five champions, the first of which was Am., Can. Ch. Carado's Reaper von Tannenwald, T.T., a multiple Best of Breed winner who at nine years of age was still winning in the Veterans Class. Then came Am., Can. Ch. Carado's Mighty Quinn, T.T., who finished with four majors owner-handled by Peggi Cogacar of Springfield, Kentucky; and Ch. Carado's Dark Crystal and Ch. Onyx Hills Extra Rowdy.

Carol then bred Carado's Satin Sidney (11 points) to Am., Can. Ch. Ebony Acres Yankee Alliance, which produced the dynamic Am., Can. Ch. Carado's Satin Classic, T.T., who became Top Rottweiler Bitch in Canada for 1986, 1987, and 1988. She was also No. 3 Rottweiler, either sex, in 1986. She is lovingly owned by Suzanne Sosne and Carol Kravets.

To introduce some new lines, Carol acquired the German import, Bessy vom Flosserloch. Bessy was bred to Am., Can. Ch. Carado's Mighty Quinn, from which came some extremely promising puppies, including Can. Ch. Carado's Sudden Impact, back-to-back Best of Winners and Best of Opposite Sex over specials when only seven months old; Carado's Pop 'N' Fresh, who when shown for the second time in Canada went Winners Bitch, Best of Opposite Sex, and Best Puppy in breed; and last but not least, Carado's Mighty Essex, owned by Jonathan and Cynthia Chester of Amherstburg, Ontario, being shown in both obedience and conformation at the same shows, proving that with proper breeding and work, this can be done.

CHAFARD

Chafard Rottweilers are owned by Sylvie Fafard of St. Eulalie, Quebec. Mrs. Fafard began breeding Rotties in 1984 and is keeping her kennel a small one as far as production is concerned, limiting the number of breedings to just one or at the most two each year. Great emphasis is placed upon quality, and all litters are bred from titled parents.

Through 1988, Chafard had produced five Canadian champions: Zeta de Chafard, Winter Mallochi of Chafard,

Vedette de Chafard, Xcel Rambo de Chafard, Xterminator of Chafard, and two C.D. dogs, Zonan de Chafard, and Yes She Candy of Chafard.

From Sylvie Fafard's breeding program, Can. Ch. Xcel Rambo de Chafard achieved his championship in three consecutive days from the Junior Puppy Class at only eight-and-one-half months old, going Best of Winners on each occasion. Before one year of age, Rambo had twice won Best Puppy in Show (the first Rottie to have won two such awards), plus five Bests in Puppy Group.

Can. Ch. Xterminator of Chafard completed his Canadian Championship from the Senior Puppy Class at only 10½ months of

Above: Ch. Darby's Solitaire von Meadow, by Ch. McCoy von Meadow ex Ch. Miss Ellie von Meadow, taking Best of Winners. Owner, Sheena Marchand. *Left:* Wyreglen's Clancy, owned by F. Mueller and C.E. MacPherson, Uxbridge, Ont., Canada.

271

Am., Can. Ch. Carado's Satin Classic, T.T., with her mother Carado's Satin Sidney in July, 1986. Photo courtesy of Carole Kravets, Windsor, Ont., Canada.

age. He has won Best in Puppy Group four times. He is owned by Shirley Robert.

Can. Ch. Vedette de Chafard was another to make the title in three consecutive days of showing, taking Best of Winners twice and Best of Opposite Sex at only 15 months.

Sylvie Fafard is currently president of the *Club Rottweiler du Quebec.*

FINNROTTI

Finnrotti Kennels, registered, are owned by Markus Maenpaa of Nipigon, Ontario. This gentleman has a most interesting story behind his interest in the breed: in the 1950s, his father trained the first Rottweiler (a bitch) in Finland for police work. The family moved to Canada in 1956, where Markus purchased his first Rottweiler from Oscar Scholz in May, 1972. This was Asta v. Fichtental, by Rodsden's Sabre v. Fichtental ex Ch. Northwind's Carla. She was never bred nor shown and she died in 1979.

The next bitch was purchased by Markus from Lars Renkola in October, 1985. Her name is Princess Geisha, and she is by Am., Can. Ch. Borris vom Grenelandring, U.D.T., ex Ch. Finnberg's Belinda.

Through her, Markus became involved with obedience training as well as showing. She now has her Canadian C.D.X. and eight points in conformation, plus one leg of her American C.D. She is registered in both Canada and the United States and will soon be working on her utility title.

In October, 1988, Finnrotti Kennels imported an 11-week-old male from Finland. The breeder is J.A.U. Yrjola, the Breed Warden for the past 25 years. The pup's name is Joukonheimo Sulla (by Rocky ex Joukonheimo Ofelia). Markus describes him as a "magnificent male weighing 92 pounds at nine months. He also has an excellent temperament and is very showy in the ring." His Canadian registrations have come through, and Markus intends also to register him with the American Kennel Club. Sulla already had four points towards his Canadian title. A note of interest is that this dog's uncle, Rudi, won the Specialty Show in Finland in 1988, where there were more than 156 Rottweilers in competition.

On New Year's Eve, 1988, Markus' bitch Geisha presented him with his first litter of Rottweiler puppies, 11 of them, eight of whom survived. Two bitches from this litter were kept for future breeding to Sulla, to be the foundation of the Finnrotti breeding program. The kennel name was established in 1988. The kennel reflects the Finnish background characterized by sound temperament, intelligence and excellent conformation.

Markus Maenpaa belongs to the Canadian Kennel Club, the Thunder Bay Kennel and Training Club, the Lakehead Kennel Club, the Sovereign Rottweiler Club, the Rottweiler Club of Finland, and the Rottweiler Club of Canada.

JANLYNN

Janlynn Rottweilers at Saskatoon, Saskatchewan, are owned by Mr. and Mrs. D.G. Flury, who had their first Rottweiler litter in November, 1975. The

Top: Can. Ch. Mink Hollow's Amber Jewel, by Ch. Bryloukis Evil's Guardian Ninja ex Ch. Heidegruen's Celito, C.D. Handled by S. Smith; bred by K. Becker. *Bottom:* Ch. Rivy's Samson De Deveaux taking second in a strong Working Group at Hawaiian Dog Fanciers' event in October, 1988. Handled by Sue Cates for owner Lia Mesquit, Waimanalo, HI.

parents of these puppies were a champion dog and a champion bitch, the dog of Rintelna background and the bitch from Rodsden and Jeheriss descent. With this first litter their original line was established.

In their second litter, one of the bitches from the first litter, Can. Ch. Janlynn's Natasha, C.D.X., produced one of Canada's leading Top Winning Rottweilers, Can. Ch. Wathaman's Adventurous Griffin, C.D., who was a multiple Best in Show and Group placing dog. These first two litters combined

produced seven Canadian champions.

To introduce and establish another line which they felt would be compatible with their earlier one, the Flurys added Can. Ch. Cantess Wendigo to their kennel, the No. 2 Rottweiler in Canada in 1979. He was a son of Arras vom Kohlerwald from Ch. Don-Ari's Brigitte. Presently, with eight generations of Janlynn bitches and a combined program of linebreeding and outcrossing, Janlynn Rottweiler lines have become established, emphasizing temperament, working ability, and conformation.

At the April, 1985, Rottweiler Club of Canada Specialty Show, with 89 entries, two of Janlynn's dogs fared especially well, winning Best of Opposite Sex (Ch. Janlynn's Minto) and Winners Dog (Janlynn's Nibi). Then Nibi went on to gain Canadian championship and C.D. at his very next dog show.

Can. Ch. Janlynn's Quasar has been a multiple Group and Best of Breed dog and is proving himself well as a sire. From the pointed bitch, Janlynn's Pied Piper, Can. C.D., Quasar has become an especially exciting young bitch for whom hopes are high.

At this time, 24 Canadian championships, 22 C.D. degrees, two C.D.X. titles, and one Utility Dog degree have been earned by Janlynn Rottweilers in very limited showing. But most important of all, Janlynn Rottweilers are serving their owners well as pets in many family homes, on farms working cattle, and in security work.

KARANATA

Karanata Rottweilers officially became a kennel, with the registration of this name, in 1985. They are owned by Sam Cannata of Sunderland, Ontario. Mr. Cannata, however, has been an admirer of this breed since the early 1970s.

In high school, Sam befriended a fellow student whose family was involved with Great Pyrenees. Sam accompanied them to a dog show one day in Toronto, and at this gathering his eye fell upon a large,

Can., Am. Ch. Wyreglen's Archangel and Arthur Rihel at Bushy Run K.C. where Archangel won Best of Breed. Owned by F. Mueller and C.E. MacPherson.

powerfully built, black and tan dog. So striking was this majestic dog that it left an indelible impression on Sam Cannata's mind.

The first of Sam's Rottweilers was acquired in 1980, Rotnoir's Shadow, who came to him as a puppy. A substantial bitch, she was 25 inches in height at the shoulder and weighed 105 pounds. Her pedigree traced back to some well-known names. Her first breeding was to a Konigsberg dog, who had the great Harras von Sofienbusch strongly behind him. Sadly, this litter was almost completely wiped out by parvovirus.

Next time around, Shadow was bred to Ch. Fairvalley's Kluge, who had completed his title at age ten

months and was considered to be one of the very best Rotties of his day in Canada. This time the puppies were more fortunate. Among others they included Ch. Karanata's Apache Dancer, C.D.X., No. 1 Rottweiler in Canada of his day, owned by Irene Machnik. A litter brother also finished the following year, and both are siring puppies of outstanding type and quality.

Following several years of inactivity with the Rotties, Sam now has a most promising bitch acquired from Brit Nichols. Expectations are high for this one, Carthage vom Kyffhaeuser, and she will surely be heard from in the future.

Von Hawthorne's Magna F, C.D. Dam of Ch. Von Hawthorne's Murry M, No. 5 Am. Rottie in 1988. "Maggie" is by Ch. Fritzi T. von Hawthorne, C.D., ex Ch. Radio Ranch's Axel v. Notara. Owner, Alice J. Hahn.

KONIGSBERG

Konigsberg Rottweilers are owned by Peter and Tammy Mehnert, who reside in Lindsay, Ontario, Canada. The Mehnerts have a kennel based on outstanding dogs from Germany and a very nice bitch from England. Peter Mehnert, a founding member of the Rottweiler Club of Canada, has been breeding Rottweilers since the mid-1960s.

Conformation and working ability are the qualities for which the Mehnerts strive in their breeding program. The recent imports and present studs at the kennel are Falko von Hause Nonn, SchH. III, AD, V-rated, whose pedigree goes back to Blit v. Schlob Westerwinkel, Quick v.d. Solitude,

Erno v. Wellesweiler, and the great Harras von Sofienbusch.

Cliff von der Moosheide is another German import, who came in third at the World Championship in Amsterdam, Holland. He is the son of Bandit von Geiersberg and is a grandson of Athos vom Letiten Heller. His lines go back to Hasso v. Oelberg, Igor v. Hause Henseler, and Fetz v. Oelberg.

Also among the stud dogs, there is Eike vom Uhlsmeer, SchH. II, many times V-rated, who goes back to Morris v. Rauchfang, Burga v. Rauchfang, Elko v. Luckshot, Benno v. Allgauer Tor and the well-known Dux v. Hungerbuhl.

MAASAI

Maasai Rottweilers are owned by Thelma Boyd and located in Alberta Beach, Alberta, Canada. This is the home of a very renowned Rottweiler, Canadian Ch. and OTCH Davinghof's Aqtar Terror Shai, T.D., who was born November 14, 1984, bred by Ingrid Paul and handled by Debbie Van Meer.

"Actor," as he is called, was one of Thelma Boyd's first Rotties, who has accomplished many things within a short length of time. As well she should, his owner takes tremendous pride in him. "Actor" was Canada's No. 1 Obedience Rottweiler and No. 1 Working Dog in 1986. He also was No. 1 Obedience Rottie in 1987. A young champion, this wonderful Rottie achieved his OTCH by the age of two years. Thelma Boyd now has two bitches, one with puppies from whom she hopes for more good things.

MY VALLEY

My Valley Kennels in Calgary, Alberta, are so named for the lovely Assiniboine Valley of Manitoba, where the owner of these Rottweilers, Mrs. Barb Berard, grew up. "My Valley" comes from a statement made by a great-uncle of Barb's who died alone near his small cabin rather than leave his precious home in the hills of the Assiniboine. When a concerned relative asked him to spend the winter in town, the aging gentleman remarked "I'll never leave my valley." He never did.

There have been no litters as yet from this kennel, but a breeding plan is underway. Following a search of two years, Mrs. Berard feels that she may have found what she has been looking for in a foundation bitch. Barb feels that the dam is of ultimate importance in any breeding program and that she should possess superior substance. She has noted that there seems to be a trend toward rather small-boned, less-than-athletic appearing females who are losing type. Mrs. Berard feels very strongly that the "she's good enough for a brood bitch" attitude is harmful and that the dam's quality should receive at least equal consideration as that afforded the stud dog.

The culmination of Barb's search for a bitch she really liked was the purchase of Lojabo's Autumn Jessica, a bitch strong in Swedish bloodlines who joined the kennel early in 1988. Her maternal grandsire is closely bred on the famous Fandango's "F" litter from Sweden, while her maternal granddam is from Fairvalley and the first Cantass litter bloodlines. On her sire's side she carries Chris von Wildeberg and Benno lines along with some splendid females.

My Valley's foundation dog will be a son of Trollegen's Frodo, Can. Ch. Lowindy's Flist von Ae, C.D., T.T., whose dam is Ch. Panamint Haunting Melody, C.D.

Of particular interest to Mrs. Berard is the beautiful temperament of her Rottweiler. A proper working specimen must be under self-control at all times and have the ability to "come down" from a high stress situation very quickly.

Barb is involved in public education for the care of canine companions as well as the promotion of a positive community attitude towards the Rottweiler. "Jessie" and "Ebon" are first-rate

ambassadors in the education campaign, participating regularly in parades and educational booths.

PRAIRIESKY

Prairiesky Kennels are located in Warren, Manitoba, and owned by Corrinne Walker and Ken Wainwright. A relatively new addition to the dog fancy, the kennel is just starting to make its mark on the world of pure-bred dogs.

The philosophy behind the operations at Prairiesky Kennels is one of bringing out the inherent, natural working abilities of the Rottweiler. The natural drives and working temperament of the dogs are channeled through obedience,

Ch. Einmin Lyric v. Rottdan taking 4 points, owner-handled by Rita McMahon, first time in the ring! Freyan Rottweilers, Lakeport, CA.

young male from German import parents, Can. Ch. Alf vom Steilen Fels and Can. Ch. Dany vom Giesenend, V-1 rated. Vitro has just recently entered the conformation ring and is well on his way to compete successfully for the C.D. title and hopefully for the more advanced ones in time.

Prairiesky's breeding program is based on linebreeding in the famous German sire, Int. Ch. Ives Eulenspeigel, Europasieger 1977, SchH. III. It is anticipated that the future generations will mirror the qualities, both conformation and working, which Ives consistently produced in Europe.

RITZLUND

Ritzlund Rottweilers, Labelle, Quebec, are principally a breeding kennel owned by Doug and Kathy Nimmo. All their dogs are imported from Germany, and all are registered with the Canadian Kennel Club. Some are also registered with the American Kennel Club for the purpose of being shown in the United States.

The Nimmos are striving to maintain and better the breed in all aspects, feeling that a Rottweiler's best qualities are his character and temperament. The breed's intelligence is very high, and the dogs love showing off what they can accomplish. The breed's devotion to family and friends, adults and children is absolute. They also adapt very well to many different environments and situations.

It is quite easy to see that the Nimmos are completely in love with this breed, and why. As they put it, "we could not ask for a better type of dog."

ROBOROTT

Roborott Rottweilers are owned by Dr. P.K. St. John, D.V.M., and his wife Shelley of Welland, Ontario. This is a relatively new kennel which initially concentrated on conformation dogs but more recently has developed an increased interest in the Rottweiler as a working dog.

Am., Can. Ch. Cannon River Stowaway, Am., Can. C.D., T.T., has won several Bests of Breed. Stowaway is by Ch. Rodsden's Berte v. Zederwald C.D.X., ex Cannon River Showboat. Owner, Mike Liberato, handler, Vicki Barker.

tracking and conformation training.

Corinne and Ken spend considerable amounts of time educating new owners and the general public about the breed. From mall displays to visiting senior citizen homes, the Rottweiler is presented as a faithful friend and an important member of the family.

Prairiesky's breeding program is still in its early stages. The foundation bitch, Can. Ch. Wolfsanger's Ashburg, C.D., achieved her Canadian championship at only 11 months of age. With but a limited showing, she won several Bests of Breed before terminating her show career to become a mother.

Another addition to Prairiesky is Vitro vom Teufelhund, a robust

It was in the mid-1980s when the St. Johns adopted a sickly ten-day-old Rottweiler pup with anal atresia and megacolon. By the time she was three months of age, she had been through four minor surgeries and had been examined by two prominent veterinary surgeons in Canada. The St. Johns bottlefed this pup for over two months, through her good days and the bad ones. She meant the world to them, and she was a real fighter. Unfortunately, at about 12 weeks of age the pup died from septicemia, secondary to her bowel problem. Needless to say, the St. Johns were devastated at the loss of the dog they loved so dearly.

The void in their home was soon filled by Rommell, who became Can. Ch. Arrowback's Jaro Blakey, a male puppy from the No. 1 Rottweiler in Canada during 1987, Can., Bda. Ch. Rotterre Bardolph Buckenberg. He was purchased as a pet but as he grew and matured his handsome quality made the show circuit seem inevitable. Rommell finished his Canadian championship shortly after two years of age in limited showing and then went on to regularly take Best of Breed and even had a Group III placing. This cherished companion and friend has far exceeded his owners hopes and expectations for him.

Rommell started the avalanche effect. It was not long after his first points that Roborott Rottweilers became a registered kennel name, and the second acquisition occurred. This was Luger Legolas von Kruse, who became Rommell's sidekick. The most recent addition to the kennel is Eichehaus Baronin von Darak, a beautiful daughter of Am., Can. Ch. Goldeiche Ara von Brader, Am. C.D., ex Von Braders Breena Medellin, C.D. At just seven months, "Bara" went Best of Winners and Best of Opposite Sex for a three-point major at an important show in Toronto. She is the St. Johns' hope for the future and will be the foundation bitch of their kennel.

Dr. St. John comments that, "As a veterinarian, I have already learned a great deal about the medical problems confronting our breed. As a kennel owner, I know that over the years it will be our aim to breed only Rottweilers of exceptional conformation yet not to neglect the working ability and stamina of the Rottweiler. I must admit at this point the backbone of our kennel is my wife, Shelley, whose love and devotion to our Rottweilers will propel us through good times and hard times."

Currently, Dr. and Mrs. St. John plan to import a German bitch which will fit well into their breeding program along with being ready for Schutzhund. The St. Johns' prospects for breeding are unlimited. Rommell has lately sired a litter with a Ch. Artus von

Am., Can. Ch. Cannon River Destroyer, C.D., T.T., is owned by Phillis Clark of Clearlake, WI.

279

Adelshof daughter as the dam, which puppies they are anxious to follow along over the next few months. Luger Legolas has, as his most prominent asset, an excellent head and strong German lines in his background and will be bred to combine Berno vom Remchingen and Eulenspiegel. In addition, Bara, representing as she does the lines of Eiko v. Schwaiger Wappen and Birch Hills Governor, will make the selection of stud dog fairly easy and hopefully very successful for her puppies.

The St. Johns place great emphasis on Schutzhund work, too, and are proud that their dogs train with one of Canada's best known trainers in Schutzhund, Gottfried Dildei.

ROTTERRE

Rotterre Rottweilers, registered, incorporate the best in working and conformation dogs. Owned by J. Jacqueline Stephenson of

Shelburne, Ontario, this kennel was started under a different registered kennel name and for another breed. While those dogs were very successful, they were *not* Rottweilers, and the latter being the breed which had come to *really* intrigue this lady, Jacqueline simply was not satisfied until the Rottie became part of her life.

So it was in 1980 that Jacqueline Stephenson took the step of acquiring her first Rottweiler, Abbie, who grew up to become Ch. Rodsden Abbatab of Stepshire, T.T. Her parents were Am., Can. Ch. Rodsden's Elko Kastanienbaun, C.D.X., T.D., Can. C.D.; and Am. Ch. Rodsden's Red Pepper v.h. Walor. Abbie was the perfect foundation brood bitch, and at nine years of age she still looks and acts only about half that.

In 1983, Abbie was bred to Am. Ch. Gasto vom Liebersbacherhof, C.D.X., T.D., and produced the outstanding "B" litter consisting of

The foundation bitch of Zolty Rottweilers, this is an informal pose by Am., Can. Ch. Kitty von Kokiak, Am., Can. C.D., SchH. I, who is a Best in Specialty winner at the A.R.C. Region V Specialty and has multiple Breed and Group successes to her credit. Owner, Bob Csolti, Chico, CA.

Ch. Radio Ranch's X-Styx Charon, a son of the great Ch. Radio Ranch's Axel v. Notara, owned by Radio Ranch Rottweilers, Pamela C. Brown and Jennifer Hughes.

Brogan, Beckon, Breezy, and Buck. Brogan became Ch. Rotterre Broken Bough. Beckon became Ch. Rotterre Be Beckon. Breezy became Ch. Rotterre Breezy Brae. And Buck became Canada's No. 1 Rottweiler for 1987, Best in Show, Best in Specialty Show, Can., Bda., Am. Ch. Rotterre Bardolph Buckenberg, T.T. "Bucky" was on the Sovereign Rottweiler Club Honor Roll (Canada), the Medallion Rottweiler Club Honor Roll (U.S.A.), and was a *Dog World* Award Winner. All these Rotties were extremely successful in the show ring. All were of tremendous credit to their breeder-owner.

Since retirement a few years ago from the show ring, Beckon is living an active life with her new owners, on a farm with cattle and working show horses. Brogan, Breezy, and Buck are virtually retired from the show ring as well and enjoying themselves traveling and being house and working farm dogs. Brogan and Buck continue to stand at stud. They are producing exceptional puppies in limited breeding, with the newest additions to Rotterre being Breezy's young male, Bruiser, and Buck's newest female offspring, Burly and brother Booker.

ROTTFIRE

Rottfire Rottweilers at Little Britain, Ontario, are owned by Wendy and Frank Van Dersel, who are fairly new additions to the Rottie Fancy but obviously off to a good start. Rottfire was founded in February, 1989. To date the Van Dersels have not yet raised a litter, but have one planned for the near future.

This couple owns a most handsome young dog in Ch. Wyreglen's Archie Odin, who was bred by Caroline MacPherson and born in February, 1984. Odin earned his Canadian championship at age 18 months, his Canadian C.D.

at 28 months; then, in 11 shows as a special, he accounted for five times Best of Breed and three times Best of Opposite Sex. A year later he completed his Canadian C.D.X. and will soon be starting in utility and tracking. Obviously the Van Dersels are thrilled at all this

dogs and excellent ambassadors of goodwill for the breed.

VON DAMIEN

Von Damien Rottweilers, registered, Port Perry, Ontario, are owned by Mike and Irene Jackman (formerly Machnik). It was in 1983

Ch. Epic's Dynamo, T.T., bred and handled by Bob Hogan; owned by Peter and Lisa Kaloostian, winning the Working Group at Wampanoag in July, 1988, under judge Melbourne Downing. A multiple and Group-placing Rottie.

success with a dog whom they had purchased only as a pet.

The female at Rottfire is Valkyrie Wyreglen de Chafard, who was purchased from Sylvie Fafard with the intention of making her the foundation bitch at this promising new kennel.

Both these Rotties are house

when Irene noticed an advertisement in a local newspaper that she purchased a seven-month-old Rottweiler puppy bitch, which she started out by taking to obedience classes, where the puppy excelled. Irene had for many years shown horses and was accustomed to showing and handling animals, and by the time the puppy was 13 months old she had completed her C.D. with an average score of 192.5.

In June, since it was too hot to do obedience work, the young bitch was sent out to try her luck on the conformation circuit. Two weeks later she had become Can. Ch. Karenata's Apache Dancer, C.D.; and by the age of two years, the C.D. had become a C.D.X!

Owing to her success in the show ring, Irene decided to keep Dancer active in Obedience, and also to send her out as a special. By the end of 1984, Dancer had earned high enough placements in breed and obedience competition to become the No. 1 Rottweiler overall (combined obedience and conformation record, Rottweiler Club of Canada standings).

Dancer has passed along her intelligence, good movement, and correct type to her offspring. To date her credits include, as a producer, three champions, two obedience title holders, and more who are pointed.

Mike also has been working with the Rotties, and it was he who acquired an obedience title on the first Von Damien home-bred champion. This is Can. Ch. Damien's A Sly Guy, C.D., who is now doing well in Schutzhund training and work.

Von Damien Kennels have, as Irene remarks, "expanded by leaps and bounds during the past few years." Their current Rotties include Sly Guy, Can. Ch. Commandant Axel von Kruse, Can. Ch. Barlin's Abraxus von Damien, Jane vom Stommeln (a pink-papered German import), Damien's Akaylie (major pointed) and Forute von Damien (also major pointed).

At this time, Von Damien Kennels are in the process of importing a multiple V-rated, SchH. III male whom they hope soon to bring to Canada.

WYREGLEN

Wyreglen Rottweilers, permanently registered, at

Uxbridge, Ontario, are owned by Caroline MacPherson and Fred Mueller, who started out in 1972 raising and showing Wire Fox Terriers. On the lookout for a medium-sized guard dog that would fit well into their household, they quickly discovered and soon decided upon a Rottweiler.

In 1979, they found the bitch

Above: Can. Ch. Milo's An Uncommon Love, C.D., with 5-month-old Milo's Stormwarning. Owners, Heather Hayes and Mike Helliher. *Below:* Family portrait of multi-titled Roma Rotties!

Copperdot's Bronze Medal, a homebred owned by Diane D. Gibson, Tinton Falls, NJ. Taking points towards his title at Southern Maryland K.C. in 1988. By Ch. Trifecta's Barbarian v. Murph, C.D., ex Ch. Copperdot's Best Gemini.

puppy they had sought at Fairvalley, the long-established Ontario kennel of Mr. and Mrs. William H.C. Marsh. After two interviews, Caroline and Fred were allowed to purchase Latin Lottie. Her obedience days were long. However, Lottie finally did manage to train her owners and went on to gain her C.D.X.

Lottie's next hurdle was the T.D. She dragged her owners through that with vigor. Lottie's American C.D. was a somewhat painful experience. After a bath with a very mild dog shampoo, she broke out in hives the morning of the final trial. She squealed when the collar was placed on her neck, and her owners were thankful when the

judge allowed her to be shown on the collar's dead ring. Lottie subsequently placed second in the Novice Class, a major and appreciated triumph considering the circumstances.

Whelping box life for Lottie began after a visit, in December, 1983, to Int., Can. and Am. Ch. Bronco v. Rauberfield, SchH. III, FH, at Srigo Kennels in New Jersey. The "A" litter produced four males who are now all champions: Wyreglen's Archimage, Archibald, Archon Odin, and the one Caroline and Fred kept at home, their well-loved Archangel. Three of the four have finished their C.D. titles, and Odin has his C.D.X.

Ch. Wyreglen's Archangel visited the United States with Bronco's owner, Felicia Luburich. She entered "Artie" in four classes, two each at the American Rottweiler Club and Colonial Rottweiler Club Specialties; the Sweepstakes and a Regular Class. He won all four.

Felicia introduced Caroline and Fred to Art and Willey Rihel, who took Artie to his American championship in style. As Caroline says, "They showed and treated him like a prince."

In December, 1984, Lottie's return visit to Bronco produced a litter of 11. They are spread from Texas to Bermuda and include Am. Ch. Wyreglen's Broad Horizons, owned by Jack Sweeney in New Jersey; Can. Ch. Best of Both Worlds, owned by Victor Lim of Bermuda (with two majors in that country); and Caroline and Fred's own Can. Ch. Wyreglen's Bitte Schoen. Lottie has now qualified for and was inducted into the Hall of Fame by the Sovereign Rottweiler Club of Ontario.

Next Lottie was bred to the Canadian Top Rottweiler of 1987, Can., Bda. Ch. Rotterre Bardolph Buckenberg for a litter of six puppies. All the pups were very nice, and the males excelled again. The number one brood bitch spot is now passed on to Lottie's daughter, Ch. Wyreglen's Bitte Schoen. Lottie will always hold first place in the hearts of her owners; she knows it however, and expects to be treated accordingly.

Bitte was bred to Can., Bda. Ch. Rotterre Bardolph Buckenberg, and the line continues. The seven puppies were all of better than good quality, and Bitte showed her strength in the females.

Pick bitch Dinasty went to Sylvie Fafard of Chafard Kennels in Quebec. Dinasty showed good type and strong, bold behavior patterns, but was unfortunately killed by a car before she made her name. Second pick was purchased by the Fairvalley Kennels, and "if Duchess can leave a cat alone," she will begin her show career soon. The owner's pick was from the heart, the lovable and now Can. Ch. Wyreglen's Dancing Shadow. Dancer is living up to her name, prancing through her first American competition to a four-point major in bitches and on to Best of Winners.

Caroline and Fred are looking ahead to tracking fields and obedience rings, and they wish to thank all the wonderful people who helped them along the way.

THE CANADAN KENNEL CLUB OFFICIAL BREED STANDARD FOR THE ROTTWEILER

Origin and Purpose—The Rottweiler was developed from the dogs used by the Roman legions to herd and guard the cattle brought by them to feed their legions. The butchers of Rottweil, Germany, developed the dogs to drive cattle to market and to protect their money bags which were tied around the dogs' necks. It was an arduous task to drive the cattle, and a strong dog with staying power, full of self will and physical strength was needed. In the beginning of the 20th century, these dogs were found particularly well suited as a police dog, a function they still fulfill especially in Europe.

General Appearance—The ideal Rottweiler is an above medium-

sized, robust, and powerful dog, black with clearly defined rich tan markings. His compact build denotes great strength, agility, and endurance. Males are characteristically larger, heavier boned and more masculine in appearance.

Temperament—The Rottweiler should possess a fearless expression with a self-assured aloofness that does not lend itself to immediate and indiscriminate friendships. He has a strong willingness to work. In examining a Rottweiler, one should bear in mind that this dog reacts with alertness to his master and his surroundings, and in performing

The foundation bitch at Von Dorow Rottweilers, Ch. Merrymoore's Imp von Dorow, T.T., taking a Group placement at Lake Charles, LA, in 1984. Owned by Nancy C. Estes.

CALCASIEU KENNEL CLUB
LAKE CHARLES LOUISIANA
AUGUST 18 1984
WORKING GROUP 4
JUDGE
MR LEE A REASIN
PHOTO BY
PETRULIS

Am., Can. Ch. Wilderness Kobuk v. Furstwald with his dam, Am., Can. Ch. The Chena Wilderness. Owner-breeder, JoAnn Harnish.

be present on neck and thighs. The Rottweiler should be exhibited in a natural condition without trimming, except to remove whiskers, if desired. The colour is always black with rich tan to mahogany markings. The borderline between the black and the colour should be clearly defined. The markings should be located as follows: a spot over each eye; on cheeks; as a strip around each side of the muzzle, but not on the bridge of the nose; on throat; a proportionate triangular mark on either side of the breastbone not to exceed 25 percent of the forechest; on forelegs from carpus downward to toes; on inside of rear legs showing down the front of the stifle and broadening out to front of rear legs from hock to toes but not eliminating the black from the back of the legs; under tail. Black pencilling markings on the toes. The undercoat is grey or black. Quantity and location of markings are important. Insufficient or excessive markings should be penalized.

Head—Of medium length, broad between the ears; forehead line seen in profile is moderately arched. The cheekbones and stop are well developed. The length of the *muzzle* should not exceed the distance between the stop and the occiput. The *skull* is preferred dry; however, some wrinkling may occur when the dog is alert. The bridge of the muzzle is straight. The muzzle is broad at the base with slight tapering towards the tip but not snipey. The *nose* is broad rather than round, with black nostrils. The lips are always black with the corners tightly closed. The flews should not be too pronounced. The inner mouth pigment is dark. A pink mouth is to be penalized. The teeth are 42 in number; 20 upper and 22 lower. They are strong and should be correctly placed meeting in a scissors bite—lower incisors touching the inside of the upper incisors. *Eyes* should be of medium size, moderately deep set, almond shaped with well-fitting lids. The

his function in life, the Rottweiler is not expected to submit to excessive handling by strangers. However, the judge shall dismiss from the ring any shy or vicious Rottweiler. A dog shall be judged fundamentally shy if, refusing to stand for examination, it shrinks away from the judge; if it fears an unexpected approach from the rear; if it shies at sudden or unusual noises to a marked degree. A dog that attacks or attempts to attack, without provocation, either the judge, or its handler, is definitely vicious. An aggressive or belligerent attitude towards other dogs shall not be deemed viciousness.

Size—Dogs 24–27 in (60–68 cm). Bitches 22–25 in (55–63 cm).

Proportion should always be considered rather than height alone. The length of the body, from the breastbone (sternum) to the rear edge of the pelvis (ischium), is slightly longer than the height of the dog at the withers, the most desirable proportion being as 10 to 9. Depth of chest should be fifty percent of the height.

Coat and Colour—Outer coat is straight, coarse, dense, medium length, lying flat. Undercoat must

iris should be of uniform colour, from medium to dark brown, the darker shade always preferred. **Ears** should be pendant, proportionately small, triangular in shape, set well apart and placed on skull so as to make it appear broader when the dog is alert. The ear should terminate at approximately mid-cheek level. When correctly held, the inner edge will lie tightly against the cheek.

Neck—Powerful, well muscled, moderately long with slight arch and without loose skin.

Forequarters—The shoulder blade should be long and well laid back at a 45-degree angle. The elbows are tight and under the body. The distance from the withers to the elbow and the elbow to the ground is equal. The legs are strongly developed with straight, heavy bone. They are not set close together. The pasterns are strong, springy and almost perpendicular to the ground. Feet are round, compact with well-arched toes, turning neither in nor out. Pads are thick and hard. Nails are short, strong and black. Dewclaws may be removed.

Body—The topline is firm and level, extending in a straight line from the withers to the croup. The brisket should be deep, reaching to the elbow. The chest is roomy and broad with a well-developed forechest. The ribs are well sprung. The loins short, deep, and well muscled. The flank should not be tucked up. The croup is broad, of medium length and slightly sloping.

Hindquarters—The angulation of the hindquarters balances that of the forequarters. The slope of the pelvis from the horizontal is between 20–30 degrees. The bone of the upper thigh is fairly long and the thigh is broad and well muscled. The stifle joint is moderately angulated. The lower thigh is long, powerfully muscled leading to a strong hock joint. The metatarsus is perpendicular to the ground. Viewed from the rear, the hind legs are straight and

perpendicular to the ground. The feet are somewhat longer than the front feet, with well-arched toes turning neither in nor out. Dewclaws must be removed.

Tail—The tail is normally carried in a horizontal position giving the appearance of an elongated topline. It is carried above the horizontal when the dog is excited. The tail is normally docked short close to the body. The set of the tail is more important than length.

Gait—The Rottweiler is a trotter; the motion is harmonious, sure, powerful and unhindered, with strong forereach and a powerful

Ch. Pioneer's Image of Evermor finishing her title in grand style with a 4-point major and Best of Opposite Sex at Farmington Valley, handled by breeder Sheryl Hedrick. Owner, Janna Morgan, Aurora, CO.

Ch. Copperdot's Best Gemini, by Ch. Arras vom Hasenkamp, ex Gibson's Bubbles, bred and owned by Dianna D. Gibson. Handled by William T. Wynn, III. Lina Basquette is awarding Best of winners to this splendid dog in 1986 on the way to the title.

BEST OF
WINNERS
ROCKLAND COUNTY
KENNEL CLUB
1986
/ASHBEY

rear drive. Front and rear legs are not thrown either in or out, as the imprint of the hind feet should touch that of the forefeet. In a trot, the forequarters and hindquarters are mutually co-ordinated while the back remains firm. As speed increases, the legs will converge under the body towards the centre line.

Faults—The foregoing is a description of the ideal Rottweiler. Any structural fault that detracts from the ideal must be penalized to the extent of the deviation. Included as faults are: pink mouth, wavy coat, insufficient markings, undercoat showing through outercoat. Faults considered serious are: lack of proportion, undersize, oversize, level bite, yellow eyes, eyes not of same colour, eyes unequal in size or shape, hairless eyelids, excessively short coat, curly or open coat, lack of undercoat, white markings any place on dog (a few white hairs do not constitute a marking), excessive markings, light-coloured markings, up to four missing pre-molars.

Disqualifications—Undershot, overshot, more than four missing pre-molars and/or any other missing tooth, long coat, any base colour other than black, total absence of markings.

288

Rottweilers in Australia

THE BEGINNING

Australia and the Rottweiler were introduced to one another after at least one false start, in 1962, when word was received that Captain Roy Smith of the famed Ritelna Rotties in Great Britain was emigrating to Australia and that almost without doubt he would be bringing at least a dog or two with him.

This news was heard with particular pleasure by working-dog fanciers Mr. and Mrs. Doug Mummery. During the late 1950s, they had traveled to Hawaii, the mainland United States, Canada, the United Kingdom, and the European continent in search of an outstanding working Rottweiler to bring to Australia as a foundation sire for now world famous Heatherglen Kennels. It was difficult, but the Mummerys succeeded in finding exactly the dog they wanted, Balthasar of Mallion, and they persuaded the owner to sell him. They were thrilled, as this son of Rudi Eulenspiegel of Mallion from Quinta Eulenspiegel of Mallion was exactly the dog that they had envisioned—handsome, excellently bred, and with extraordinary working instincts and ability even for a Rottweiler. They were elated and arranged that he be shipped to

them in Australia along with some others they had purchased. But how quickly that happiness turned to sorrow when the magnificent Zhar was overcome by the heat aboard the ship coming across the Red Sea and succumbed to heat exhaustion.

For a long time the Mummerys did not attempt to bring over another dog (hardly to be wondered at following so deep and hurtful a disappointment). But when they heard that Captain Smith was coming to their country and bringing a pair of Rottweilers with him, the urge to try it again became very strong.

Captain Smith, it developed, had chosen a dog and a bitch to make the trip to Australia. The bitch, having been bred prior to starting the journey, whelped her puppies in the quarantine kennels at Perth. This was the first litter of Rottweilers actually to be born on Australian soil. Sadly, of the six puppies born, it was only possible for Captain Smith to locate a suitable home for one, due to which the others were put to sleep. The survivor, a bitch puppy, went to a Dutch policeman, Mr. De Jonge, who was migrating to South Australia, where he took her with him.

When he had learned this

> "Australia and the Rottweiler were introduced to one another after at least one false start, in 1962, when word was received that Captain Roy Smith of the famed Ritelna Rotties in Great Britain was emigrating to Australia . . ."

Top: Ezygo Queen, age 10 months, by Aust. Ch. Stromhall Nobelius ex Brabantsia Raiko. The Van Helvoorts, Gidgegannup, Western Australia. *Bottom:* A famous Top Producer Rottweiler dam, Ch. RC's Gator Bel von Meadow, T.T., is an outstanding Top Producer of Champions. Photo courtesy of Rebecca L. Chriscoe. Owned by Vickie Chriscoe, bred by Donna M. Wormser. Kostlich-Von Ursa Rottweilers, Micanopy, FL.

Top: Aust. Ch. Stromhall's Lord Lutz being evaluated by Herr K. Altpeter of Germany. Lord Lutz was Best Exhibit in Show that day. Photo courtesy of Patricia Hall. *Bottom:* Aust. Ch. Stromhall Pick A Pack. Best Exhibit, R.C. of New South Wales Championship Show, Germany. Another example of P. Hall's Stromhall breeding program in Australia.

Aust. Ch. Kuhnheit Herr Cossack, with three sons: future Aust. Ch. Kuhnheit Herr Lucifer, Aust. Ch. Kuhnheit Herr Imposter, and Kuhnheit Black Cossack. Owner, Rosemary Adler, Southern River, Western Australia.

information, Mr. Mummery promptly placed an order for a bitch puppy from the next litter by Rintelna the Dragoon ex Rintelna the Chatelaine. We dare say that anticipation was high as he looked forward to the arrival of his long awaited Rottweiler of U.K. parentage.

Finally the puppies were born in July, 1963. This was officially the Rintelna "F" litter. Accordingly, the puppy was named Rintelna the Fatale.

During this same year, Mr. Mummery also decided it was time for another attempt at bringing a mature dog for himself from the U.K. His selection this time was a male known as Pilgrimsway Loki. More fortunate than Zhar had

been, Loki arrived by ship from the U.K. in good shape. Eventually he and Fatale produced the first litter of Rottweiler pups born in Victoria.

The Heatherglens, owned by the Mummerys, and the Rotvels, owned by Mrs. J. Pherrson, were the first kennel prefixes under which Rottweilers were exhibited in Australia. Only for a short while did they remain the only ones, however, as interest in the breed and admiration for the dogs quickly led to further constructive activity. Others from the earlier period were Auslese Kennels, registered to Mr. and Mrs. J. Pettengell, and Jimnan Kennels, registered to Mrs. J. Stewart.

The year 1972 proved to be a busy one for Rottie development, during which Mr. and Mrs. K. Terry registered Kerusgal Kennels; Mr. E. Warren and Mr. B. Wheeler, the Kalataras Kennels; and Mr. and Mrs. G. Bitris made it official for Korobeit. Thus it was that Rottweilers were on their way in Australia with Victoria the focal point of activity during that period.

DEVELOPMENT IN VICTORIA

The leadership behind the move to form the Rottweiler Club of Victoria began in May, 1971, for the purpose of directing and protecting the future of the Rottweiler breed there. David Slater and Brian and Pat Dyson were the trio who started the movement when they attended an informal barbecue party at the Dyson home in May, 1971. The plan and ideas evolved and met with high enthusiasm for the 32 guests, resulting in a business meeting being called for the next month to finalize plans and set the ball rolling.

The first slate of officers drawn up at this first business meeting was as follows: president, Mr. Tony Syme; vice-presidents, Mr. Brian Dyson and Mr. Peter Wilson; secretary, Mr. David Slater; assistant secretary, Mrs. Diane Wilson; treasurer, Mr. Keith Lovell; committee members, Mrs. Jean Miller, Mr. Ken Hendrick, Mr.

Murray Harding, Miss Juanita Drever, and Mr. Wayne Hetherington.

It was agreed during this same meeting that Mr. F. Watkins be invited to serve as patron of this new club, a position which he has held and fulfilled admirably over the years. Another early decision was that the club emblem should be that of the breed's "home territory," Rottweil, Germany, where its true early development had taken place. Permission for this was granted by the "powers that be" of Rottweil, and the emblem since has become the club badge. The new club grew at an astonishing rate of speed, quite in keeping with what was taking place everywhere among Rottweilers, both in their own numbers and those of the people owning them.

The club sponsored its first official function, a competition for dogs owned by members, with Mr. Keith Cronchey officiating, making that gentleman the first person to judge Rottweilers at an Australian dog show.

The Victoria Club held its first open parade in 1972. This event was judged by Mr. Murray; 47 Rottweilers appeared in competition, with the coveted award of Best Exhibit in Parade won by Mr. and Mrs. Dyson's Brentano Heidi, followed by Best of Opposite Sex to Mrs. Pherrson's Rotvel Troy.

Other milestones were culminated in March, 1975, when Graham Head officiated as judge at the Rottweiler Club of Victoria's first Championship Specialty Show with an entry of 61 dogs, truly a beautiful presentation of the cream of the crop of the breed where quality is concerned.

Mrs. G. Terry had the honor of taking the Best Adult in Show Award with Uplands Lados. Mr. B.J. Henderson's Auslese Contessa was Best of Opposite Sex to the winner.

Australia's first two Rottweilers to gain championship honors did so in 1969. The first was a dog, Australian Ch. Rintelna the

General, owned by J.M. Pettengall. The second (and at the same time the first bitch), Australian Ch. Heatherglen Cliquot, was also owned by Mr. Pettengall.

It was in 1972 that a change took place in the officials of the Rottweiler Club of Victoria: the election as president of Mrs. Diane Taylor; and as secretary, the election of Mrs. Pat Hall. They succeeded the very successful reign of Tony Syme and Brian Dyson, who brought the club through seven years of progress.

ROTTWEILERS IN NEW SOUTH WALES

Rottweilers lost no time in gaining the attention of the dog-loving public in New South Wales, quickly receiving recognition and

Head study of the great Aust. Ch. Stromhall Lord Lutz, bred, owned, and handled by Patricia Hall.

Top: This splendid Rottweiler in Australia is Hanahaus Heather, by Bragi Poetical Justice (of Germany) ex Crista von Rika (of the U.S.). Owned by the Van Helvoorts, Barrabadeen Stud, Gidgegannup, Western Australia. *Bottom:* R.C. of Victoria's Obedience Team at work. Photo courtesy of Patricia Hall.

Top: Ch. Graf Hasso v. Alpen Haus, owned by Laura Krutsch, Round Top, NY. *Bottom:* Brabantsia Raiko in May, 1986. By Guiding Flame ex Aust. Ch. Brabantsia Tanja. Another splendid Rottie from the Barrabadeen Stud.

Ch. Garen's Fourth X A Charm, C.D., T.T. Charm is the foundation bitch at Garen's Rottweilers, and she is a daughter of Am., Can. Ch. Donnaj Vt. Yankee of Paulus, C.D.X., T.T., ex Rodsden's Belle. Her owners are Gary F. and Karen L. Sims, St. Charles, MO.

was the excellent bitch Australian Ch. Rotvel Nova.

Renee Edwards and Kevin Whatson were the next to bring additional Rottweilers to New South Wales, theirs from Mrs. Gail Terry's Kerusgal Kennels, namely Australian Ch. Kerusgal Black Anvil, C.D., and Kerusgal Black Bruin.

It was in September, 1975, that plans got underway to start a Rottweiler Club of New South Wales for the purpose of educating the public and promoting the breed. As help in accomplishing this, several different courses were followed, including the stationing of a Rottweiler with a person collecting funds for Guide Dogs for the Blind (these were posted at busy locations where a maximum number of people pass through each day). Rottweilers also went as visitors to prisons and institutions where they did obedience presentations. These measures helped acquaint the public with the personality and intelligence of Rottweilers. It was also felt that the formation of a breed specialty club would bring together people of mutual interests, which would prove beneficial to all.

In the beginning, meetings of the Rottweiler Club of New South Wales were held in private homes, as funds were noticeably lacking at this early stage of the game. Since holding a parade is one prerequisite towards the granting of a new club's affiliation, this was undertaken successfully. Winner of the parade, owned by Mr. and Mrs. Elick, was Australian Ch. Rotvel Zeon.

Then came the real "biggie," the first Championship Show of the Rottweiler Club of New South Wales. A full year's hard work went into planning for it, with triumph the ultimate result! Best in Show and Runner Up were, respectively, littermates from Victoria: Australian Ch. Anverdons Peter Pan, owned by Mr. Fisher; and Australian Ch. Anverdons Tara, owned by Mr. and Mrs. Bugeja. The breed judge was Mr. Tony Valli.

approval there. John Pereghy is generally credited with having the first Rottweiler brought to New South Wales, in 1966, from Heatherglen Kennels. Unfortunately this dog died of bloat. But, Mr. Pereghy's enthusiasm did continue, leading to the eventual purchase of a dog from Rotvel Kennels.

Then Mrs. Jackson, from Paddington, brought in Marthleen Camilla from South Australia, who was the first Rottie of her sex generally seen in New South Wales. She was, however, only shown occasionally.

Australian Ch. Montoya Cybelle, C.D.X., soon arrived, brought in by Mrs. Tina Scheltema. Following soon thereafter, to this same lady,

SOUTH AUSTRALIA

South Australia also has a nucleus of dedicated Rottweiler fans. Their specialty club was organized in the 1970s. Its first president was Mr. Murray Montgomerie, with Mrs. Carlene Naughton as the first secretary. Later these positions were filled by Mr. Peter Oates and Mr. John Blebin.

The first open parade of this club was in 1977, won by Kemmelberg Shivalee. Its first Championship Show was in 1972, Australian Ch. Tayvelka Noble Marcus winning Best Exhibit for Mr. and Mrs. Borg.

QUEENSLAND

Those first two Rottweilers (the dog and the bitch) who originally accompanied Captain Roy Smith when he migrated to Australia from the U.K. automatically became the first two of the breed in Queensland when their owner settled and made it his home after coming from England to Perth. The Rintelna prefix was registered for Australia to Captain Smith. One of his Rotties, Rintelna the Chatelaine, was sold to a Perth fancier; thus she returned to Western Australia.

It was in 1974 that Rottweiler enthusiasm became increasingly evident, a situation which has been steadily on the rise ever since. Thus, here too, the need was for the guidance of a breed club, as a result of which the Rottweiler Club of Queensland was formed in 1982.

Brisbane is the center of Queensland breed activity, thus the proposed club chose that city to be its home. The first president and first secretary were Mr. and Mrs. Graeme Everett. By the year 1983, Canine Council figures state that 402 Rottie pups were registered that year.

Rintelna the Dragoon, one of the original U.K. imports, won the Brisbane Royal Challenge Certificate for dogs in 1966, when no bitches were entered. The following year both a dog and a bitch competed and were awarded C.C.s; they were Rintelna the Grenadier and Rintelna the Gorgeous. Grenadier repeated in 1968, with no award in bitches that year, as only one of that sex was shown.

NORTHERN TERRITORY

There are ardent Rottweiler fans to be found in the Northern Territory as in the other Australian areas. Among them are Mrs. Judith Lattaway, Norweiler Rottweilers; and Mr. Wayne Roddom, Rodonburg Kennels.

In 1976, the first registration of a Rottweiler from this territory took place. This was Auslese Pouilly Fuise, owned by Mrs. Pfitzner and sired by Ch. Rintelna the General ex Ch. Heatherglen Cliquot.

Ortrud vom Alpen Haus at age 10 weeks. Owned by Laura Krutsch, Alpen Haus Rottweilers.

Am., Can. Ch. Black Maria von Dorow, by Am., Can. Ch. Rodsden's Berte v. Zederwald, C.D.X., from Ch. Merrymoore's Imp von Dorow. Owner, Kathy Lingman-Shane, Thunder Bay, Ont., Canada. Breeder, Nancy C. Estes, Midland, TX.

The breed made its appearance in the show ring at the North Australian Society's championship event in July, 1969. This young dog, Auslese Dragoon, won Best Junior All Breeds in Show under Dr. Spira, a widely respected authority from New South Wales. Quite an exciting debut for the breed in Northern Territory competition.

Australian Ch. Korobeit Kahn, by Uplands Wolfgang ex Austerman Bingo and owned by N.B. Coles, completed title in May, 1978.

WESTERN AUSTRALIA

The history of Rottweilers in Western Australia has been supplied by Jo and Keith Peckham of Rivervale. We truly appreciate their regional coverage for this book. We also thank Mrs. E. Goedemondt and Mrs. R. Adler for their helpfulness.

Mrs. J. Peckham tells us that the establishment of the Rottweiler in Western Australia began in 1972 through the activity of Brabantsia Kennels, owned by Mr. F. Goedemondt. Although his initial attempts are said to have been somewhat inhibited by his original lines, his imported stock of 1976, 1977, made this kennel one of the most influential in Western Australia by 1980. The imports of the period referred to were Chesara Dark Rustler (U.K.) and Friofater (Holland). Rustler still appears in many pedigrees.

During the year following Rustler's arrival came Guiding Flame and his litter sister, Gilda Debruse, followed by Chesara Dark Syrus in 1980. Guiding Flame and Gilda Debruse were of the Von Marchenwald line in Germany, their sire being Hasso von Marchenwald, and their dam, Owlcroft Anitra. Many champions have resulted from these lines—locally, interstate, and overseas. It is Guiding Flame to whom Joan Peckham tells us credit must go for the establishment of a distinctive type in Western Australia and to whom credit should be recorded for the greatest influence on the breed there to date.

In 1974, another notable kennel was established by Mrs. Adler, the now famous Kuhnheit Rottweilers. Mrs. Adler claims that Arrumarrut Simba has been the greatest influence on the establishment of this line. He sired four litters for her kennel, from which two bitches and one dog became its foundation. The dog was Kuhnheit Herr Cossack who, along with the bitch Kuhnheit Frau Cougar, earned championship. The other bitch, Kuhnheit Frau Brunhild, was used as a security dog. So far as can be verified, Kuhnheit Kennels have produced nine show champions and five C.D.-titled dogs.

Mrs. Adler's breeding has been notably successful over the years in show competition, with numerous major victories to its credit. As of 1990, Mrs. Adler's Ch. Kuhnheit Frau Huntriss was the only Rottie bitch to win Best Exhibit in Show at an all-breed championship show in Western Australia.

The Kuhnheit line is unique in Western Australia for the production of natural bobtails, three of whom are champions, namely Aust. Ch. Kuhnheit Frau Evita, Herr Imposter, and Herr Rocky. Since the threat of a law against all tail-docking exists in Australia, Mrs. Adler must be happy indeed with these natural bobtail lines.

Over a period of years, offspring from these two foundation Rottweiler Kennels were virtually the only lines in the show ring in Western Australia, and it is only since the mid-1980s that a major influx of new blood has appeared there in the ring. In fact, to Jo Peckham's knowledge, the only Rottie not from these kennels to take a major award prior to 1984 was Ch. Antwell Bia, bred by Mrs. J. Antoine, and owned by Keith Peckham. Bia took Best of Opposite Sex in Show at an all-breed championship show in 1983, making her one of only two Rottie bitches to have taken that honor there.

During 1984, Western Australia was treated to a visit from a young Victorian dog, Korolla Boris (owned by Ross and Tracey Chavesse), a most beautiful dog who presented to Western Australia a type different from its own. He took Western Australia by storm while he was there, winning many Bests of Breed and major awards in the years during which he was shown. Unfortunately, he was used at stud only a couple of times while in Western Australia, and perhaps even more unfortunately none of his progeny have been shown there. However, when he returned East it was with the titles Aust. Ch. Korolla Boris, C.D.X., E.T.

Taking over for Boris in the ring

was Ch. Brabantsia Rupert, owned by P. Alder and V. Green, a typical Brabantsia boy who certainly took his share of Bests of Breed and major awards and became the top winning Rottie of Western Australia in 1986. Among Rupert's special victories was that of Best Exhibit in Show at the second Western Australia Members Competition in 1986.

Jo Peckham continues reviewing the Rottweilers of Western Australia with words of praise for Australian Ch. Russpeck von Ranolph, owned by P. and K. Arangiom, a small but lovely boy well admired by the judges. Ranolph was Best Exhibit in Show

Kennrich Vic-Tory, bred and owned by Kennette and Richard Tabor of Chesapeake, VA. Whelped in 1987, Vic-Tory was sired by Kimbo vom Siedlerpead, SchH. I, ex Ch. Radio Ranch's Casablanca Pia.

Ch. Radio Ranch's Casablanca Pia, by Ch. Radio Ranch's X-tra Special ex Ch. Centurian's Ivy League. Bred by Leslie Fulcher, owned by Kennrich Rottweilers, Kennette and Richard Tabor.

very hard and dry and maybe a smoother outline than we had been used to seeing." Noble was shown only a few times in his first two years in Western Australia, owing to his owner-handler Keith Peckham's serious traffic accident. Noble was a very difficult dog for the novice to handle, due to his strong temperament and high fighting instincts, which did not endear him to the hearts of the other exhibitors. Therefore, it was not until Miss Tonya Syme came to live for a short time in Western Australia that Noble was campaigned consistently for seven months. Under Tonya's expert handling, he went through the show ring like a whirlwind. He gained his title in six challenges. All told, he actually gained his title more than twice over and was virtually always Best of Breed. As of 1990, Noble still holds the record for major awards by a Rottweiler, including Best Exhibit in Show at major championship shows, in Western Australia. It would seem entirely fair to say that Noble put Rottweilers on the map in Western Australia.

Hot on Noble's heels for this honor is P. Alder and V. Green's Aust. Ch. Rotvel Alpine Ferryman, who is winning up a storm as a close second to Noble's record for major awards. Ferryman is a New South Wales bred dog who is a more "dry" type and, like Noble, a treat to watch in the ring. Additionally, Ferryman is a thorough gentleman in and out of the ring, making him a tremendously popular winner. Ferryman has also taken a Best Exhibit in Show at a major championship event. As the record shows, this award has only gone to four male Rottweilers at championship shows in New South Wales, namely Aust. Ch. Brabantasia Faro, Aust. Ch. Stromhall Nobelius, Aust. Ch. Rotvel Alpine Ferryman, and Aust. Ch. Kuhnwert Herr Rocky. Congratulations to these four and to the many who will follow them in the future.

at the first Western Australia Members Competition and was also the only offspring of Antwell Bia to be made a champion.

Over this same period, another dog who was doing well in the ring was Aust. Ch. Janendorf Sensation, a big boy and a beautiful-moving dog. He certainly did his owner-handler, Pat Scott, proud. "Bill," as he is affectionately known, also has a C.D. under his belt.

During 1987, Australian Ch. Stromhall Nobelius, bred by P. and G. Hall in Victoria, and owned by the Peckhams, was campaigned in Western Australia. Jo Peckham says of this, "again a different type from what we have seen in the past,

Regarding the females, Jo Peckham relates that the two top-winning bitches of modern times are Aust. Ch. Heroden Betty and Aust. Ch. Brabantasia Madora. Betty, owned by P. and D. Scott, is a consistent C.C. and Best of Breed winner and has a fair share of Group and Best in Show awards. This is no mean feat for a Rottie bitch in Australia, as they are constantly shown against top-winning dogs. "Duchess," as Betty is known, is an "on-her-toes" bitch who is beautifully controlled by her owner-handler, Pat Scott. She moves around the ring like she owns it, according to Jo Peckham, and is a hard one to pass up.

Madora, we understand, is also a lovely bitch, ultra-feminine, with a very smooth outline. She too has taken numerous major awards and Bests of Breed, and it is claimed by her handler, Mrs. Goedemondt, that she is the top-winning Western Australia Rottie bitch in the ring at this time.

Mrs. Peckham has attempted to send us a chronological scenario of the top-winning Rottweilers in Western Australia, which now brings us to Ch. Stromhall Lord Lore, bred by P. and G. Hall, and owned by K. and J. Peckham. Lord was a stunning dog right from the start, and he has surely made his presence strongly felt.

While still a "minor," Lord achieved runner-up to Best Exhibit in Show at the second Western Australia Members Competition. A beautiful and masculine dog, Lord has what his owners consider to be the ultimate honor of being Mrs. Muriel Freeman's (U.S.A.) selection for Best Exhibit in Show out of 257 Rottweiler entries at the New South Wales Rottweiler Club's Specialty Championship Show in June, 1988. Lord returned home to Western Australia to win Best Exhibit in Show at the Rottweiler Club of Western Australia's Inaugural Open Parade, judged by Mrs. Honey Gross-Richardson, under whom his owners were also highly pleased to win as she has a deep interest in the breed and has a Rottie in her household of German Shepherds.

Mrs. Peckham goes on to mention Mr. and Mrs. Smirk's boy, Poirot Tomahawk, imported from the United Kingdom, as being a most welcome addition to the bloodlines in Western Australia. "Duke" is a lovely dog who endears himself to everyone. To Mrs. Peckham's knowledge, this is the only internationally imported Rottweiler in Western Australia outside of the Brabantsia imports.

Another dog believed to have left a strong stamp on the breed is Brabantsia Raiko, belonging to R. and D. Scott. Prior to his having been tragically shot by a neighbor, this dog managed to sire three

Ch. Wyreglen's Broad Horizons, owned by F. Mueller and C.E. MacPherson, Uxbridge, Ont., Canada.

champions, namely Aust. Ch. Janendorf Sensation, Aust. Ch. Russpeck Dark Danton, and Aust. Ch. Guntzler Rockville Lad—a fine effort within a short period of time.

Other well-known champions who Mrs. Peckham feels deserve mention here include Aust. Ch. Ooyella Samson, owned by C. and M. Frame, a striking dog who in his day won two major awards when these were difficult to attain. He

"Dr." Bruno in one of his "just-for-fun impersonations' is ready for the day's first patient. Owned by Janice DelFarno.

also has been a successful sire of some admired dogs, and he is always very welcome on pedigrees, as he has produced progeny with very good hip status, being known to have upgraded hips in Western Australia. Ch. Russpeck Dark Danton, owned by R. and I. Barnard, has notable wins which include a Best of Breed at the Perth Royal Show in 1988.

Aust. Ch. Brabantsia Demayne, owned by P. Alder and V. Green, was a top-winning bitch of her day. Aust. Ch. Guntzler Rockville Lad was owner-handled in the ring.

Aust. Ch. Failsafe Boadecia, owned and bred by R. and C. Axten, is a bitch who did well from the past. Another owned by the Axtens, Aust. Ch. Auslese Droll E.T., SchH. III, is the only Rottweiler in Australia to have a Schutzhund III title. Aust. Ch. Kuhnheit Herr Hagar, owned and bred by R. Adler, was a very handsome young dog really "knocking them dead" in the ring some years back but who was killed by a snake bite at age 15 months—a sad loss to the breed.

Again our thanks to Jo and Keith Peckham for all this "on the spot" information from Western Australia, which we deeply appreciate. Jo remarks in closing that she has probably left out some Rottweilers who should have been included, and if so, she extends her apologies.

HELSINGBORG

Helsingborg Rottweilers are a quite recently formed project, a merging of the mutual interest in the breed shared by Robert and Rosemary Van Helvoort and Pat and David Scott at the Barrabadeen Stud, a famous and successful horse farm in Bidgegannup, Western Australia, where the Van Helvoorts raise Holsteiner horses. The farm sits in the hills just outside Perth in Western Australia.

During 1987, Pat and David Scott, who were Rottweiler breeders, were appointed farm managers of the Barrabadeen Stud. It was the interest of Mrs. Van Helvoort in the dogs that led to the joint ownership with the Scotts of the Helsingborg Rottweilers.

Pat and David Scott had purchased their first dogs in 1983. Farm managers at the time, they found that the breed adapted admirably to farming conditions and to the Australian bush. So favorably impressed were they that two other Rotties soon joined their family. It was those Rottweilers who aroused the admiration of Rosemary Van Helvoort, causing the eventual joint kennel.

The Scott's foundation dogs were

Brabantsia Raiko ("Benny");
Janendor's Sensation ("Bill"), and
Heroden Betty ("Duchess"). Benny,
whelped in 1983, sired seven
litters. Of these, three of his
progeny became Australian
champions: Ch. Janendorf
Sensation, C.D., Russpeck Dark
Danton, and Ch. Guntzler Rockville
Lad. Guntzler Stuka is also well on
his way to becoming an Australian
champion. Benny had an eventful if
short life. Shown only once, he
broke his leg badly at age 15
months, necessitating his
retirement from the ring. Fond of
walking in the bush, he strayed
onto a neighboring farm and was
one of two dogs shot by the farmer.
At the age of four years, Ben's
wounds proved fatal.

Bill, whelped in June, 1985,
experienced many highs and lows
in his show and obedience careers:
Best of Breed and Best Exhibit in
Group 6 and Best Junior in Group 6
at 17 months under judge Mrs. E.
Robshaw, Western Australia, 1986;
Best of Breed and Runner Up to
Best Exhibit in Group 6 under Mrs.
H. Spira (New South Wales), 1988.
An attempt at an endurance trial in
1988 saw Bill complete 20
kilometers, finishing with a lower
pulse rate (68) than he started with
(84). Unfortunately, needing a
second command for his jump, he
failed the trial. His owners are
hoping for a better result in this
year's attempt. He did earn his C.D.
in 1989.

Next comes tracking. Bill enjoys
pulling the Rottweiler Club of New
South Wales cart and is something
of a celebrity, having pulled the
cart through the streets of Perth for
the 1988 Perth Royal Show Street
Parade. Deciding that "show biz"
was for him, he willingly proved
his style again on Exhibition Day at
the Perth Royal Show in 1988,
thereby helping the Rottweiler
Club of Western Australia to
receive second place in exhibition,
which was a tremendously great
honor. Bill has sired three litters
thus far—from Reichmaster
Morgen and Russpeck Frau
Anneke, to whom he was mated in

1987, and Brabazon Astart (a
daughter of Aust. Ch. Ooyella
Samson) in 1988.

Duchess (born in May, 1985) was
purchased by the Scotts at 15
months of age. She produced her
first litter at 19 months, bred to
Aust. Ch. Russpeck von Ranolph.
None of these puppies were shown,
owing to the Scotts' decision to sell
all three of them as pets.

Duchess began her show career
at the age of two years. In March,
1987, under Mrs. Anne Mitchell,
she received her first Challenge
Certificate and was runner up to
Best of Breed Aust. Ch. Stromhall
Nobelius, the latter gaining his
final Challenge Certificate that
day. In July, 1987, under American
judge Dr. Robert Moore, Duchess
received Best of Breed, Best
Australian-bred in Show, Group,
and her final Challenge Certificate.

Aust. Ch.
Stromhall
Skana, C.D.X.,
Best of Breed at
the Melbourne
Royal, 1982, and
Challenge Bitch
at the Sydney
Royal, 1982.
Owned, bred
and handled by
Patricia Hall.

This is Lee Mckenney's beloved Margo (Ashby v. Foxcroft, C.D., ex Grand Matriarch of True Lee Rottweilers). An A.R.C. Producer of Merit; Medallion R.C. Honor Roll.

Now a champion, Duchess received numerous Bests of Breed under both International and Australian judges. Duchess had had an impressively worthy show career. She is now taking a respite from the ring with her third litter, this by Ch. Rotvel Alpine Ferryman.

Helsingborg Harskarrina (Mitzi), a Duchess daugher by Australian Ch. Ooyella Samson, was purchased by the Van Helvoorts and is presently being shown by Robert Van Helvoort, who has found his wife's enthusiasm for the breed to be contagious. The Van Helvoorts had previously owned a Labrador Retriever, which they had loved, but in 1984 Rosemary saw, at the Perth Royal, a beautiful

and gentle Rottie bitch with whom she was deeply impressed; that admiration was enhanced by the Scotts' arrival, when they had been appointed to manage the farm, with their own three wonderful Rottweilers.

Barrabadeen Stud and Helsingborg Rottweilers seem to complement one another very nicely. Importation of Holsteiner horses from Germany began in the 1970s, and recent years have brought tremendous gratification in the show ring plus the quite overwhelming opportunity which they have now received to export horses back to Germany. That the Rottweilers are well started on the road to equally exciting success is quite certain.

RUSSPECK

Russpeck Rottweilers are located in Rivervale, Western Australia, where they are owned by Jo and Keith Peckham, who have been involved with the breed since the late 1970s. The Peckhams breed only on a small scale, being deeply concerned with overpopulation in the breed. A litter, therefore, is never planned until such a time as good homes are awaiting the arrival of the puppies.

Russpeck started off with local bloodlines for the first few litters, which produced for them two champions: Aust. Ch. Russpeck von Ranolph, by Aust. Ch. Kuenheit Herr Hager ex Aust. Ch. Antwell Bia; and Aust. Ch. Russpeck Dark Danton, by Brabantsia Raiko ex Ooyella Juliana. Ranolph was a handsome boy and a popular winner when he went through in 1986.

It was in 1984 that the Peckhams decided to bring some new blood into Western Australia, for which they chose the respected Stromhall line from Victoria. Their first of these was Aust. Ch. Stromhall Nobelius, who became a magnificent dog and who holds the record as the winner of most major awards among Rottweilers in Western Australia.

Soon after purchasing Noble, the

Peckhams realized what a treasure they had, which led to their ordering another male from Pat Hall's Stromhall Kennels, this one Aust. Ch. Stromhall Lord Lore. "Lord" had been winning major awards from Minor Puppy Classes and has been Best Exhibit in Show at three events. He was Muriel Freeman's Best Exhibit in Show when she judged at the New South Wales Rottweiler Club Championship Specialty (which drew an entry of 257 from all parts of Australia). Needless to say, the Peckhams were overjoyed to have gained so prestigious an award from so highly regarded a judge. As frosting on the cake, Lord since then has won Best Exhibit in Show at the Rottweiler Club of Western Australia Open Parade in both 1988 and 1989, although he was only three years old in 1989.

Both of these dogs have been used for breeding and their owners are delighted with them and their prepotency in their offspring, who are now coming into their own.

STROMHALL

Stromhall Rottweilers are owned by Pat and George Hall in East Wandin, Victoria. The foundation bitch here was Australian Ch. Anverdons Olympia, C.D., from the "greatest of the old time dogs" (quoting Pat Hall), Australian Ch. Heatherglen Franz, C.D.X. "Olympia" was bred to one of Mr. and Mrs. Mummery's imports, Chesara Dark Nobleman (U.K.), which litter produced Stromhall's foundation sire, Aust. Ch. Stromhall Torrey, U.D., T.D. This is the dog on whom Pat Hall bases all her breeding, right up to present times.

It is Pat Hall who imported the first Rottweiler from the United States to Australia, the magnificent dog Powderhorn Fetz of Wencrest, who has been a tremendous asset to the kennel and whose bloodlines combined with those of Torrey have produced quality and type to please the most discerning fancier.

Since starting as a Rottweiler breeder, Pat Hall has truly

achieved exciting successes with her dogs. As an example, there is Australian Ch. Stromhall Pick A Pack, who was Best Exhibit in Show, graded "excellent" by judge Herr Kurt Lohnert from Germany at the Rottweiler Club of New South Wales Championship Show in 1988. Australian Ch. Stromhall Lord Lutz's win of Best Exhibit in Show, graded "excellent" by judge Herr Klaus Altpeter from Germany at the Rottweiler Club of New South Wales Championship Show in 1989, was another highlight.

Stromhall Rottweilers have also won Best Exhibit in Show at the Rottweiler Club of Victoria Specialty Championship Show in 1980 (Aust. Ch. Stromhall Torrey, U.D., T.D., also Best Junior).

Kostlich Ebony Pistol v. Ursa, by Ch. Beaverbrook Kreiger, C.D., ex Ch. Gator's Cookie Bella von Ursa. Owned by Rebecca L. Chriscoe and Paul R. Girouard.

Head study of Int. Ch. Green Mtn's Flora, C.D., the multi-titled bitch who has brought home fantastic honors to Little Flowers Kennels, Mr. and Mrs. Frank Fiorella, Boxford, MA. Flora was bred by Anthony Atalla.

Rottweilers in the Netherlands

During the past 12 years, and the writing of several books about this breed, I have done considerable research on the Rottweiler. Increasingly I have noted with admiration the type, substance, soundness and quality of the dogs coming from the Netherlands in the photographs I have seen, imports I have noted, and comments of other fanciers whose opinions I respect.

During a recent dog show weekend, it was by pleasure to have occasion to discuss European Rottweilers with my friend Frank Fiorella, owner of Little Flower Kennels in Massachusetts. Knowing how frequently he and Mrs. Fiorella visit Europe, I, of course, wanted and received some opinions to share with my readers.

The Fiorellas are both members of the Netherlands Kennel Club and of the A.D.R.K., thus they have a finger firmly on the pulse of what is taking place in the Netherlands and in Germany. Frank constantly has an eye out for quality dogs to bring back to the States, and there is little he misses as he watches the judging and the dogs as they relax around the show grounds or in their kennels.

One of the Rottweilers possessing special merit in Frank's opinion is Duuck van de Nedermolen, a stunning dog extremely difficult to fault, who belongs to Eigenaar, G.A.J. Kuijpers, Hoogaloon, the Netherlands.

Frank has recently enjoyed what must be considered a major triumph in his discovery and successful negotiation of the purchase of a stunning, extremely worthwhile dog named Barto V/T Straotje, who had to his credit in Europe such honors as HH, TC, I.P.O. following his name, which is preceded by Netherlands, Belgium, Europe, Luxembourg, International (working and conformation combined), Ch. and 1988 Netherlands Club Best in Show Dog. Barto's career has moved right along smoothly under the new ownership of Mr. Fiorella, too, as he is already an American and Canadian champion with an American T.D.

Barto's breeding is of the finest, his parents being Dingo vh Mamoriem SchH. I, HD, and Dutch, International Ch. Quinto V/T Straotje, HD, TC, I.P.O.—an impressive background to pass along to future generations. V/T Straotje Kennels, from which Barto came, have long been respected for the superb quality of Rottweilers

"Increasingly I have noted with admiration the type, substance, soundness, and quality of the dogs coming from the Netherlands . . ."

Left top: Am., Can., Mex. Ch. Elton's Northwind Ero completing his Mexican championship and winning Group first at Mexicali in January, 1989, under judge Antonio Montero, owner-handled by Pat Elton. Ero is a grandson of Int. Ch. Rodsden's Njord v.h. Brabant and Ch. Northwind's Jasmine.

Left middle: Powderhorn's Zero of Wencrest, C.D., owned by Ray and Joann Hurley.

Left bottom: First in Brood Bitch Class, Golden State R.C. Specialty 1983. Ch. Taba v.d. Keizerslanden, Dutch import, owned by Powderhorn/Wencrest Rottweilers, Inc.; Ch. Powderhorn's Kapt of Wencrest, C.D., T.T., owned by Jim and Sue Johnson; and Ch. Powderhorn's Gwen of Wencrest, owned by Connie Colnot.

Above: Elessar's Cuno of Ebonstern, by Am., Can. Ch. Ebonstern Ivan v.d. Liebe ex Am., Can. Ch. Rodsden's Beorn. Co-owned by Cheryl Wheeler and Erick Lund.

Right top: Carol Woodward with Am., Can Ch. Kitty von Kodiak, Am., Can. C.D., SchH I. Kitty is the dam of the Woodwards' Ch. Zana von Siegerhaus and Ch. Zolti von Siegerhaus. She is owned by Bob and Kathy Csolti.

Right middle: Ch. Epic's Adulteress, T.T., at 13 months winning Best in Sweepstakes at the Colonial R.C. Specialty. Bob and Rose Hogan, Epic Kennels, Chepachet, RI.

Right bottom: Ch. Hans v.h. Brabantpark, Dutch import, Top Ten Rottweiler. Owned by Powderhorn/Wencrest Rottweilers.

Below: The great European winner, Can., Am., Int. Ch. Barto v.t. Straotje, T.D., I.P.O. III, came to Little Flower Kennels following a career in Europe which made him the most titled Rottweiler there at the time. He quickly resumed his winning career for his new owners, and lost no time in adding American, Canadian conformation titles, and American Tracking Dog degree to his ever-growing title. This photo captures Barto's first major in the U.S., Best of Winners, in August, 1988, handled by Bill Burrell for the Fiorellas.

Top: Can. Ch. Jimick's Ainabella is owned by Chuck and Jan Freudenberg at Euphoria Kennels, Cordova, TN. *Bottom:* We are grateful to Frank Fiorella for sharing with us the great Hol. Ch. Duuck van der Nedermolen. A fantastic dog, Duuck was an outstanding winner during 1982–84. Owned by G.A.J. Kuijpers, Hoogerland, Netherlands.

to be found there. Barto has done them proud as a Best in Show dog at such events as the Klubsieger where he defeated another Best in Show dog.

Barto had been judged prior to leaving for America by the noted authority Herr Hedke, at the Club Show in Belgium, where he spared no words of praise for this dog in enumerating his many superior qualities. Naturally it took some time and doing to persuade his former owners, Tom and Wil Emmers, to part with such a "once in a lifetime" sort of dog. Frank feels that his cause was helped through the efforts of the folks at Rodsden in the United States and

at Brabantpark in the Netherlands, to which he is grateful. We wish Barto many happy years in the States.

Barto is a true working Rottweiler, never seeming more content than when tracking, competing in obedience, and honing his protective skills. He is a significant figure in the Rottweiler World Competition breeding program.

Ever since starting to compile information for my Rottweiler books, I have been aware of the superiority of Netherlands-produced members of this breed. For example, who could possibly forget the contributions of the

Stromhall Nayah, owned by Clara Hurley and Michael S. Grossman, was bred at the Stromhall Kennels in Australia, and took Winners Bitch for new owners in the U.S. at the Medallion Specialty. Nayah is a daughter of the great Aust. Ch. Stromhall Torrey, U.D., T.D.

The 3-times Best in Show Ch. Alina's Abelbear of Wesley, winning his second such victory with best friend and handler Bob Hogan. "Genero" belongs to Dr. and Mrs. Leo Minisce.

splendid Rodsden import, Ch. Falco v. Brabantpark, who sired several dozen champions, or the Powderhorn/Wencrest importation, Dutch and Belgian Ch. Oscar v.d. Brabantpark, who was five years old when imported to this California kennel but who gained many show honors including that of becoming the Top Rottweiler in the country for the year 1979. He was also a Top Producer in the U.S., and a son of his, Powderhorn's Fetz of Wencrest, was the first Rottweiler to go from the United States to Australia, to Patricia Hall, where he is making notable contributions.

Obviously, Mrs. Hurley and Mr. Grossman were well satisfied with their Brabantpark dogs, as more imports from there have followed, including Dutch and Luxembourg

Ch. Quanto v.h. Brabantpark, full brother to Oscar from a later litter. At the time of his fifth year, Quanto started out in a big way for a brief six-month show career, which was abruptly ended by an accident, which made it impossible for him to be campaigned further. Nonetheless, although only shown for half the time period, Quanto made it to No. 3 Rottie for the entire year in the United States.

Ch. Donar v.d. Hoeve, C.D., joined the Powderhorn/Wencrest family, again with exciting results. Interestingly, the first three Specialty winners for the Hurley-Grossman kennels were Oscar, Quanto, and Donar, all three from the Netherlands. At this time it is Nelson who is carrying the Brabantpark banner high over the United States.

Top: **Ch. Radio Ranch's Riggons v. Bethel. Bred by Bob Bolden and owned by David A. Gallo, M.D. Photo courtesy of Barbara Hoard, Virginia Beach, VA.**
Bottom: **Mirko v. Sofienbusch, German import, owned by Powderhorn/ Wencrest Rottweilers, Inc.**

Ch. Crioula da Onca, bred by Meena R. Freitas, owned by Canil Baruki's, Brazil.

Rottweilers in Brazil

Some of the world's most devoted and enthusiastic dog fanciers are to be found throughout South America, and we are happy to tell you about some of the leading Rottweiler breeders in Brazil, where activity is especially keen. Our neighbors to the south have a really strong desire not only to import animals of highest quality but to breed their own as well. With this in mind, breeders from South America are visiting the United States and Europe with increasing frequency in order to learn first-hand where to find and purchase the best and to become personally acquainted with leading owners in order to assure them of the high ideals and their ambitions for success with their own dogs. These folks are never satisfied with second best, aiming only for superior dogs, and they are willing to invest considerable amounts of money, energy, and study in order to obtain the finest available stock from which to work. We have deep admiration for South American breeders and for the progress they have already made and are continuing to make in their respective breeds.

Working dogs are among the most popular in that part of the world; thus Rottweilers are high on the list of favorites. On the following pages we tell of some breeders, owners, and exhibitors who have made their presence strongly felt.

Bruckenheim Kennels are owned by Caio Brandao Pinto, Belo Horizante, Minas Gerais, Brazil. Caio has been a Rottweiler breeder since the early 1980s. His kennel is conspicuous for breeding and showing the largest number of prize-winning Rottweilers in Brazil, and his dogs have won 25 all-breed Bests in Show, plus numerous Reserve Bests in Show in addition to Working Group and Best of Breed placements.

Throughout his childhood, Caio longed for a dog; but, even though an only child who really needed the companionship of a pet, he was not permitted to have one. Thus as soon as he was grown up, and following the loss of both parents, he decided that the time had come to acquire that long-yearned-for dog.

It is a great compliment that Caio Brandao Pinto gained much of his early information about this breed from my first work on the breed, *The Book of the Rottweiler*.

With the encouragement of his future wife, with whom he was going at the time, and her enjoyment of talking by the hour about that impressive breed of dog with the solemn name "Rottweiler," he decided that he

"Our neighbors in the south have a really strong desire not only to import animals of highest quality but to breed their own as well."

22 meyer

Apollo vom Bruckenheim is holder of the titles: Junior Champion, Champion, and Grand Champion. He is one of Brazil's most outstanding Rottweilers.

was entitled to indulge himself in a hobby which, although extravagant, was one he had long anticipated.

Glower Duarte and Gwen Larsen, from Curitiba and Itapecerica da Serre (State of Sao Paulo), respectively, were two friends and Rottweiler breeders with whom he had been in touch. He had recently visited them and discovered that they had puppies available; Caio felt that their breeding met the requirements indicated in the book.

He put aside all former doubts and phoned to make the reservations, and a few days later, he was active again in the business of porridges and vitamins, an occupation which had previously concerned him only during the early years of his first marriage

when he was involved with the care of three lively babies, Daniel, Melissa, and Janaina.

Caio took particular pride in Konig do Atuba, whom he called "Nero." This was a beautiful youngster, a son of Devilles Know, imported from the United States, whose parents were Trollegen's Fable and Ron Dar's Stephanie. Nero's dam was Inge vom Schwaiger Wappen; imported from West Germany, she was the daughter of Condor Zur Klamm and Aki vom der Hembachbrucke.

Elly av. Valhall, nicknamed "Xuxa," was a 90-day-old puppy, when acquired, who especially excelled in face and chest, with a handsome head and other conspicuously superior qualities. She became the Brazilian

Rottweiler Champion in 1985. Xuxa was born to a Swiss female dog, Pamele, whose parents were Gass and Beauty-Belina, the sire a Brazilian Rottweiler named Bacchus vom Lukmanier who was the son of Thor von Circle and Aretha v. Hessel's Haus Am Berg.

Mr. Pinto says of these two, "Nero and Xuxa were two surprising dogs. Xuxa paved the way for the success of the Rottweiler in Brazil, as it had not yet become a winning breed in that country when she made her appearance." She was the Best Brazilian Rottweiler and one of the Best Ten in her Group in 1985.

In 1986, Nero was the Best

National Rottweiler, and the seventh among all-breeds. After being Young Champion, Champion, Grand Champion, International Beauty Champion, and Grand National winner, he was ranked Show Reserve in the Inca Dog Show held in Lima, Peru, in 1988, one of the venues of the World Show.

Nero and Xuxa also caused a lot of new breeders to appear in Brazil who now have important positions in the Rottweiler fancy and who made their start under the influence of this famous pair!

Among many important and noteworthy kennels in Brazil is Berg-Phanter, whose owner was

Braz. Ch. Baruki's Cigano, by Gr. Ch. Jumkes do Atuba ex Braz. Ch. L'Tula do Laio, pictured winning *Mehor da Raca* (Best of Breed) under Jayme Martinello, handled by Marcelo Chagas for Canil Baruki's. Photo by Luiz Arriuda.

Konig do Atuba is a well-known winner in Brazil, answering to his friends as "Nero."

assisted in making his first acquisition by Mr. Pinto. Later on, in a bold move for the time, Berg-Phanter joined forces with Bruckenheim in order to send Xuxa to Germany, where she was bred to Osco vom Schwaiger Wappen, producing ten puppies.

Xuxa's offspring were very beautiful, mostly with prominent frame and stature. However, while in Germany, Mr. Pinto had the opportunity to see Rottweilers "with massive snouts such as I have never seen in Brazil, not even in Xuxa's offspring, which were above average." Thus the decision was made to import a Rottweiler capable of producing dogs with such snouts and other desirable features. We assume that these "massive snouts" refer to the strength of foreface.

Not long afterward, Raudi vom Zimmerplatz—a Rottweiler who was destined to leave his prints on many Brazilian pedigrees—arrived there at age eight weeks. Raudi was the Best National Rottweiler in 1988, the first in the Working Group, and third among all-breed. He is a well-known stud dog, and many of his offspring have been Best in Show in various parts of the country. Raudi belongs to the Leistungszucht group, and his parents are Duuck van de Nedermolen (Netherlands) and Simmy vom Schwaiger Wappen (West Germany), whose owner is Ingeborg Kugel-Staiger, from Calv-Stammheim, West Germany.

Xuxa has produced such successful dogs as Negra vom Bruckenheim, belonging to Heloise Marchesi from Ribeirao Preto, and two other dogs, both Grand Champions belonging to Mr. Pinto

Braz. Ch. Crioula da Onca, by Gr. Ch. Bacchus v. Lukmanier ex Gr. Ch. Asturias da Sete Ramchos, is a splended example of the quality Rottweiler to be found at Canil Baruki's (Baruki's Kennel).

and Linda Witkoff, respectively, and Astor, who has been Best in general (all-breed) show.

It was in Rome during the autumn of 1988 when Mr. Pinto's car was moving fast towards the German embassy in the Vatican. He was on his way to lunch, at one o'clock, with the Ambassador Alfonso Arinos, who had asked that he not be late. He was thinking about things that had happened the evening before when suddenly his thoughts were interrupted by a most "breathtaking sight, the most beautiful Rottweiler I had ever seen accompanied by a glorious blue-eyed young lady who were just passing by." The driver unfortunately did not understand the cries to stop the car, and so the dog and the young lady

Raudi vom Zimmerplatz, by Duuck van der Nedermolen ex Simmy vom Schwaiger Wappen, came to Bruckenheim Kennels, Caio Brandoa Pinto, M.G., Brazil, at age 8 weeks; he is to be found in many Brazilian pedigrees. Best National Rottweiler in 1988; first in Working Group; No. 3 all-breeds.

disappeared into the traffic; but it was an experience which will never be forgotten as the impression of the most outstanding Rottweiler he ever had seen is printed so clearly on Mr. Pinto's mind.

Eventually Mr. Pinto became more concerned about aspects other than the ugly and the beautiful. He needed to know more about the complex genetics of the Rottweiler, such as temperament; structural and motor problems; thigh and femur malformation; white spots; lack or excess of teeth; and all other disorders affecting this wonderful breed.

The Pinto kennel had grown and new dogs were imported from Germany and the Netherlands, not always with good results. Mr. Pinto

had all his dogs x-rayed and found a slight side malformation (dysplasia) in Nero and Astor, as well as in Xuxa, whose problem was in both sides, thus requiring more attention. Xuxa was bred only twice, the first time with no knowledge of her problem; and only because of her distinctive breed features was she mated a second time. One offspring from that second litter survived, the others having been victims of the corona virus, the vaccination for which was not yet available in Brazil.

To Brazilian breeders, Caio Pinto tells us, "dysplasia is tantamount to leprosy." The "uninformed dealers" are at the root of this misconception. Since it is not recessive but a quantitative process, it is not enough that the sire and dam are healthy. It is necessary to follow up several past and future generations in order to minimize this problem.

Joys and disappointments apart, Mr. Pinto decided to retire from competition. Now he is exclusively devoted to the work of breeding. Meanwhile he has adopted two Siberian tigers which have cost him three lawsuits and two weeks in the newscasts. One of his neighbors photographed the tigers moving freely in the Pinto backyard and went to court demanding their detention ... and just when his dogs were becoming accustomed to the tigers.

Baruki's Kennel of Rottweilers in Rio de Janeiro started its activities in 1982 with the union of two breeders, Mr. Marcelo Paes de Mello and Mar Juarez Magno.

The following year their stud dog, Ch. Bacchus von Luckmanier, came to be the winner of the breed in the National Rankings, producing outstanding quality in his offspring. Among other famous winners, his progeny includes the female who led the breed in the 1985 National Ranking, Ch. Elly v. Valhal. The owners of Baruki's are the breeders of numerous champions and are certainly succeeding in their goal of bettering the breed in Brazil.

Miriam Shikata Yasuhara owns the Dai-Goro Kennels in São Paulo. Having loved dogs ever since earliest childhood, and having enjoyed the companionship of many ranging from pure-breds to strays of mixed heritage, all dearly loved and enjoyed, it is hardly very surprising that when she saw a Rottweiler for the first time it was love at first sight.

Her passion for Rottweilers began around the close of the 1970s, when Miriam and her husband, Carlos, were looking through a dog magazine together. It was there that they saw a handsome Rottweiler pictured and decided that they would like to have one.

After many difficulties (in those

days it was not easy to find Rottweilers of quality whose owners were willing to sell them), they did succeed in obtaining a foundation bitch, with whose first litter the Dai-Goro Kennels began.

First, some importations were brought from Germany for the Yasuharas, these led by S.A. Ch. Nora v. Liebersbacherhof. She became the first Rottweiler bitch to win an all-breed Best in Show in Brazil. Following Nora came Arras von der Hamalnd Route, who is a European *Sieger*, A.D.R.K.

Braz. Ch. Nordic da America do Sol, "Zillo," who is a popular representative of the breed in Brazil.

Klubsieger, and Westdeutscher *Sieger*, and who is living up well to the hopes of becoming a marvelous producer. Just recently one more addition to the "family" arrived at the Dai-Goro household, Pia v. Schilfeck, Ubt, VFH, Ch., SchH. III, who will soon begin her Brazilian show career. On her first appearance, she went Best of Breed over specials. Finally, there is a young home-bred dog just starting out in competition, Dai-Goro's Debor, who is the pride and joy of his owners.

Also in São Paulo, Bill and Linda Witkoff have the Lymington Kennel, which they opened in 1982 with the purchase of a foundation bitch, Anitra. She produced many outstanding puppies and her owners found that they really loved the breeding and raising of Rottweiler litters, or at least the

ones produced by Anitra. Since then they have found that breeding Rottweilers is not quite so easy as Anitra made it seem, that one must know a great deal about the breed and that it requires much hard work. The Witkoffs have now raised 16 litters, this hobby being of tremendous interest to them. They are most careful in rearing and socializing the puppies as well as working with them in obedience. Three of their young dogs are well advanced in their obedience training.

Lymington Kennels have achieved some good success in the show ring. Most enjoyable of all for the Witkoffs is watching the dogs they have bred succeed in both obedience and conformation. Basically they feel strongly that character, temperament and soundness are the primary assets

Etza of Herburger's, by Herburger's Count Rivelino ex Anik of Herburger's, is owned by Bruno and Rosangela Tausz.

Above: Arras vom der Hamaland-Route. By Iwan v. Fusse der Eifel ex Rona v. Stein Koff. Owned by Dai Goro's Kennel, Brazil.
Below: Pia vom Schilfeck, owned by Dai Goro's Kennel, San Paulo, Brazil. By Cliff vom Waldhuck ex Nadja vom Schilfeck.

Elfi von der Argarten, by Hassan vom Konigsgarten ex Angelina von der Argarten. Owned by Bruno and Roseangela Tausz.

of a working breed such as the Rottweiler, thus they are happy that their dogs possess these qualities.

There is a lake at Lymington where, as Mrs. Witkoff puts it, "all the dogs swim like fish." Their wonderful guard dog and companion, Yves, who is badly dysplastic, remains fit and well at the age of five years with his constant swimming. Because of Yves, the Witkoffs believe that they were the first Rottweiler breeders in their area to initiate testing for hip dysplasia, and also because of this dog whom they dearly love, they are well aware of the seriousness of the problem.

The Lymington Kennel owners have been members of the Golden State Rottweiler Club and, both being Californians, they appreciate

their contacts there and the helpfulness of their fellow breeders who worked with them for the formation of the Rottweiler Club of São Paulo.

Another outstanding breeder from São Paulo is Monica Soares Armond, who in 1985 was the happy owner and exhibitor of a beautiful Miniature Schnauzer. Attending one of the all-breed shows, she was introduced to a breed she never before had seen— a Rottweiler, whose lovely attitude and firm character enchanted her. She decided then that this would come to be her breed and that she would become involved with these dogs.

Monica found and bought an outstanding bitch from the Baruki's Kennel, Ch. Ebony da Onca, followed by Ch. Baruki's Cywa.

By this time the friendship was well established between her and the Baruki's owners, who were very helpful at the beginning towards getting her kennel off to a splendid start. One year later, Ebony's brother, Magnum da Onca, arrived and became the guardian angel of the house.

In 1985, Monica had her baby daughter, and she was presented by Baruki's Kennel with a marvelous female, Baruki's Dahana, who had proven a superb brood bitch.

Loving the breed as they do, the Armonds are fighting for the good conscience of new breeders where hip dysplasia and other genetic defects are concerned. Along with Miriam Yasuhara, Monica is tremendously helpful with Rottweiler activities in São Paulo.

In Rio de Janiero, there are the Tarbendorf Kennels of Mr. Bruno Tausz, who owns the Farbendorf Kennels with his wife Rosangela. Rio is often referred to as "Brazil's visiting card," where there are so many beautiful places that it is almost impossible to count. In this lovely setting, one finds the Farbendorf Kennels living up to their surroundings as one of Brazil's best-equipped breeding, boarding, and obedience training operations.

It is a pleasure, we are told, to hear Bruno talk about his passion, the Rottweiler, which goes so far that he wrote an interesting and informative book on the breed which is now in its third edition. His interest in dogs began in 1945, when he was presented with "Billy," a German Shepherd, who was his entry into the world of dog ownership. Later came Budo von Rheiland, and since then the dogs have grown to be a part of the family life.

No longer a part-time hobby, the kennel is now a pleasant full-time occupation for both Mr. and Mrs. Tausz. The switch to Rottweilers from Shepherds was made circa 1978-79.

Numerous German imports from leading German bloodlines were made by Mr. Tausz, giving him the breeding program, which is paying off large dividends of success in the show rings. Since 1984, Mr. Tausz has been licensed to judge Working breeds and Group.

Interestingly, Mr. Tausz holds an honorary membership in the military police for important contributions to the corporation. Many are the classes he has given and continues to give for judging applicants as well as dog fanciers. He insists on, and calls to the attention of new fanciers, serious study of temperament and the necessity for hip dysplasia examinations for all members of the breed. His work and general interest in careful selective breeding reflect the concern of this "Italian-born Brazilian" who, himself and with his family, dedicates time and thought to their dearly loved occupation, the raising and training of superb Rottweilers.

Braz. Ch. Ebony da Onca, by Gr. Ch. Bacchus v. Lukmamier ex Asturias do Sete Ramchos. Bred by Canil Baruki's; owned by Tasmom's Kennel, Brazil.

Purchasing Your Rottweiler

The purchase of any dog is a matter deserving of considerable thought and study prior to actually taking the step. This is especially true of the Rottweiler, which is a very special breed with strong and definite characteristics of temperament and behavior, making these dogs not suitable for everyone. We are sure that our readers are aware of this and have given it due consideration. We assume that you are among those who have weighed all the pros and cons, and that you still remain strong in feeling a Rottweiler is the breed for you, a decision made following thoughtful deliberation and despite whatever problems you may also be assuming.

A first step towards a happy association in the world of Rottweiler owners is a good association with the person who has sold you your dog. The importance of this cannot be overemphasized; thus, to the study of dogs, must be added the study of the various people offering puppies for sale.

As with any astronomical rise in popularity, such as Rottweilers have "enjoyed" during the recent past, problems become part of the picture. Unscrupulous people jump on the band wagon with the thought of making money on the popularity of and demand for the dogs—a very unhealthy situation from the buyer's point of view as such people can be amazingly without conscience in their dealings.

One of the most respected ladies in the Rottweiler world, Ms. Felicia E.H. Luberich of Srigo Kennels at East Brunswick, New Jersey, comments on buying a Rottweiler in the world today, being fearful of the harm already done the breed and that which may still follow unless unscrupulous, "purely for the money" type breeding and those who conduct this activity become extinct. Warns Ms. Luberich: "In starting out with an ownership of a dog, the purchaser of a 'new' breed is wise to 'make haste slowly'. I know that it is difficult for the novice, which all of us were at one time, to get started correctly. But future success depends largely on one's doing so, thus the novice should be extremely wary. It is not easy, in the beginning, to sort out *opinion* from *fact*. Many people are quite free to express their opinion; but be sure of the background and quality from which that person speaks before classifying the information passed along by him as being factual. Everyone is willing to expound on the breed; but not

Opposite: These two young members of the "B" litter at J. Jacqueline Stephenson's Rotterre Kennel in Shelburne, Ont., are splendid examples of the type and quality for which this kennel has become famous.

These adorable Rottie pups are by Urban Eulenspiegel, SchH. I, ex Ch. Ridgerunner's Rowdy Rover, U.D. Bred by Richelle Uyeda and Claire Inouye, Richmark Rottweilers, Honolulu, HI.

everyone is qualified by actual *knowledge* to do so. Prepare and defend yourself from such people by studying, reading, learning and observing everything you can about the Rottweiler, in order that you will be able to make by yourself a qualified judgement of all these 'opinions' which will be fed to you as fact.

"Be wary also of what you read in advertisements. Remember that these ads are simply for the purpose of promoting the dog or dogs owned by the people paying for them, and that the statements made sometimes are widely exaggerated. Bear this in mind, for while many advertisers are extremely scrupulous and exact in their claims, some do tend to get carried away with glowing accounts of their dogs' successes which are misleading. Be on the watch!

"Bear in mind, too, that the people from whom it is most

difficult to make a purchase are frequently the ones from whom you will get the best quality.

"Over-eagerness to make a sale should cause one to wonder if the seller is interested in the right dog for the right person, as should be the case; or just anxious to push the dog out the door, whether it is likely to bring satisfaction or not. So watch out for high pressure salesmanship. With the demand as great as it has been these past few years for Rottweilers, the breeders whose customers are happy and satisfied with their purchases usually have a waiting list and are not scrambling for buyers."

Felicia also cautions about imports: "Regarding imports, some of what is offered for sale from Europe that appears to be a great 'bargain' is something with problems which may not be immediately evident to the purchaser. These can include bitches who upon arrival turn out

to be sterile or semi-sterile, who kill their puppies, and who have insufficient or bad milk. Some bitches who are supposedly in whelp turn out not to be, despite all the claims that they were bred. And some have had an injury that is in remission but which shows up after awhile. In males, they can arrive sterile, be an intermittent breeder or a non-breeder, or can be a dog who produces puppies with a high rate of birth defects. In addition to these various risks, prices are astonishingly high owing to the great demand from people with more money than knowledge. These usually from America or the Orient."

Felicia then makes the following very important statement: "Remember that when purchasing your Rottweiler you are not buying just the dog; but the dog should include the interest and helpfulness for the well-being of the seller. So as you contemplate a purchase, bear this thought in mind: The advice and help which can set you on the right track in making difficult decisions entirely on your own are priceless in value. A good friend is always valuable, but when the care, health and future of your dog is concerned, then it becomes invaluable.

"When you find a breeder whose dogs you like and admire, and whose general attitude develops a feeling of warmth and confidence, that is the place to purchase a puppy—not from someone who probably could not care less about that puppy's future or the pleasure it does or does not bring to a new owner. So do not be misled by high pressure, but look for the true concern of the seller for the *dog*. Do not allow yourself to be hustled into a deal by any of the well-known pressure selling tactics. A reluctance to sell is probably going to lead to higher satisfaction on the part of the new owner than the puppy someone is rushed into buying by a lot of extravagant 'time is running out' salesmanship."

You will find in this book the names of a large number of

respected kennels and breeders in various areas. Other sources of information are the American Kennel Club, 51 Madison Avenue, New York, N.Y., 10010, and the Kennel Club of Great Britain, 1 Clarges Street, Piccadilly, London, W1Y 8AB, which can give you names and addresses in your home area and the secretary of the local Specialty Club. The latter method is especially recommended, as people who have had unfortunate incidents in purchasing from a kennel seem very apt to tell the circumstances of what took place to the Parent Specialty Club or one serving the area in which that person lives.

Your first step in searching for your puppy is to make appointments at kennels specializing in your breed, where you can visit and inspect the dogs,

Spoiled and loved at Powsell's Rottweilers, this is Powsell's Laughter of Sara at age 4 months. She is a daughter of Powsell's Risen Son ex Anja von Esta Klasse. Deborah Moneque, owner.

Tri-Lee's Dark Shadow is another promising Ara-Champagne puppy at the kennels of Don and Norma White in Solon, IA.

both those available for sale and the kennel's basic breeding stock. You are looking for an active, sturdy puppy with bright eyes and intelligent expression and who is friendly and alert; avoid puppies who are hyperactive, dull, or listless. The coat should be clean and thick, with no sign of parasites. The premises on which he was raised should look (and smell) clean and be tidy, making it obvious that the puppies and their surroundings are in capable hands. Should the kennels featuring the breed you intend to own be sparse in your area or not have what you consider attractive, do not hesitate to contact others at a distance and purchase from them if they seem better able to supply a puppy or dog who will please you—*so long as it is a recognized breeding kennel of that breed.* Shipping dogs is a regular practice nowadays, with comparatively few problems when one considers the number of dogs shipped each year. A reputable,

well-known breeder wants the customer to be satisfied; thus, he will represent the puppy fairly. Should you not be pleased with the puppy upon arrival, a breeder, such as described, will almost certainly permit its return. A conscientious breeder takes real interest and concern in the welfare of the dogs he or she causes to be brought into the world. Such a breeder also is proud of a reputation for integrity. Thus on two counts, for the sake of the dog's future and the breeder's reputation, to such a person a *satisfied* customer takes precedence over a sale at any cost.

If your puppy is to be a pet or "family dog," the earlier the age at which it joins your household the better. Puppies are weaned and ready to start out on their own, under the care of a sensible new owner, at about six weeks old; and if you take a young one, it is often easier to train it to the routine of your household and to your requirements of it than is the case with an older dog which, even though still technically a puppy, may have already started habits you will find difficult to change. The younger puppy is usually less costly, too, as it stands to reason the breeder will not have as much expense invested in it. Obviously, a puppy that has been raised to five- or six–months old represents more in care and cash expenditure on the breeder's part than one sold earlier; therefore he should be, and generally is, priced accordingly.

Top: Puppies from Hawaii at age 4 weeks. They are by Ch. Rivy's Samso De Dedeaux ex Rivy's Delilah De Dedeaux. Owned by Lia Mesquit, Waimanalo, HI. *Middle left:* How a future big winner looks at 10 weeks. Ch. RC's Magnum Force von Ursa, T.T., with owner, Roy Chriscoe, grew up to be No. 1 A.R.C. Bitch for 1982 and a Producer of Champions. *Middle right:* Ch. Powderhorn's Clu of Wencrest owned by Anie Grimaldi and Powderhorn/ Wencrest Rottweilers, Inc. *Bottom:* Innocenti's famous Select Am., Can. Ch. Goldeiche Ara von Brader, C.D., at 8 weeks of age.

There is an enormous amount of truth in the statement that "bargain" puppies seldom turn out to be that. A "cheap" puppy, raised purely for sale and profit, can and often does lead to great heartbreak, including problems and veterinarian's bills which can add up to many times the initial cost of a properly reared dog. On the other hand, just because a puppy is expensive does not assure one that is healthy and well reared. There have been numerous cases where unscrupulous dealers have

331

sold, for several hundred dollars, puppies that were sickly, in poor condition, and such poor specimens that the breed of which they were supposedly members was barely recognizable. So one cannot always judge a puppy by price alone. Common sense must guide a prospective purchaser, plus the selection of a *reliable*, well-recommended dealer whom you know to have well-satisfied customers or, best of all, a specialized breeder. You will probably find the fairest pricing at the kennel of a breeder. Such a

person, experienced with the breed in general and with his or her own stock in particular, through extensive association with these dogs, has watched enough of them mature to have obviously learned to assess quite accurately each puppy's potential—something impossible where such background is non-existent.

One more word on the subject of pets. Bitches make a fine choice for this purpose as they are usually quieter and more gentle than the males, easier to house train, more affectionate, and less inclined to

roam. If you do select a bitch and have no intention of breeding or showing her, by all means have her spayed, for your sake and for hers. The advantages to the owner of a spayed bitch include avoiding the nuisance of "in season" periods which normally occur twice older because this simple operation almost entirely eliminates the possibility of breast cancer ever occurring. It is recommended that all bitches eventually be spayed—even those used for show or breeding when their careers have ended—in order

A Liebenswert Rottie pup with "Baby," an orphaned fawn who helped to raise two Rottie litters at Pat Storer's kennel.

yearly—with the accompanying eager canine swains haunting your premises in an effort to get close to your female—plus the unavoidable messiness and spotting of furniture and rugs at this time, which can be annoying if she is a household companion in the habit of sharing your sofa or bed. As for the spayed bitch, she benefits as she grows that they may enjoy a happier, healthier old age. Please take note, however, that a bitch who has been spayed (or an altered dog) *cannot be shown at American Kennel Club dog shows once this operation has been performed.* Be certain that you are *not* interested in showing her before taking this step.

If you are thinking in terms of a

dog to show, obviously you must have learned about dog shows and must be in the habit of attending them. Much can be learned about a breed at ringside at these events. Talk with the breeders who are exhibiting. Study the dogs they are showing.

If you are located in an area where dog shows take place only occasionally or where there are long travel distances involved, you will need to find another testing ground for your ability to select a worthy show dog. Possibly, there are some representative kennels raising this breed within a reasonable distance. If so, by all means ask permission of the owners to visit the kennels and do so when permission is granted. You may not necessarily buy then and there, as they may not have available what you are seeking that very day, but you will be able to see the type of dog being raised

there and to discuss the dogs with the breeder and perhaps reserve one from a future litter. This is frequently done, and it is often worth waiting for a puppy, unless you have seen a dog with which you truly are greatly impressed and which is immediately available.

The only place from which to purchase a show prospect is a breeder who raises show-type stock; otherwise, you are almost certainly doomed to disappointment as the puppy matures. Show and breeding kennels obviously cannot keep all of their fine young stock. An active breeder-exhibitor is, therefore, happy to place promising youngsters in the hands of people also interested in showing and winning with them, doing so at a fair price according to the quality and prospects of the dog involved. Here again, if no kennel in your immediate area has what you are seeking, do not hesitate to contact top breeders in other areas and to buy at long distance. Ask for pictures, pedigrees, and a complete description. Heed the breeder's advice and recommendations, after truthfully telling exactly what your expectations are for the dog you purchase. Do you want something with which to win just a few ribbons now and then? Do you want a dog who can complete his championship? Are you thinking of the real "big time" (*i.e.*, seriously campaigning with Best of Breed, Group wins, and possibly even Best in Show as your eventual goal)? Consider it all carefully in advance; then honestly discuss your plans with the breeder. You will be better satisfied with the results if you do this, as the breeder is then in the best position to help you choose the dog who is most likely to come through for you. A breeder selling a show dog is just as anxious as the buyer for the dog to succeed, and the breeder will represent the dog to you with truth and honesty. Also, this type of breeder does not lose interest the moment the sale has been made but, when necessary, will be right there to assist you with beneficial advice and suggestions based on years of experience.

As you make inquiries of at least several kennels, keep in mind that show-prospect puppies are less expensive than mature show dogs, the latter often costing close to four figures, and sometimes more. The reason for this is that, with a puppy, there is always an element of chance, the possibility of its developing unexpected faults as it matures or failing to develop the excellence and quality that earlier had seemed probable. There definitely is a risk factor in buying a show-prospect puppy. Sometimes all goes well, but occasionally the swan becomes an ugly duckling. Reflect on this as you consider available puppies and young adults. It just might be a good idea to go with a more mature, though

more costly, dog if one you like is available.

When you buy a mature show dog, "what you see is what you get," and it is not likely to change beyond coat and condition, which are dependent on your care. Also advantageous for a novice owner is the fact that a mature dog of show quality almost certainly will have received show-ring training and probably match-show experience, which will make your earliest handling ventures much easier.

Well-known British Rottweiler breeder Violet Slade with puppies at her Potterspride Kennels, Saffronwalden, Essex.

Frequently it is possible to purchase a beautiful dog who has completed championship but who, owing to similarity in bloodlines, is not needed for the breeder's future program. Here you have the opportunity of owning a champion, usually in the two-to-five-year-old range, which you can enjoy campaigning as a special (for Best of Breed competition) and which will be a settled, handsome dog for you and your family to enjoy with pride.

If you are planning foundation for a future kennel, concentrate on acquiring one or two really superior bitches. These need not be top show-quality, but they

should represent the Rottweiler's finest producing bloodlines from a strain noted for quality, generation after generation. A proven matron who is already the dam of show-type puppies is, of course, the ideal selection; but these are usually difficult to obtain, no one being anxious to part with so valuable an asset. You just might strike it lucky, though, in which case you are off to a flying start. If you cannot find such a matron available, select a young bitch of finest background from top-producing lines who is herself of decent type, free of obvious faults, and of good quality.

Great attention should be paid to the pedigree of the bitch from whom you intend to breed. If not already known to you, try to see the sire and dam. It is generally agreed that someone starting with a breed should concentrate on a fine collection of topflight bitches and raise a few litters from these before considering keeping one's own stud dog. The practice of buying a stud and then breeding everything you own or acquire to that dog does not always work out well. It is better to take advantage of the many noted sires who are available to be used at stud, who represent all of the leading strains, and, in each case, to carefully

Could anyone possibly resist that face? Ch. Misty Lakes Afternoon D'Light owned by Dr. Eric and Amelia Jimeniz.

select the one who in type and pedigree seems most compatible to each of your bitches, at least for your first several litters.

To summarize, if you want a "family dog" as a companion, it is best to buy it young and raise it according to the habits of your household. If you are buying a show dog, the more mature it is, the more certain you can be of its future beauty. If you are buying foundation stock for a kennel, then bitches are better, but they must be from the finest *producing* bloodlines.

When you buy a pure-bred dog that you are told is eligible for registration with the American Kennel Club, you are entitled to receive from the seller an application form which will enable you to register your dog. If the seller cannot give you the application form, you should demand and receive an identification of your dog, consisting of the name of the breed, the registered names and numbers of the sire and dam, the name of the breeder, and your dog's date of birth. If the litter of which your dog is a part is already recorded with the American Kennel Club, then the litter number is sufficient identification.

Do not be misled by promises of papers at some later date. Demand a registration application form or proper identification as described above. If neither is supplied, do not buy the dog. So warns the American Kennel Club, and this is especially important in the purchase of show or breeding stock.

Left top: Am., Can. Ch. Noblehaus Explorer, T.T., Top-Winning Rottweiler of 1988, defeating more dogs in one year than any in the history of the breed to the time. Owners, Patricia and Mark Schwartz, West Nyack, NY.

Left middle: Am., Can. Ch. Rodsden's Lindenwood Hero, owned by Jim and Roxanna McGovern, Port Crane, NY.

Left bottom: Relaxing at home after a big weekend is the High Scoring Champion of Record at the 1988 A.R.C. Specialty, Highest Scoring and new C.D. at the Oakland Dog Training Club Trial and A.R.C. Select, Select Ch. Eischenwals's Basil v. Axel. Owners, tired and proud, are Pat Deridivania and Robert Baston, Oakland, CA.

Below: Concord's Tandem of Lakeview at 10 months. By Ch. Kev-Mar Tuff Stuff v. Wilhaus ex Concor's Isis. Owner, T.J. Oldham.

Owning a Rottweiler

The purchase of a dog never should be taken lightly, nor entered into in an offhand thoughtless manner. It should be thought out carefully, with due consideration given to whether or not you *really* will enjoy dog ownership, your schedule and way of life, by whom and how the dog will be maintained, and all the positive and negative points which cover your life as a dog owner. These should be weighed ahead of time, not after the purchase has been made. Were this policy followed, there would be far fewer abandoned dogs and dogs looking for new homes, overcrowding the animal shelters, as is the case today.

When it is a Rottweiler whose purchase you are contemplating, this advance soul-searching becomes of still greater necessity, for in assuming responsibility for a Rottweiler you are undergoing entry into the ranks of people who do not take dog ownership lightly and who are prepared to spend time with and on the new canine member of the family.

Rottweilers are truly special dogs. They are not suitable for a casual relationship with their owners. Rather they are demanding both of your time and company and of the sharing of your home and lifestyle.

If you are right for the breed and it for you, then the relationship between you and your Rottweiler will be highly rewarding. But if you do not want or expect to enjoy the company of your dog on a daily basis, then you will be happier with a less demanding breed that prospers equally well with or without companionship from its humans.

Sharing the life of the human (or humans) he loves is truly a "must" for a well-adjusted and happy Rottweiler. The breed is not one which blithely loves the world, or to which any human is as good as his owner. Being among the most loyal and devoted of breeds, the Rottweiler develops very strong attachments. Being with you is a greater need for such a dog than it is for one whose attitude toward even its own humans is more casual than the Rottweiler's attitude toward all humans. The tremendous devotion and loyalty of Rottweilers to their owners make them incomparable as natural protectors. But at the same time they create a deep need for your attention. This is often expressed in their constant seeking of your company, their reluctance to leave your side, and their habitual following you from place to place even at home—dogging your

"Sharing the life of the human (or humans) he loves is truly a 'must' for a well-adjusted and happy Rottweiler. The breed is not one which blithely loves the world, or to which any human is as good as his owner."

339

1988 Klubsiegerin and Best in Show Cita von der Nonnenhohle from the 18th Annual A.D.R.K. Klubsieger Show at Rottweil, Germany. Photo courtesy of Frank Fiorella.

proving the enjoyment brought by association with this canine friend.

The most important word to be used in connection with the rearing of your Rottweiler is "socialization." Right from earliest puppyhood, while still in the nest, each puppy should be picked up, petted and talked to frequently, becoming accustomed to being handled. As soon as the puppies are getting on their feet, they should be played with, loved and cuddled by family and friends. As maturity progresses, the more time you and the puppies spend together, or the entire family spends with them, the better for future personality and temperament. The basic need of a well-adjusted adult Rottweiler is to have been taught to love humans and to enjoy their company right from the time they become aware of the world around them.

It is cruel to keep a Rottweiler shut off by himself or confined exclusively to kennel life. If you acquire a Rottweiler, please keep this fact in mind. Always remember that sharing family life is the ideal situation for a Rottweiler, and even if you come to own a large kennel of them, a routine should be arranged in which each dog gets to spend a fair amount of time with you in the house—if possible, all of it! The more time that a Rottweiler spends with the family he loves, the better adjusted and more thoroughly satisfactory a companion he will become. To repeat an earlier statement—if you want a dog who will require the least minimum of your time, do not choose a Rottweiler lest you find yourself with a poorly adjusted and unhappy dog.

As you are deciding about the Rottweiler's suitability for your particular way of life, do keep in mind that this is a big, strong, muscular dog—truly a powerhouse for its size. Without question, so strong and muscular a dog could quite easily, unintentionally (just in playing) throw a less-than-robust person to the ground. Bear this in

footsteps, so to speak, rather than going off on their own pursuits. Mutual companionship between a Rottie and its person is life-blood to the dog. Without it he will not be at his best, nor will he develop his natural instinct toward that true Rottweiler character which makes the breed so very special to those who understand the demands.

The temperament of Rottweilers varies, ranging from the reserved "one-man dog" to the quite outgoing one. They are affectionate with friends and family, wary (but not unfriendly) until their approval has been earned, and seem to possess an almost inborn sense of humor. They are considered by those who know them to be "fun animals," a fact which the majority of Rottweiler owners can attest to with a long series of stories,

mind if your family includes someone infirm or along in years in order to guard against an unfortunate accident. In addition, be wary with small children unless they and the Rottweiler are accustomed to one another from baby/puppyhood, as the dog needs to be aware that rough play with an infant or toddler is not in order.

Obviously, no dog of this size and power can go untrained in, at the very least, simple obedience. This should be started by you at home before the puppy is past a few months of age; and make certain that "come," "stay," "sit," "heel," and just plain "No" become familiar words which are understood by the young dog. Join a training class with the puppy as soon as his age makes him acceptable. Follow the advice of the person from whom the puppy was purchased to locate a good trainer. Remember that rough,

cruel, or heavy-handed training should be avoided. It is not difficult to control dogs as intelligent as Rottweilers through verbal reprimands when needed and lots of praise when your instruction is obeyed. While upon some very rare occasions there may be a need for physical correction, it should be handled with kindness, not in bad temper. In other words, the dog should obey your commands not out of fear but from the desire to earn your pleasure and praise. Patience, time, and realization of the dog's intelligent anxiousness to please should bring about the desired result.

It is true of Rottweilers, as with other breeds, that some are suitable and trustworthy with small children (and vice-versa) while others are not. Due to the Rottweiler's power and strength, it becomes absolutely imperative

Powsell's Laughter of Sara at 4 months. Owner, Deborah Moneque.

that you impress upon your children and your Rottweiler that you expect a strong sense of love and respect for one another. Rottweilers in their intelligent wisdom seem to realize that babies and toddlers must be treated gently, a fact which your own attitude should make clear. Children, on their part, should love and respect their dog, treating it not as an object for abuse and torment but as a friend. There should always be mutual dependence between dog and child. No child should ever be permitted to mistreat any dog. But when the dog is one so big and so strong, it is especially important for the child's sake as well as the dog's that the dog be gently, never hurtfully, enjoyed. This also applies to your children and their friends.

Do not misunderstand me, please. I am not saying that a Rottweiler is anything other than a wonderful pet for your child. But knowing the irresponsibility of far too many parents where animals and children are concerned, I am simply pointing out that these dogs deserve the affection and devotion which they give to your children returned to them in equal amounts

OWNING A ROTTWEILER

from these children. Even the most patient of dogs sometimes can be tried beyond endurance by a child who has not been brought up with this belief; in which case, when the dog is big and strong and powerful, a tormenting child could possibly (although not very likely) bite off more than he can handle.

No youngster could have a more faithful and loving guardian than a Rottweiler, as this dog is formidable in appearance, inherently a guardian of its people, and in case of a dangerous situation ready without hesitation to protect its young friend even if the cost is its own life.

If yours is a family that enjoys an assortment of pets, there should not be any problem with a Rottie already "in residence" as long as the introductions are handled tactfully and the established household member is not made to feel jealous or neglected. The arrival of a newcomer on the scene should be made pleasant for the whole family, with lots of petting and admiration showered on the *senior* member of the household, making it very clear that this new arrival is in no way a replacement for the established pet. It is always easier to bring in a puppy or kitten than it is to bring in a mature dog or cat who may have some thoughts and attitudes of his own about

sharing with other pets. In addition, a member of the opposite sex is less apt to be resented than a dog of the same sex. Like most of life's little problems, this one, too, can almost certainly be handled and the adjustment smoothly made. Remember that a lot will depend on your not making the older animal feel that the newcomer is taking precedence in your affections.

It hardly seems necessary to caution that the newcomer to the household not be left alone with the older dog until you have made absolutely certain that no problems are likely to arise. When you add to your animal family, be alert and on the spot for the first couple of days to be sure that all is going well.

Left: Foxy's Deep Desire at age 4 months. By Am., Can. Ch. Donnaj Herr I Am, C.D., T.T., ex Ch. Fraulein Gretchen von Fox, C.D., T.T. Bred by Maria Fox, who co-owns with the Mancinos. *Below:* Iwan vom Fusse der Eifel with owner Heinz Esser; photo taken at the Klubsieger Show in Rottweil in 1988. Iwan was awarded Top Stud Dog. Photo courtesy of Frank Fiorella.

As a Rottweiler owner, you will find that, from the time your dog feels at home and that this is his place in the world, you will have a reliable, hard working and dependable guardian for your home, your property, the members of your family, and your own person. This has been bred into these dogs for generation after generation over as long a period of time as there have been Rottweilers. It is a situation which you must promptly get under control lest you find yourself living the life of a hermit, with visitors, delivery people, household help and gardeners exceedingly wary about setting foot on your premises.

Obviously, and true of every breed of dog, Rottweilers should not be allowed to run free, unattended, even on your own property. They should be walked on a lead (which provides them with the best form of exercise) and they should have a shady, comfortable fenced area in which to stay when outside the house. A dog running loose is never safe from harm and can become involved in all sorts of dangerous situations. Giving a dog his freedom is pretty much outlawed in our modern society. The well-cared-for dog is the one whose owner provides proper facilities, where he is free from chance of harm from cars, from other dogs, from irate neighbors—some of whom cannot bear to see a dog set paw on their property and will react promptly. Your dog should be protected from all these dangers—and in a way from himself, as he cannot get into any troublesome situations when he is in the house, the kennel or his carefully fenced-in area (which should be locked to make certain that no one comes along to leave the gate ajar).

There are people who fear Rottweilers and are overly in awe

Tri-Lee's Drummer Boy at age 4 months. By Ch. Goldeiche Ara von Brader ex Ch. Tri-Lee's Champagne. Bred and owned by Don and Norma White, Solon, IA.

Visiting
Grandma's
place. Eight-
week-old
puppies,
granddaughters
and grandsons
of Can. Ch. JB's
Black Phantom
Kaluha.
Alouette
Rottweilers,
Pitt Meadows,
B.C., Canada.

of the size and strength of such a dog. This puts the person off to a bad start immediately, since dogs do sense that attitude and may take advantage of the situation.

The acquisition of so power-packed a dog as a Rottweiler brings with it an obligation to accept a strong sense of responsibility for that dog and his behavior. A neglected, untrained Rottweiler can be far more dangerous to the public than a small dog, just by the matter of sheer strength if nothing else. This is a subject for serious thought as you contemplate the guardianship of one. The hysteria against dogs of several breeds has sadly grown to a high pitch during recent years, with feeling against these breeds mounting day by day. We definitely

do not want the Rottweiler among them. It is the duty of any and all Rottweiler owners to see that the dog is reared under proper circumstances, obedience trained, and taught that he *must* obey and that he must be a worthy canine citizen. This is not all that hard to manage. You owe it to yourself, your dog, and the breed to avoid letting the dog become a menace or nuisance in any way. Non-dog owners and "anti-dog" groups have their rights too, a fact which must not be forgotten. Your dog should be well able to conduct himself like a *good* canine citizen, but it is up to *you*, the owner, to assure his doing that. We do *not* want incidents which are a discredit to the breed taking place. Yet, it can happen all too easily—so beware.

Right: Panamint Zepher v. Riggons at age 4 months represents the 11th generation of Barbara Hoard's Panamint breeding program. *Below:* Powderhorn's Naga of Wencrest and Powderhorn's Giri of Wencrest. Owned by John and Jenny Wright and Powderhorn/ Wencrest Rottweilers, Inc.

Responsibilities of Ownership

RESPONSIBILITIES TO THE BREED

Contributed by Dr. Evelyn M. Ellman

Dr. Ellman has been an admirer, owner, and fancier of the Rottweiler breed since childhood in Germany, and her husband Jack, after being introduced to these intelligent and beautiful dogs by her, quickly shared her feelings.

The Ellmans' "Rottweilers von Stolzenfels" are bred "for Nobility and Utility," which has long been the motto of the von Stolzenfels Kennels. A deep-rooted feeling towards the integrity of the breed and an enthusiastic, steady desire to improve on previous achievements, to breed excellent companions and to produce champion-quality dogs have been the goals of the Ellmans right since the start of their breeding program. Quality rather than quantity is foremost on Dr. Ellman's mind as she plans each breeding.

Producing good dogs, says Dr. Ellman, requires total dedication to the chosen breed. Breeding is hard work. It demands good facilities, and much time and money are involved. It necessitates almost endless general study of all things canine and the systematic study of bloodlines. A lot of time and even more patience are needed for the on-going education of prospective owners and fanciers of the breed. The sale of a puppy should always be the beginning of a relationship, never the end of a transaction.

The public needs better education about breeders and what to expect of them prior to the purchase of a puppy. Unfortunately, many prospective purchasers are not aware of which questions should be asked, or of what it involves to own a dog of this size and type. A Rottie is, as we have often noted, a special dog for special people—one who definitely does *not* fit everyone's lifestyle.

It is the breeder's responsibility to educate the customer in what it takes to raise a Rottweiler puppy correctly and to maintain an adult of the breed. Many purchasers know that Rottweilers are very intelligent but frequently are unaware that training makes them better dogs. They also do not know that training must commence at a young age. At von Stolzenfels, puppy training starts at eight weeks and by 11 to 12 weeks they know the rudiments of basic obedience commands like heel, sit, down, stay, and come. Achieving this requires a lot of time and patience, but the work pays off greatly in the many years of the

> "The public needs better education about breeders and what to expect of them prior to the purchase of a puppy. Unfortunately, many prospective purchasers are not aware of which questions should be asked, or of what it involves to own a dog of this size and type."

to their initial owners and do not transfer their loyalty quickly nor easily to a second owner, something the Ellmans have experienced first-hand when they imported Ossy vom Stuffelkopf at age 18 months. It took Ossy almost a year to accept them totally as her new "family." She would lie down a short distance away and consistently observe the Ellmans but would only come for petting or hugging when especially encouraged to do so, never licking nor kissing. Then finally one night the barrier seemed to drop and all that love and devotion held back for so long overwhelmed her as she showered her owners, now fully acknowledged, with kisses, and from that day on, her affection never ceased.

Above: **Janka von der Silberdistel at age 18 months. Sired by Casar vom Eisplatz, SchH. III, A.D., Gekort, ex Niky vom Steinkopf, SchH. I, Gekort. Owners, E. and M. Johnson.** *Right:* **Radio Ranch's Ch. Astro vom Chrisstenbrad, a Canadian import owned by Pam Weller.**

dogs' lives as household members, making it unnecessary for them to be kept as kennel dogs or, worse yet, outside dogs.

Bringing up a puppy in the house without constant crating requires a lot of supervision and education. But prospective puppy owners must be made aware of how investigative and inquisitive Rottweilers are, and what it takes to put them on the right path so that they, sooner or later, will not be returned to their breeder, or, worst of all, become "throw away" dogs. For this reason, if no other, it is imperative that one consider very carefully before taking the step into Rottweiler ownership. Rottweilers become very attached

neighborhood that has not been burglarized. Five-month-old Gamma is responding well to his initial training for narcotics search and seizure, and has become protective of his owner's two-year-old toddler and half-year-old baby. It is good to hear that Adda, in Massachusetts, was instrumental in literally catching and holding a Peeping Tom who had been a longtime plague in the neighborhood, despite all the efforts of the police to catch him. Thankfully, Adda did not hurt herself when jumping through the closed window!

The many photos of dogs raised at von Stolzenfels, which arrive each Christmas from their owners,

Left: Could there possibly be a more endearing puppy? Wyreglen's Collier Boy owned by F. Mueller and C.E. MacPherson. *Below:* Can. Ch. Roma Star v. Stolzenfels with owner Jan Bourghton. Eight-month-old Roma was bred by Jack P. and Dr. E. M. Ellman.

Breeding good dogs and staying in touch with the pup's owners through the years can be a most rewarding experience. You share with them the happy, and sometimes the very sad, hours which they experience with their dogs. At the Ellmans, hardly a day passes when the phone does not ring with the "parents" of one of the Rottweilers whom they had bred reporting in.

It is always welcome news to hear what the dogs are doing: that Shadow, who lives in St. Thomas, loves to sit with his master in the hammock, enjoying the breeze from Magens Bay; and that Shadow and Thunder guard their beautiful St. Thomas home so well that theirs is the only house in the

Above: Ch. Arrowback's Jaro Blakey at age 2 years. Owned by Dr. P.K. and Shelley St. John, Roborott Kennels, Welland, Ont., Canada. *Right:* Two of the Rottweilers owned by Mr. and Mrs. John M. Reed, Black Forest, CO. These 10-week-old littermates are Reed's Daemon von Lukegaroo and Reed's Toscha

utterly fascinating. Soon he had struck up a friendship with an older mare; daily he would go to the pasture and sit beside the fence waiting for her to appear. Soon the mare and younger horses would notice him and break out from the woods, galloping to the fence. Viking would stand and crane his neck upward and the mare would hang hers down, enabling them to "wash" one another's faces. After just gazing into the mare's face for awhile, Viking would get up and trot home. Still a year later, when the horses were moved off the property, Viking returned periodically several times daily to "their" spot.

A Von Stolzenfels's puppy was sold to a family who owns a large sailing motor yacht. Much time was spent cruising the East Coast waters of the U.S and the Caribbean Basin during the winter. Appropriately they renamed the dog Diesel, and he immediately grew "sea legs," adjusting beautifully to living on the yacht. He learned very quickly where he had to go to defecate (which can be quite a problem for a big dog on a ship). He also learned to be extremely careful to stay away from the few spots where he could fall through and go overboard. He, nevertheless, got himself into

are a source of great pleasure. Well remembered are such occasions as when one owner, Ray Cobb, trained his Dynamo von Stolzenfels to a SchH. III title with exceptionally high scores, and when, despite worries, Dr. Ann Norton's big male Rottie named Turri did indeed tolerate a kitten being added to his household—Turri and the kitten became fast friends, playing and sleeping together devotedly.

From personal memories, there was the time of the move to Augusta, Maine, where horses lived on the property. At this period, Nello von Sillahop, called "Viking," was in residence— formerly a city dweller who had never seen a horse. He found them

serious trouble when a big fishing lure and hook caught his attention; in an unobserved moment, he got the sharp hook stuck through his upper lip in such a manner that it penetrated almost an inch. This must have hurt quite a bit. Yet he stood perfectly still while his owner snipped off the part of the hook sticking out of his lip in order to, hopefully, push the remaining part through and out of his lip. Then, when this did not succeed, he sat quietly without crying or fussing, waiting patiently for the boat to get into harbor to seek a veterinarian to remove the hook. Needless to say, he never touched another fishing hook.

Sometimes the Ellmans sit in front of the fireplace enjoying the cozy warmth. It is then that they contemplate the many years that they have spent with Rottweilers, and all the things they have taught the dogs, and that they in turn have taught the Ellmans. Some were glory days, like the time seven out of eight Von Stolzenfels's dogs present at a Medallion Specialty, being judged by a famous German judge, won their class or were in the ribbons, or the days when one received another High Score in trial. Some days were filled with great joy—observing a mother playing gently with her puppies.

Then there were those days that were filled with anxiety and great sadness when one of the faithful dogs had reached the end of his lifetime and the Ellmans had to say a fond and tearful goodbye.

"How much poorer our life would have been if we could not have accepted the love and devotion our dogs gave us from the first day of their life to the last. That's what it is all about to be a dedicated breeder!"

MORE ROTTWEILER OWNERS AND THEIR DOGS

We feel that proper understanding of a breed is enhanced the more one learns of its character, its intelligence, and

Above: Select Ch. Eischenwald's Basil v. Axel, C.D., with handler Robert Hanley. Owned by Pat Derdivanis and Robert Baston, Oakland, CA. Photo, Fox and Cook.
Left: At 7-weeks age, Roma's Ultimate TNT v. Mirko has big things to look forward to in the future we are very sure. From the Martins' Mirko-Ultra litter at Roma.

its suitability for many ways of life. A long-time friend of ours, a breeder of outstanding Beagles, surprised her many friends some years back when she added Rottweilers to her canine family and eventually changed over to Rotties entirely.

This lady, Mary Jo Czarny, was a resident of Florida when we first met her; she moved later to Swansea, Massachusetts, where she remained over a number of years; then returned to the South where she and her husband, Michael, settled in Florida.

Mary Jo could be said to have "discovered" Rottweilers while she was living in Massachusetts. There she became interested in the training of dogs for police work, which she did most successfully. The first Swansea police dog was a gift to the police department from Mary Jo. Since that time, the police department there has developed a limited training program in its own facility, and Mary Jo has been fulfilling other needs in her chosen profession of working with dogs. She is finding that the Rottweiler interest perfectly suits her present way of life, just as working with drug-identifying police dogs in Florida and the training of the dogs for police work in New England gave her much pleasure when she was younger.

When she had settled in Florida again, Mary Jo found that she missed the dogs whom she had left behind in Swansea and rather

Top: **HawkHaven puppies at age 2 months. Barbara Kellett, owner, Crystal Lake, IL.**
Middle: **Powderhorn's Noel of Wencrest, owned by Lois Elaine Smith and Powderhorn/Wencrest Rottweilers, Inc.**
Bottom: **Three little 21-day-old Rotties all in a row. Jake, Dylan, and Bud are by Ryatti Degen v. Camas Valley ex Strudel von Trostheim.**

regretted having parted with them before making the move. Because of this, it was necessary for her to start almost entirely over in Florida, which she did with the importation of a handsome German-born Rottie male, Fetz von Hegestrauch, V-rated in conformation, excelling in temperament and with a pedigree showing a solid Schutzhund lineage behind him. Fetz arrived here with his SchH. III degree, FH, I.P.O. III, and since then has attained his Canadian Ch. and C.D., American C.D.X. and T.D., both American majors, and is getting started on American U.D. In Canada, Fetz won two Group firsts, a Group third, and at the same time was High-Scoring American Dog. He does love the obedience ring, much preferring it to conformation.

As an example of the gentleness of this dog, Mary Jo tells of the squirrel half drowned in their swimming pool which Fetz saved, gently bringing it from the water (so gently that not a mark was on the squirrel anywhere) and watching over it while Mary Jo worked to bring it around. Now the squirrel lives in the yard but gives the pool a very wide berth.

All of Mary Jo's dogs have been obedience trained and have earned degrees. She finds that Rotties really enjoy working at obedience, and it is her opinion

Top: **Ch. Cannon River Oil Tanker after going Best in Show at the 1988 A.R.C. Specialty. Photo by Mitchell.**
Middle: **An exquisite head study of Best in Show Ch. Pioneer's Beguiled, by Ch. Graudstark's Luger, C.D., ex Ch. Robil Marta von Donnaj. Bred and owned by Virginia Aceti and Sheryl Hedrick, the first all-breed Best in Show Rottie.**
Bottom: **At the Monmouth County K.C. in 1987, 4 winning littermates: Ch. Copperdot's Bo von Hohler; Copperdot's Bronze Medal; Gretchen von Schlenger; and Copperdale Best Katrina Dee. Owner, Diana D. Gibson.**

that more folks should start theirs out in this manner even before letting them set foot in a conformation ring.

Now the Czarnys are looking for a suitable lady Rottie to breed to Fetz, which will bring Mary Jo full circle with the dogs as she again becomes a breeder.

CHILDREN AND ROTTWEILERS

Perhaps not everyone thinks of a Rottweiler as the suitable breed for a youngster in Junior Showmanship, especially when that youngster is, say, only six-years old. Yet, a young lady named Chrissy Sanders, who lives in West Virginia, proved that this combination can indeed work out very well.

While still a first-grader, Chrissy not long ago showed her Rottweiler, Sascha, at a dog show in Zanesville, Ohio. Competing against nine other youngsters in the Junior Class, this talented little girl handily won first prize, resulting in her eligibility to compete against the winner of the Senior Class, where eight had

Top: Rottweilers easily learn to do such things as shake hands. This is judge John Von Baron with his favorite friend. Owner, Judy M. Sample, Bakersfield, CA.
Middle: Liebenswert Cajun Coonazz, C.D., T.T., H.I.C., with his water buddy, Jay Swindle. Owner, P.J. Storer.
Bottom: Obvious devotion! Ch. Misty Lakes Awol Kid gazes adoringly at Dan Jimeniz. Owner, Dr. and Mrs. Eric Jimeniz.

Left: Scott Alkus and Dirk von Trostheim. California boy, California dog, California flower. Photo courtesy of Sharon Alkus, Santa Clarita, CA.
Below: Two fast friends at Camas Valley Rotties! Dan and Debby Kutz, owners, Springdale, WA.

competed. Here her competition came from a 17-year-old. Chrissy, however, prevailed.

Sascha was three years old at the time and outweighed her young handler by about 40 pounds, which did not in the least trouble Chrissy. She and Sascha grew up together and a very strong rapport developed between the two—as so frequently develops between a Rottie and its favorite person.

Chrissy, being an only child, has strongly relied upon Sascha as a playmate and companion. She is, thus, in no way intimidated by the dog's size, and the dog works with her most smoothly and with great cooperation.

It seems very likely that Chrissy will grow up a dedicated dog fancier owing to her experiences with Sascha, and we look forward to see her with other winning Rottweilers, too, as time progresses.

Right: Five-week-old puppies at Powsell's Kennels, owned by Deborah Moneque. By Ch. Powsell's Rambo De Jaco ex Powsell's Sara von Ester Klase.
Below: Briarwood's Rhett Butler at 9 weeks, by Ch. Marksman von Turick, C.D., ex Gina Marie's Class Act. Breeder, L. Herring.

The Care of Your Rottweiler Puppy

The moment you decide to be the new owner of a puppy is not one second too soon to start planning for the puppy's arrival in your home. Both the new family member and you will find the transition period easier if your home is geared in advance of the arrival.

The first things to be prepared are a bed for the puppy and a place where you can pen him up for rest periods. Every dog should have a crate of its own from the very beginning, so that he will come to know and love it as his special place where he is safe and happy. It is an ideal arrangement, for when you want him to be free, the crate stays open. At other times you can securely latch it and know that the pup is safely out of mischief. If you travel with him, his crate comes along in the car; and, of course, in traveling by plane there is no alternative but to have a carrier for the dog. If you show your dog, you will want him upon occasion to be in a crate a good deal of the day. So from every consideration, a crate is a very sensible and sound investment in your puppy's future safety and happiness and for your own peace of mind.

When you choose the puppy's crate, be certain that it is roomy enough not to become outgrown.

The crate should have sufficient height so the dog can stand up in it as a mature dog and sufficient area so that he can stretch out full length when relaxed. When the puppy is young, first give him shredded newspaper in the crate as a bed; the papers can be replaced with a mat or turkish towels when the dog is older. Carpet remnants are great for the bottom of the crate, as they are inexpensive and in case of accidents can be quite easily replaced. As the dog matures and is past the chewing age, a pillow or blanket in the crate is an appreciated comfort.

Sharing importance with the crate is a safe area in which the puppy can exercise and play, an area where he can be outside in safety which should be fenced in prior to the dog's arrival at your home. This area does not need to be huge, but it does need to be made safe and secure. If you are in a suburban area where there are close neighbors, stockade fencing works out best, as then the neighbors are less aware of the dog and the dog cannot see and bark at everything passing by. If you are out in the country where no problems with neighbors are likely to occur, then regular chain-link fencing is fine. For added

"Every dog should have a crate of its own from the very beginning, so that he will come to know and love it as his special place where he is safe and happy."

Right: Sam and Sabra, promising puppies from Germany's respected Vom Fusse der Eifeland Kennel, by the magnificent German stud, Falco von der Tente, Int. Ch. Bundsieger '83, Klubsieger 1984, SchH. III. Owner, Little Flower Kennel, Boxford, MA.

Opposite top: Ch. and Gr. Ch. Bacchus v. Lukmamier, by Thor v. Circle ex Aretha v. Wessel's Haus Am Berg, an important Rottweiler at Canil Baruki's in Brazil. *Opposite bottom:* Bachhus v. Lukmamier with friend. Dai Goro's Kennel, Brazil.

precaution in both cases, use a row of concrete blocks or railroad ties inside against the entire bottom of the fence; this precludes or at least considerably lessens the chances of your dog digging his way out.

Be advised that if yours is a single dog, it is very unlikely that it will get sufficient exercise just sitting in the fenced area, which is what most of them do when they

walks, a game of ball, and other such activities, are part of your daily program as a dog owner.

If your fenced area has an outside gate, provide a padlock and key and a strong fastening for it, and use them, so that the gate cannot be opened by others and the dog taken or turned free. The ultimate convenience in this regard is, of course, a door (unused

are there alone. Two or more dogs will play and move themselves around, but one by itself does little more than make a leisurely tour once around the area to check things over and then lie down. You must include a daily walk or two in your plans if your puppy is to be rugged and well. Exercise is extremely important to a puppy's muscular development and to keep a mature dog fit and trim. So make sure that those exercise periods, or

for other purposes) from the house around which the fenced area can be enclosed, so that all you have to do is open the door and out into his area he goes. This arrangement is safest of all, as then you need not be using a gate, and it is easier in bad weather since then you can send the dog out without taking him and becoming soaked yourself at the same time. This is not always possible to manage, but if your house is arranged so that you could

Seven-week-old brother and sister sired by Am., Can., Mex. Ch. Quick von Siegerhaus, C.D., Z.T.P.R., ex Can., Mex. Ch. Leibgarde's "Heidi" vom Hochfeld, Am. T.T., Mex. T.T. Breeders and photographers, the Mitchells.

The puppy will need a collar (one that fits now, not one to be grown into) and a lead from the moment you bring him home. Both should be an appropriate weight and type for his size. Also needed are a feeding dish and a water dish, both made preferably of unbreakable material. Your pet supply shop should have an interesting assortment of these and other accessories from which you can choose. Then you will need grooming tools of the type the breeder recommends and some toys. Equally satisfactory is Nylabone®, a nylon bone that does not chip or splinter and that "frizzles" as the puppy chews, providing healthful gum massage. Avoid plastics and any sort of rubber toys, *particularly those with squeakers* which the puppy may remove and swallow. If you want a ball for the puppy to use when playing with him, select one of very hard construction made for this purpose and do not leave it alone with him because he may chew off and swallow bits of the rubber. Take the ball with you when the game is over. This also applies to some of those "tug of war" type rubber toys which are fun when used with the two of you for that purpose but again should *not* be left behind for the dog to work on with his teeth. Bits of swallowed rubber, squeakers, and other such foreign articles can wreak great havoc in the intestinal tract—do all you can to guard against them.

Too many changes all at once can be difficult for a puppy. For at least the first few days he is with you, keep him on the food and feeding schedule to which he is accustomed. Find out ahead of time from the breeder what he feeds his puppies, how frequently, and at what times of the day. Also find out what, if any, food supplements the breeder has been using and recommends. Then be prepared by getting in a supply of the same food so that you will have it there when you bring the puppy home. Once the puppy is accustomed to his new

do it this way, you would never regret it due to the convenience and added safety thus provided. Fencing in the entire yard, with gates to be opened and closed whenever a caller, deliveryman, postman, or some other person comes on your property, really is not safe at all because people not used to gates are frequently careless about closing and latching them *securely.* Many heartbreaking incidents have been brought about by someone carelessly half-closing a gate (which the owner had thought to be firmly latched) and the dog wandering off. For greatest security a fenced *area* definitely takes precedence over a fenced *yard.*

surroundings, then you can switch the type of food and schedule to fit your convenience, but for the first several days do it as the puppy expects.

Your selection of a veterinarian should also be attended to before the puppy comes home, because you should stop at the vet's office for the puppy to be checked over as soon as you leave the breeder's premises. If the breeder is from your area, ask him for recommendations. Ask you dog-owning friends for their opinions of the local veterinarians, and see what their experiences with those available have been. Choose someone whom several of your friends recommend highly, then contact him about your puppy, perhaps making an appointment to stop in at his office. If the premises are clean, modern, and well equipped, and if you like the veterinarian, make an appointment to bring the puppy in on the day of purchase. Be sure to obtain the puppy's health record from the breeder, including information on such things as shots and worming that the puppy has had.

JOINING THE FAMILY

Remember that, exciting and happy an occasion as it is for you, the puppy's move from his place of birth to your home can be, for him, a traumatic experience. His mother and littermates will be missed. He quite likely will be awed or frightened by the change of surroundings. The person on whom he depended will be gone. Everything should be planned to make his arrival at your home pleasant—to give him confidence and to help him realize that yours is a pretty nice place to be after all.

Never bring a puppy home on a holiday. There is just too much going on with people and gifts and excitement. If he is in honor of an "occasion," work it out so that his arrival will be a few days earlier, or perhaps even better, a few days later than the "occasion." Then your home will be back to its

normal routine and the puppy can enjoy your undivided attention. Try not to bring the puppy home in the evening. Early morning is the ideal time, as then he has the opportunity of getting acquainted and the initial strangeness should wear off before bedtime. You will find it a more peaceful night that way. Allow the puppy to investigate as he likes, under your watchful eye. If you already have a pet in the household, keep a careful watch that the relationship between the two gets off to a friendly start or you may quickly find yourself with a lasting problem. Much of the future attitude of each toward the other will depend on what takes place that first day, so keep your

"A photographer's nightmare: five 7-week-old Rottie puppies into one clay pot." Photographer Mitchell reveals that,"this shot took 2 rolls of film and the patience of 3 puppy-stuffers." Sired by Ch. Donar von Reishoff from Von Danna Dynasty Royalhaus. Owner, P. Palecek.

mind on what they are doing and let your other activities slide for the moment. Be careful not to let your older pet become jealous by paying more attention to the puppy than to him, as that will start a bad situation immediately.

If you have a child, here again it is important that the relationship start out well. Before the puppy is brought home, you should have a talk with the youngster. He must clearly understand that puppies are fragile and can easily be injured; therefore, they should not be teased, hurt, mauled, or overly rough-housed. A puppy is not an inanimate toy; it is a living thing with a right to be loved and handled respectfully, treatment which will reflect in the dog's attitude toward your child as both mature together. Never permit your children's playmates to mishandle the puppy, tormenting the puppy until it turns on the children in self-defense. Children often do not realize how rough is too rough. You, as a responsible adult, are obligated to assure that your puppy's relationship with children is a pleasant one.

Do not start out by spoiling your puppy. A puppy is usually pretty smart and can be quite demanding. What you had considered to be "just for tonight" may be accepted by the puppy as "for keeps." Be firm with him, strike a routine, and stick to it. The puppy will learn more quickly this way, and everyone will be happier as a result. A radio playing softly or a

Top: **A promising 4-week-old male at Powsell's Kennel of Deborah Moneque. This youngster is by Ch. Degan's Talker von Meadow ex Powsell's Dorcas (a Yankee daughter).**
Middle: **Czirga vom Haus Kalbas, a 10-week-old puppy bitch with Ch. Krueger vom Odenwald, U.D.T., SchH. III, both owned by Paula Gampp.**
Bottom: **Ch. Liebenswert Cafe Ole, C.D., T.T., H.I.C.; Liebenswert Frier, T.T., H.I.C.; and Command Roxanna, C.D.X., T.T., H.I.C., enjoying a swim in Alleyton, TX.**

dim night light are often comforting to a puppy as it gets accustomed to new surroundings and should be provided in preference to bringing the puppy to bed with you—unless, of course, you intend him to share the bed as a permanent arrangement.

SOCIALIZING AND TRAINING

Socialization and training of your puppy should start the very day of his arrival in your home. Never address him without calling him by name. A short, simple name is the easiest to teach as it catches the dog's attention quickly; avoid elaborate call names. Always address the dog by the same name, not a whole series of pet names; the latter will only confuse the puppy.

Use his name clearly, and call the puppy over to you when you see him awake and wandering about. When he comes, make a big fuss over him for being such a good dog. He thus will quickly associate the sound of his name with coming to you and a pleasant happening.

Several hours after the puppy's arrival is not too soon to start accustoming him to the feel of a light collar. He may hardly notice it; or he may struggle, roll over, and try to rub it off his neck with his paws. Divert his attention when this occurs by offering a tasty snack or a toy (starting a game with him) or by petting him. Before long he will have accepted the strange feeling around his neck and no longer appear aware of it. Next comes the lead. Attach it and then immediately take the puppy outside or otherwise try to divert his attention with things to see and sniff. He may struggle against the lead at first, biting at it and trying to free himself. Do not pull him with it at this point; just hold the end loosely and try to follow him if he starts off in any direction. Normally his attention will soon turn to investigating his surroundings if he is outside or you have taken him into an unfamiliar room in your house; curiosity will take over and he will become

interested in sniffing around the surroundings. Follow him with the lead slackly held until he seems to have completely forgotten about it; then try with gentle urging to get him to follow you. Don't be rough or jerk at him; just tug gently on the lead in short quick motions (steady pulling can become a battle of wills), repeating his name or trying to get him to follow your hand which is holding a bite of food or an interesting toy. If you

have an older lead-trained dog, then it should be a cinch to get the puppy to follow along after *him*. In any event the average puppy learns quite quickly and will soon be trotting along nicely on the lead. Once that point has been reached, the next step is to teach him to follow on your left side, or heel. This will not likely be accomplished all in one day; it should be done with short training periods over the course of several days until you are satisfied with the result.

First day on the lawn, these delightful Rottie babies are by Ch. Degan's Talker von Meadow ex Powsell's Dorcas. They belong to D. Moneque.

Top left: From a painting of a typical "Dutch" puppy from the Jo-Bea Rottweilers at Ont., CA, done by artist Diana Moore. *Top right:* These 7-week-old pups by Am., Can. Ch. Trifecta's Barbarian v. Murph, C.D., ex Von Hottenstein's The Boss, make an adorable reception committee. Bred by Nancy Reynolds. *Below:* An orphan fawn with some Liebenswert "M" puppies. Gentleness is all the approach to raising puppies, as owner Pat Storer reminds us.

During the course of house training your puppy, you will need to take him out frequently and at regular intervals: first thing in the morning directly from the crate, immediately after meals, after the puppy has been napping, or when you notice that the puppy is looking for a spot. Choose more or less the same place to take the puppy each time so that a pattern will be established. If he does not go immediately, do not return him to the house as he will probably relieve himself the moment he is inside. Stay out with him until he has finished; then be lavish with your praise for his good behavior. If you catch the puppy having an accident indoors, grab him firmly and rush him outside, sharply saying "No!" as you pick him up. If you do not see the accident occur, there is little point in doing anything except cleaning it up, as once it has happened and been forgotten, the puppy will most likely not even realize why you are scolding him.

The puppy should form the habit of spending a certain amount of time in his crate, even when you are home. Sometimes the puppy will do this voluntarily, but if not, he should be taught to do so, which is accomplished by leading the puppy over by his collar, gently pushing him inside, and saying firmly, "Down" or "Stay." Whatever expression you use to give a command, stick to the very same one each time for each act. Repetition is the big thing in training—and so is association with what the dog is expected to do. When you mean "Sit," always say exactly that. "Stay" should mean *only* that the dog should remain where he receives the command.

"Down" means something else again. Do not confuse the dog by shuffling the commands, as this will create training problems for you.

As soon as he has had his immunization shots, take your puppy with you whenever and wherever possible. There is nothing that will build a self-confident, stable dog like socialization, and it is extremely important that you plan and give the time and energy necessary for this, whether your dog is to be a show dog or a pleasant, well-adjusted family member. Take your puppy in the car so that he will learn to enjoy riding and not become carsick, as dogs may do if they are infrequent travelers. Take him anywhere you are going where you are certain he will be welcome: visiting friends and relatives (if they do not have housepets who may resent the visit), busy shopping centers (keeping him always on lead), or just walking around the streets of your town. If someone admires him (as always seems to happen when one is out with puppies), encourage the stranger to pet and talk with him. Socialization of this type brings out the best in your puppy and helps him to grow up with a friendly outlook, liking the world and its inhabitants. The worst thing that can be done to a puppy's personality is to shelter him. By always keeping him at home away from things and people unfamiliar to him, you may be creating a personality problem for the mature dog that will be a cross for you to bear later on.

FEEDING YOUR ROTTWEILER

Time was when providing nourishing food for dogs involved a far more complicated procedure than people now feel is necessary. The old school of thought was that the daily ration must consist of fresh beef, vegetables, cereal, egg yolks, and cottage cheese as basics with such additions as brewer's yeast and vitamin tablets on a daily basis.

During recent years, however, many minds have changed regarding this procedure. Eggs, cottage cheese, and supplements to the diet are still given, but the basic method of feeding dogs has changed; and the change has been, in the opinion of many authorities, definitely for the better. The school of thought now is that you are doing your dogs a favor when you feed them some of the fine commercially prepared dog foods in preference to your own home-cooked concoctions.

The reason behind this new outlook is easily understandable. The dog food industry has grown to be a major one, participated in by

Von Dorow at 3½ months. By Am., Can. Ch. Tulake's Apollo ex Ch. Merrymoore's Imp von Dorow. Owner, Nancy C. Estes.

some of the best known and most respected names in America. These trusted firms, it is agreed, turn out excellent products, so people are feeding their dog food preparations with confidence and the dogs are thriving, living longer, happier, and healthier lives than ever before. What more could one want?

There are at least half a dozen absolutely top-grade dry foods to be mixed with broth or water and served to your dog according to directions. There are all sorts of canned meats, and there are several kinds of "convenience foods," those in a packet which you open and dump out into the dog's

Right: Ch. Milo's Storm Warning at age 9 weeks, by Can. Ch. Simsberg's Kuno ex Can. Ch. Kyladies Imagination, C.D. Mike Kelliher, owner. *Below:* A very promising baby Rottie at age 12 weeks: the future Ch. Camas Valley Cassandra owned by D. and D. Kutz.

dish. It is just that simple. The convenience foods are neat and easy to use when you are away from home, but generally speaking a dry food mixed with hot water (or soup) and meat is preferred. It is the opinion of many that the canned meat, with its added fortifiers, is more beneficial to the dogs than the fresh meat. However, the two can be alternated or, if you prefer and your dog does well on it, by all means use fresh ground beef. A dog enjoys changes in the meat part of his diet, which is easy with the canned food since all sorts of beef are available (chunk, ground, stewed, and so on), plus lamb, chicken, and even such concoctions as liver and egg, plain liver flavor, and a blend of five meats.

There is also prepared food geared to every age bracket of your dog's life, from puppyhood on through old age, with special additions or modifications to make it particularly nourishing and beneficial. Previous generations never had it so good where the canine dinner is concerned, because these commercially prepared foods are tasty and geared to meeting the dog's gastronomic approval.

Additionally, contents and nutrients are clearly listed on the labels, as are careful instructions for feeding just the right amount for the size, weight, and age of each dog.

With these foods the addition of extra vitamins is not necessary, but if you prefer there are several kinds of those, too, that serve as taste treats as well as being beneficial. Your pet supplier has a full array of them.

Of course there is no reason not to cook up something for your dog if you would feel happier doing so. But it seems unnecessary when such truly satisfactory rations are available with so much less trouble and expense.

How often you feed your dog is a matter of how it works out best for you. Many owners prefer to do it once a day. It is generally agreed that two meals, each of smaller quantity, are better for the digestion and more satisfying to the dog, particularly if yours is a household member who stands around and watches preparations for the family meals. Do not overfeed. This is the shortest route to all sorts of problems. Follow directions and note carefully how your dog is looking. If your dog is overweight, cut back the quantity of food a bit. If the dog looks thin, then increase the amount. Each dog is an individual and the food intake should be adjusted to his requirements to keep him feeling and looking trim and in top condition.

From the time puppies are fully weaned until they are about twelve weeks old, they should be fed four times daily. From three months to six months of age, three meals should suffice. At six months of age the puppies can be fed two meals, and the twice daily feedings can be continued until the puppies are close to one year old, at which time feeding can be changed to once daily if desired. If you do feed just once a day, do so by early afternoon at the latest and give the dog a snack, a biscuit or two, at bedtime.

Remember that plenty of fresh water should always be available to your puppy or dog for drinking. This is of utmost importance to his health.

ALL DOGS NEED TO CHEW

Puppies and young dogs need something with resistance to chew on while their teeth and jaws are developing—for cutting the puppy teeth, to induce growth of the permanent teeth under the puppy teeth, to assist in getting rid of the puppy teeth at the proper time, to help the permanent teeth through

the gums, to assure normal jaw development and to settle the permanent teeth solidly in the jaws.

The adult dog's desire to chew stems from the instinct for tooth cleaning, gum massage and jaw exercise—plus the need to vent periodic doggie tensions.

Dental caries (decay), as it affects the teeth of humans, is virtually unknown in dogs; but tartar accumulates on the teeth of dogs, particularly at the gum line, more rapidly than on the teeth of

Van Gailingen's Made To Order and Matinee Idol at age 1 year. Breeder-owner, C.M. Thompson.

Top:
Bergenhof's Gunther von Nelson, by Best in Show-winning Ch. Nelson von het Brabantpark ex Select Ch. Sophe von Bergenhof. Joan Harrison, owner.
Bottom: **Ch. Altar's Gunner of Woodland. Owner, Arthur Coia.**

humans. These accumulations, if not removed, bring irritation and then infection, which erodes the tooth enamel and ultimately destroys the teeth at the roots. Most chewing by adult dogs is an effort to do something about this problem for themselves.

Tooth and jaw development will normally continue until the dog is more than a year old—but sometimes much longer, depending upon the breed, chewing exercise, the rate at which calcium can be utilized and many other factors,

known and unknown, which affect the development of individual dogs. Diseases, like distemper for example, may sometimes arrest development of the teeth and jaws, which may resume months or even years later.

This is why dogs, especially puppies and young dogs, will often destroy property worth hundreds of dollars when their chewing instinct is not diverted from their owner's possessions, particularly during the widely varying critical period for young dogs. Saving your possessions from destruction, assuring proper development of teeth and jaws, providing for "interim" tooth cleaning and gum massage, and channeling doggie tensions into a non-destructive outlet are, therefore, all dependent upon the dog's having available something suitable when his instinct tells him to chew. If your purposes, and those of your dog, are to be accomplished, what you provide for chewing must be desirable from the doggie viewpoint, have the necessary functional qualities, and, above all, be safe for your dog.

It is very important that dogs not be permitted to chew on anything they can break or indigestible things from which they can bite sizeable chunks. Sharp pieces, such as those from a bone which can be broken by a dog, may pierce the intestine wall and kill. Indigestible things which can be bitten off in chunks, such as toys made of rubber compound or cheap plastic, may cause an intestinal stoppage; if not regurgitated, they are certain to bring painful death unless surgery is promptly performed.

Strong natural bones, such as 4- to 8-inch lengths of round shin bone from mature beef—either the kind you can get from your butcher or one of the varieties available commercially in pet stores—may serve your dog's teething needs, if his mouth is large enough to handle them effectively.

You may be tempted to give your puppy a smaller bone and he may not be able to break it when you do, but puppies grow rapidly and the power of their jaws constantly increases until maturity. This means that a growing dog may break one of the smaller bones at any time, swallow the pieces and die painfully before you realize what is wrong.

Many people have the mistaken notion that their dog's teeth are like those of wild carnivores or of dogs from antiquity. The teeth of wild carnivorous animals and those found in the fossils of the dog-like creatures of antiquity have far thicker and stronger enamel than those of our contemporary dogs.

All hard, natural bones are highly abrasive. If your dog is an avid chewer, natural bones may wear away his teeth prematurely; hence, they then should be taken away from your dog when the teething purposes have been served. The badly worn, and usually painful, teeth of many mature dogs can be traced to excessive chewing on natural bones.

Contrary to popular belief, knuckle bones that can be chewed up and swallowed by the dog provide little, if any, useable calcium or other nutriment. They do, however, disturb the digestion of most dogs and cause them to vomit the nourishing food they need.

Never give a dog your old shoe to chew on, even if you have removed all the nails or metal parts, such as lace grommets, buckles, metal arches, and so on. Rubber heels are especially dangerous, as the dog can bite off chunks, swallow them, and suffer from intestinal blockage as a result. Additionally, if the rubber should happen to have a nail imbedded in it that you cannot detect, this could pierce or tear the intestinal wall. There is always the possibility, too, that your dog may fail to differentiate between his shoe and yours and chew up a good pair while you're not looking. It is strongly recommended that you refrain from offering old shoes as chew toys since there are much safer products available commercially.

Dried rawhide products have become available during the past few years. They don't serve the primary chewing functions very well, they are a bit messy when wet from mouthing, and most dogs chew them up rather rapidly—but they have been considered safe for dogs until recently. Now, more and more incidents of death, and near death, by strangulation have been reported to be the result of partially swallowed chunks of rawhide swelling in the throat. Currently, some veterinarians have been attributing cases of acute constipation to large pieces of

Carado's Mighty Essex and Carado's Tamara v. Quinn. Photo courtesy of Carole Kravets, Windson, Ont., Canada.

Above: Among the handsome and talented crowd: Pepperhaus Black Brat; Pepperhaus Arco von Warstar, C.D.X.; Langhoffen's Esse, C.D.X., H.I.C., T.D.I.; Welkerhaus Early Edition, U.D.; Am., Can. Ch. Fraulein Anka von Ascothaus; and Pepperhaus Black Gayla, C.D., H.I.C.
Below: Bryloukis "F" Edition, by Am., Can. Ch. Bryloukis Alexander ex Ch. Eltre Christel aus Kiros. Bred by Bryloukis Rottweilers.

incompletely digested rawhide in the intestine.

The nylon bones, especially those with natural meat and bone fractions added, are probably the most complete, safe and economical answer to the chewing need. Dogs cannot break them or bite off sizeable chunks; hence, they are completely safe. And being longer lasting than other things offered for the purpose, they are economical.

Hard chewing raises little bristle-like projections on the surface of the nylon bones to provide effective interim tooth cleaning and vigorous gum massage, much in the same way your tooth brush does for you. The little projections are raked off and swallowed in the form of thin shavings, but the chemistry of the nylon is such that they break down in the stomach fluids and pass through without effect.

The toughness of the nylon provides the strong chewing resistance needed for important jaw exercise and effective help for the teething functions; however, there is no tooth wear because nylon is non-abrasive. Being inert, nylon does not support the growth of microorganisms; and it can be washed in soap and water, or it can be sterilized by boiling or in an autoclave.

There are a great variety of Nylabone® products available that veterinarians recommend as safe and healthy for your dog or puppy to chew on. These nylon pooch pacifiers—Nylabone®, Nylaball®—can't splinter, chip, or break off in large chunks; instead, they are frizzled by the dog's chewing action, and this creates a toothbrush-like surface that cleanses the teeth and massages the gums. At the same time, these hard-nylon therapeutic devices channel doggie tension and chewing frustation into constructive rather than destructive behavior. Check your local pet shop for the *only* chew products made of flavor-impregnated solid nylon; and be

Left: Bryloukis Extra Special, Can. C.D.X., by Am. Ch. Trollegen's Ammon ex Trollegen's Faith; bred by Cynthia Ronay. *Below:* Am., Can. Ch. Rowehaus A. Erwin Rommel, handled by Sid Lamont, finished his title at age 5 years, after working at it for a few months. Owner, D.K. Loving.

sure to ask about the various sizes, shapes, and flavors that are manufactured for your dog's needs. If you want a soft, chewy play toy, look for Gumabone® wherever Nylabone® products are sold. These flexible nylon bones are designed to provide entertainment for you and your dog, and they are great aids for teaching your canine companion how to retrieve.

Nothing, however, substitutes for periodic professional attention to your dog's teeth and gums, not any more than your toothbrush can do that for you. Have your dog's teeth cleaned by your veterinarian at least once a year—twice a year is better—and he will be healthier, happier and a far more pleasant companion.

Top: Mutual admiration: Rosemary Van Helvoort and Helsingborg Harskarrina gaze with obvious approval at one another. Owners, Barrabadeen Stud, Gidgegannup, Western Australia.
Bottom: Two 4-week-old pups from Lakeview Rottweilers of Tonya Jones Oldham, Dawson Springs, KY.

Breeding Your Rottweiler

Conscientious breeders feel quite strongly that the only possible reason for producing puppies is the ambition to improve and uphold quality and temperament within the breed—definitely *not* because one hopes to make a quick cash profit on a mediocre litter, which never seems to work out that way in the long run and which accomplishes little beyond perhaps adding to the nation's heartbreaking number of unwanted canines. The only reason ever for breeding a litter is, with conscientious people, a desire to improve the quality of dogs in their own kennel or, as pet owners, to add to the number of dogs they themselves own with a puppy or two from their present favorites. In either case, breeding should not take place unless one definitely has prospective owners for as many puppies as the litter may contain, lest you find yourself with several fast-growing young dogs and no homes in which to place them. Remember, too, that Rotties have large litters.

THE BROOD BITCH

Your Rottweiler bitch should not be bred until she is at least eighteen months of age; has been X-rayed for hip dysplasia; and has received a preliminary evaluation by the Orthopedic Foundation of America (O.F.A.) indicating her hips are normal at the time the X-ray was taken. Many people prefer to show their bitches before breeding them. When you have decided what will be the proper time, start watching at least several months ahead for what you feel would be the perfect mate to best complement your bitch's quality and bloodlines. Subscribe to the magazines which feature your breed exclusively and to some which cover all breeds in order to familiarize yourself with outstanding stud dogs in areas other than your own, for there is no necessity nowadays to limit your choice to a local dog unless you truly like him and feel that he is the most suitable. It is quite usual to ship a bitch to a stud dog a distance away, and this generally works out with no ill effects. The important thing is that you need a stud dog strong in those features where your bitch is weak, a dog whose bloodlines are compatible with hers. Compare the background of both your bitch and the stud dog under consideration, paying particular attention to the quality of the puppies from bitches with backgrounds similar to your bitch's. If the puppies have been of the type and quality you admire,

"The only reason ever for breeding a litter is, with conscientious people, a desire to improve the quality of dogs in their own kennel..."

Above: "The Gang." These Rottie puppies are all littermates, 6 dogs and 5 bitches. By Ch. Lindenwood's Bounce ex Ch. Tobant's Iza Winner. Breeder, Craig Ames.
Below: A 10-week-old daughter of Shikara von Dular ex Denel's Instigator v. Eisen.

then this dog would seem a sensible choice for yours, too.

Stud fees may be a few hundred dollars for a particularly successful sire. It is money well spent, however. *Do not* ever breed to a dog because he is less expensive than the others unless you honestly believe that he can sire the kind of puppies who will

be a credit to your kennel and your breed.

Contacting the owners of the stud dogs you find interesting will bring you pedigrees and pictures which you can then study in relation to your bitch's pedigree and conformation. Discuss your plans with other breeders who are knowledgeable (including the one who bred your own bitch). You may not always receive an entirely unbiased opinion (particularly if the person giving it also has an available stud dog), but one learns by discussion so listen to what they say, consider their opinions, and then you may be better qualified to form your own opinion.

As soon as you have made a choice, phone the owner of the stud dog you wish to use to find out if this will be agreeable. You will be asked about the bitch's health, soundness, temperament, and freedom from serious faults. A copy of her pedigree may be requested, as might a picture of her. A discussion of her background over the telephone may be sufficient to assure the stud's owner that she is suitable for the stud dog and that she is of type, breeding, and quality herself, capable of producing the kind of puppies for which the stud is noted. The owner of a top-quality stud is extremely selective in the bitches permitted to be bred to his dog, in an effort to keep the standard of his puppies high.

As the time for her season draws near, you should take the bitch to your veterinarian to be checked over. Be sure to have her checked for worms, make sure that she is up-to-date on all her shots, and attend to any other tests, such as brucellosis, the stud owner may have requested. At this time it is very important to have your veterinarian run a titer for parvovirus, to make certain that your bitch has developed the immunity to pass on to her puppies.

Check out which airport will be most convenient for the person meeting and returning the bitch, if she is to be shipped, and also what airlines use that airport. You will find that the airlines are also apt to have special requirements concerning acceptance of animals for shipping. These include weather limitations and types of crates which are acceptable. The weather limits have to do with extreme heat and extreme cold at the point of destination, as some airlines will not fly dogs into temperatures above or below certain levels, fearing for their safety. The crate problem is a simple one, since, if your own crate is not suitable, most of the airlines have specially designed crates available for purchase at a fair and moderate price. It is a good plan to purchase one of these if you intend to be shipping dogs with any sort of frequency. They are made of fiberglass and are the safest type to use for shipping.

Normally you must notify the airline several days in advance to make a reservation, as they are able to accommodate only a certain number of dogs on each flight. Plan on shipping the bitch on about her eighth or ninth day of season, but be careful to avoid shipping her on a weekend when schedules often vary and freight offices are apt to be closed. Whenever you can, ship your bitch on a direct flight. Changing planes always carries a certain amount of risk of a dog being overlooked or wrongly routed at the middle stop, so avoid this danger if at all possible. The bitch must be accompanied by a health certificate which you must obtain from your veterinarian before taking her to the airport. Usually it will be necessary to have the bitch at the airport about two hours prior to flight time. Before finalizing arrangements, find out from the stud's owner at what time of day it will be most convenient to have the bitch picked up promptly upon arrival.

Some people feel that the trauma of the flight may cause the bitch to not conceive; and, of course, undeniably there is a slight risk in shipping which can be

avoided if you are able to drive the bitch to her destination. Be sure to leave yourself sufficient time to assure your arrival at the right time for her for breeding (normally the tenth to fourteenth day following the first signs of color);

Von Gailingen's Matinee Idol, Am., Can. C.D., relaxing on the lawn. Owner, C.M. Thompson.

and remember that if you want the bitch bred twice, you should allow a day to elapse between the two matings.

The moment you notice the swelling of the vulva, for which you should be checking daily as the time for her season approaches, and the appearance of color,

immediately contact the stud's owner and settle on the day for shipping or make the appointment for your arrival with the bitch for breeding. If you are shipping the bitch, the stud fee check should be mailed immediately, leaving ample time for it to have been received when the bitch arrives and the mating takes place. Be sure to call the airline, making her reservation at that time, too.

Do not feed the bitch within a few hours before shipping her. Be certain that she has had a drink of water and been well exercised before closing her in the crate. Several layers of newspapers, topped with some shredded newspaper, make a good bed and can be discarded when she arrives at her destination; these can be replaced with fresh newspapers for her return home. Remember that the bitch should be brought to the airport about two hours before flight time, as sometimes the airlines refuse to accept late arrivals.

If you are taking your bitch by car, be certain that you will arrive at a reasonable time of day. Do not appear late in the evening. If your arrival in town is not until late, get a good night's sleep at your motel and contact the stud's owner first thing in the morning. If possible, leave children and relatives at home, as they will only be in the way and perhaps unwelcome by the stud's owner. Most stud dog owners prefer not to have any unnecessary people on hand during the actual mating.

After the breeding has taken place, if you wish to sit and visit for awhile and the stud's owner has the time, return the bitch to her crate in your car (first ascertaining, of course, that the temperature is comfortable for her and that there is proper ventilation). She should not be permitted to urinate for at least one hour following the breeding. This is the time when you attend to the business part of the transaction. Pay the stud fee, upon which you should receive your breeding certificate and, if you do not already have it, a copy of the stud dog's pedigree. The owner of the stud dog does not sign or furnish a litter registration application until the puppies have been born.

Upon your return home, you can settle down and plan in happy anticipation a wonderful litter of puppies. A word of caution! Remember that although she has been bred, your bitch is still an interesting target for all male dogs, so guard her carefully for the next week or until you are absolutely certain that her season has entirely ended. This would be no time to have any unfortunate incident with another dog.

Von Gailingen's Made to Order, Am., Can. C.D. A homebred owned by Van Gailingen Rottweilers.

"Bruno," owned by Janice DelFarno, masquerades in cap and goggles.

THE STUD DOG

Choosing the best stud dog to complement your bitch is often very difficult. The two principal factors to be considered should be the stud's conformation and his pedigree. Conformation is fairly obvious; you want a dog that is typical of the breed in the words of the standard of perfection. Understanding pedigrees is a bit more subtle since the pedigree lists the ancestry of the dog and involves individuals and bloodlines with which you may not be entirely familiar.

A novice in the breed often finds the correct interpretation of a pedigree at first difficult to grasp. Study the pictures and text of this book to find names of important bloodlines and members of the breed. Also make an effort to discuss the various dogs behind the proposed stud with some of the more experienced breeders, starting with the breeder of your own bitch. Frequently these folks will be familiar with many of the dogs in question, will be able to offer opinions of them, and may have access to additional pictures which you would benefit by seeing. It is very important that the stud's pedigree be of suitable bloodlines for the bitch you plan on breeding to him. Do not rush out and breed to the latest winner with no thought of whether or not he can produce true quality. By no means are all great show dogs great producers. It is the *producing* record of the dog and the dogs and bitches from which he has come, that should be the basis on which you make your choice.

Breeding dogs is never a money-making operation. By the time you pay a stud fee, care for the bitch during pregnancy, whelp the litter,

377

Fancy Bavaria von Stolzenfels, Am., Can. C.D., by Ch. Imors Bulli von Stolzenfels ex Herta Cicka Stolzenfels, C.D. Owners, Ken and Renae Rook. Breeders, J. and E. Ellman.

and rear the puppies through their early shots, worming, and so on, you will be fortunate to break even financially once the puppies have been sold. Your chances of doing this are greater if you are breeding for a show-quality litter which will bring you higher prices, as the pups are sold as show prospects. Therefore, your wisest investment is to use the most suitable dog available for your bitch regardless of the cost; then you should wind up with more valuable puppies. Remember that it is equally costly to raise mediocre puppies as it is top ones, and your chances of financial return are better on the latter.

It will be your decision as to which course you follow when you breed your bitch, as there are three options: linebreeding, inbreeding, and outcrossing. Each of these methods has its supporters and its detractors! Linebreeding is breeding a bitch to a dog belonging originally to the same canine family, being descended from the same ancestors, such as half brother to half sister, grandsire to granddaughter, niece to uncle (and vice-versa) or cousin to cousin. Inbreeding is breeding father to daughter, mother to son, or full brother to sister. Outcross breeding is breeding a dog and a bitch with no or only a few mutual ancestors.

Linebreeding is probably the safest course, and the one most likely to bring results, for the novice breeder. The more sophisticated inbreeding should be left to the experienced, longtime breeders who throroughly know and understand the risks and the possibilities involved.

You should *never* breed to an unsound dog or one with any serious disqualifying faults according to the breed's standard. Not all champions by any means pass along their best features; and by the same token, occasionally you will find a great one who can pass along his best features but never gained his championship title due to some unusual circumstances. The information you need about a stud dog is what type of puppies he has produced, and with what bloodlines, and whether or not he possesses the bloodlines and attributes considered characteristic of the best in your breed.

If you go out to buy a stud dog, obviously he will not be a puppy, but rather a fully mature and proven male with as many of the best attributes as possible. He will be an expensive investment, but if you choose and make his selection with care and forethought, he may well prove to be one of the best investments you have ever made.

Of course, the most exciting of all is when a young male you have decided to keep from one of your litters, due to his tremendous show potential, turns out to be a stud dog such as we have described. In this case he should be managed with care, for he is a valuable asset that can contribute inestimably to this breed as a whole and to your own kennel specifically.

If you are the proud owner of a promising young stud dog, one that you have either bred from one of your own bitches or that you purchased after much deliberation, do not permit him to be used for the first time until he is at least eighteen months of age; has been X-rayed for hip dysplasia and has received a preliminary evaluation by the Orthopedic Foundation of America (O.F.A.) indicating his hips at the time of the X-ray are normal. To receive a permanent O.F.A. number for normal hips, the dog must be two years of age or older.

Your young stud must permit help with the breeding, as later there will be bitches who will not be cooperative. If right from the beginning you are there helping him and praising him, whether or not your assistance is actually needed, he will expect and accept this as a matter of course when a difficult bitch comes along.

Things to have handy before introducing your dog and the bitch are K-Y jelly (the only lubricant which should be used) and a length of gauze with which to muzzle the bitch should it be necessary to keep her from biting you or the dog. Some bitches put up a fight; others are calm. It is best to be prepared.

The accepted litter is one live puppy. It is wise to have printed a breeding certificate which the owner of the stud dog and the owner of the bitch both sign. This should list in detail the conditions of the breeding as well as the dates of the mating.

Upon occasion, arrangements other than a stud fee in cash are made for a breeding, such as the owner of the stud taking a pick-of-the-litter puppy in lieu of money.

This should be clearly specified on the breeding certificate along with the terms of the age at which the stud's owner will select the puppy, whether it is to be a specific sex, or whether it is to be the pick of the entire litter.

Almost invariably it is the bitch who comes to the stud dog for the breeding. Immediately upon having selected the stud dog you wish to use, discuss the possibility with the owner of that dog. It is the stud dog owner's prerogative to refuse to breed any bitch deemed unsuitable for this dog. Stud fee and method of payment should be stated at this time and a decision reached on whether it is to be a full cash transaction at the time of the mating or a pick-of-the-litter puppy, usually at eight weeks of age.

Ch. Gretchen of Dugins Farms was bred by Diane Johnston of Rainhart Rottweilers, Greenbank, WA.

If the owner of the stud dog must travel to an airport to meet the bitch and ship her for the flight home, an additional charge will be made for time, tolls, and gasoline based on the stud owner's proximity to the airport. The stud fee includes board for the day on the bitch's arrival through two days for breeding, with a day in between. If it is necessary that the bitch remain longer, it is very likely that additional board will be charged at the normal per-day rate for the breed.

Be sure to advise the stud's owner as soon as you know that your bitch is in season so that the stud dog will be available.

As the owner of a stud dog being offered to the public, it is essential that you have proper facilities for the care of visiting bitches. Nothing can be worse than a bitch being insecurely housed and slipping out to become lost or bred by the wrong dog. If you are taking people's valued bitches into your kennel or home, it is imperative that you provide them with comfortable, secure housing and good care while they are your responsibility.

Going into the actual management of the mating is a bit superfluous here. If you have had previous experience in breeding a dog and bitch, you will know how the mating is done. If you do not have such experience, you should not attempt to follow directions given in a book but should have a veterinarian, breeder friend, or handler there to help you with the first few times. You do not turn the dog and bitch loose together and await developments, as too many things can go wrong and you may altogether miss getting the bitch bred. Someone should hold the dog and the bitch (one person each) until the "tie" is made and these two people should stay with them during the entire act.

If you get a complete tie, probably only the one mating is absolutely necessary. However, especially with a maiden bitch or one that has come a long distance for this breeding, a follow-up with a second breeding is preferred, leaving one day in between the two matings. In this way there will be little or no chance of the bitch missing.

Once the tie has been completed and the dogs released, be certain that the male's penis goes completely back within its sheath. He should be allowed a drink of water and a short walk, and then he should be put into his crate or somewhere alone where he can settle down. Do not allow him to be with other dogs for a while as they will notice the odor of the bitch on him, and, particularly with other males present, he may become involved in a fight.

Handsome head study of Judge John Von Baron owned by Judy Sample, Bakersfield, CA.

PREGNANCY, WHELPING, AND THE LITTER

During pregnancy, your bitch should be treated normally. Controlled exercise is good and necessary for the bitch throughout her pregnancy, tapering it off to just several short walks daily, preferably on lead, as she reaches her seventh week. As her time grows close, be careful about her jumping or playing too roughly.

The theory that a bitch should be overstuffed with food when pregnant is a poor one. A fat bitch is never an easy whelper, so the overfeeding you consider good for her may well turn out to be a hindrance later on. During the first few weeks of pregnancy, your bitch should be fed her normal diet. At four to five weeks along, calcium should be added to her food. At seven weeks her food may be increased if she seems to crave more than she is getting, and a meal of canned milk (mixed with an equal amount of water) should be introduced. If she is fed just once a day, add another meal rather than overload her with too much at one time. If twice a day is her schedule, then a bit more food can be added to each feeding.

A week before the pups are due, your bitch should be introduced to her whelping box so that she will be accustomed to it and feel at home there when the puppies arrive. She should be encouraged to sleep there but permitted to come and go as she wishes. The box should be roomy enough for her to lie down and stretch out in but not too large, lest the pups have more room than is needed in which to roam and possibly get chilled by going too far away from their mother. Be sure that the box has a "pig rail"; this will prevent the puppies from being crushed against the sides. The room in which the box is placed, either in your home or in the kennel, should be kept at about 70 degrees Fahrenheit. In winter it may be necessary to have an infrared lamp over the whelping box, in which case be careful not to place it too low or close to the puppies.

Newspapers will become a very important commodity, so start collecting them well in advance to have a big pile handy for the whelping box. With a litter of puppies, one never seems to have papers enough, so the higher the pile to start with, the better off you will be. Other necessities for whelping time are clean, soft turkish towels, scissors, and a bottle of alcohol.

You will know that her time is very near when your bitch becomes restless, wandering in and out of her box and out of the room. She may refuse food, and at that point her temperature will start to drop. She will dig at and tear up the newspapers in her box, shiver, and generally look uncomfortable. Only you should be with your bitch at this time. She does not need

Tasmon's DaHanna Luger. By Ciddo v. Schwetzinger, SchH. III, ex Baruki's DaHamma. Owned by Tasmon's Kennels, Brazil.

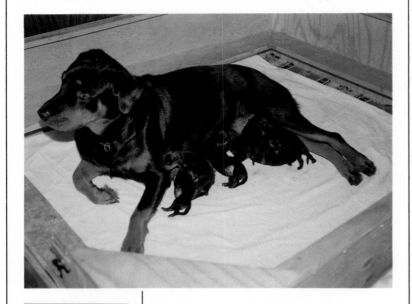

Above: Ch. Katryn the Great von Ursa, C.D.X., with one of her families. This lovely bitch is owned by Zornhaus Rottweilers, Wilton Manors, FL.
Below: The future Am., Can. Ch. Von Worley's Alexander, Am., Can. C.D., with brother Panzer. Owners, D. and J. Worley.

spectators; and several people hanging over her, even though they may be family members whom she knows, may upset her to the point where she may harm the puppies. You should remain nearby, quietly watching, not fussing or hovering; speak calmly and frequently to her to instill confidence. Eventually she will settle down in her box and

begin panting; contractions will follow. Soon thereafter a puppy will start to emerge, sliding out with the contractions. The mother immediately should open the sac, sever the cord with her teeth, and then clean up the puppy. She will also eat the placenta, which you should permit. Once the puppy is cleaned, it should be placed next to the bitch unless she is showing signs of having the next one immediately. Almost at once the puppy will start looking for a nipple on which to nurse, and you should ascertain that it is able to latch on successfully.

If the puppy is a breech (*i.e.,* born feet first), you must watch carefully for it to be completely delivered as quickly as possible and for the sac to be removed quickly so that the puppy does not drown. Sometimes even a normally positioned birth will seem extremely slow in coming. Should this occur, you might take a clean towel, and as the bitch contracts, pull the puppy out, doing so gently and with utmost care. If, once the puppy is delivered, it shows little signs of life, take a rough turkish towel and massage the puppy's chest by rubbing quite briskly back and forth. Continue this for about fifteen minutes, and be sure that the mouth is free of liquid. It may be necessary to try mouth-to-mouth breathing, which is begun by pressing the puppy's jaws open and, using a finger, depressing the tongue which may be stuck to the roof of the mouth. Then place your mouth against the puppy's and blow hard down the puppy's throat. Rub the puppy's chest with the towel again and try artificial respiration, pressing the sides of the chest together slowly and rhythmically—in and out, in and out. Keep trying one method or the other for at least twenty minutes before giving up. You may be rewarded with a live puppy who otherwise would not have made it.

If you are successful in bringing the puppy around, do not immediately put it back with the mother as it should be kept extra

warm. Put it in a cardboard box on an electric heating pad or, if it is the time of year when your heat is running, near a radiator or near the fireplace or stove. As soon as the rest of the litter has been born, it then can join the others.

An hour or more may elapse between puppies, which is fine so long as the bitch seems comfortable and is neither straining nor contracting. She should not be permitted to remain unassisted for more than an hour if she does continue to contract. This is when you should get her to your veterinarian, whom you should already have alerted to the possibility of a problem existing. He should examine her and perhaps give her a shot of Pituitrin. In some cases the veterinarian may find that a Caesarean section is necessary due to a puppy being lodged in a manner making normal delivery impossible. Sometimes this is caused by an abnormally large puppy, or it may just be that the puppy is simply turned in the wrong position. If the bitch does require a Caesarean section, the puppies already born must be kept warm in their cardboard box with a heating pad under the box.

Once the section is done, get the bitch and the puppies home. Do not attempt to put the puppies in with the bitch until she has regained consciousness, as she may unknowingly hurt them. But do get them back to her as soon as possible for them to start nursing.

Should the mother lack milk at this time, the puppies must be fed by hand, kept very warm, and held onto the mother's teats several times a day in order to stimulate and encourage the secretion of milk, which should start shortly.

Assuming that there has been no problem and that the bitch has whelped naturally, you should insist that she go out to exercise, staying just long enough to make herself comfortable. She can be offered a bowl of milk and a biscuit, but then she should settle down with her family. Freshen the whelping box for her with

newspapers while she is taking this respite so that she and the puppies will have a clean bed.

Unless some problem arises, there is little you must do for the puppies until they become three to four weeks old. Keep the box clean and supplied with fresh newspapers the first few days, but then turkish towels should be tacked down to the bottom of the box so that the puppies will have traction as they move about.

If the bitch has difficulties with her milk supply, or if you should be so unfortunate as to lose her, then you must be prepared to either hand-feed or tube-feed the puppies if they are to survive. Tube-feeding is so much faster and easier. If the

Southwind Dempsey of True Lee, son of Ch. Altar's Gunner of Woodland ex Ashby v. Foxcroft, C.D. Bred by Lee McKenney. Owned by Priscilla Drake Qua, Khetaqua Kennels, Center Ossipee, NH.

Nacht Music von Siegerhaus, Am., Can. C.D., with her first (and only) litter. Roma Rottweilers, Gary and Roberta Martin, Chico, CA.

bitch is available, it is best that she continues to clean and care for the puppies in the normal manner, excepting for the food supplements you will provide. If it is impossible for her to do this, then after every feeding you must gently rub each puppy's abdomen with wet cotton to make it urinate, and the rectum should be gently rubbed to open the bowels.

Newborn puppies must be fed every three to four hours around the clock. The puppies must be kept warm during this time. Have your veterinarian teach you how to tube-feed. You will find that it is really quite simple.

After a normal whelping, the bitch will require additional food to enable her to produce sufficient milk. In addition to being fed twice daily, she should be given some canned milk several times each day.

When the puppies are two weeks old, their nails should be clipped, as they are needle sharp at this age and can hurt or damage the mother's teats and stomach as the pups hold on to nurse.

Between three and four weeks of age, the puppies should begin to be weaned. Scraped beef (prepared by scraping it off slices of beef with a spoon so that none of the gristle is

included) may be offered in very small quantities a couple of times daily for the first few days. Then by the third day you can mix puppy chow with warm water as directed on the package, offering it four times daily. By now the mother should be kept away from the puppies and out of the box for several hours at a time so that when they have reached five weeks of age she is left in with them only overnight. By the time the puppies are six weeks old, they should be entirely weaned and receiving only occasional visits from their mother.

Most veterinarians recommend a temporary DHL (distemper, hepatitis, leptospirosis) shot when the puppies are six weeks of age. This remains effective for about two weeks. Then at eight weeks of age, the puppies should receive the series of permanent shots for DHL protection. It is also a good idea to discuss with your vet the advisability of having your puppies inoculated against the dreaded parvovirus at the same time. Each time the pups go to the vet for shots, you should bring stool samples so that they can be examined for worms. Worms go through various stages of development and may be present in a stool sample even though the sample does not test positive in every checkup. So do not neglect to keep careful watch on this.

The puppies should be fed four times daily until they are three months old. Then you can cut back to three feedings daily. By the time the puppies are six months of age, two meals daily are sufficient. Some people feed their dogs twice daily throughout their lifetime; others go to one meal daily when the puppy becomes one year of age.

The ideal age for puppies to go to their new homes is between eight and twelve weeks, although some puppies successfully adjust to a new home when they are six weeks old. Be sure that they go to their new owners accompanied by a description of the diet you've been feeding them and a schedule of the shots they have already received and those they still need. These should be included with the registration application and a copy of the pedigree.

SOME REMARKS ABOUT PARVO

Rottweilers are strong, healthy dogs who would seem likely to have few problems with health. Yet it has struck me with considerable impact that a very great number of Rottweiler puppies and young dogs lose their lives at an early age due to parvovirus.

It would hardly seem fair to say that they are more susceptible to this dread disease than other breeds, for after all why *should* that be the case? Yet, when working on the kennel stories I have been electrified by the frequency with which losses from parvo have been noted.

Since Rotties do seem to be especially susceptible to this very serious disease, I am including a resume of the advisable innoculation schedule for your puppies with vaccine information. *Please do not be neglectful.* Someone who is new to puppy ownership or who has never had the misfortune and the heartbreak of an encounter with this illness may not quite realize the seriousness of it, and it is to them that this is particularly directed in the hope of helping them to avoid the sadness of losing a single puppy.

It has been discovered that weak immune systems in Rottweilers (Doberman Pinschers, too, we understand) cause these lovely dogs to be especially susceptible to virus-related illnesses. Therefore, added protection should be given to your Rottweiler puppy.

A wise schedule begins vaccination at age eight weeks, repeated every three weeks, until the puppy is 17 weeks old. The dog then should be vaccinated at six-month intervals until it reaches two years of age, by which time its immune system should be fully functioning.

We have also learned that one reason so many vaccinated dogs are proving unprotected, despite their vaccination record, is the presence of a recently discovered mutant virus, against which the formerly used vaccines are proving ineffective. Now, to handle this virus, a new vaccine has been developed at Fort Dodge

laboratory. This new vaccine provides cross protection (protection from all presently existing forms of the virus) and is proving highly successful. We have learned from a highly knowledgeable authority that this new vaccine should be used to achieve optimum protection from the dreaded parvovirus. The name of this vaccine is KF11. It is a modified live virus and has been found more effective than any killed virus to date. Do consult with your veterinarian about this new vaccine, which has already well proven its worth.

Von Gailingen's "M" litter at age 4 months. Bred and owned by C.M. Thompson.

Above: Von Gailingen's Matinee Idol, Am., Can. C.D., going Best in Sweepstakes at the 1988 National under celebrated breeder-judge Mrs. Dorothea M. Gruenerwald. Owner, C.M. Thompson.
Below: Half-sisters: Seren's Holiday Magic v. Ara and Landgrave Stella v. Brabant placing at the A.R.C. National Specialty 1988.

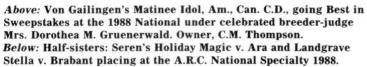

Top: Antren's Bustin' Loose taking Best of Winners at Wallkill, NY, handled by Karen DiCicco, Antren Rottweilers, Lynbrook, NY.
Bottom: Apache Hill's Calendar Girl, owned by Mike Winters and Irene F. Castillo. By Am., Can. Ch. Rodsden's Berte v. Zederwald, C.D.X., from Ch. Excalibur's B Apache War Song, C.D.

386

The Making of a Show Dog

If you have decided to become a show dog exhibitor, you have accepted a very real and very exciting challenge. The groundwork has been accomplished with the selection of your future show prospect. If you have purchased a puppy, it is assumed that you have gone through all the proper preliminaries concerning good care, which should be the same if the puppy is a pet or future show dog, with a few added precautions for the latter.

GENERAL CONSIDERATIONS

Remember the importance of keeping your future winner in trim, top condition. Since you want him neither too fat nor too thin, his appetite for his proper diet should be guarded, and children and guests should not be permitted to constantly feed him "goodies." The best treat of all is a small wad of raw ground beef or a packaged dog treat. To be avoided are ice cream, cake, cookies, potato chips, and other fattening items which will cause the dog to put on weight and may additionally spoil his appetite for the proper, nourishing, well-balanced diet so essential to good health and condition.

The importance of temperament and showmanship cannot possibly be overestimated. They have put many a mediocre dog across, while lack of them can ruin the career of an otherwise outstanding specimen. From the day your dog joins your family, socialize him. Keep him accustomed to being with people and to being handled by people. Encourage your friends and relatives to "go over" him as the judges will in the ring so this will not seem a strange and upsetting experience. Practice showing his "bite" (the manner in which his teeth meet) quickly and deftly. It is quite simple to slip the lips apart with your fingers, and the puppy should be willing to accept this from you or the judge without struggle.

Most judges prefer that the exhibitors display the dog's bite and other mouth features themselves, which is sensible considering the missing teeth disqualification. Judging includes a careful look at the back of the mouth and the proper observation of the "bite." There have been incidences where judges have been bitten; this should always be guarded against by the exhibitor. But the old-fashioned judges still persist in doing it themselves, so the dog should be ready for either possibility.

Take your future show dog with

"The importance of temperament and showmanship cannot possibly be overestimated. They have put many a mediocre dog across, while lack of them can ruin the career of an otherwise outstanding specimen."

Gaines
Presents
The 1988 United States
Western Regional
Dog Obedience Championship
in conjunction with
The Pacific Obedience Association
3

Gaines
Western
Regional
1988

Above:
Langhoffen's Esse, C.D.X., H.I.C., T.D.I., earned an average score at Gaines of 195.5. Bred by Coco Steinford, from Ch. Alexandros G. Broadway ex Langhoffen's Camber, C.D.X., T.D. Owned and trained by Sandy Peppers-Phillips.
Right: **Grunhaus Rottweilers: Harmony Marie, Havanna v. Jansen, and Izadora.** Owner, Danielle Greene.

things with which he will come in contact at dog shows, so it is wiser to keep him up-to-date on all protective shots and then let him become accustomed to being among dogs and dog owners. Also, a dog who is never among strange people, in strange places, or among strange dogs may grow up with a shyness or timidity of spirit that will cause you real problems as his show career draws near.

Keep your show prospect's coat in immaculate condition with frequent grooming and daily brushing. When bathing is necessary, use a mild dog shampoo or whatever the breeder of your puppy may suggest. Several of the brand-name products do an excellent job. Be sure to rinse thoroughly so as not to risk skin irritation by traces of soap left behind, and protect against soap entering the eyes by a drop of castor oil in each before you lather up. Use warm water (be sure it is not uncomfortably hot or chillingly cold) and a good spray. Make certain you allow your dog to dry thoroughly in a warm, draft-free area (or outdoors, if it is warm and sunny) so that he doesn't catch cold. Then proceed to groom him to perfection.

A show dog's teeth must be kept clean and free of tartar. Hard dog

you in the car, thus accustoming him to riding so that he will not become carsick on the day of a dog show. He should associate pleasure and attention with going in the car, van, or motor home. Take him where it is crowded: downtown, to the shops, everywhere you go that dogs are permitted. Make the expeditions fun for him by frequent petting and words of praise; do not just ignore him as you go about your errands.

Do not overly shelter your future show dog. Instinctively you may want to keep him at home where he is safe from germs or danger. This can be foolish on two counts. The first reason is that a puppy kept away from other dogs builds up no natural immunity against all the

information of this type with you.

Accustom your show dog to being in a crate (which you should be doing with a pet dog as well). He should relax in his crate at the shows "between times" for his own well-being and safety.

MATCH SHOWS

Your show dog's initial experience in the ring should be in match show competition. This type of event is intended as a learning experience for both the dog and the exhibitor. You will not feel embarrassed or out of place no matter how poorly your puppy may behave or how inept your attempts at handling may be, as you will find

Left: Ch. Apache Hill's Peyote Odyssey, C.D., T.T., bred and owned by Apache Hill. *Below:* Connie's Rana von Ursa, by Am., Can. Ch. Bryloukis Great Expectations, C.D., ex Connie's Wilderness Ursa, C.D. Breeder and owner, Connie T. Thomas.

biscuits can help toward this, but if tartar accumulates, see that it is removed promptly by your veterinarian. Bones for chewing are not suitable for show dogs as they tend to damage and wear down the tooth enamel.

Assuming that you will be handling the dog yourself, or even if he will be professionally handled, a few moments each day of dog show routine is important. Practice setting him up as you have seen the exhibitors do at the shows you've attended, and teach him to hold this position once you have him stacked to your satisfaction. Make the learning period pleasant by being firm but lavish in your praise when he responds correctly. Teach him to gait at your side at a moderate rate on a loose lead. When you have mastered the basic essentials at home, then hunt out and join a training class for future work. Training classes are sponsored by show-giving clubs in many areas, and their popularity is steadily increasing. If you have no other way of locating one, perhaps your veterinarian would know of one through some of his other clients; but if you are sufficiently aware of the dog show world to want a show dog, you will probably be personally acquainted with other people who will share

others there with the same type of problems. The important thing is that you get the puppy out and into a show ring where the two of you can practice together and learn the ropes. It is foolish to spend the higher entry fees on point shows for an untrained youngster.

POINT SHOWS

Entries for American Kennel Club point shows must be made in advance. This must be done on an official entry blank of the show-giving club. The entry must then be filed either personally or by mail with the show superintendent or the show secretary (if the event is being run by the club members alone and a superintendent has not been hired, this information will

Right: Three top placements in the Puppy Class to litter sisters by Brando vom Dattelner Hof ex Lyndale's Cindy Vondez. Owner, Lana Young. *Below:* The great Am., Can. Ch. Noblehaus Explorer, T.T., receiving Award of Merit. Bred and owned by Mark Schwartz.

appear on the premium list) in time to reach its destination prior to the published closing date or filling of the quota. These entries must be made carefully, must be signed by the owner of the dog or the owner's agent (your professional handler), and must be accompanied by the entry fee; otherwise they will not be accepted. Remember that it is not when the entry leaves your hands that counts, but the date of arrival at its destination. If you are relying on the mails, which are not always dependable, get the entry off well before the deadline to avoid disappointment.

A dog must be entered at a dog show in the name of the actual owner at the time of the entry closing date of that specific show. If a registered dog has been acquired by a new owner, it must be entered in the name of the new owner in any show for which entries close after the date of acquirement, regardless of whether the new owner has or has not actually received the registration certificate indicating that the dog is recorded in his name. State on the entry form whether or not transfer application has been mailed to the American Kennel Club, and it goes without saying that the latter should be attended to promptly when you purchase a registered dog.

In filling out your entry blank, type, print, or write clearly, paying particular attention to the spelling of names, correct registration numbers, and so on. Also, if there is more than one variety in your breed, be sure to indicate into which category your dog is being entered.

The **Puppy Class** is for dogs or bitches who are six months of age and under twelve months and who are not champions. The age of a dog shall be calculated up to and inclusive of the first day of a show. For example, the first day a dog whelped on January 1st is eligible to compete in a Puppy Class at a show is July 1st of the same year; and he may continue to compete in Puppy Classes up to and including a show on December 31 of the same year, but he is *not* eligible to compete in a Puppy Class at a show held on or after January 1 of the following year.

The Puppy Class is the first one in which you should enter your puppy. In it a certain allowance will be made for the fact that they *are* puppies, thus an immature dog or one displaying less than perfect showmanship will be less severely penalized than, for instance, would

Top: Ch. Powderhorn's Clu of Wencrest, owned by Angie Grimldi and Powderhorn/Wencrest Rottweilers, Inc. *Middle:* Am., Can. Ch., Can. OTCH, Winterhawk's Chief Justice, won all his titles handled by owner Jane Justice. *Bottom:* Select Am., Can. Ch. Goldeiche Ara von Brader, Am., Can. C.D. owned by Dale and Karen Innocenti; and Select Am., Can., Ch. Von Bruka Fiona, bred and owned by Bruce and Karen Billings. Both received "Select" designation at the 1987 A.R.C. National Specialty.

Above:
Roberta's Buddy De Pattiz, Am., Can. C.D.X., Am. T.D. Owners, Gary and Roberta Martin.

be the case in Open. It is also quite likely that others in the class will be suffering from these problems, too. When you enter a puppy, be sure to check the classification with care, as some shows divide their Puppy Class into a 6-9 months old section and a 9-12 months old section.

The **Novice Class** is for dogs six months of age and over, whelped in the United States or Canada, who *prior to the official closing date for entries* have *not* won three first prizes in the Novice Class, any first prize at all in the Bred-by-Exhibitor, American-bred, or Open Classes, or one or more points toward championship. The provisions for this class are

confusing to many people, which is probably the reason exhibitors do not enter in it more frequently. A dog may win any number of first prizes in the Puppy Class and still retain his eligibility for Novice. He may place second, third, or fourth not only in Novice on an unlimited number of occasions, but also in Bred-by-Exhibitor, American-bred and Open and still remain eligible for Novice. But he may no longer be shown in Novice when he has won three blue ribbons in that class, when he has won even one blue ribbon in either Bred-by-Exhibitor, American-bred, or Open, or when he has won a single championship point.

In determining whether or not a dog is eligible for the Novice Class, keep in mind the fact that previous wins are calculated according to the official published date for closing of entries, not by the date on which you may actually have made the entry. So if in the interim, between the time you made the entry and the official closing date, your dog makes a win causing him to become ineligible for Novice, change your class *immediately* to another for which he will be eligible, preferably either Bred-by-Exhibitor or American-bred. To do this, you must contact the show's superintendent or secretary, at first by telephone to save time and then in writing to confirm it. The Novice Class always seems to have the fewest entries of any class, and therefore it is a splendid "practice ground" for you and your young dog while you are getting the "feel" of being in the ring.

Bred-by-Exhibitor Class is for dogs whelped in the United States or, if individually registered in the American Kennel Club Stud Book, for dogs whelped in Canada who are six months of age or older, are not champions, and are owned wholly or in part by the person or by the spouse of the person who was the breeder or one of the breeders of record. Dogs entered in this class must be handled in the class by an owner or by a member of the immediate family of the owner. Members of an immediate family for this purpose are husband, wife, father, mother, son, daughter, brother, or sister. This is the class which is really the "breeders' showcase," and the one which breeders should enter with particular pride to show off their achievements.

The **American-bred Class** is for all dogs excepting champions, six months of age or older, who were whelped in the United States by reason of a mating which took place in the United States.

The **Open Class** is for any dog six months of age or older (this is the only restriction for this class). Dogs with championship points compete in it, dogs who are already champions are eligible to do so, dogs who are imported can be entered, and, of course, American-bred dogs compete in it. This class is, for some strange reason, the favorite of exhibitors who are "out to win." They rush to enter their pointed dogs in it, under the false impression that by doing so they assure themselves of greater attention from the judges. This really is not so, and some people feel that to enter in one of the less competitive classes, with a better chance of winning it and thus

earning a second opportunity of gaining the judge's approval by returning to the ring in the Winners Class, can often be a more effective strategy.

One does not enter the **Winners Class.** One earns the right to compete in it by winning first prize in Puppy, Novice, Bred-by-Exhibitor, American-bred, or Open. No dog who has been defeated on the same day in one of these classes is eligible to compete for Winners, and every dog who has been a blue-ribbon winner in one of them and not defeated in another, should he have been entered in more than one class (as occasionally happens), *must* do so. Following the selection of the

Above: Thatcher von Trostheim, by Am., Can. Ch. Harras vom Sachsen ex Strudel von Trostheim, handled by Patti Holt for owner Sharon Alkus. *Left:* Rosendorn's Notorious, T.T., was bred by Johann Emedi and is owned by John and Teresa Petzold.

NEW C.D.X.

TRUCKEE MEADOWS
SEPT 1987 FOX & COOK
VICKY 408-728-3787

Am., Can. Ch. Roberta's Buddy De Pattiz, Am., Can. C.D.X., Am. T.T. Owned by Gary and Roberta Martin.

championship points.

Winners Dog and Winners Bitch are the awards which carry points toward championship with them. The points are based on the number of dogs or bitches actually in competition, and the points are scaled one through five, the latter being the greatest number available to any one dog or bitch at any one show. Three-, four-, or five-point wins are considered majors. In order to become a champion, a dog or bitch must have won two majors under two different judges, plus at least one point from a third judge, and the additional points necessary to bring the total to fifteen. When your dog has gained fifteen points as described above, a championship certificate will be issued to you, and your dog's name will be published in the champions of record list in the *Pure-Bred Dogs/American Kennel Gazette*, the official publication of the American Kennel Club.

The scale of championship points for each breed is worked out by the American Kennel Club and reviewed annually, at which time the number required in competition may be either changed (raised or lowered) or remain the same. The scale of championship points for all breeds is published annually in the May issue of the *Gazette*, and the current ratings for each breed within that area are published in every show catalog.

When a dog or bitch is adjudged Best of Winners, its championship points are, for that show, compiled on the basis of which sex had the greater number of points. If there are two points in dogs and four in bitches and the dog goes Best of Winners, then *both* the dog and the bitch are awarded an equal number of points, in this case four. Should the Winners Dog or the Winners Bitch go on to win Best of Breed or Best of Variety, additional points are accorded for the additional dogs and bitches defeated by so doing, provided, of course, that there were entries specifically for Best of Breed competition or Specials, as these

Winners Dog or the Winners Bitch, the dog or bitch receiving that award leaves the ring. Then the dog or bitch who placed second in that class, unless previously beaten by another dog or bitch in another class at the same show, re-enters the ring to compete against the remaining first-prize winners for Reserve. The latter award indicates that the dog or bitch selected for it is standing "in reserve" should the one who received Winners be disqualified or declared ineligible through any technicality when the awards are checked at the American Kennel Club. In that case, the one who placed Reserve is moved up to Winners, at the same time receiving the appropriate

specific entries are generally called.

If your dog or bitch takes Best of Opposite Sex after going Winners, points are credited according to the number of the same sex defeated in both the regular classes and Specials competition. If Best of Winners is also won, then whatever additional points for each of these awards are available will be credited. Many a one- or two-point win has grown into a major in this manner.

Moving further along, should your dog win its **Variety Group** from the classes (in other words, if it has taken either Winners Dog or Winners Bitch), you then receive points based on the greatest number of points awarded to any member of any breed included within that Group during that show's competition. Should the day's winning also include Best in Show, the same rule of thumb applies, and your dog or bitch receives the highest number of points awarded to any other dog of any breed at that event.

Best of Breed competition consists of the Winners Dog and the Winners Bitch, who automatically compete on the strength of those awards, in addition to whatever dogs and bitches have been entered specifically for this class for which champions of record are eligible. Since July 1980, dogs who, according to their owner's records, have completed the requirements for a championship after the closing of entries for the show (but whose championships are unconfirmed) may be transferred from one of the regular classes to the Best of Breed competition, provided this transfer is made by the show superintendent or show secretary *prior to the start of any judging at the show.*

This has proved an extremely popular new rule, as under it a dog can finish on Saturday and then be transferred and compete as a Special on Sunday. It must be emphasized that *the change must be made prior to the start of any part of*

Above: Littermates Ch. Von Hawthorne's Max Otto-C and Von Hawthorne's Brutus-C combine for Best of Breed and Best of Winners. Owner, Alice J. Hahn.
Below: Tonka Bear taking second in Novice Obedience class with a qualifying 194.5. Owners, Jon and Caron Rosender.

BEST of BREED
COLUMBIANA
COUNTY K C INC
B.KURTIS   JUNE 1987

Above: Ch. Myran's Excalibur, owned by Brenda and John Jayne and Mike and Pam Donley, is by Ch. Birch Hill's Minuteman, C.D., ex Rhoda Dolli vom Nordon, C.D. Bred by Dawn Lawver. *Right:* Ch. Von Hottenstein's Fandango ranked No. 2 Bitch, A.R.C. System, for 1988. Owner, Charles Williams, Jr., and Barbara Ester.

Non-regular classes are sometimes included at the all-breed shows, and they are almost invariably included at Specialty shows. These include Stud Dog Class and Brood Bitch Class, which are judged on the basis of the quality of the two offspring accompanying the sire or dam. The quality of the latter two is beside the point and should not be considered by the judge; it is the youngsters who count, and the quality of *both* are to be averaged to decide which sire or dam is the best and most consistent producer. Then there is the Brace Class (which, at all-breed shows, moves up to Best Brace in each Variety Group and then Best Brace in Show) which is judged on the similarity and evenness of appearance of the two brace members. In other words, the two dogs should look like identical twins in size, color, and conformation and should move together almost as a single dog, one person handling with precision and ease. The same applies to the Team Class competition, except that four dogs are involved and, if necessary, two handlers.

The Veterans Class is for the older dog, the minimum age of whom is seven years. This class is

the day's judging, not for just your individual breed.

In the United States, Best of Breed winners are entitled to compete in the Variety Group which includes them. This is not mandatory; it is a privilege which exhibitors value. (In Canada, Best of Breed winners *must* compete in the Variety Group or they lose any points already won.) The dogs winning *first* in each of the seven Variety Groups *must* compete for Best in Show. Missing the opportunity of taking your dog in for competition in its Group is foolish, as it is there where the general public is most likely to notice your breed and become interested in learning about it.

judged on the quality of the dogs, as the winner competes in Best of Breed competition and has, on a respectable number of occasions, been known to take that top award. So the point is *not* to pick out the oldest dog, as some judges seem to believe, but the best specimen of the breed, exactly as in the regular classes.

Then there are Sweepstakes and Futurity Stakes sponsored by many Specialty clubs, sometimes as part of their regular Specialty shows and sometimes as separate events on an entirely different occasion. The difference between the two stakes is that Sweepstakes entries usually include dogs from six to eighteen months of age with entries made at the same time as the others for the show, while for a Futurity the entries are bitches nominated when bred and the individual puppies entered at or shortly following their birth.

JUNIOR SHOWMANSHIP COMPETITION

Entry in Junior Showmanship Classes is open to any boy or girl who is at least ten years old and under seventeen years old on the day of the show. The Novice Junior Showmanship Class is open to youngsters who have not already won, at the time the entries close, three firsts in this class. Youngsters who have won three firsts in Novice may compete in the Open Junior Showmanship Class. Any junior handler who wins his third first-place award in Novice may participate in the Open Class at the same show, provided that the Open Class has at least one other junior handler entered and competing in it that day. The Novice and Open Classes may be divided into Junior and Senior Classes. Youngsters between the ages of ten and twelve, inclusively, are eligible for the Junior division; and youngsters between thirteen and seventeen, inclusively, are eligible for the Senior division.

Any of the foregoing classes may be separated into individual classes for boys and for girls. If

such a division is made, it must be so indicated on the premium list. The premium list also indicates the prize for Best Junior Handler, if such a prize is being offered at the show. Any youngster who wins a first in any of the regular classes may enter the competition for this prize, provided the youngster has been undefeated in any other Junior Showmanship Class at that show.

Junior Showmanship Classes, unlike regular conformation classes in which the quality of the dog is judged, are judged solely on the skill and ability of the junior handling the dog. Which dog is best is not the point—it is which youngster does the best job with the dog that is under consideration. Eligibility requirements for the dog being shown in Junior Showmanship, and other detailed information, can be found in *Regulations for Junior Showmanship*, available from the American Kennel Club.

A junior who has a dog that he or she can enter in both Junior Showmanship and conformation classes has twice the opportunity for success and twice the opportunity to get into the ring and

Chirlyn's Any Day Now, by Ch. Razdy's Akemo Grandem C.D., ex Ch. Darby's Solitaire vom Meadow, taking Reserve Winners from the Puppy Bitch Class. Breeder-owner, Sheena R. Marchand.

Ch. Misty Lakes Awol Kid, handled exclusively by Gwendolyn Wolforth. Owned by Eric Jimenez, M.D., and Amelia M. Jimeniz.

work with the dog, a combination which can lead to not only awards for expert handling, but also, if the dog is of sufficient quality, for making a conformation champion.

PRE-SHOW PREPARATIONS

Preparation of the items you will need as a dog show exhibitor should not be left until the last moment. They should be planned and arranged several days in advance of the show in order for you to remain calm and relaxed as the countdown starts.

The importance of the crate has already been mentioned and should already be part of your equipment. Of equal importance is the grooming table, which very likely you have also already acquired for use at home. You should take it along with you to the shows, as your dog will need last minute touches before entering the ring. Should you have not yet made this purchase, folding tables with rubber tops are made specifically for this purpose and can be purchased at most dog shows, where concession booths with marvelous assortments of "doggy" necessities are to be found, or at your pet supplier. You will also need a sturdy tack box (also available at the dog show concessions) in which to carry your grooming tools and equipment. The latter should include: brushes; combs; scissors; nail clippers; whatever you use for last minute clean-up jobs; cotton swabs; first-aid equipment; and anything you are in the habit of using on the dog, including a leash or two of the type you prefer, some well-cooked and dried-out liver or any of the small packaged "dog treats" for use as bait in the ring, an atomizer in case you wish to dampen your dog's coat when you are preparing him for the ring, and so on. A large turkish towel to spread under the dog on the grooming table is also useful.

Take a large thermos or cooler of ice, the biggest one you can accommodate in your vehicle, for use by "man and beast." Take a jug of water (there are lightweight, inexpensive ones available at all sporting goods shops) and a water dish. If you plan to feed the dog at the show, or if you and the dog will be away from home more than one day, bring food for him from home so that he will have the type to which he is accustomed.

You may or may not have an exercise pen. While the shows do provide areas for exercise of the dogs, these are among the most likely places to have your dog come in contact with any illnesses which may be going around, and having a pen of your own for your dog's use is excellent protection. Such a pen comes in handy while you're traveling; since it is roomier than a crate, it becomes a comfortable place for your dog to relax and move around in, especially when you're at motels or rest stops. These pens are available at the show concession stands and come in a variety of heights and sizes. A set of "pooper scoopers" should also be part of your equipment, along with a package of plastic bags for cleaning up after your dog.

Bring along folding chairs for the members of your party, unless all of you are fond of standing, as these are almost never provided by the clubs. Have your name stamped on the chairs so that there will be no doubt as to whom the chairs belong. Bring whatever you and your family enjoy for drinks or snacks in a picnic basket or cooler, as show food, in general, is expensive and usually not great. You should always have a pair of boots, a raincoat, and a rain hat with you (they should remain permanently in your vehicle if you plan to attend shows regularly), as well as a sweater, a warm coat, and a change of shoes. A smock or big cover-up apron will assure that you remain tidy as you prepare the dog for the ring. Your overnight case should include a small sewing kit for emergency repairs, bandaids, headache and indigestion remedies, and any personal products or medications you normally use.

In your car, you should always carry maps of the area where you are headed and an assortment of motel directories. Generally speaking, Holiday Inns have been found to be the nicest about taking dogs. Ramadas and Howard Johnsons generally do so cheerfully (with a few exceptions).

Have everything prepared the night before the show to expedite your departure. Be sure that the dog's identification and your judging program and other show information are in your purse or briefcase. If you are taking sandwiches, have them ready. Anything that goes into the car the night before the show will be one thing less to remember in the morning. Decide upon what you will wear and have it out and

ready. If there is any question in your mind about what to wear, try on the possibilities before the day of the show; don't risk feeling you may want to change when you see yourself dressed a few moments prior to departure time!

In planning your outfit, make it something simple that will not detract from your dog. Remember that a dark dog silhouettes attractively against a light background and vice-versa. Sport clothes always seem to look best at dog shows, preferably conservative in type and not overly "loud" as you do not want to detract from your dog, who should be the focus of interest at this point. What you wear on your feet is important.

Antren's Broadway Rhythm taking a 4-point major at Westchester K.C., handled by Karen DiCicco, Antren Rottweilers.

Many types of flooring can be hazardously slippery, as can wet grass. Make it a habit to wear rubber soles and low or flat heels in the ring for your own safety, especially if you are showing a dog that likes to move out smartly.

Your final step in pre-show preparation is to leave yourself plenty of time to reach the show that morning. Traffic can get amazingly heavy as one nears the immediate area of the show, finding a parking place can be difficult, and other delays may occur. You'll be in better humor to enjoy the day if your trip to the show is not fraught with panic over fear of not arriving in time!

THE DOG SHOW

Always show your dog with an air of pride. If you make mistakes in presenting him, don't worry about it. Next time you will do better. Do not permit the presence of more experienced exhibitors to intimidate you. After all, they, too, were once newcomers.

The judging routine usually starts when the judge asks that the dogs be gaited in a circle around the ring. During this period the judge is watching each dog as it moves, noting style, topline, reach and drive, head and tail carriage, and general balance. Keep your mind and your eye on your dog, moving him at his most becoming gait and keeping your place in line without coming too close to the exhibitor ahead of you. Always keep your dog on the inside of the circle, between yourself and the judge, so that the judge's view of the dog is unobstructed.

Calmly pose the dog when

Top: **Way-Mar's Rocky Raccoon, U.D., T.T., is a son of Ch., OTCh. Roger's Summer Thunder ex Ch. Way-Mar's Disco Dawg. Owner, Barbara Kiefer.**
Middle: **Der Fruchtwald DD Bernherdt and Der Fruchtwald Barouka. Co-owners, Janice Lynch and Barbara and Bill Baker.**
Bottom: **Von Hottenstein's Heartbreaker, by Am., Can. Ch. Trifecta's Barbarian v. Murph, C.D. Owner Nancy Reynolds. Co-owner, Nancy Quail.**

requested to set up for examination. If you are at the head of the line and many dogs are in the class, go all the way to the end of the ring before starting to stack the dog, leaving sufficient space for those behind you to line theirs up as well, as requested by the judge. If you are not at the head of the line but between other exhibitors, leave sufficient space ahead of your dog for the judge to examine him. The dogs should be spaced so that the judge is able to move among them to see them from all angles. In practicing to "set up" or "stack" your dog for the judge's examination, bear in mind the importance of doing so quickly and with dexterity. The judge has a schedule to meet and only a few moments in which to evaluate each dog. You will immeasurably help yours to make a favorable impression if you are able to "get it all together" in a minimum amount of time. Practice at home before a mirror can be a great help toward bringing this about, facing the dog so that you see him from the same side that the judge will and working to make him look right in the shortest length of time.

Listen carefully as the judge describes the manner in which the dog is to be gaited, whether it is straight down and straight back; down the ring, across, and back; or in a triangle. "In a triangle" means the dog should move down the outer side of the ring to the first corner, across that end of the ring to the second corner, and then back to the judge from the second corner, using the center of the ring in a diagonal line. Judges like to see the dog in an uninterrupted triangle, as they are thus able to get a better idea of the dog's gait.

It is impossible to overemphasize that the gait at which you move your dog is tremendously important and considerable study and thought should be given to the matter. At home, have someone move the dog for you at different speeds so that you can tell which shows him off to best advantage. The most becoming

action almost invariably is seen at a moderate gait, head up and topline holding. Do not gallop your dog around the ring or hurry him into a speed atypical of his breed. Nothing being rushed appears at its best; give your dog a chance to move along at his (and the breed's) natural gait. For a dog's action to be judged accurately, that dog should move with strength and power, but not excessive speed, holding a straight line as he goes to and from the judge.

As you bring the dog back to the judge, stop him a few feet away and be sure that he is standing in a becoming position. Bait him to show the judge an alert expression, using whatever tasty morsel he has been trained to expect for this purpose or, if that works better for you, use a small squeak-toy in your hand. A reminder, please, to those using liver or treats: take them with you when you leave the ring. Do not just drop them on the ground where they will be found by another dog.

True Lee's Shining Star, C.D., T.T., by True Lee's Shenendoah ex True Lee's Fair Exchange, owned by Bob Condon, taking an Obedience placement at Providence County.

Top: Family portrait. Am., Can. Ch. Von Bruka Indra v. Yden, Am., Can. C.D., T.T., winning Brood Bitch Class with her children: Ch. Yden's Blythe Spirit; Bda. Ch. Pioneer's Bounder v. Yden; and Baron O.J. v. Yden, C.D.X. *Middle:* Winning Best in Sweepstakes at the Golden State R.C. Specialty in June, 1988, John Dine's Ain't Misbehavin' at age 9 months. Owner, Nadine Jaquez. *Bottom:* Camas Valley Ruben Alexander, U.D., SchH. I, was bred by Dan and Debby Kutz and is owned by Monica and David Lundgren. By Ch. Camas Valley Kaiser Kutz ex Ch. Camas Valley Cassandra.

Your Rottweiler and Obedience

For its own protection and safety, every dog should be taught, at the very least, to recognize and obey the commands "Come," "Heel," "Down," "Sit," and "Stay." Doing so at some time might save the dog's life and in less extreme circumstances will certainly make him a better behaved, more pleasant member of society. If you are patient and enjoy working with your dog, study some of the excellent books available on the subject of obedience and then teach your canine friend these basic manners. If you need the stimulus of working with a group, find out where obedience training classes are held (usually your veterinarian, your dog's breeder, or a dog-owning friend can tell you) and you and your dog can join. Alternatively, you could let someone else do the training by sending the dog to class, but this is not very rewarding because you lose the opportunity of working with your dog and the pleasure of the rapport thus established.

If you are going to do it yourself, there are some basic rules which you should follow. You must remain calm and confident in attitude. Never lose your temper and frighten or punish your dog unjustly. Be quick and lavish with praise each time a command is correctly followed. Make it fun for the dog and he will be eager to please you by responding correctly. Repetition is the keynote, but it should not be continued without recess to the point of tedium. Limit the training sessions to ten- or fifteen-minute periods at a time.

Formal obedience training can be followed, and very frequently is, by entering the dog in obedience competition to work toward an obedience degree, or several of them, depending on the dog's aptitude and your own enjoyment. Obedience trials are held in conjunction with the majority of all-breed conformation dog shows, with Specialty shows, and frequently as separate Specialty events. If you are working alone with your dog, a list of trial dates might be obtained from your dog's veterinarian, your dog breeder, or a dog-owning friend; the AKC *Gazette* lists shows and trials to be scheduled in the coming months; and if you are a member of a training class, you will find the information readily available.

The goals for which one works in the formal AKC Member or Licensed Trials are the following titles: Companion Dog (C.D.), Companion Dog Excellent (C.D.X.), and Utility Dog (U.D.). These degrees are earned by receiving

"Never lose your temper and frighten or punish your dog unjustly. Be quick and lavish with praise each time a command is correctly followed. Make it fun for the dog and he will be eager to please you by responding correctly."

Select Ch. Eischenwald's Basil v. Axel, C.D., showing off his new Specialty medal. Owners, Pat Derdivanis and Robert Baston.

three "legs," or qualifying scores, at each level of competition. The degrees must be earned in order, with one completed prior to starting work on the next. For example, a dog must have earned C.D. prior to starting work on C.D.X.; then C.D.X. must be completed before U.D. work begins. The ultimate title attainable in obedience work is Obedience Trial Champion (OTCh)

When you see the letters C.D. following a dog's name, you will know that this dog has satisfactorily completed the following exercises: heel on leash and figure eight, heel free, stand for examination, recall, long sit, and long down. C.D.X. means that tests have been passed on all of those just mentioned plus heel free and figure eight, drop on recall, retrieve on flat, retrieve over high jump, broad jump, long sit, and long down. U.D. indicates that the dog has additionally passed tests in

scent discrimination (leather article), scent discrimination (metal article), signal exercise, directed retrieve, directed jumping, and group stand for examination. The letters OTCh are the abbreviation for the only obedience title which precedes rather than follows a dog's name. To gain an obedience trial championship, a dog who already holds a Utility Dog degree must win a total of one hundred points and must win three firsts, under three different judges, in Utility and Open B Classes.

There is also a Tracking Dog title (T.D.) which can be earned at tracking trials. In order to pass the tracking tests the dog must follow the trail of a stranger along a path on which the trail was laid between thirty minutes and two hours previously. Along this track there must be more than two right-angle turns, at least two of which are well out in the open where no

Above: This is probably the author's favorite photo in our book. An Obedience demonstration "Sit and Stay" executed by the Rottweiler Club of Victoria's Demonstration Team. Photo courtesy of Patricia Hall.

Right: Carado's Pied Piper at age 7 months, by Ch. Sriroco's MacArthur Park ex Inga von Tannenwald. Photo courtesy of Carole Kravets, Ont., Canada.

fences or other boundaries exist for the guidance of the dog or the handler. The dog wears a harness and is connected to the handler by a lead twenty to forty feet in length. Inconspicuously dropped at the end of the track is an article to be retrieved, usually a glove or wallet, which the dog is expected to locate and the handler to pick up. The letters T.D.X. are the abbreviation for Tracking Dog Excellent, a more difficult version of the Tracking Dog test with a longer track and more turns to be worked through.

Top: Proud new winner of A.R.C. Select at the 1988 Specialty, under judge Robert Moore. Select Ch. Eischenwald's Basil v. Axel, C.D. Robert Hanley, handler; Pat Derdivanis and Robert Baston, owners. *Bottom:* Am., Can. Ch. Cannon River Destroyer, C.D., T.T., by Ch. Cannon River Oil Tanker ex Cannon River Showboat, with his Best in Show ribbons and trophies from the Lakehead K.C. All-Breed Championship Show. Owner, Mrs. Phyllis Clark of Clear Water, WI.

Specialty Clubs in the U.S.

As had been the case in Germany some 33 years previous, the first Specialty Club for Rottweilers in the United States got off to a stormy start.

In this case, the first American Rottweiler Club was founded in California in 1940, owing to the interest and efforts of Barbara Hoard Dillon and Noel Jones, the latter's backyard proving the location for many early matches held by this organization. Earliest members included, in addition to the two just mentioned, Nancy and Andrew Cooper plus some other folks who had high hopes for the Club's anticipated bright future. At the time of its inception, this was intended to become the parent club for Rottweilers and was coming along nicely when a new group joined up, which promptly set about elimination of many of the original people who had worked and planned for its future success. The new clique has been described as getting the membership down to about half a dozen people, all of their own group, rotating the officers, and accepting no new applications for memberships. This obviously is not the road to success, and it left the breed at a sad disadvantage when the numbers of these dogs and people interested in them started to soar.

It was not until the summer of 1971 that delegates of the various local clubs devoted to Rottweilers, which had been formed to fill the void during the intervening years, held an informal meeting to consider, discuss and plan for the organization of a *new* national, or parent, club for Rottweilers. A constitution and by-laws which had been approved by the American Kennel Club were put into effect, and charter memberships became available to interested individuals immediately.

William Stahl, a long-time Rottweiler breeder and exhibitor who had been one of the delegates that helped formulate plans for this new parent club and who had been one of the founders of the highly successful Colonial Rottweiler Club, was elected the first president of this American Rottweiler Club, which at that time consisted of 359 charter members.

That the new club has prospered, stepping in and admirably filling its position as parent club of this now tremendously popular breed, is a fact which speaks clearly for itself. The breed standard needed and received prompt, careful attention. The one in use until that time had been approved back in 1935, when the breed was originally admitted for competition at A.K.C. dog

"That the new club has prospered, stepping in and admirably filling its position as parent club of this now tremendously popular breed, is a fact which speaks clearly for itself."

407

Ch. Lindenwood's Bouncer, C.D., T.T., taking placement in the Novice B Obedience Class at Medina K.C. Handler, Bill Michels; co-breeder-owner, Linda Michels.

popular and extremely successful.

The first Independent Specialty Show of the American Rottweiler Club took place during spring, 1981, in Massachusetts. Its success was a triumph and it has been followed by equally outstanding events ever since.

The American Rottweiler Club takes its obligations to the fancy very seriously, making every effort to provide educational material and information to all. One of the Club's most notable projects has been the *Rottweiler Pictorial*, which is an idea conceived by Mrs. Dorothea Gruenerwald while serving as president of the club during the late 1970s. This is a veritable treasure-trove of several hundred pictures and three-generation pedigrees of Rottweilers who have been important in the development of the breed in the U.S. It grows larger with each new edition and now includes an invaluable gallery of Producers of Merit. Then there is the "illustrated standard" already mentioned, plus a free (except for a stamped, self-addressed envelope) booklet chock-full of useful information for the new or prospective Rottie owner. This can be obtained by a request to Mrs. Doris Baldwin, P.O. Box 23741, Pleasant Hill, California 94523.

shows, and was based partially on the standard then effective in Germany. As time had passed, the German breed standard was constantly being updated while the A.K.C. Standard simply remained status quo.

Not only was a *new* standard drawn up and approved; but it also was illustrated in the hope of making all details clear to even the novice reader and clarifying any perhaps mistaken impressions existing in the minds of breeders and/or judges. This "illustrated standard" is a feature of our previous T.F.H. book, *The World of Rottweilers*.

A promptly inaugurated match show program has proved both

Opposite top left: **Barry vom Whithaus, age 10½ months, with his breeder-handler Bobbie Whitman. Barry won Best Senior Puppy at the Greater Jacksonville R.C. Specialty. He is a son of Int. Ch. Santo vom Schwaiger Wappen, SchH. III, C.D.X., T.D.I., ex Ch. Henni vom Bakkes, SchH. I.** *Opposite top right:* **Am., Can. Ch. Windcastle's X-tra Special, T.T., by Am., Can. Ch. Donnaj Herr I Am, C.D., ex Am., Can. Ch. Gatstuberget's Katarina, T.T. Owned by Carolyn and Bert Kaufmann.** *Opposite bottom left:* **Windcastle's Valentino was the Grand Sweepstakes Winner at the Golden State R.C. Specialty in 1988. Owner, Windcastle Rottweilers.** *Opposite bottom right:* **Doroh's Renaissance at 19 months. A fifth generation homebred with 7 points towards championship. Breeder-owner-handlers, D.A. and V. Wade.**

The American Rottweiler Club also offers a bi-monthly newsletter, which has grown from a six-page brochure to a 60-page or so magazine of reference. It has on at least two occasions been honored with awards from the Dog Writers Association of America.

MEDALLION ROTTWEILER CLUB

The Medallion Rottweiler Club in Illinois is one of the oldest for the breed in the United States and has been holding well-attended Specialty shows since 1969. Its first Independent Specialty took place in 1977. Medallion also introduced the custom of holding Futurity Stakes for Rottweilers in this country; the first occurred in 1979.

Medallion publishes many useful items for Rottie fanciers: a Tenth Anniversary Year Book and a Twentieth Anniversary Year Book, a bi-monthly newsletter, and a "New Member Information Kit" which supplies a wide range of information which one needs to become active in breed matters.

COLONIAL ROTTWEILER CLUB

The Colonial Rottweiler Club, founded in May, 1956, held its first Specialty show in 1959. It continues to do so annually, usually on the early May weekend of Bucks County and Trenton all-breed events. Colonial also sponsors an important Sweepstakes each year.

GOLDEN STATE ROTTWEILER CLUB

California's Golden State Rottweiler Club is another with a long record of service to the breed, having held its first annual Specialty show in 1969. This, too, is a service organization for Rottie fans. Its *Guardian Newsletter* reaches hundreds of members and subscribers around the world.

WESTERN ROTTWEILER CLUB

Another of the long-time-in-existence breed organizations, Western Rottweiler Club was founded in 1962. A booklet issued by them, *On Owning a Rottweiler*, has been enormously successful and helpful to new folks in the breed.

ROTTWEILER CLUB ADDRESSES:

ALOHA STATE ROTTWEILER CLUB
Richelle Uyeda, Secretary
2505 Saul Place
Honolulu, HI 96816

AMERICAN ROTTWEILER CLUB
Kay Peltier, Secretary
1012 Franklin Lane
Billings, MT 59101

BLUE BONNET ROTTWEILER FANCIERS
Linda Herrscher, Secretary
3401 Greenbriar Lane
Plano, TX 75074

CAROLINA ROTTWEILER CLUB OF GREATER RALEIGH
Cathleen Hancock, Secretary
Route 3, Box 121-B
Apex, NC 27502

CHICAGOLAND ROTTWEILER CLUB
Bernard M. Clay, Secretary
118 South Mayfield Avenue
Chicago, IL 60644

COLONIAL ROTTWEILER CLUB
Marilyn Piusz, Secretary
Route 1, Box 192F, Black Street
Johnstown, NY 12095

DOGWOOD ROTTWEILER CLUB OF METROPOLITAN ATLANTA
Cat Klass, Secretary
4704 Brownsville Road
Powder Springs, GA 30073

Bottom left: Am., Can. Ch. Altar's Mingen Magic v. Amars, T.T., is owned by Johann and Joseph Emedi. *Bottom right:* Can. Ch., OTCh. Kyladie's Kismet Kato, owned by Perry and Bernie Eitzen, was in the top 3 Obedience dogs in Canada for 3 consecutive years.

"The first Independent Show of the American Rottweiler Club took place during Spring, 1981, in Massachusetts. Its success was a triumph and it has been followed by equally outstanding events ever since."

EMERALD VALLEY
ROTTWEILER CLUB OF
GREATER CLEVELAND
   Marilyn Faught, Secretary
   11821 Erwin Avenue
   Cleveland, OH 44135

GOLD COAST ROTTWEILER
CLUB
   Theresa Riddle, Contact
   6584 Patricia Drive
   West Palm Beach, FL 33413

GOLDEN STATE ROTTWEILER
CLUB
   Samantha Mooney, Secretary
   725 Pleasant View
   Glendale, CA 91202

GREAT LAKES ROTTWEILER
CLUB OF MICHIGAN
   Pat Mays, Secretary
   32455 Nottingham Knoll
   Farmington Hills, MI 48018-4525

GREATER NEW YORK
ROTTWEILER CLUB
   Karen Di Cicco, Secretary
   10 Oceanview Road
   Lynbrook, NY 11563

GREATER OZARKS
ROTTWEILER CLUB
   Carol Owens, Secretary
   Route 2, Box 122
   Mansfield, MO 65704

GULFSTREAM ROTTWEILER
CLUB OF GREATER MIAMI
   Valerie Dombrowski, Secretary
   805 N.W. 9 Street
   Homestead, FL 33030

HI-DESERT ROTTWEILER
CLUB
   Mariella Reno, Secretary
   7102 7th Street
   Hesperia, CA 92345

HOOSIER ROTTWEILER CLUB
   Barbara Grisell, Secretary
   15707 Oak Road
   Carmel, IN 46032

HOUSTON AREA ROTTWEILER
FANCIERS
   Deborah Whelan, Secretary
   3426 Kennonview Drive
   Houston, TX 77068

INLAND EMPIRE
ROTTWEILER CLUB
   Karen Thompson, Secretary
   58793 Arcadia Trail
   Yucca Valley, CA 92284

MEDALLION ROTTWEILER
CLUB
   Geraldine Kittner, Secretary
   1629 Roosevelt Road
   Rockford, IL 61111

NATIONAL CAPITAL
ROTTWEILER CLUB
   Barbara Grasso, Contact
   P.O. Box 110
   Orlean, VA 22128

NEW ENGLAND ROTTWEILER
FANCIERS
   Doreen LePage, Secretary
   960 South Main Street
   Pascoag, RI 02859

NORTH LOUISIANA
ROTTWEILER CLUB
   Karen L. Slusarczyk, Contact
   606 Carrolton Street
   Bossier, LA 71112

NORTHWEST OHIO
ROTTWEILER CLUB
   Mary Runyan, Secretary
   3905 Walbridge Road
   Walbridge, OH 43465

NORTHWEST ROTTWEILER
FANCIERS
   Lauren Baur, Secretary
   1201 East 71st Street
   Tacoma, WA 98404

ORANGE COAST ROTTWEILER
CLUB
   Lisa Bonsteel, Secretary
   P.O. Box 2782
   Fullerton, CA 92633

OREGON TRAIL ROTTWEILER
CLUB
   Sharon Smith, Secretary
   18090 N.W. Avalon Drive
   Portland, OR 97229

ROCKY MOUNTAIN
ROTTWEILER CLUB
   Valerie Dombrowski, Contact
   2154 Sumac Street
   Longmont, CO 80501

Top: Can. Ch. Arrowback's Jaro Blakey takes Best of Breed at Oakville and District K.C. in September, 1988, at 22-months of age. Owner, Dr. P.K. and Shelley St. John.
Middle: Best in Show, Am., Can. Ch. Don Ari's Harras was Triple VI rated at the Canadian Sieger Show under A.D.R.K. rules with A.D.R.K. judges. Owner, Marlin Easton.
Bottom: A glorious fivesome: Can. Ch. Wathaman's Garth The Invader, C.D.; Can. Ch. Haramita Zoe Freesia Aroma; Can. Ch. Haramita Kyladies Son O'Garth, C.D.; Can. Ch. Bravamar's Brittany; and Ch. Wyndhurst's Bold Apollo.

Above: Powsell's Hanna, 22-month-old bitch owned by Powsell Rottweilers, Lake Worth, FL. Photo by Pat Pohlman, photographer, Boynton Beach, FL.
Below: Ch. Imor von Stolzenfels, C.D., at age 9 years. Owners, Jack P. and Dr. Evelyn M. Ellman, Augusta, MI.

ROTTWEILER CLUB OF ALASKA
Katie Nolan, Secretary
P.O. Box 140242
Anchorage, AK 99514

ROTTWEILER CLUB OF CANADA
Katrin Becker, Secretary
R.R. 2
Cochrane, Alberta, Canada
T0L0W0

ROTTWEILER CLUB OF KANSAS CITY
Debbie Leavitt, Secretary
Route 4, Box 116
Leavenworth, KS 66048

ROTTWEILER CLUB OF KNOXVILLE
Karen Riddle, Secretary
Route 1, Box 417-A, Lovelace Road
Fall Branch, TN 37656

ROTTWEILER CLUB OF LAS VEGAS
Jeanne Peterson, Secretary
551 Ellen Way
Las Vegas, NV 89104

ROTTWEILER CLUB OF MAINE
Judith Gagner, Secretary
1662 Essex Street
Bangor, ME 04401

SIERRA ROTTWEILER OWNERS
1600 Tarzyn Road
Fallon, NV 89406

SOUTHERN NEVADA ROTTWEILER CLUB
Karen Ransdell, Secretary
P.O. Box 28677
Las Vegas, NV 89126

SOUTHWESTERN ROTTWEILER CLUB
Paula Cingota, Secretary
3761 Rudnick Road
Jamul, CA 92035

SUNSHINE STATE ROTTWEILER CLUB
Debbie Faulds, Secretary
12215 S.W. 109 Lane
Miami, FL 33186

TEXAS ROTTWEILER CLUB
Debbie Gallegos, Secretary
3306 John Glenn
San Antonio, TX 78217

UNITED STATES ROTTWEILER
CLUB
  Eckart Salquist, Contact
  15700 Golden Star
  Riverside, CA 92506

WASATCH ROTTWEILER
ASSOCIATION
  P.O. Box 1473
  Sandy, UT 84091

WESTERN PENNSYLVANIA
ROTTWEILER CLUB
  Peggy Laskovich, Secretary
  3230 Cedar Ridge Road
  Allison Park, PA 15101

WESTERN ROTTWEILER
OWNERS
  Debbie Dolinajec, Secretary
  P.O. Box 1754
  Lafayette, CA 94549

WILLAMETTE ROTTWEILER
CLUB
  LaVerne Hensley, Secretary
  Route 1, Box 1768
  Clatskanie, OR 97016

Above: Yden's Ama Morgen, C.D., by Int. Ch. Bronco vom Rauberfeld, SchH. III, ex Am., Can. Ch. von Bruka Indra v. Yden, C.D., T.T., here is backpacking in the mountains at 12 months of age. Owner, Y. M. Forest.
Bottom left: Von Gailingen's Matinee Idol, Am., Can. C.D., in the mood for a romp. "Rudi" belongs to C. M. Thompson.
Bottom right: Am., Can. Ch. Carado's Reaper v. Tannenwald at age 15 months. Carole Kravets, owner.

Rottweilers Then and Now

By Dorothea Gruenerwald

Dorothea Gruenerwald is one of the most respected fanciers of the Rottweiler breed. As a breeder, exhibitor, and now as a judge, she has been a most helpful director of the American Rottweiler Club, having served in many capacities, including president, with outstanding success. Her devotion to the breed and her work on its behalf have gained for her tremendous admiration among her peers.

We are honored and delighted to bring our readers Mrs. Gruenerwald's comments on how the Rottweiler, as a breed, has fared from the late 1950s until the present, and her prophesies for the future. Her remarks are of particular value, owing to her great love of Rottweilers, her in-depth knowledge, and her intelligent, unbiased point of view.

Welcome, Dorothea, to our pages; we thank you for supporting our endeavors.

—A.K.N.

Before moving to Colorado Springs in 1964, we bred Aphra (then five years old) to an outstanding male which Joan Klem had just imported from Germany— BS Ch. Harras vom Sofienbusch, SchH. I. Aphra had a one-puppy litter, by Caesarean, which I hand-raised—sleeping on the living room couch for five weeks! We named her Lorelei.

This was the beginning of Von Gruenerwald Rottweilers.

In the late 1960s, Rottweilers were virtually unknown at all-breed shows, particularly in Colorado. We had purchased Nick vom Silahopp and started exhibiting in conformation. Because of the scarcity of entries in our area, some of the clubs in Colorado, Wyoming, and New Mexico combined the sexes to provide majors for Rottweilers. When we took Lorelei to her first big show in Oakland, California (March, 1966), the total class entry of 27 dogs and bitches was the largest ever—a five-point major. Handled by my good friend, Ann Maurer, the unknown young homebred Rottweiler from Colorado Springs won Winners Bitch and Best of Winners. What a thrill it was when she duplicated this win at the Chicago International Show the following

Opposite: **TJ's Tasha of Lakeview at age 1 year. 1988 A.R.C. Club Sweepstakes 9– 12 Months Puppy Bitch winner. By Brando vom Dattelner Hof, SchH. II, F.H., ex Lyndale's Cindy Vondez. Owner, T.J. Oldham.**

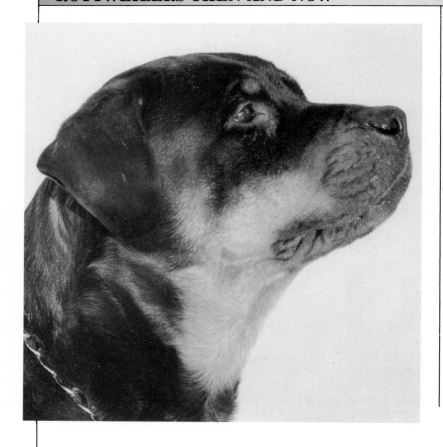

month for another five points.

Breeding on a very small scale was inevitable. A litter every other year was about all we could fit into a busy schedule. Nicky and Lori's lineage combined two strong German lines that "nicked" well, producing six champions from three litters. In the early 1970s, we found an eight-acre farm where I established a state-approved breeding kennel. The one major disadvantage was that it was six miles from our home. This necessitated employing people to live on the premises and take care of the dogs. (Lorelei was not a "dog" so she and Nicky lived at home.)

We traveled to New Mexico, Wyoming, Texas, Illinois, and California to compete. I gradually learned to exhibit, and over the years finished six of my own dogs. My husband was supportive of my growing interest in the breed and

Above: The English import, Corylus Wanda at Panelma is a foundation bitch at Wyndhurst Kennels, owned by Nicola Lundregan and Rick Field, Alta., Canada.
Below: Int. Ch. Green Mtns's Flora ("Rachel" to her friends), handled by Bill Burrel in a class with other competitors at the World Show in 1988. Rachel won!

encouraged me to make numerous cross-country trips to the C.R.C., M.R.C., and G.S.R.C. annual shows. For me it was always educational to see the outstanding Rottweilers of the day. Additionally, I made several trips to Holland, Germany, and Finland to attend the International Friends of the Rottweiler Congresses.

The years went very swiftly. There was never a doubt that adding up the plusses and minuses (of which there are both when involved in the breeding of any kind of animal) would result in a successful record for the effort expended. Today, the number of Von Gruenerwald title holders stands at 33. Two of my dogs are Bronze Producers and one a Silver Producer (American Rottweiler Club system).

With the growing popularity of the breed, I instinctively decided that it was time to curtail my own breeding program. The statistics are the same across our country, i.e., the difficulty of finding suitable homes for Rottweilers, the profusion of backyard breeders, and most of all the hard-sell advertising. My last litter was whelped in 1985, and the next year I sold my kennel. At present, we have only two Rottweilers at home. In retrospect, I would never maintain another kennel, as it is too unfair to the dogs.

Top: Ch. Vira von der Grurmannsheide by Ferro vom Amselhof, SchH. III, F.H., ex Elsa vom Sachsen, SchH. I. A consistent winner of Best of Breed and Group victories. Owned by Borrasco Kennels, Rick and Teri Mutschler. *Left:* Ch. Yden's Blythe Spirit, no coward, winning first in the 12–15 Months Bitch Class at the 1987 Colonial R.C. Specialty. Owner-handler, Yvette M. Forest.

Scharf and Linde are members of the Brocton Arch Therapy Dog Group; they really enjoy entertaining and the attention and fondling they receive afterwards. Owner, Norma Dikeman.

Over 30 years ago (April, 1959) my husband brought home our first Rottweiler—a five-month-old bitch named Abingdon Aphrodite. It was the beginning of a total commitment to a breed then virtually unknown but now in the top ten of A.K.C. registrations.

At the time, we owned a mountain cattle ranch in Colorado and wanted a dog for companionship. At the Chicago International Kennel Club Show we fell in love with the

Rottweilers, and shortly thereafter located a breeder who had a litter of puppies out of her champion Rottweiler. Seemingly, we were destined to find the last puppy bitch in the litter.

When we lived in a high-rise apartment on Chicago's near north side, a young Rottweiler was a challenge. We walked her three or four times a day, in all kinds of weather, and quite unconsciously on our part she became the most "socialized" Rottweiler we ever

15th floor of an apartment building! But we did have her hips x-rayed for H.D. This was several years before the O.F.A. was founded. In the opinion of our veterinarian, her hips were normal, and ten years later when we submitted the old x-ray, O.F.A. confirmed his reading—Aphra's number is R036.

For the last several years I have been judging fun and sanctioned matches and American Rottweiler Club Regional Specialty Sweepstakes. This has been a wonderful extension of an involvement in the breed which my husband and I chose many years ago.

Left: **Panzern's Arri Oil Patch Blu, owned and handled by Claire Coker, and Panzern's Bell of Arcrosanti, owned and handled by Sharon Wood, co-owned by Pansy Roberts.** *Below:* **True Lee Traum v. Gunner, C.D., by Ch. Altar's Gunner, C.D., ex Ashby v. Foxcroft, C.D. Bred by Lee McKenney; owned by Pat Luccid.**

owned. In and out of public elevators, through the lobby, the garage, over gratings in sidewalks, past peak traffic on Lake Shore Drive, chasing tennis balls on the beaches of Lake Michigan, and long walks on a neighboring golf course became routine. Everywhere we went, people would ask, "What kind of dog is that?" The second most asked question invariably was, "Why did you decide to buy a Rottweiler?"

One day while walking Aphra, my husband met a young boy who instantly recognized the breed; his family owned one of Aphra's littermates. The only difference, he said, was that his Rottweiler walked funny in the rear. What a sad way to learn about hip dysplasia.

Although there were several A.K.C. all-breed shows in the Chicago area where Rottweilers were being exhibited, I was too preoccupied with my singing career to be interested in showing. In the summer months, Aphra and I would board the California Zephyr and head for Colorado and the mountains, where she would tree porcupines and swim in the beaver ponds. She had a wonderful life.

From time to time, we thought about breeding Aphra; the primary obstacle was raising a litter on the

**Can. Ch.
Wynhurst's
Jessie is owned
by Donna
Telford and
Clyde Stevens.**

IN THE SHOW RING

In 1958, Rottweilers ranked 72nd in A.K.C. standings. There were so few Rottweilers that every owner knew every dog and owner in their immediate area and beyond. There was a genuine camaraderie at shows, with owners handling to the best of their ability. Amateur handling was the norm, the proud owners doing the best they could in the ring—and the few A.K.C.-licensed judges tolerating their assignments. Many considered Rotties a filler or junk breed. Many were admittedly afraid of the dogs—one judge called them "Rottenwilders!"

In the 1960s and 1970s, it was quite possible to owner-handle a Rottweiler to its championship title. It is not common today. The paid or professional handler has replaced most owner-handlers. This is unfortunate, since there is no greater thrill than to know that the dog, not the handler, deserved those ribbons. Too often, there is a distinctly impersonal atmosphere at all-breed shows—with novices huddled to one side and the seasoned veterans and handlers clustered together, barely conscious of newcomers to the breed.

The standard for the Rottweiler approved by the A.K.C. in 1935 had no disqualifications, and some judges were hesitant to dismiss a vicious dog. The late O.L. Harriman was bitten on the nose by a large male Rottweiler at a local Colorado Springs show, but chose not to dismiss the dog, and instead gave him BOB. This would not be tolerated today. The A.K.C. has wisely chosen to provide for the safety of judges; no matter what breed, any dog which cannot be examined by the judge is excused; any dog that attempts to bite the judge is automatically disqualified.

The ring deportment of today's Rottweiler, for the most part, has improved. With the proliferation of professional handlers in the Rottweiler rings, owners who still wish to exhibit their own dogs have learned to be more professional in their presentation. Most dogs have been conditioned to be thoroughly examined, i.e., proper dentition, testicles, shoulder layback, etc. Unfortunately, it is usually the novice exhibitor without sufficient conformation class training who brings a young, unsocialized dog into competition and suffers the embarrassment and consequences of being excused or disqualified; or, the eager exhibitor with a newly acquired German import that rushes the dog into the A.K.C. conformation ring without sufficient retraining. In Germany, these dogs are not conditioned to submit to hands-on examination, and they are confused and at a distinct disadvantage if they are shown in breed too soon.

We see this even at matches where young dogs lacking self-confidence or of unstable temperament are being shown. It is recommended that owners not rush their dogs into conformation competition. Some Rottweilers take longer to mature than others, both physically and mentally. It is far better to wait until your Rottweiler is emotionally mature and ready to win than to waste money and effort prematurely. I used to believe that it was an occupational hazard associated with judging to be bitten by a cantankerous Rottweiler, but not any more! The warning look in the eye, the "talking," the muttering or low growl of a large male or even a puppy is not to be condoned today by A.K.C. rules and regulations.

OBEDIENCE, TRACKING, SCHUTZHUND

Years ago, few Rottweilers competed in obedience. Many felt that a Rottweiler with an obedience degree after its name was one who had not measured up to expectations, conformation-wise, or had been neutered—or both. They were a distinct group.

Nowadays, many owners are training their dogs for high-scoring obedience competition. There has been a tremendous increase in obedience degrees awarded to Rottweilers during the intervening years. The number of degrees, ranging from C.D. to U.D., grows every year. At last count, there were four OTCH (Obedience Title Champion) Rottweilers.

Along with the growing number of obedience-titled dogs are those with dual titles, a Ch. in front and a C.D., C.D.X., or U.D. behind the name. The challenge of obtaining a championship and an obedience title is meaningful, as it is indicative of combining beauty with brains. The list is growing every year. The "working Rottweiler" will not be lost in the breed as long as there are owners and trainers willing to spend the time necessary to develop these inherent traits.

Ideally, the one-on-one relationship between owner and canine begins around the dog's seventh week of age. This is especially true of the Rottweiler breed. While few behavioral studies have been done with respect to the formative stages of a developing Rottweiler, it is imperative that *all* young dogs receive some form of obedience training. The most important decision you will make is to enroll your Rottweiler in a quality obedience training class at an early age. Whether or not you obtain an obedience degree on your dog is of secondary importance.

Tracking degrees, both T.D. and T.D.X., are appearing on more pedigrees than in the past. Puppies can be taught to track with a little

Can. Ch. Milo's An Uncommon Love, C.D., at age 1½ years. By Can. Ch. Kyladies Javelon Janus, C.D., ex Can. Ch. Kyladies Imagination, C.D. Owned by Heather Hayes.

Ch. Wyndhurst's Dark Nemis, owned by Kathy Bardick, is winning her class in the 1988 Canadian National Specialty.

separate Rottweiler clubs for the sport have been formed in various parts of the U.S.

TYPE

While some will argue that there is still a lack of uniformity of type in the breed, this lack was more obvious many years ago. There was a uniformity of type in certain areas of the U.S., but there were definite regional differences. Dogs on the West Coast were generally taller and heavier boned than those on the East Coast. West Coast dogs had darker mahogany markings, in some instances almost an absence of markings. East Coast dogs were better presented in the show ring, but many lacked the substance of their relatives to the West. Midwestern dogs were of a distinct type because of the prevalence of Rodsden breeding.

In their country of origin, Germany, Rottweilers were bred as working dogs. They were not considered a showy or elegant breed. Yet, today, the showy Rottweiler often places in the ribbons. A dog with "ring appeal" may sometimes take a Group or B.I.S. but may not necessarily be correct in type.

To add to the dilemma of lack of uniformity in type, during the past five to ten years there has been a surge of German imports. While American-bred Rottweilers used to be status symbols, today the imported Rottweiler has replaced the American-bred dog in prestige. These imports are usually distinctly different in type, and breeder-judges especially are quick to spot a "German" dog in the ring, invariably placing it higher than the American-breds. However, in my opinion, while many German imports have helped correct some of the breed's problems, there are many dogs who have brought new problems. Of particular concern currently is the more protruded, rounded eye seen in a great many imported dogs. Not only is this distracting to the overall impression of the head, but it is difficult to eradicate in a

patience and fortitude, and they enjoy it. However, climate and training locations are factors to consider. The motivation to track your dog is rewarding by itself—with or without a Tracking degree.

While the sport of Schutzhund has played an important part in the breeding of the total Rottweiler in Germany for many, many years, in the U.S. it was primarily a sport engaged in with German Shepherd Dogs. But this too has changed. Schutzhund training and trials are becoming more popular with Rottweiler fanciers. As more Rottweilers with Schutzhund Titles are imported from European countries, the interest in the sport is rapidly growing. Since the American Kennel Club does not sanction Schutzhund Trials,

Above: Can. Ch. Contessa Christina of Alouette, taking Best of Breed at Mount Cheam K.A. Dog Show, October, 1988.
Below: Powderhorn's Oreo of Wencrest, C.D., owned by Debbie and Terry Longobardo and Powderhorn/Wencrest Rottweilers, Inc.

Above: Ch. Tri-Lee's Champagne, bred and owned by Don and Norma White, is finishing her championship under Robert Stein at Town and Country K.C. in 1987, handled by Delores Burkholder.
Below: Robin Bell's Powderhorn's Kier of Wencrest

Top left: Ch. Fine Brin's von Nordon, C.D., age 3 years, taking points towards the title. Valerie T. Hellmann, handler. *Top right:* Ch. Radio Ranch's Bad Girl taking Best of Winners and Best of Opposite Sex at Troy K.C. in 1982. Owner, P.C. Brown.

breeding program. Since it is fashionable to breed to German studs, the rounded eye may soon replace the almond eye called for in our standard.

Another concern is the bright pink mouth seen in many imports. Since lack of mouth pigment is now considered a fault in Germany, many dogs with pink lips or jaws are being sent to the U.S.

Perhaps the most noticeable change in general type has been the gradual change in overall size. While the height called for in our standard has not been changed significantly, it is my opinion that too many dogs and bitches are presented in the show ring at the bottom of the height standard rather than at the top.

Rottweilers of the 1960s and 1970s are a rarity. Many fanciers ask: Where are the big, beautiful head, the dark, almond eyes, the

heavy bone? Most females are too refined compared to years ago.

In my opinion, an "elegant" bitch is not a typical working Rottweiler. She might win under some judges looking for "expression," but she does not reflect the purpose for which she was bred.

Movement is better in some areas of the country than in others, possibly related to the greater opportunity to exercise the dogs or depending on the owners' real interest to exercise themselves!

Many exhibitors in the earlier days were not objective of their dog's movement and could not understand why judges would overlook their "promising" dog or bitch. Had they stood back and permitted someone else to move their dog, they would have seen and better understood the lack of reach and drive, the dippy topline when moving, and the east-west fronts and cow-hocked rears!

Today, with more Rottweilers in the Classes and much stiffer competition, more attention is being given to basic structural defects. The top breeders are giving particular thought to correcting these obvious defects, and we see more structurally correct dogs in the show ring.

HEALTH PROBLEMS

The Rottweiler, like most other large breeds, is prone to hip dysplasia, and the breed no doubt would have suffered the fate of the German Shepherd Dog were it not of the establishment of the Orthopedic Foundation for Animals (O.F.A.) in the mid-1960s.

Although the awareness of the condition and the need to x-ray all breeding stock was accepted slowly at first, conscientious breeders have supported the x-raying of all breeding stock and have bred only O.F.A.-certified dogs and bitches. This early awareness may have prevented a disaster in the breed.

Obviously, the backyard breeders and puppy mills are not interested in requiring breeding stock to be x-rayed clear. This places a great responsibility on the part of the new owner to research thoroughly the background of both the sire and dam for hip certification when considering the purchase of a puppy or adult Rottweiler.

Over the ensuing years, as the popularity of the breed has increased, so have the growing number of additional health problems, i.e., elbow dysplasia, cataracts and retinal disorders, Von Willebrands disease, ruptured cruciate ligaments, immune

Bottom left: Ch. Bastel's Zeke vom Scuilla, by Ch. Be My Brother vom Scuilla ex Hiede Follow Shaw vom Scuilla. Owners, Michael and Rosemarie Kennedy. *Bottom right:* Obstgarten's Alexander v. Axel in June, 1988. Owned by Obstgarten Rottweilers, Dinuba, CA.

deficiency syndrome, neuromuscular dystrophy, and hypothyroidism. Particularly distressing is the undisputable fact (though not researched to my knowledge) that Rottweilers are extremely cancer-prone.

It used to be that new owners were told the average lifespan of a Rottweiler was ten years. In 1985, the American Rottweiler Club, through its bi-monthly newsletter, conducted an informal health and mortality survey. The results of this survey indicated an average lifespan of only seven years.

CLUB INVOLVEMENT

The Rottweiler Club of America, formed in 1948 on the West Coast, was the first A.K.C.-recognized club for the breed. It would have become the parent club but, due to lack of support and internal conflict, the club virtually ceased to exist by 1966.

During the mid-1950s and early 1960s several local clubs were formed. Composed of owners who resided in close proximity to the club area, these clubs offered educational meetings, matches and other events where members could share the unique experience of owning an unknown breed called the Rottweiler.

On the East Coast, the Colonial Rottweiler Club was established in 1956 in the Philadelphia–Trenton area. In 1959 the Medallion Rottweiler Club was organized in the Chicago area. On the West Coast, two clubs were founded in 1962: Western Rottweiler Owners in the San Francisco Bay area, and Golden State Rottweiler Club in the Los Angeles area. Because these clubs were the only active ones, the membership profile became regional rather than local as new owners were attracted to the breed.

In 1971, a small group of members from three Specialty clubs formed the American Rottweiler Club, which was destined to become the parent club of the breed. The formation of this club, encouraged by the A.K.C., was to reflect national rather than regional or local membership. Currently, A.R.C. members are found in almost all 50 states, in European and Scandinavian countries, Canada, Australia, and South Africa.

During the 1980s, matching the sudden spurt in popularity of the breed, there again has been a growing trend towards the formation of local clubs. There are numerous local clubs, in addition to the aforementioned Specialty clubs. The sincere interest of these small groups in preserving and improving the breed is remarkable. With limited budgets they publish monthly or bi-monthly newsletters. Many are involved in rescue and home-finding projects for

Antren's Bustin' Loose taking Best of Winners at Westbury K.A. Handler, Karen DiCicco for Antren.

unwanted and abandoned Rottweilers.

Many are working towards A.K.C. sanctioning. Most have adopted a code of ethics whereby they hope to maintain the integrity of the breed and its breeders. The involvement of all the clubs reflects the determination to maintain the positive image of the breed at a time when breed-specific laws threaten the very existence and ownership of our dogs.

READING MATERIAL ON THE BREED

When we obtained our first Rottweiler, there was very little written information on the breed. Other than scant reference to Rottweilers in generalized dog books, there were no published breed books.

During the late 1960s, the Colonial Rottweiler Club published three English translations of A.D.R.K. material which covered studies of the breed history in Germany, stud book records, and an anniversary book. While informative, they lacked up-to-date information on owning, raising, and training the dogs.

Over the years, the most readily available reading material has been provided by the various club newsletters. Articles and experiences shared in solving breeding, reproductive, health, and training problems can be found in these newsletters.

The anniversary book published by Medallion, Colonial, and Golden State Rottweiler Clubs provides pictures and statistics on their individual Specialty winners and are important additions to any owner's library.

Western Rottweiler Owners publishes a concise, educational pamphlet entitled "On Owning a Rottweiler." Several years ago they published a translation of a Dutch book on Rottweilers.

Four Rottweiler pictorials published by the American Rottweiler Club have included hundreds of pictures and three-

generation pedigrees on titled dogs (champions, obedience, Schutzhund, Producers of Merit, etc.)

Powderhorn Press has published numerous translations of books on the breed from Denmark, Finland, Holland and Germany. Rottweiler critiques and O.F.A. alphabetical listings are available; all important additions to an owner's library.

And, of course, T.F.H. has published several books on the breed including Miss Nicholas's widely read first volume, *The Book of the Rottweiler* (1981) and her second opus, *The World of Rottweilers* (1986); both volumes are available through the publisher. *The Rottweiler* by Richard F. Stratton was published in 1985 by T.F.H. and it, too, is available.

Ch. Kennrich's Soaring Zena, by Int. Ch. Amon vom Filmteich, SchH. III, ex Ch. Radio Ranch's Casablanca Pia. Owned by Anna and Dennie McCormack, Lebanon, NJ.

Top left: Am., Can. Ch. Myran's Eon of Excalibur, bred by Dawn Lawver and owned by Brenda and John Jayne. *Top right:* Wilson's Tru Held Dillion, bred by Dan and Debby Kutz, is owned by Barney and Jeanne Wilson. By Ch. Eiko v. Schwaiger Wappen, C.D.X., SchH. III, ex Ch. Camas Valley Hildagard v. Kutz.

THE NEXT THIRTY YEARS

Perhaps the hardest facts to accept are the frightening scenarios which face the breed and its owners. The meteoric rise in popularity has spawned undesirable owners—witness the daily newspaper and TV accounts of the mauling of children and adults by loose-running Rottweilers; the number of dogs found in the local pounds; the dogs protecting drug dealers and other dubious persons, and last but not least, the traveling breeder-salesman in the Rocky Mountain region peddling six- to seven-week-old puppies, promising to send A.K.C. papers which never arrive.

The steady rise on the A.K.C. list of most popular breeds has only made matters worse. But we really can't point the finger only at the puppy mills and backyard breeders when we hear high-profile owners brag that they co-own over 200 Rottweilers. There are too many breeder-owners with a "get-rich quick attitude" making a living by raising puppies. They profess to know better, but by their actions they are contributing to the proliferation of mediocre dogs. All one has to do is glance at the 12 or more pages of Rottweiler advertisements in a national dog magazine to get the complete picture of what has happened to the breed.

The negative press is not indigenous to the U.S. Articles in the *London Times* indicate that after a recent rash of Rottweiler attacks on children puppy sales in Britain plummeted, with owners of adult dogs having them euthanized rather than face insurance cancellations.

It is difficult to project how and when the "fad" of Rottweiler ownership will diminish. Popularity cycles (Dobermans,

German Shepherds, and some working breeds who have been at the top in the past) are predictable and usually run their course. The real question is whether or not the working qualities and stability of the breed will remain unchanged—will there be a nucleus of breeder/owners with some representative specimens of the breed to carry on?

Breed-specific laws in the U.S. may force ownership to decline, particularly when the cost of a liability insurance premium may become prohibitive. At the present time, there are breed-specific laws on the books in several areas of the U.S. These, for the most part, have been directed at pit bulls; but, if the vicious image of the Rottweiler continues in the media, our breed will be the next to suffer.

This gloomy picture is one which has taken time to develop. Everyone in some way contributed

to it, innocently or not. We weren't super-careful where we placed each puppy. We didn't follow up on each owner, did not try to guide them with a sound breeding program or with health problems. We did not make a conscious effort to present the positive image of the breed, and instead thought it macho if our male was aggressive. We did not seriously obedience-train our dogs at an early age, nor correctly socialize them.

While I am no longer breeding, I still look to the future with a feeling of hope that among the new, smaller breeders there will be those who will preserve and improve the breed. I especially look to the small local clubs to attract newcomers, to have a positive influence on them, and to lead them through educational seminars and meetings.

We may then have come full circle.

Bottom left: Ch. Kennrich's Soaring Zena, bred by Kennette and Richard Tabor, Kennrich Kennels, Chesapeake, VA.
Bottom right: Von Hochfeld Margot vom Haux, by Oleo vom Schmidall, SchH. III, (a Nero son) ex Von Hochfeld Celestial Charm, is a splendid bitch in whom owner Janice M. Lynch takes tremendous pride.

Index

Note: Page numbers in *italic* indicate an illustration. All titles and awards have been eliminated from the dog's name for the reader's convenience.